VALUE FOR MONEY

BUDGET AND FINANCIAL MANAGEMENT REFORM IN THE PEOPLE'S REPUBLIC OF CHINA, TAIWAN AND AUSTRALIA

VALUE FOR MONEY

BUDGET AND FINANCIAL MANAGEMENT REFORM IN THE PEOPLE'S REPUBLIC OF CHINA, TAIWAN AND AUSTRALIA

EDITED BY ANDREW PODGER, TSAI-TSU SU, JOHN WANNA, HON S. CHAN AND MEILI NIU

Australian
National
University

PRESS

Published by ANU Press
The Australian National University
Acton ACT 2601, Australia
Email: anupress@anu.edu.au
This title is also available online at press.anu.edu.au

A catalogue record for this
book is available from the
National Library of Australia

ISBN(s): 9781760461799 (print)
9781760461805 (eBook)

Cover design and layout by ANU Press

Contents

List of figures

List of tables

Abbreviations

AIC	Akaike information criterion
ANAO	Australian National Audit Office
APM	Active Participation Model
APS	Australian Public Service
APSC	Australian Public Service Commission
ASEAN	Association of Southeast Asian Nations
BL	Budget Law (China)
BOO	build–operate–own
BOT	build–operate–transfer
CAC Act	*Commonwealth Authorities and Corporations Act 1997*
CBA	cost–benefit analysis
CCP	Chinese Communist Party
CDIC	Central Discipline Inspection Commission
CDRF	China Development and Research Foundation
CFAR	Commonwealth Financial Accountability Review
COAG	Council of Australian Governments
CPI	consumer price index
CRF	Consolidated Revenue Fund
DBFOM	design, build, finance, operate and maintain
DBR	departmental budget reform
DGBAS	Directorate-General of Budget, Accounting and Statistics
dibao	rural minimum living stipend scheme
ERC	Expenditure Review Committee

EU	European Union
FMA Act	*Financial Management and Accountability Act 1997*
GAO	Government Accountability Office (US)
GDP	gross domestic product
GFC	Global Financial Crisis
GFRS	government financial reporting system
HECS	Higher Education Contribution Scheme
HELP	Higher Education Loan Programme
HRM	human resource management
IGR	intergenerational report
IMF	International Monetary Fund
INTOSAI	International Organization of Supreme Audit Institutions
IPPG	Institution of Public Policy and Governance
IT	information technology
JCPAA	Joint Committee of Public Accounts and Audit
JSA	Job Services Australia
JSCI	Job Seeker Classification Instrument
KPI	key performance indicator
LBC	Legislative Budget Center
LIC	local investment corporation
MAC	Management Advisory Committee
MFP	multifactor productivity
MoF	Ministry of Finance
MP	Member of Parliament
MRT	Mass Rapid Transit (Taipei)
MTFF	medium-term fiscal framework
NAO	National Audit Office
NGO	non-governmental organisation
NPM	New Public Management
NSW	New South Wales

OECD	Organisation for Economic Co-operation and Development
OLS	ordinary least squares
OT	operate–transfer
PAC	Public Accounts Committee
PAP	Private Affordable Preschools (China)
PBB	performance-based budgeting
PBO	Parliamentary Budget Office
PBP	Participatory Budgeting Project
PBS	portfolio budget statement
PDB	performance-determined budgeting
PEFO	Pre-Election Fiscal Outlook
PEO	Performance Evaluation Office (China)
PFM	public financial management
PGPA Act	*Public Governance, Performance and Accountability Act 2013*
PIB	performance-informed budgeting
PM	prime minister
PM&C	Department of the Prime Minister and Cabinet
PPIP Act	*Promotion of Private Participation in Infrastructure Projects Act 2000*
PPP	public–private partnership
PRB	performance-reported budgeting
PRC	People's Republic of China
PS Act	*Public Service Act 1999*
R&D	research and development
RMB	renminbi
ROT	rehabilitate–operate–transfer
RRC	Revenue Review Committee
SAI	supreme audit institution
SBIC	Schwarz Bayesian Information Criterion
SBIR	Small Business Innovation Research

SER	self-evaluation report
SII	Statute for Industrial Innovation
SOE	state-owned enterprise
SUI	Statute for Upgrading Industries
TPD	Third Plenum Decisions
UK	United Kingdom
US	United States
VAGO	Victorian Auditor-General's Office
VAR	vector autoregressive
VAT	value-added tax

Contributors

Zizhou Bu is a specialist at the Human Resources Department of the China Life Insurance Company Ltd. He received his PhD from the School of Public Policy and Management at Tsinghua University, Beijing.

Hon S. Chan is a Professor in the Department of Public Policy, City University of Hong Kong. His research focuses on civil service reforms, cadre personnel management and performance evaluation and management in China. He has published extensively in major journals in the field.

Ming Huei Cheng is Postdoctoral Fellow of Political Science at the National Taiwan University. Her research interests include metropolitan governance, local corruption and renewable energy policy.

Kai-Hung Fang is Associate Professor in the Department of Public Policy and Management at Shih-Hsin University, Taipei. He received his PhD from the Graduate School of Public and International Affairs at the University of Pittsburgh. His major research interests include local government, local public finance and public policy. He has published or taught courses on subjects including public administration, local government, public finance and budgeting and qualitative methods.

Zahirul Hoque (PhD, FCPA, FCMA) is Professor of Management Accounting/Public Sector and Head of the Department of Accounting and Data Analytics at La Trobe University, Melbourne. He is also the Executive Director of the Centre for Public Sector Governance, Accountability and Performance at La Trobe University. He has held positions at Deakin University, Charles Darwin University, Griffith University, Victoria University of Wellington and Dhaka University in Bangladesh. He is the founding editor-in-chief of the *Journal of Accounting*

& Organizational Change. His research interests include management accounting, public sector management, accounting in developing economies and non-governmental organisation and non-profit accounting.

Yilin Hou is Professor at the Maxwell School of Citizenship and Public Affairs at Syracuse University in New York. He holds an MA and PhD in public administration from Syracuse University. His research interests and publications cover fiscal policy and institutions, state and local taxation, intergovernmental fiscal relations and intellectual development of public budgeting.

Hsini Huang is an Assistant Professor of Public Affairs and Political Science at National Taiwan University. She received her PhD in the School of Public Policy at Georgia Institute of Technology, USA. She is well trained in the field of the economics of innovation, economic geography and science and technology policy. She has published articles in the *Cambridge Journal of Regions, Economy and Society*, *Science and Public Policy* and *Research Policy*. She is currently working on a research project that examines the distribution and outcomes of government funding for science and technology research in Taiwan.

Dr Wendy Jarvie is Adjunct Professor at the School of Business at the University of New South Wales in Canberra, where she undertakes research into the role of evidence, innovation and learning in public policy. She was previously deputy secretary in the employment and education departments in the Australian Public Service. She has also managed evaluations and strategy development at the World Bank in Washington, DC.

Dr Nailing Kuo is Associate Professor at the Graduate Institute of Public Affairs and Department of Political Science, National Taiwan University. Her research interests include public budgeting, public accountability and governance.

Yu-Ying Kuo is Professor of Public Policy and Management and Dean of Academic Affairs at Shih Hsin University, Taipei. Her research interests include public policy, cost–benefit analysis and government budgeting. She is the editor of *Policy Analysis in Taiwan* (Policy Press, 2015).

Dr Trish Mercer is a Visiting Fellow in the Australia and New Zealand School of Government at The Australian National University in Canberra. Her academic research is grounded in her policy, program and service delivery experiences as a senior executive for some 20 years in the Australian Public Service. Her focus is on bridging academic theory and practitioner experience, and she has developed a number of social policy case studies both for publication and for public policy workshops.

Dr Meili Niu is a Professor in the School of Government, Sun Yat-sen University, and the Deputy Director of the Center for Chinese Public Administration Research. Her research focuses on public budgeting and finance. She has over 10 years' experience working as a consultant and adviser to Chinese governments and congresses on budgetary reforms and policy evaluation. She serves on the editorial board of several academic journals, including the *Journal of Public Administration* (Chinese), the *Journal of Public Budgeting, Accounting, & Financial Management*, *Perspectives on Public Management & Governance* and *State and Local Government Review*.

Des Pearson was Auditor-General of Victoria from 2006 to 2012 and Auditor-General of Western Australia from 1991 to 2006. He was a convenor of the Australasian Council of Auditors-General from 1997 to 1999, a member of the Auditing and Assurance Standards Board from 1997 to 2000 and a member of the Australian Accounting Standards Board from 2005 to 2008. Mr Pearson is a Life Member and Fellow of CPA Australia and the Australian Institute of Management, Western Australia, and a National and Victorian Fellow of the Institute of Public Administration Australia. He is also the Chair of the Advisory Board of the Centre for Public Sector Governance, Accountability and Performance at La Trobe University, Australia.

Andrew Podger is Honorary Professor of Public Policy at The Australian National University. He was previously a senior public servant in the Australian Government, with roles including Public Service Commissioner, Secretary of the Department of Health and Aged Care, Secretary of the Department of Housing and Regional Development and Secretary of the Department of Administrative Services. He was also national president of the Institute of Public Administration Australia from 2004 to 2010.

Tsai-Tsu Su is Professor and Director at the Graduate Institute of Public Affairs, National Taiwan University, where her teaching and research are focused on public budgeting, administrative reform and policy analysis. Professor Su received her PhD from Carnegie Mellon University,

Pittsburgh, and taught at the State University of New York at Stony Brook before returning to Taiwan. She has served as a committee member or consultant to various government agencies and was the president of the Taiwan Association for Schools of Public Administration and Affairs for two terms.

Hsin-Fang Tsai is an Assistant Professor of Public Administration and Management at Chinese Culture University, Taipei. She is well trained in the field of public economics, public finance and budgeting. Her research interests include public budgeting, public finance and political economy.

Youqiang Wang is Professor at the School of Public Policy and Management of Tsinghua University, Beijing. He holds PhDs in economics (University of Maryland) and mathematics (University of Ohio). His research interests include public economics, governance and leadership management.

John Wanna is the Sir John Bunting Chair of Public Administration in the Australia and New Zealand School of Government and Professor in the School of Politics and International Relations, College of Arts and Social Sciences, at The Australian National University.

Christine Wong is Professor of Chinese Studies and Director of the Centre for Contemporary Chinese Studies at the University of Melbourne. She has published widely on China's public finance, intergovernmental fiscal relations and their implications for governance, economic development and welfare. Her recent research is focused on economic reform under Chinese President Xi Jinping and the institutional constraints to modernising governance in China.

Mike Woods is Professor of Health Economics at the University of Technology Sydney and a visiting scholar at The Australian National University. His research interests are in health system reform, aged care and economic reform. He was formerly the deputy chairman of the Australian Productivity Commission and was presiding commissioner on more than 20 national inquiries into aspects of economic reform.

Hanyu Xiao is a Postdoctoral Fellow at the College of Liberal Arts and Social Sciences at the City University of Hong Kong. His research interests include public budgeting and finance management, corruption and environmental leadership.

Ping Zhang is Assistant Professor in the School of International Relations and Public Affairs at Fudan University, Shanghai. He got his PhD in public administration and policy from the University of Georgia. His research interests include property taxation, intergovernmental fiscal relations and local governance.

Dr Zaozao Zhao is an associate researcher at the National Academy of Economic Strategy in the Chinese Academy of Social Sciences. She was also a visiting scholar at the University of Georgia in 2006 and at the University of Kansas in 2016–17. Dr Zhao's research focuses on public budgeting and financial management, performance budgeting, auditing and inflation. She has been the principal investigator or a core researcher in major projects funded by the National Natural Science Foundation of China, the Chinese Ministry of Finance, the Chinese Academy of Social Sciences and the National Development and Reform Commission.

1

How political institutions, history and experience affect government budgeting processes and ways of achieving 'value for money'

Andrew Podger, Tsai-tsu Su, John Wanna, Meili Niu and Hon S. Chan

All governments face the challenge of scarce resources, requiring budgetary management processes for identifying the resources required by and available to government, and then for allocating them and ensuring their use or deployment represents value for money. Such budgetary and financial management processes need to routinely inform decision-making and protect the integrity of the way public resources are used—with some public accountability to indicate that their uses are properly authorised and reflect the policies of legitimate government leaders. The processes ideally should also facilitate assessments of how well the resources have been used, and of whether and how efficiently expenditures have achieved the objectives of the policymakers.

These common challenges are, however, addressed in very different contexts: different institutional frameworks with different historical trajectories and notions of governance; different levels of prosperity and stages of economic development; different aggregates of spending or proportions of societal resources available to government and different societal needs and priorities; and different scales of population and government administration. There is no ideal model, and even countries with the most advanced and mature economies and long-established political systems are under constant pressure to improve the systems and processes that help to balance priorities, impose reliable controls, ensure accountability and deliver efficient and effective services.

This does not preclude opportunities for different countries to learn from each other, but it should caution scholars and practitioners to first appreciate the different contexts and to recognise that any lessons drawn from other jurisdictions must be carefully adapted to the learning country's own context. Often in exercises in policy transfer, insufficient attention is given to the contextual contours. Another important aspect of transfer is the appreciation of pathways and sequencing—whether reform proposals can be implemented incrementally step-by-step or require radical punctuated changes to institutional arrangements, and what preconditions are required for reforms to be successful.

The chapters in this book explore budgeting and financial management in three very different jurisdictions: Australia, the People's Republic of China (PRC) and the Republic of China (Taiwan). These activist and, at times, innovative jurisdictions are keen to analyse and reflect on each other's policy achievements and patterns of public provision. They are keen to learn more about each other as their economic and social engagement continues to deepen. They are also conscious that fundamental differences exist in terms of economic development, global strategic positioning and levels and philosophies of political development; to an extent, these differences are representative of differences among countries around the globe.

While Australia as a continent is geographically large, its population (just over 24 million) is only slightly larger than Taiwan's. Australia's budgetary and financial systems are much more established and institutionalised than those of the PRC or Taiwan, which are relatively recent in origin. Its public budgetary processes present a comprehensive coverage of revenue and expenditures, it has firm controls to ensure accountability and to avoid fraud and corruption and it has extensive processes to promote efficiency and effectiveness. Its public finance operates within a political framework that was established more than a century ago, drawn from experience in the nineteenth century in both the United Kingdom and the United States, with a parliamentary democracy and a federal system of government. As a pioneer of budgetary reform, its resulting budgetary and financial management systems were extensively refined in the 1980s and 1990s as Australia drew on and helped shape the ideas of 'New Public Management' (NPM), emphasising 'management for results' or value for money. Australia is a relatively wealthy country whose population has high expectations of what government should deliver. Many current demands on government relate to complex social, economic and environmental issues raising new challenges for budgeting and financial management as well as for longer-term policymaking. More recent developments within its internal systems try to address these challenges by, for example, adding much longer-term projections into the budgetary process and linking financial management not only to current performance, but also to organisational capability for future performance.

The PRC is huge both geographically and in terms of population (over 1.3 billion). It is in the process of a huge transition from its former command economy to a state-guided market economy with associated structural changes to the role of government and to the political institutions that control and manage government. It seems intent on maintaining its authoritarian one-party political system, delivering high rates of economic and social development while facilitating decentralised administration, allowing considerable discretion at provincial, municipal, county and district levels. China has become a middle-income country in an extraordinarily short period of time, but with wide dispersion of income and wealth, great pressures on government to manage urbanisation on an unprecedented scale and increasing demands for public services comparable with those in more developed countries. China has been building budget and financial management processes that can support these developments, strengthening controls over revenue and expenditures, ensuring more comprehensive coverage, better linking of policy with financing, addressing concerns about fraud and corruption and introducing aspects of performance management. The task is immense and the achievements to date remarkable, but the system has a long way to go to become openly transparent and publicly accountable. One implication of such a huge transition is the need to consider carefully the sequencing and adaptation of reforms to budgeting and financial management introduced elsewhere.

Taiwan is also a young country in transition, although it is now firmly an upper–middle income successful democracy (possibly the most free and democratic society in Asia), with reasonably comprehensive if traditional budget systems and reliable financial management controls linked to its particular (relatively new) political institutions. It is, however, still in the process of matching government revenue to the expenditures necessary to meet the demands of a more wealthy population. The country is not large geographically or in terms of population (just under 24 million), and government is not as decentralised as in the PRC (and it does not have a federal structure like Australia's), so the financial control framework is in many respects relatively simple. The country is now enhancing the system, drawing on developments in more developed countries, such as more performance-based approaches. It is also experimenting in such fields as participatory budgeting aimed to complement the democratic political framework it has established.

Budgeting approaches

Factors that contribute to successful public sector budgeting include:

- the comprehensive coverage of revenue and expenditures that ensures decision-makers can set macroeconomic fiscal policies and also determine priorities across all government activities
- the reliability of estimates of revenue and expenditures in the budget year and beyond
- the quality of analytical support to inform budget decision-making and ensure policy and financing are firmly integrated
- political-administrative cultures or disciplines of budgetary control involving important internal and external strictures
- the monitoring and scrutiny processes that ensure expenditure is consistent with budget decisions
- the regular monitoring and evaluation of performance, ensuring budgetary processes promote performance and value for money
- robust processes that ensure the accountability of those in authority to the wider public.

John Wanna in Chapter 2 presents a description of Australian budgeting as it operates in practice, going beyond official formal descriptions. He draws attention to the federal structure under which each of the six sovereign states (and two territories) has its own budget process separate from the Commonwealth's. There are nonetheless strong similarities and long-shared histories, and a considerable degree of coherence is promoted by the extent of revenue transfers from the Commonwealth and by the intergovernmental machinery that helps to align key policies and promote fiscal discipline.

Key strengths in the Australian system(s) include the comprehensive coverage, reliability of the estimates, extensive analytical capacity to support decision-makers, processes to ensure accountability to the legislature and the public and the monitoring and scrutiny process. Wanna suggests, however, that performance information is not nearly as influential in budget decision-making as might be inferred from Australia's efforts over more than 30 years to pursue NPM's emphasis on program budgeting and managing for results. Rather, the main emphasis continues to be on aggregate expenditure control and the overall fiscal balance. Performance information perhaps has more impact on management decision-making than on political decision-making. Wanna also identifies weaknesses in the legislature's oversight of the budget and of the performance of government agencies and programs, notwithstanding the recent establishment of the Parliamentary Budget Office.

Mike Woods in Chapter 3 examines Australia's recent efforts to go beyond a medium-term approach to budgeting (budget year plus three forward years) to draw on much longer-term projections. These efforts draw on New Zealand initiatives and are similar to those in a number of other Organisation for Economic Co-operation and Development (OECD) countries; they are aimed at informing decision-makers of longer-term forces and promote consideration of early action that might ameliorate their fiscal impact. In the Australian context, the main focus has been on demographic change and its likely impact on social security, health and aged care expenditures. A key initiative has been the regular publication of an intergenerational report (IGR), but Woods is concerned that this has increasingly become a political document to support the ruling government's existing policy prescriptions rather than an objective analytical report to inform the public as well as the government and the legislature and to promote sound discussion and debate. Some senior government officials suggest that the IGR documents have not been as influential as they were expected to be, but this may reflect the lack of receptivity from recent governments rather than flawed processes. Woods suggests nonetheless that the IGR be more comprehensive in its coverage, including state as well as Commonwealth budget implications, be prepared by a more independent authority and be systematically updated as a platform for debating such key long-term policy agendas as productivity reform.

Christine Wong highlights in Chapter 4 the enormous challenges now facing the Chinese leadership under President Xi Jinping, with the country having reached middle-income status, no longer able to rely on exports and investment for growth and facing increasing domestic pressures. The agenda for 'deepening reform' set by the leadership in late 2013 is aimed at further restructuring the roles of government and the market and modernising governance. A key element is reform of China's fiscal system, including a standardised and transparent budget management system, tax reform to support new policy priorities and clearer division of responsibilities between central and local governments.

Wong describes earlier measures taken to develop a more comprehensive budget management system with more centralised control of revenues and a new financial management information system, but implementation at subnational levels, where 85 per cent of public expenditures takes place, stalled, perhaps because administrators were simply overwhelmed by the task as revenues grew exponentially and the central government decided to greatly expand expenditures in support of a 'harmonious society'. The 2013 agenda is intended to correct the situation, with the new Budget Law (BL) aimed to rein in local government debt and extrabudgetary revenue, improve transparency and strengthen accountability. Central to the BL is its comprehensiveness, but its success is dependent both on the analytical capacity at the centre and on implementation at subnational levels. Broader fiscal reform is also highly dependent on realigning and rationalising intergovernmental fiscal relations—an agenda requiring strong and sustained support from the top.

Tsai-Tsu Su identifies a number of problems with Taiwan's public budget system today in Chapter 5. The system has been through major reforms associated with the country's democratisation and, subsequently, with a drive for increased efficiency through NPM ideologies. The system is carefully controlled by the centre (the Directorate-General of Budget, Accounting and Statistics and the Ministry of Finance) and, while the legislature has further to go in reviewing the executive's budget proposals, it has made great strides since the authoritarian era in budget review, promoting transparency and open government. Similar to the Australian experience, in Taiwan, the budget control emphasis remains on the aggregate bottom line rather than on performance despite the NPM agenda, although a key challenge remains for the country to increase revenue so that government is able to meet more of the legitimate demands of a high- to middle-income country. Budget execution controls and accounting and audit also focus more on the legality of the expenditures rather than performance or value for money.

While local government has a degree of autonomy in Taiwan, it is regulated by the centre and comes under the *Budget Act*, *Financial Statement Act* and the *Audit Act*. Moreover, its budgetary and accounting personnel are appointed by the central government, which also issues instructions on budget preparation and execution. On the other hand, the reliance of local government on revenue transfers from the centre and the willingness of the centre to provide financial support to prevent bankruptcy seem to discourage local government from expanding its own revenue or exercising fiscal discipline, and hence may justify the centre's imposition of tight controls. This dilemma is not unique to Taiwan, as evident from the earlier chapters on Australia and the PRC, but may be particularly acute in Taiwan, which does not have the degree of local autonomy seen in the PRC or Australia's federal system.

Su also draws attention to two examples of recent budget reform initiatives. The first concerns local government trials of 'participatory budgeting'. Different models have been used, each aimed to provide opportunities to involve citizens in budget priority setting. There are risks of 'pork-barrelling' for political gain, but also opportunities for genuine and informed public involvement in selecting local projects. The second initiative concerns a shift to performance auditing, described in more detail by Fang and Su in Chapter 10.

Financial management systems

Financial management systems complement the budget processes, ensuring expenditures are lawful and consistent with the purposes for which they were authorised, and that those responsible for those expenditures are held accountable. Increasingly, financial management is also designed to promote value for money—that performance as well as compliance is given priority. Associated with good financial management are organisational capability and governance arrangements that support current and future performance through continuous improvement.

Andrew Podger in Chapter 6 describes the evolution of Australia's financial management system, particularly since it first gave more emphasis to performance and 'management for results' in the 1980s. The most recent development is the *Public Governance, Performance and Accountability Act 2013*, which replaced earlier legislation to provide an umbrella for the financial management of all Commonwealth organisations (state government developments vary but generally follow a similar trajectory). This umbrella ensures consistency by articulating common principles or objectives and by promoting cooperation across government while allowing variations in governance structures and the way the principles are applied. The accountability arrangements are closely integrated with the budget cycle and emphasise performance. It is also intended to enhance performance by granting degrees of 'earned autonomy' whereby organisations with a strong performance record may face less onerous central controls. A key development in the new legislation is the requirement for corporate plans that promote organisational capability for future as well as current performance. Another development is increased emphasis on risk management.

Podger confirms the many strengths of the Australian system, which has been a model of NPM since the 1980s, but notes that reality has not so far fully reflected the rhetoric of 'management for results'. There are significant potential advantages in the latest legislation, but risks also that practice will continue to fall short of intentions. A key challenge is to achieve a public sector culture of high performance and a focus on learning and results that is not easy given political factors that impose strong incentives for short-term, risk-averse behaviour. Like Wanna, Podger identifies a disconnection between politicians and administrators, with performance information seeming to have limited impact on political decisions and mainly informing decisions by managers. Perhaps there is insufficient appreciation by both politicians and administrators of the need for political leaders to determine the performance indicators that reflect their political objectives. Podger also stresses the extent to which Australia's reforms since the 1980s have built on sophisticated systems of civil service and financial management established and maintained over the previous 80 years that have nurtured a professional culture of integrity and accountability.

In Chapter 7, **Meili Niu** explores the use of performance-based budgeting (PBB) at the municipal level in China, addressing some of the concerns Christine Wong identifies in Chapter 4 about the implementation of financial management reforms at subnational levels. While encouraged by the central government, PBB reform has mostly been a bottom-up exercise led by local-level finance departments without direct powers over the local line departments. Niu examines the case of the education department in municipal Guangzhou (a city with a population of over 10 million). PBB reform in China focuses on 'program spending', which mostly involves capital projects such as construction, renovation and purchasing major equipment; the other categories of expenditure—employee costs and 'operational expenses'—are still determined centrally by the human services department that controls staffing and by formulae linked to employee numbers. For the education department, program spending still represents around 20 per cent of its budget (down from 40 per cent), although the city's population growth is slowing. Niu's research shows that, notwithstanding directions from the finance department to apply PBB to program spending, line agencies tend only to 'adopt' the policy, paying lip-service to the requirement rather than taking the policy seriously in their internal decisions on which projects to pursue. For a while, however, the education department went further, 'implementing' the policy by applying more rigorous evaluation techniques and using external expertise to improve their own resource allocation decisions. The key contributing factors were the leadership attitude within the Department of Education and the respect it had from the finance department for its expertise and experience. When these changed, PBB was no longer pursued seriously by the education department.

Hanyu Xiao in Chapter 8 examines the problem of misuse of public resources by public officials through extravagant position-related expenditures—on travel, cars and hospitality. He finds that informal rules or culture often outweigh the formal rules in China, undermining efforts to curb this misuse. He recommends action to ensure formal and informal rules complement each other, requiring on the one hand that the formal rules do not take frugality too far, making it hard for officials to do their jobs, and, on the other hand, that a culture of excessive deference to authority and excessive emphasis on personal material gain must also change. The financial management framework and stronger rules on position-related consumption represent an essential discipline in promoting efficient and effective use of public resources and ethical behaviour. The Australian financial management legislation's emphasis on principles, and its explicit requirement for 'economic, efficient, effective and ethical' use of resources, is intended similarly to influence informal as well as formal rules to promote ethical behaviour.

Performance auditing and evaluation

The audit function is critical to accountability, informing the legislature and public whether expenditure has been lawful and proper and in line with the purposes for which it was authorised, and whether it has been accurately and fully reported. The independence of the audit function is critical to its credibility. Around the world, there has been a shift in the role of audit to go beyond compliance to also address performance and value for money, presenting a number of challenges for audit offices. This shift is the subject of chapters here on Australian and Taiwanese experience.

Zahirul Hoque and **Des Pearson** explore in Chapter 9 the shift in Australia, which has been one of the pioneers of this international development. They highlight the contribution of performance auditing not only to the promotion of value for money, but also to the capacity of the legislature to oversee the executive and hold it to account for its performance. This is facilitated by the close relationship between the auditor-general—technically operating within the executive arm of government—and the legislature and its public accounts committee (the Joint Committee of Public Accounts and Audit, or JCPAA, as it is known in the Australian Parliament). The shift to performance auditing in Australia was gradual, the initial, small steps taken in the 1970s, and it was built on the auditor-general's strong reputation for compliance auditing. It required significant restructuring of the audit organisation to gain the necessary expertise and to build new relationships with the organisations being audited. It was also not without its critics who were concerned about the subjectivity of performance auditing and the risk of the auditor-general becoming embroiled in political debates. Hoque and Pearson refer to efforts in Australia to avoid this risk by focusing closely on the policy objectives as articulated by the government and by assessing performance strictly against these, without commenting on the policies themselves.

Hoque and Pearson identify some of the contributions made by performance auditing to improve performance management and reporting by government organisations in Australia, including at the state level as well as the Commonwealth. They also draw attention to the way the auditor-general's own performance is evaluated and reported on to the legislature. They see the Australian experience as providing some lessons for other countries, but also note areas where the Australian practice could be improved further, including through more systematic follow-up by the legislature of executive responses to performance audit reports.

Kai-Hung Fang and **Tsai-tsu Su** in Chapter 10 present a description of Taiwan's move to performance auditing, highlighting similar challenges to those identified by Hoque and Pearson. The shift in Taiwan has been more recent than in Australia and the National Audit Office (NAO) is still building the necessary expertise and the new relationships that are required with the organisations subject to audit, but significant progress is being made under the current leadership of the NAO. The challenges emerging parallel those faced in Australia, relating not only to expertise and relationships, but also to managing the subjectivity of performance auditing and the need to avoid politicisation. So far, Fang and Su report that feedback both from within the NAO and from outside has been mixed. The NAO's leadership, however, is determined to take the shift further, from 'oversight' (compliance) to 'insight' (performance) and on to 'foresight' (using performance to identify emerging trends and help agencies to address longer-term issues). In the meantime, more effort seems to be required to improve the quality of the performance audits rather than emphasise quantity, and to improve relationships with audited organisations by the NAO presenting itself more as a trusted independent management consultant offering advice rather than an authority issuing firm judgments and instructions.

The Taiwanese approach is also affected by its unique political institutional arrangements. Separate from the executive, legislative and judicial arms (or 'Yuans') of government, Taiwan has a Control Yuan (focusing on the efficiency of executive agencies and fraud and corruption) to which the NAO is responsible, and an Examination Yuan (which regulates the merit principle in the civil service). The NAO's independence from the executive is arguably a little firmer under this arrangement than that of the auditor-general in Australia; its relationship with the legislature is through the role of the Control Yuan, which is appointed by the president and approved by the Legislative Yuan.

Capital and municipal financing

While the two chapters in this section of the book focus only on Taiwan's experience, the issues involved will be familiar to practitioners and scholars in Australia and the PRC, and in other countries struggling with infrastructure investments and managing decentralised or federated government systems.

Resource allocation must reflect political judgments, but these do need to be informed by expert analysis and should not be distorted by intergovernmental arrangements that blur accountability. That said, distinguishing the respective responsibilities of different levels of government is not easy, and central governments worldwide are taking more responsibility to collect taxes and then 'buy-in' to policy fields that might otherwise be left to subnational governments. Managing shared responsibilities has become an increasingly important challenge.

Yu-Ying Kuo and **Ming Huei Cheng** examine in Chapter 11 Taiwan's recent experience in employing public–private partnerships (PPPs) for investing in infrastructure. Taiwan's approach has been systematic and highly expansionary, aimed at both economic stimulation after the 2008 Global Financial Crisis (GFC) and providing high-priority infrastructure needed for the next stage of Taiwan's economic growth. The processes have been set out in legislation and a large program of major projects announced by the government and included in national budgets. PPPs are also supported by tax incentives and planning concessions. The 12 projects in the 'i-Taiwan' program involve a total budget of nearly NT$4 trillion (or over A$150 billion) of which 30 per cent is private investment. The legislated processes provide a sound basis for decision-making, and Kuo and Cheng conclude that PPPs have saved the government significant money and made better use of public land and existing infrastructure, delivering better public services while stimulating the economy. They identify some problems and weaknesses, however, particularly from trying to implement so many projects simultaneously and not properly evaluating projects on completion to see that they delivered the cost–benefit advantages claimed at the approval stage. They also express some unease that the attractiveness of private investment may lead budget-constrained governments to relax scrutiny, with a risk of increased costs to the public in the future.

Hsin-Fang Tsai explores Taiwan's fiscal decentralisation reforms in Chapter 12 and how they have operated in the climate of austerity since the GFC. From studies of five municipalities, she finds strong resistance to measures to reduce services to the public or to raise taxation despite central government pressure for municipalities to take more responsibility for their fiscal position. Instead, the municipalities prefer to rely on central government transfers and grants, and central government decisions on taxes and services, and to focus their efforts on less controversial measures such as increasing user-pays charges, changing land use to promote development and generate revenue and relying more heavily on private investment for infrastructure (via PPPs).

The Ministry of Finance's 2014 'Local Fiscal Consolidation Project' promoted local fiscal autonomy and better control of debt, presenting strategies to increase self-financing and reduce expenditure and debt, and offering financial counselling. However, with local governments' own revenue averaging around 50 per cent of their total revenue, resistance to the finance ministry's agenda was perhaps not unexpected or surprising; it was always going to be easier for local government to blame the centre for insufficient transfers and grants. Nonetheless, some improvements were made through non-tax revenue increases and through expenditure restraint without direct cuts in services. Also, the increased transparency about local debt included in the finance ministry's approach has also imposed a useful discipline allowing closer media scrutiny of local governments' fiscal performance.

Evaluation of policy implementation to improve results

As countries look to give more emphasis to performance in their budgeting and financial management arrangements, the role of policy evaluation is critical, along with the related question of how evaluation is linked to resource allocation decision-making. Examples presented demonstrate practices in the three countries, identifying both strengths that might be replicated more widely and gaps and weaknesses that need to be addressed.

Wendy Jarvie and **Trish Mercer** describe in Chapter 13 Australia's experience in the case of employment services. These were outsourced to private providers and community organisations nearly 20 years ago, at that time both improving outcomes for unemployed people and reducing costs to government. Jarvie and Mercer explore the monitoring and evaluation processes used over the following years to ensure continuous improvement in results and value for money, and to help the Department of Employment address changing labour market conditions, client needs and the behaviour of employment service providers. Among the lessons they draw from this mostly positive experience are: the importance of a long-term approach to data collection, monitoring and evaluation; high levels of in-house and contracted analytical expertise (addressing the risk that outsourcing 'hollows out' internal capacity for informed purchasing); regular use of performance data by decision-makers; strong audit and fraud controls; and transparency of the performance management system and the confidence of the providers in its integrity.

Important for those in other countries looking to similar reforms is that the Australian success did not come easily. It required a complex system of management with an intense focus on the performance of the outsourced providers, and an acceptance of experimentation and risk management. It seems likely also that this drew on the experience of the earlier regime of government provision. Podger's findings in Chapter 6 also suggest that the positive experience revealed by Jarvie and Mercer has not been widely replicated across Australian departments and programs and is rightly now a priority for further effort.

Zaozao Zhao provides case studies in Chapter 14 to describe and analyse the important role of third parties in China's performance budgeting reform process. This provides essential expertise where it is lacking in-house, allowing local governments in China to successfully introduce performance-based budgeting when many other developing countries have struggled to do so. The use of third parties also ensures a greater degree of independence of the evaluations and means the process is not just internal to the relevant government and finance departments, but also acknowledges the importance of a broader public and political dimension to resource allocation decisions. There are nonetheless challenges for the third parties in exercising independence in their evaluation work, and for departments in fostering greater transparency and public participation given the central role of the Communist Party in China's authoritarian framework.

Nonetheless, the challenge of having both objective evaluation and political decisions of priorities is common to all three jurisdictions and by no means confined to authoritarian regimes. In theory, balance is achieved in democratic regimes such as Australia's and Taiwan's by a degree of separation of politics and administration: administrators are required to be professional and impartial but also responsive to the (elected) government and subject to its lawful direction, including on policy priorities. Transparency also helps to ensure political decision-making is properly informed and does not disregard objective evaluation and analysis. Like China, Australia makes extensive use of external experts to assist with performance evaluation, but there are commercial and political pressures to constrain the level of independence of evaluation findings; there are also often pressures on internal advisers to tailor evaluations and advice to the preferences of political leaders.

Ping Zhang, **Zizhou Bu**, **Youqiang Wang** and **Yilin Hou** provide a case study evaluation in Chapter 15 to illustrate how evaluation could greatly improve resource allocation in China. Their example concerns the equity of funding in China for school education. They use data from local counties across China to analyse the factors that affect intraprovince equity of education funding. They find that recent measures by the central and provincial governments aimed at improving equity have had some positive impacts in terms of dampening the growth in inequality, but disparities are still growing between developed and less developed counties. The study reveals that, if the transfers are to do more than just dampen growing inequality, they will need to be increased. While the authors note the need for more research, the analysis provides an important demonstration of the potential value of careful evaluation of government policies in promoting greater effectiveness and efficiency.

Hsini Huang and **Nailing Kuo** also provide a case study evaluation, in Chapter 16, their case being the effect of public research and development (R&D) subsidies on private R&D investment in Taiwan. They report how previous research has influenced policy in Taiwan, shifting R&D subsidies from tax incentives to direct support because this was shown to be a more effective means of addressing the market failure that constrains R&D investment. Huang and Kuo's research suggests the government should now go further, better tailoring the direct subsidies to sectors and activities where the 'additionality' effect of the subsidies is more certain. The evidence they present suggests this is most likely in high-technology fields and where the agency distributing the funds has considerable expertise in the fields concerned. Responding to this evaluation evidence will require further policy development and administrative effort, and consideration in future budget processes.

Lessons and challenges

In the final chapter (Chapter 17), **Andrew Podger** provides a summary of the challenges common to all three jurisdictions (and probably therefore to other countries) that can be drawn from the book, and identifies some of the lessons that can be shared. These cover the very concept of 'value for money', the drivers of reform, the question of sequencing reform measures, the relationship between politics and administration, institutional roles and relationships and the importance of leadership.

Conclusion

While the contexts vary significantly, all three jurisdictions are placing considerable effort on improving budgetary and financial management processes to deliver better value for money. The trend in all three is towards a greater focus on performance and associated arrangements for monitoring, evaluation and auditing, although there are marked differences in how far each country has gone so far.

In all three, these reforms are closely linked to broader economic, social and/or political transformations and, indeed, are proving critical to their success. Accordingly, it is important to look further than the many technical advances described in this book. They, and the broader agendas to which they are contributing, will only be successful if both political and administrative leadership commitments are sustained, and if appropriate cultures are in place and continuously nurtured.

2

Government budgeting and the quest for value-for-money outcomes in Australia

John Wanna

Government executive budgeting in Australia is fundamentally premised on parliamentary scrutiny and endorsement. This provides not only the formal legality for all public finance, but also a degree of transparency, information-sharing and the possibility of investigation. Governments legally require authorisation from the legislature for imposing taxation or raising other revenue and for spending from its consolidated revenue fund. Four key empowering clauses in the Australian Constitution apply to government financing: Section 51 (currency, taxes, borrowing, spending and property acquisition), Section 56 (the financial initiative of the executive), Section 83 (monies only legally drawn from the Treasury if appropriated lawfully) and Section 90 (the Commonwealth's exclusive power to impose customs and duties). Other sections specify how money bills must be handled, but these four important sections constitute the Commonwealth's principal financial powers. While the subnational jurisdictions follow similar budgetary procedures, they have no such constitutional stipulations.

Each year in May, annual budget statements including any new policy proposals announced in separate documentation are presented to parliament for approval. These documents remain the executive's intended budget and are not initiated or 'owned' by the legislature, but the bicameral parliament is formally required to appropriate all expenditures and authorise any changes to revenue to ensure their legality. Parliament is not required to 'pass' the budget documents (merely noting these various documents, which are formally 'tabled' and therefore become public documents), but instead authorises a small number of very skeletal appropriation bills giving legal effect to expenditures, and then deliberates any other subsequent revenue and expenditure measures separately. Other than receiving these appropriation bills initiated in the lower house and legally passing them through both houses (or rejecting aspects of them), the Constitution is silent on any other roles for parliament (or the executive) in presenting budgets. However, the Constitution does insist that the bill covering the 'ordinary annual services of the government' shall deal only with those items (effectively, the base budget for the Commonwealth), and this has meant that, since 1965, a separate appropriation bill (Bill No. 2) has been reserved for other items of new spending, capital injections or transfers to the states. Since the late 1990s, the parliament has received a third appropriation bill containing the budgets of the legislature itself and a few independent officers of the parliament (e.g. the auditor-general and the parliamentary budget officer). Additional appropriations for entitlements (special appropriations) and for additional estimates can be passed at other times or later in the budget year.

It is the executive's primary responsibility to steer its budget through the legislature (or secure as much of it as it can through the Senate, where the government of the day often does not command a majority in the upper house). Approval is not automatic or necessarily expected. There have been many instances where governments have not received approval for key measures included in their proposed budget and a few occasions when the budget has met with fierce resistance and a sequence of measures have been rebuffed (e.g. in 1975, 1993 and 2014) (see Young 1996). In recent years, governments have provided more transparency with their budget documentation, trying to keep parliament better informed, but the material has also become highly technical, especially with the transition to accrual reporting of budgets and multiple budgetary balances (fiscal, underlying, headline). However, some useful information once produced in previous decades has been discontinued—for example, historical time-series of functional outlays, senior executive remunerations, maintenance and some smaller capital works. Over the past 30 years, budgets have become less compliance based and more managerial in orientation as

Australia moved from line-item funding with firm central input controls to one-line budgeting on a results basis (using an outputs and outcomes framework for the Commonwealth's own-use spending, approximating 20 per cent of total expenses). There were many accompanying budgetary reforms associated with this transition to a results-based budgetary process (see Wanna et al. 2000, 2010; Blöndal 2008; Di Francesco and Alford 2016); some have been retained and built on (e.g. the link to corporate plans, consistent 'line of sight' reporting, resource agreements, one-line budgets for operating costs, budgetary offsets and efficiency dividends), but many others were tried and soon discarded (e.g. multiagency portfolio budgets, the annual capital charging of departments, individual agency bank accounts, the devolution of forward and budget estimates calculations to line agencies, purchasing and property management and cashed provisions for depreciation). Reporting on progress with budgetary implementation and an annual reconciliation statement of the final budget outcome is now more seamless and interconnected under the *Charter of Budget Honesty Act*, which mandates reporting requirements and consistency over the entire budgetary cycle. This Act provides a consistent set of statutory reporting requirements for budget estimates against eventual actuals.

It should also be remembered that, in population terms, Australia is a relatively small federation, a continental country with an imperious national government (but often limited in its constitutional powers) and eight relatively active subnational governments (six states and two territories). This implies, first, that Australia has not one unitary budgetary system, but nine differentiated processes across the jurisdictions, each with their own priorities, characteristics and often timing; and second, with a high degree of fiscal centralisation, the federal government is highly active in providing intergovernmental financial transfers under various 'agreed' funding criteria (often termed 'executive federalism' because most of this activity involves interexecutive bargaining, not in the various legislatures). These transfers can involve direct untied grants, tied grants for specific purposes stipulated by the Commonwealth, matching project grants for which both levels of jurisdiction agree to joint funding and performance-related national partnership payments through the Council of Australian Governments (COAG) (previously, federal governments have provided some special grants to activities within the states' responsibilities but these have now been declared *ultra vires* by the High Court).

From a budgetary perspective, there are three main problems with this fragmented federalist system of budgeting: 1) the economies and demographics of the various states can move at different speeds, making national management difficult for the federal government and its budget settings; 2) states and territories can actively work against the fiscal strategies of the federal government with different spending and funding priorities or expansionary/contractionary tensions; and 3) the states' budgetary positions have become increasingly dependent on the largesse of the federal government, which is guided by redistributive 'horizontal equalisation' principles. This redistributive aspect establishes a perverse logic whereby a state wishing to increase its tax take within its own jurisdiction can subsequently be penalised by receiving lower federal funding from Canberra (a particularly vexing problem that besets the distribution of the nationally collected 10 per cent goods and service tax and pits the larger/richer jurisdictions against the smaller/weaker ones).

This chapter briefly introduces budgeting and budgetary management in Australia, focusing on the federal level. It then explores the various stages of the budget cycle, beginning with the pre-authorisation period before the budget is presented to parliament, the authorisation stage conducted in public through the legislature, followed by the post-authorisation stage where various formal evaluations occur, asking what degree and types of value-for-money investigations are made (routinely or exceptionally). It concludes by examining the strengths and weaknesses of the Australian budgetary management system according to the level of integrated accountability, the coherence of the monitoring and scrutiny processes and performance improvement.

Australia's budgetary processes

Budgetary processes in Australia are a combination of top-down orchestration and bottom-up estimations of base budgets. Top-down factors may involve some strategic framing, the issuance of fiscal guidelines, decisions about key government priorities (usually expressed in writing and communicated through such devices as the prime minister's charter letters to ministers and senior agency heads), politically imposed aggregate expenditure limits or savings measures and even privatisations or asset sales. It also includes a medium-term fiscal framework (MTFF) covering the budget year plus three further out-years, tabled in parliament, which forms the 'hard' basis of future budgets, as well as a mid-year economic and fiscal update that revises estimates and can be used to rein in spending. Bottom-up processes tend to take place throughout the budgetary year, involving the monitoring of all expenses within tolerance parameters, calculation and recalibration of actuals, revision of estimates and re-agreeing estimates between central and line agencies. Colloquially, this has led to the adoption of what is often termed a 'measures and pressures' approach, which also serves as a convenient methodology for budget preparation. 'Measures' include any new policy proposals, adjustments to existing policy of funding packages, expenditure tightening options, efficiency measures or any budget-balancing instruments such as tax increases, reductions in concessions or changes to eligibility criteria. 'Pressures' consist of a duality of factors: the economic growth forecasts including fiscal projections impacting on the budgetary position and inbuilt cost pressures from existing programs or spending allocations (e.g. inflation, enterprise bargaining outcomes, particular cost pressures on certain inputs and changing demographic pressures such as the age pension/aged care implications imposed by an ageing population).

The base budget of most agencies and programs is largely administratively agreed between central agency and line officials, unless cabinets insist on extraordinary cutbacks (as in 1996 and again in 2014). These administrative assessments are usually made on the assumption of maintaining the quality and level of existing services, not necessarily value-for-money criteria. This point was made in an earlier Organisation for Economic Co-operation and Development (OECD) study of Australia (Kraan et al. 2012), which explored aspects of budget reforms, spending reviews and recommendations for future improvement.[1] New policy proposals and changes to existing policy settings go to the powerful Expenditure Review Committee (ERC) of cabinet (senior ministers who act as fiscal guardians), which, by dividing bids from ministers/agencies into minor and major proposals, evaluates and ranks the merits of the various bids (producing 'one principal moment' of budgetary deliberation with a running scorecard totalling probable, possible and unlikely proposals). Once all spending decisions have been made (usually by March–April) then there is a final 'hunting season', which allows the central budget

---

1   Although this OECD study (Kraan et al. 2012) was referred to as a 'value-for-money in government' study and was part of a cross-national comparative survey, for the most part, the analysis presented was of budgetary and managerial reform initiatives. Only sections dealing with spending reviews and market testing touched on value-for-money considerations.

agency (the Department of Finance) to look for additional savings and present these options to the ERC for approval (see Hawke and Wanna 2010), followed by a review of revenue measures to establish whether any reductions or increases in revenue are warranted by the Revenue Review Committee (RRC). The final two to three weeks before the budget is tabled are spent refining the sales pitch for the budget, honing key messages, promoting the highlights, dropping selective leaks to manage expectations and briefing government ministers and backbenchers.

The main budgetary orchestrating actors include three central agencies— Treasury, the Department of Finance and the Department of the Prime Minister and Cabinet (PM&C)—that play complementary roles but also serve two powerful budgetary cabinet committees (the ERC and the RRC) and have input into various ad hoc strategic budget reviews by the most senior ministers.[2] These political and bureaucratic institutions have generally worked collaboratively and with a high degree of coordination (which is not to say they do not have occasional differences of opinion over selected aspects of the budget). The ERC has a huge workload making decisions that require the authority of the most senior members of the government, meeting over six months with an intensive period in February and March each year. The RRC has a far lighter workload and may meet perhaps only once a year, usually towards the end of the process, to decide on any tweaking of tax rates. In servicing both these cabinet committees, the Departments of Treasury and Finance provide the updated data and analytical capacities, while PM&C provides the prime minister with individual advice, monitors the budgetary assemblage and conveys the prime minister's preferences regularly to the other players. Treasury's main focus as the leading economic adviser to government is macroeconomic policy, the intersection of monetary and fiscal policy, international financial developments, microeconomic reform, taxation reform and intergovernmental transfers. The Department of Finance is the main housekeeping budgetary agency responsible for expenditure management, estimates, financial management, asset management and

---

2   Since the late 1990s, various strategic forums of the most senior ministers have been held, usually in November each year. These have included the Senior Ministers' Retreat, then the Senior Ministers' Review, then the Strategic Budget Committee, followed by the Strategic Policy and Budget Committee. These usually off-site meetings of the prime minister, deputy prime minister, treasurer and minister for finance predetermine the key strategic parameters for the upcoming budget deliberations—and have often been followed by the prime minister issuing his/her charter letters to the ministry (see Blöndal 2008; Hawke and Wanna 2010).

procurement, budgetary rules and processes. PM&C has a smaller advisory capacity on fiscal and economic policy, but has the prime minister's ear and coordinates the formulation process.

Other sources of expertise and budgetary input include the Commonwealth's line departments and agencies, the central agencies located in subnational jurisdictions, plus various specialist agencies that can influence decision-making, including (within government) the Productivity Commission (an independent long-term economic and social policy adviser; see Chapter 3 by Mike Woods in this volume), the Australian Bureau of Statistics (key statistical indicators), the Australian Taxation Office (taxation advice), the Australian National Audit Office (ANAO) (audit findings) and (outside government) key interests groups from business, unions, farmers, consumers, welfare lobbyists, think tanks and economic/fiscal consulting firms and accounting firms, the media and a diverse group of academics and professionals (e.g. doctors and psychologists on health issues or engineers on infrastructure needs).

Although Australia's budgetary timetable follows the same repetitive patterns, the central budgetary agencies tend to focus their attention on the formulation stages, whereas line agencies tend to make budgetary submissions while focusing on the implementation and review stages of the process (see Appendix 2.1). Operating across a budgetary three-year cycle of *formulation* (nominally year −1), *implementation* (year 0) and *evaluation* (year +1), Finance and Treasury's timetable usually starts around November in year −1 and goes through to the annual reports and final budget outcome midway through year +1, but their main analytical focus is concentrated on February to June in year −1.[3] Line agencies use a different timeline, which typically starts around two years prior to the budget year (years −2 and −1), with ongoing research, program reviews, evaluation, feedback from stakeholders and feedback from administration—all of which goes to inform the eventual annual budget submission from the minister, which is submitted in December. The agency then goes into more detail in preparation for the implementation year (year 0, in which the agency expends that year's annual budget allocation) and then into year +1 for further implementation and evaluation.

---

3   Australia's budgetary year follows the official financial year that starts from 1 July and runs until 30 June. Hence, both the formulation year (−1) and the implementation year (0) would run from July of one year to the end of June the next. The evaluation year (+1) can run longer than 12 months, depending on the length and magnitude of official reviews by both the ANAO and/or parliamentary committees.

Assessing value for money in the pre-authorisation stages

The degree to which value-for-money assessments are made in the pre-authorisation stages (i.e. when the executive is drafting its preferred budget in secret) is usually fragmented and focuses on specific facets of the process as information is being sought and decisions are being made. There is no overarching or comprehensive value-for-money assessment of the entire budget in this stage, and most of the tough decisions (reallocations, cuts, offsets, program lapsing) are usually not made public but are promulgated and prosecuted in secret. Governments may conduct expenditure reviews, strategic reviews or capability reviews (and usually only in small numbers), but these are not necessarily linked or integrated with budget setting, and often focus on policy–administrative alignments. So the degree to which value-for-money analyses are influential in this stage is something of a black box, and even the actors most closely involved in budget framing will not have complete knowledge of all the investigations and modifications. The economic, fiscal and political contexts tend to dictate the degree of 'toughness' or 'easiness' displayed by the central budgetary institutions.

The first phase in budgetary analysis involves the ability to accurately estimate revenue and expenses, which remain confidential throughout this period but which will subsequently be published and subject to public accountability. Internal bureaucratic analysis of the forward estimates (the MTFF) is not simply an exercise in arithmetic, because the various players are not neutral and disinterested. All budget actors are contestants, and budgetary processes have to allow for the inclusion of contestable spaces in which to weigh contending and countervailing arguments. This is often referred to in Western democracies as the 'challenge function' or the intentional tension that is institutionalised between guardian and spending actors who perform different roles but must work within and cultivate long-term relations (see Heclo and Wildavsky 1974; Kelly and Wanna 2001). The 'challenge function' may be exploited to contest the accuracy of program or administrative costings, question parameter estimates or take-up rates or challenge the behavioural assumptions of the community—all of which, even with only minor changes, can vary estimates greatly.

In making expenditure estimates, central budget agencies have distinct advantages here because they not only have an authoritative and positional advantage in setting and agreeing estimates, but also can monitor spending progress in the budgetary implementation out-year and can rein in spending to come within budget projections. So, for example, the Department of Finance has final authority over the forward estimates of agencies and of all costings to cabinet. Not surprisingly, an ANAO performance report into the accuracy of budgetary estimates found that Treasury/Finance were accurate to within 0.65 per cent over a five-year period in the late 1990s (ANAO 1999), which was three times more accurate than their UK and New Zealand counterparts and seven times more reliable than Canada. Finance routinely assesses the accuracy of its own expenditure estimates, using this as a marker of the quality of its work, and selectively publishes results in its annual reports. Estimating revenue is much harder and Treasury traditionally erred on the prudential side, using conservative estimates (possibly as a way to constrain the appetite of ministers for more spending or to eventually produce a better-than-expected budget balance). However, in recent years, in the aftermath of the Global Financial Crisis (GFC), the Treasury has routinely produced overly optimistic revenue projections, which have proved to be exaggerated (Gregory 2017). Given that successive cabinets (under the leadership of Kevin Rudd, Julia Gillard, Tony Abbott and Malcolm Turnbull) have generally fashioned their spending plans in budget formulation against these optimistic revenue projections, such misjudgments probably contributed to larger deficits than otherwise might have been expected. Some governments—most notably, the Gillard Government—have even approved major long-term policy commitments (running out to 10 years) that were largely unfunded given the sluggishness of current revenue receipts (e.g. by announcing indicative funding targets for national disability provision and major augmentations to spending on schools, both constituting nominal public commitments but without funding plans, and certainly not legislated at the time of announcement). Moreover, many infrastructure projects are announced without a detailed business plan being made public, such as with the rollout of the National Broadband Network.

Australia's confidential bidding process for new and/or revised policies provides an internal forum for potentially evaluating the likely returns on public investments (Wanna et al. 2000; Blöndal 2008). All new policies requiring additional funding are submitted to the central budget agencies for evaluation and follow preset timelines and routines. Consolidated bidding procedures allow governments to evaluate spending proposals comparatively, investigate and compare the likely costs (and benefits) of proposals, consider alternative policy designs in making value-for-money assessments and rank preferred spending priorities. Through cabinet budgetary committees, senior government ministers can weigh policies on national security, infrastructure, social programs, communications, education or the environment in a closed, secretive forum (Dowding and Martin 2017). Spending agencies may try to pad bids or 'game the system' in other ways, but the principal job of Treasury and Finance is to call their bluff, advise on the merits of the proposals versus other courses of action, challenge the costings and, if approving, recommend levels of funding (full, partial, pilot or fully offset). Central agencies may also propose alternative policy options, modified implementation or delivery methods or suggest different rollout speeds. Central officials usually analyse and approve minor bids in consultation with agencies, while the ERC handles and ranks the larger bids. The 'challenge function' is tempered in democratic societies as there is an expectation that democratically elected governments will want to spend funds on policies attractive to voters to enhance their prospects of re-election (see Posner and Blöndal 2012).

At the federal level, Australia has adopted a particular accounting technique that essentially produces a bifurcation of the expenses allocated to agencies. It separates 'departmental expenses' (their own operating or running costs) from 'administered items' (funds they administratively distribute to others, nominally allocated to capped programs). This legal separation effectively contains departmental expenses (placing caps on expenditure that can be used only for operational purposes) and reserves earmarked funds for spending programs or grants the department merely administers.[4] Departments then have an incentive to manage within their flexible 'one-line' budget (departmental expenses) as they ought to manage within budget limits and can, in theory, carry forward into next year's budget any unspent funds in their departmental allocation. At the end of the financial year, any unspent funds in the administered items category are returned to the government for reallocation. This separation

---

4   State and territory governments do not use this bifurcation, as their departments and agencies are principally not funding entities but delivery organisations. The subnational jurisdictions allocate funding to ministerial portfolios (ministerial budget statements) and within those to agencies for their operational costs, contractual expenses, grants and subsidies and any other expenses they incur. At the Commonwealth level, only the Department of Defence is relatively exempt from the bifurcation between departmental and administered items because of the complicated character of its internal financial management relations.

(following the consolidation of running costs from the 1980s) has encouraged departments to manage their own budgets conservatively and within budget allocations. Some 95 per cent of Commonwealth agencies have operated each year within budgets for their departmental expenses and regularly underspend on administered items (practising a form of prudential 'in-year' budgetary management).

Australian governments have demonstrated a proficient ability to estimate the budgetary impact of smaller new policies and programs, mostly because these are relatively targeted, time-limited or funding capped. Nevertheless, they have a less than unblemished record in estimating the long-term costs of large policy projects and ones that are unlikely to lapse. Large items of defence spending, for instance, routinely exceed the initial costings in the out-years. In recent times, estimates for the National Disability Insurance Scheme (involving many support programs) were massively underestimated initially, with figures of $7 billion blowing out to over $22 billion within two years of the initial rollout. Similarly with the National Broadband Network, initial estimates put the price at $42 billion, half of which would be provided by the private sector; however, within six years, the figure had increased to $58 billion for a downscaled service and no private sector involvement eventuated. Similar blowouts occurred over the decades since the introduction of fees for tertiary education and the income-contingent loans scheme (the Higher Education Contribution Scheme/Higher Education Loan Programme [HECS/HELP]) in 1989 involving the virtual deregulation of student enrolment numbers and a mounting unsecured student loan debt on the federal government's balance sheet, reaching some $54 billion in 2017, with estimates that around one-third would never be repaid.

Assessing value for money in the legislative authorisation stages

Conventionally, the budget forms the centrepiece of the Budget Session of the Australian Parliament, commencing with a televised evening speech from the Treasurer, outlining the important points in the forthcoming budget. In the days and sometimes weeks before this speech, many of the key details of the budget, including any changes to taxation or spending, have been tactically leaked to the media as a form of expectation management to prepare for its reception. So, even though the budgetary papers may run to thousands of pages, parliamentarians and the media are generally well aware of the budget's main items even as it is being tabled. By convention, the opposition leader has the right of reply to the budget two days later, also in a televised speech; in recent years, opposition leaders have opted not to analyse or criticise the main aspects of the government's budget with which they might take issue, but instead to present an entirely alternative budget, hoping to appeal to the public with their policy proposals (effectively turning the 'budget reply speech' into a campaign rally speech).

Parliament then 'debates' the budget. In the House of Representatives, the budget session continues with stage-managed proforma speeches for and against particular budgetary measures, but more in-depth scrutiny is shown by the Senate, where the budget is referred to 'estimate hearings'— parliamentary committees with government, opposition and cross-bench senators organised on a sectoral or functional basis. These senate committees generally scrutinise the portfolio budget statements of the portfolio ministers, which contain detailed descriptions of the costs of programs and activities of the departments and agencies, including performance information. Senators and their staff prepare questions, which are asked of senate ministers—sometimes representing their own portfolios, but also being expected to stand in and answer for ministers who sit in the House of Representatives on matters pertaining to their portfolios. In addition, senior officials participate and often answer detailed or technical questions about ongoing programs or the implementation of new policy proposals. The extensively detailed 'portfolio budget statements' provide basic information and the putative 'agenda' for such scrutiny, but questions from senators can range across almost anything within the portfolio. Often this scrutiny consists of teasing out on the public record how the executive will achieve its intended objectives, what targets or performance indicators are pertinent and whether any variations in spending patterns look appropriate. Almost all the scrutiny is directed to the expenditure side of the budget and there is very little attention to the revenue side, although any additional revenue measures may be blocked for political reasons.

In recent years, the Parliamentary Budget Office (PBO) has been established, along the lines of the US Congressional Budget Office, but with a small staff of around 40 officials. The PBO undertakes research and educational activities for parliamentarians (who can ask for assistance or investigations on fiscal and budgetary matters). The office can also initiate its own investigations and produce reports for public consumption. A further function of the PBO is to undertake independent costings of policies that political parties propose close to election times and to assist parties confidentially with preparing costings of their policies (Bowen 2015).

An impartial observer would have to conclude that the Australian legislature does not exercise a rigorous efficiency eye over budgetary estimates and performance expectations at the authorisation stages, and large parts of the budget are passed without any comment or scrutiny. The lower house virtually eschews any serious budgetary scrutiny, although the theatrical spectacle can generate heated polemics. Parliament has relatively little access to alternative sources of data or analytical information with which to contest the government's carefully crafted figures. Non-government parliamentarians tend to engage in rhetorical critiques of spending proposals (that they do not go far enough, they go too far, are likely to lead to waste, low take-up, equity and fairness issues, and so on), but these subjective comments are based on little more than expedient opinions. However, the legislature *could* exercise a probing analysis of particular programs if members so desired or were prepared to expend the effort, and they could also come back to the issues at subsequent hearings.

Assessing value for money in the post-authorisation stages

Initially, post-budget monitoring is employed to gauge spending patterns against implementation schedules and milestones, especially for new policy proposals. Such compliance monitoring is not itself a value-for-money exercise, but can ensure implementation plans remain on track for acquittal. The Cabinet Implementation Unit (in PM&C) performs this limited function for nine to 18 months, but focuses mainly on deliverable activities and project management of specified spending items. Finance can also monitor spending against intended implementation plans and can warn agencies if their expenditures are either excessive or falling behind.

The auditor-general and the ANAO are the main accountability actors engaged in post–budget year evaluations—routinely conducting compliance audits (financial audits) across all agencies and programs (with extensive private auditor contractual assistance) and undertaking a small number of performance audits (which often focus on larger material outlays or complicated procurement projects). Presently, the auditor-general performs around 50 performance audits in each annual cycle. Audit staff regularly investigate the value-for-money issues under the themes of efficiency and effectiveness, but often report on administrative shortcomings rather than the value of the program to the community or whether any investment was demonstrably worthwhile. So, for example, a regional roads program will be evaluated for being on time, within budget, carefully planned and so on, but not on whether it provides value for money to the community or is worthwhile compared with other projects. In circumstances where the Commonwealth is transferring funds to subnational jurisdictions and earmarking amounts to specific functions, the auditor-general tends to ensure that legal compliance is satisfied with the discharge of the funds; although, in recent years, they have been granted the power by the parliament to conduct 'follow-the-money audits' in conjunction with state auditors (although few of these have actually been attempted to date).

Parliamentary committees using their own powers of investigation supplemented by public hearings can be active in scrutinising 'deliverables' in the post-authorisation stage (asking what was achieved, how effective was it, at what cost, what miscalculations or errors were made). The Joint Committee of Public Accounts and Audit (JCPAA) and sectoral committees (on defence, health, social services, public administration and so on) regularly probe policies or programs considered problematic or sensitive. The JCPAA, in particular, uses ANAO reports to guide its own subsequent investigations about value for money in Commonwealth outlays. However, these committees now rarely undertake in-year audits or site visits to check on progress or delivery, or really delve into the effectiveness of programs in post-year investigations. Instead, politics drives their agendas and they tend to interrogate officials in Parliament House (or other hearing venues) about problems with the program management or even policy parameters.

There are also problems in federal nations with intergovernmental transfers and shared responsibilities for policy sectors. In federal nations, subnational governments will often accept funding proposals initiated by the central government without necessarily being committed to achieving these policy objectives, or will be given money to provide infrastructure or quality social services without being formally obligated to do so.

Hence, considerable gaming can occur (e.g. over precise commitments, matching funding, the timing of resource commitments—front-ending versus back-ending), and some jurisdictions can regard gaming as an expected and legitimate part of intergovernmental relations because subnational jurisdictions enjoy only limited rights to taxation and no guaranteed shares of the taxes raised from their own residents (PM&C 2015).

In many federal nations, such as Australia, there is limited evaluation of performance where funding crosses jurisdictional boundaries, because, traditionally, neither level had the formal powers or sometimes even the inclination to monitor and hold the other to account. Subnational legislatures rarely (if ever) investigate policies/programs/grants that are specified by the national government but carried out and operationally implemented by state or provincial governments, nor do their principal accountability actors cross jurisdictional boundaries (including their jurisdictional parliamentary committees, auditors-general, commissions of audit, performance bodies or cost commissions). And, if constitutional arrangements prevent substantial institutional redesign, it is hard to make significant political headway over performance in areas of shared responsibilities. While actors can make various occasional pleas for reform—such as separating roles and responsibilities, rebalancing vertical fiscal imbalances, moving to guaranteed revenue shares or transferring responsibilities entirely to one level of government—they have had minimal practical effect. Both federal and state jurisdictions have only just enabled their respective auditors-general to investigate and audit performance over cross-jurisdictional funding arrangements—but this development remains contentious in some subnational governments.

How well does the system cohere?

In short, Australia's budgetary management system has many strengths and remaining weaknesses. The Australian system for evaluating the efficacy of public finance works partially and episodically, but is far from best practice. Defensive and risk-averse cultures across the public sector still impede transparency and the flourishing of an evaluation ethos that is both forthright and rigorous. Governments have little incentive to 'fess up' if programs are not performing or are failing to achieve their desired objectives; indeed, they are more likely to invest further resources in redesigning or rebadging the program than terminating it. The period in the immediate aftermath of a change of government tends to provide the main opportunity to abort or reconfigure underperforming programs (see Laurie and McDonald 2008). One recent initiative, to establish an intergovernmental performance review body to report on comparative state performance within federal funding envelopes, the COAG Reform Council, was quickly abolished in 2013 by the federal government with the blessing of the state premiers. However, since the 1990s, the Productivity Commission has produced the annual *Report on Services*, which attempts to calculate the comparative costs of delivering services across state and territory jurisdictions. The reports are full of detailed cost assessments and discussion of targeted achievements, but they receive little attention and the reviews have largely focused on the performance in policy sectors administered by state and territory jurisdictions, although, recently, they have been extended to include some Commonwealth programs.

In Australia, accountabilities for performance are still fragmented, piecemeal and sequential rather than combined and holistic. We have installed many windows to shed light into the system and through which to explore value-for-money questions, but they do not all cohere or form an integrated publicly available review. There are occasions when rigorous evaluations have been made in some component part of the system, particularly of new policy proposals, but there is often little longitudinal follow-through analysis that is made public. Moreover, where we have had some integrative aspects of performance review in the past, we have stripped these out in the name of convenience. For instance, the Commonwealth used to require all line agencies to report to the Minister for Finance within six months of receiving an unfavourable audit report what they had done to fix the problems and these departmental/agency reports were published and reviewed by Finance; this was ostensibly a 'closing the loop' provision, but it was abolished in the transition to outcomes-based accrual budgeting in the late 1990s. Agencies found the reporting requirements onerous but trivial in essence, did not take the exercise seriously and reputedly often reported back with defensive comments rather than real responses.

While some components of the annual budget are closely scrutinised, other areas of significant expenses are not rigorously evaluated unless they attract a dedicated (usually external) review.[5] Standing appropriations (or 'ongoing' appropriations), which constitute more than 80 per cent of annual outlays, generally receive scant or episodic attention in the budgetary process and continue indefinitely unless they are reviewed in some separate exercise. These standing appropriations include some 20 different forms of pensions and benefits and other entitlements to families and individuals, funding for demand-driven programs such as the Medical Benefits Scheme or the Pharmaceutical Benefits Scheme, grants and ongoing funding to community organisations (administered items), as well as general funding to states and territories, interest payments on debt, and so on. Moreover, many capital budgets (for infrastructure projects, major defence procurements) are not necessarily assessed in terms of value for money, nor judged according to where to make the best investment. Rural, regional and political factors all play a role here, leading to criticism from infrastructure specialists (such as Infrastructure Australia) that funds have been historically misallocated, creating inefficiencies and bottlenecks. Also, Australian politicians are sentimentally attached to their 'ribbon-cutting mentality' (arranging photo opportunities associated with the opening of events, new facilities or new infrastructure projects), which results in Australian governments spending far more on new infrastructure than their OECD comparators, but much less on basic maintenance and infrastructure upgrades (Infrastructure Australia 2015). There are steps afoot to redress problems with misallocation through bodies such as Infrastructure Australia turning the focus on to 'value capture' in the life cycle of major infrastructure projects.

Other inherent problems limiting higher performance

In comparative terms, Australia has not developed a strong evaluation culture in public policy. Governments are content to espouse their ostensible objectives when announcing policy initiatives but often do

---

5   Recently, a number of significant areas of the budget have attracted some form of independent review, often to inquire into their coherence, complexity, integration and funding trends rather than value-for-money questions. These reviews include the Ken Henry Review into taxation, Jeff Harmer's review of pensions and transfers, the Bennett Review of the sustainability of hospital and health funding and various Productivity Commission reviews of housing, gambling, education and training, and so on.

not collect data on outcomes they have embraced (e.g. environmental sustainability, safer communities and improved community capabilities, improved social cohesion and educational readiness). Many policies are politically driven and governments have invested considerable 'face' in their policies, meaning that unflattering evaluations threaten to embarrass the government or selected ministers. Under such conditions, policies may evade review or be only partially reviewed internally to avoid criticism of the policy intent or design. At the program level, activity reporting rather than measures of effectiveness tends to be collected, which is of limited use in evaluating value-for-money questions.

Across government, data have traditionally been poor and patchy, and much of it was not meaningfully comparable. As the COAG Reform Council argued before it was abolished, making evaluation judgments about the worth of programs on poor-quality data is inherently risky and problematic. Furthermore, the relationship between different sets of indicators pertaining to performance (say, waiting times in hospitals versus health outcomes) is not necessarily straightforward or consistent. Improvements in one measure may come at the cost of another, or a range of indicators measured may have almost nothing to do with one another. Governments find themselves responding to the more visible or more electorally sensitive aspects of policy rather than systemic refinement and recalibration.

In the 1980s and 1990s, many New Public Management adherents argued (and fervently believed) that devolved management with increased discretion and flexibilities in financial management would automatically lead to increased performance; yet, when it came to demonstrating improved performance, they were generally unable to convincingly prove results. The Australian Parliament repeatedly asked the federal government to produce reports evaluating the public sector reforms of the 1980s and early 1990s, and, although four reports were produced over a decade, they were largely silent on performance improvement—the best was *The Australian Public Service Reformed* (Task Force on Management Improvement 1992; but see also Wanna et al. 2000; Verspaandonk et al. 2010). And, although the Moran Review into Commonwealth administration (Moran 2010) argued for a comprehensive client-based survey of performance to be routinely undertaken, none ever appeared or has been planned. And, as already mentioned, the Productivity Commission's annual *Report on Services* provides costing data largely comparing the relative performance of state and territory provisioning, but only implicitly analyses the value for money of the various provisions themselves. Agency annual reports have in recent decades reported more information on administrative efficiencies and client service satisfaction relative to publicly announced service charters.

In contrast to some other nations, Australia has been reluctant to use performance incentives to improve performance. There is considerable scepticism in government that performance incentives work well in the public sector and widespread belief that such measures can lead to perverse consequences. For example, rewarding high performers or high-performing units (administrative units, hospitals or schools) can lead to the opposite effects system-wide—through discouragement of low performers, envy, perceptions of fairness and unfairness and fierce disputes over data/criteria/possibilities. It is not clear whether rewarding high-performing entities actually leads to improved performance in those entities, and fortune/happenstance may have been an important contributor to enhanced performance levels. Some large and some smaller programs have tried to use performance incentives to improve results, but to mixed effect (national partnership payments with performance bonuses, self-responsibility programs in Indigenous communities, parenting education for troubled families), and governments have usually been forced to pay the increments whatever the diminished levels of performance actually reported. There is also a widespread view that performance pay for officials (or personal bonuses) does not often lead to heightened individual or agency performance, and that, in their application, they can produce resentment, an undue emphasis on individualism, inflated exaggerations of personal contributions, team discouragement and even distorting of data and indicators (ANAO 1993). There are also criticisms of the politicised system of reviewing and awarding individual performance bonuses, which may reward factors not related to actual performance (seniority, reputation, sensitivity, gender, obsequiousness, regional–urban locations, etc.).

A further alternative way to promote performance being actively talked about more recently (and already used in a few policy sectors) is the notion of 'earned autonomy', where high-performing, well-managed entities such as hospitals or selective schools are given greater managerial autonomy to conduct their affairs. Such initiatives are still largely in the experimental stages and used judiciously. It is not yet clear whether 'earned autonomy' initiatives can be applied to poor-performing agencies or programs to improve levels of performance.

Conclusions

Australia has developed a sophisticated and comprehensive budget system, with robust processes and budget-setting procedures, including extensive reporting requirements. Over many decades, governments have put in place important managerial reforms to incentivise improved performance, especially since the 1980s. Many budget-related institutions or monitoring bodies are powerful players in the system and wield influence over decision-making. But, despite considerable effort to reorient the budgetary system towards performance management and an emphasis on results, there remain several weaknesses and gaps in the overall system. Arguably, Australia's systems of budgeting and resource allocation have principally been structured to maintain a certain fiscal discipline, but have paid far less attention to establishing and reporting on the value for money taxpayers receive from public policies. The entire budgetary authorisation process has traditionally been structured primarily to satisfy legal requirements rather than to demonstrate criteria of performance, productivity or effectiveness in policies and programs. In budgetary reform, governments at all levels have moved away from line-item budgeting to framing the budget allocations around expected results (e.g. outcomes, outputs, key performance indicators). Budget documentation has been extensively revised to provide results-based frameworks against which resources have been allocated. The impression given is that the government has weighed value-for-money considerations against its expected results and allocated resources accordingly. Yet, cynics might argue that these governments have merely allocated their resources along traditional (legacy) lines and then presented them cosmetically in a result-based packaging. Certainly, more performance information has been included in recent budget documentation (whereas little was included some decades ago), but it is not clear whether an assessment of performance informs the basis for resource allocation. Moreover, criticisms can be levelled that much of the performance information produced by agencies resembles promotional advertising rather than assessments of service quality.

Yet, within these changes, some improvements to administration and operations have occurred because of devolved management and increased discretion afforded to public sector executives. Managers have the capacity to make better management decisions, use alternative and contestable sources of delivery or provision and can better focus on desired results. They are far less constrained by bureaucratic rules and regulations governing management, but are still constrained by cascading accountabilities that foster an aversion to risk and openness. As a nation, we are not good at demonstrating the worth of policies or programs or, conversely, of admitting mistakes. There is a manifest hesitancy about being transparent and honest about value for money.

One important holistic reform may be for agencies to explicitly undertake value-for-money investigations of their programs and activities, setting out clearly the criteria on which they base their value-for-money analysis. They could then make the reports of these investigations publicly available, perhaps as a supplement to their annual reports and in budget submissions and bids for new resources. This would help link activity-based performance indicators and subsequent performance reporting with qualitative assessments of the worth of programs and activities. Ideally, these value-for-money reports should be open to independent assessments and critical reflection, perhaps from the ANAO, think tanks, academic centres, accounting firms and management consultants.

So, if outcome budgeting and performance reporting are meant to give legislatures and taxpayers reliable information on the value for money of public provision then there are still major gaps in our governmental systems. Governments have talked about putting a performance lens over budgetary systems for more than 30 years now, and are still talking about the same issue, with new legislation passed in 2013, but without much grounded detail of how improved reporting will occur. They have incorporated results-based corporate and strategic plans in budgetary documentation, but remain reluctant to release detailed information and assessments of performance, especially at program and subprogram levels. Australian legislatures at both state and federal levels have not really exercised their prerogatives to demand meaningful value for money. Until they do, governments will be content to offer activity reporting as a proxy for affirming public value.

References

Australian National Audit Office (ANAO). 1993. *Performance Audit into Performance Bonuses for Executives.* Canberra: ANAO.

Australian National Audit Office (ANAO). 1999. *Management of Commonwealth budgetary processes.* Report No. 38. Canberra: ANAO.

Blöndal, J. 2008. *Budgeting in Australia*. Paris: OECD Publishing.

Bowen, P. 2015. The Parliamentary Budget Office: 'Supporting Australian democracy'. Senate Occasional Lecture. Australian Senate, Parliament of Australia, Canberra.

Di Francesco, M. and J. Alford. 2016. *Balancing Control and Flexibility in Public Budgeting*. Singapore: Palgrave Macmillan. doi.org/10.1007/978-981-10-0341-7.

Dowding, K. and A. Martin. 2017. *Policy Agendas in Australia*. Singapore: Palgrave Macmillan. doi.org/10.1007/978-3-319-40805-7.

Gregory, R. 2017. 'Fiscal outcomes in a time of increasing political spin and unanticipated economic change'. Freebairn Lecture, University of Melbourne, Melbourne, May 2017.

Hawke, L. and J. Wanna. 2010. 'Australia after budget reform: A lapsed pioneer or decorative architect?' In J. Wanna, L. Jensen and J. de Vries (eds) *The Reality of Budgetary Reform in OECD Nations: Trajectories and consequences*. Cheltenham, UK: Edward Elgar. doi.org/10.4337/9781849805636.00010.

Heclo, H. and A. Wildavsky. 1974. *The Private Government of Public Money*. Berkeley, CA: University of California Press.

Infrastructure Australia. 2015. *Australian Infrastructure Audit Report*. Canberra: Australian Government.

Kelly, J. and J. Wanna. 2001. 'Are Wildavsky's guardians and spenders still relevant? New public management and the politics of government budgeting'. In L. Jones, J. Guthrie and P. Steane (eds) *Learning from International Public Management Reform*. Oxford: Elsevier. doi.org/10.1016/S0732-1317(01)11016-X.

Kraan, D., I. Hawkesworth, R. Deighton-Smith, J. Kelly and E. Job. 2012. *Value for Money in Government: Australia 2012*. Paris: OECD Publishing.

Laurie, K. and J. McDonald. 2008. *A Perspective on Trends in Australian Government Spending*. Canberra: Department of Treasury.

Moran, T. 2010. *Ahead of the Game: Blueprint for the Reform of Australian Government Administration/Advisory Group on Reform of Australian Government Administration*. [Moran Review]. Canberra: Department of the Prime Minister and Cabinet.

Prime Minister and Cabinet (PM&C). 2015. *Reform of the Federation*. Issues Paper No. 5. Canberra: Council of Australian Governments and Federal Financial Relations, Department of the Prime Minister and Cabinet.

Posner, P. and J. Blöndal. 2012. 'Deficits and democracy: Prospects for fiscal responsibility in democratic nations'. *Governance: An International Journal of Policy, Administration and Institutions* 25(1): 11–34. doi.org/10.1111/j.1468-0491.2011.01554.x.

Task Force on Management Improvement. 1992. *The Australian Public Service Reformed: An evaluation of a decade of management reform*. Canberra: AGPS.

Verspaandonk, R., I. Holland and N. Horne. 2010. *A chronology of changes in the Australian Public Service 1975–2010*. Parliamentary Library Background Paper. Canberra: Parliament of Australia.

Wanna, J., J. Forster and J. Kelly. 2000. *Managing Public Expenditure in Australia*. Sydney: Allen & Unwin.

Wanna J., L. Jensen and J. de Vries (eds). 2010. *The Reality of Budgetary Reform in OECD Nations: Trajectories and consequences*. Cheltenham, UK: Edward Elgar.

Young, L. 1996. *Minor Players? The Senate, the minor parties and the 1993 budget*. Parliamentary Fellow Monographs. Canberra: Parliament of Australia.

Appendix 2.1 Commonwealth budget timelines

The following timeline is followed in the lead-up to the presentation of the budget to Parliament.

Timeline (calendar month)	Event or review process	What occurs
September to November	Pre-budget submissions	The treasurer issues a press release calling for pre-budget submissions from interested parties. This allows for consultation with the community on priorities for the next budget.
November or December	Senior ministers' review	Portfolio ministers' new proposals and expected major pressures on agency budgets are considered, and priorities for the coming budget are established. The ministers who attend this review are the prime minister, the deputy prime minister, the treasurer and the minister for finance and administration.
February	Portfolio budget submissions	To seek funding for new policy proposals, agencies prepare portfolio budget submissions based on the outcome of the senior ministers' review. The submissions outline all major proposals that agencies wish to have funded and potential savings.
March	Expenditure Review Committee	This subcommittee of Cabinet is primarily responsible for developing the budget against the background of the government's political, social and economic priorities. It decides which of the agencies' proposals will be funded and by how much. Membership varies, but usually comprises the prime minister, the treasurer, the minister for finance and administration and one or two other ministers.
March or April	Ad Hoc Revenue Committee	The Ad Hoc Revenue Committee is also a Cabinet committee. It meets after the ERC to decide the revenue components of the budget.
April	Budget Cabinet	This is the final stage in the decision-making process. Decisions from the ERC are endorsed and the budget Cabinet agrees to present the budget to parliament.
May	Presentation to parliament ('Budget Night')	The budget is usually brought down on the second Tuesday in May. The government presents the budget papers and budget-related documents. The treasurer summarises the budget in the Budget Speech, which is traditionally presented at 7.30 pm on budget night and televised.

Timeline (calendar month)	Event or review process	What occurs
September	*Final Budget Outcome* report	The *Charter of Budget Honesty Act 1998* requires that a *Final Budget Outcome* be released no later than three months after the end of the relevant financial year. The financial statements in the *Final Budget Outcome* are similar to those in the budget but provide actual outcomes rather than estimates.
December	Mid-Year Economic and Fiscal Outlook	The mid-year half-yearly update must be released by the end of January or six months after the budget is handed down, whichever is later. It provides a full update of changing assumptions, expenses and any policy changes affecting the budget.
Three-yearly	Pre-Election Fiscal Outlook (PEFO)	The *Charter of Budget Honesty Act 1998* requires that a PEFO be released in election years. The purpose of the PEFO is to update information on the economic and fiscal outlook before an election. A PEFO must be released publicly within 10 days of the issue of the writ for a general election, and must contain spending and revenue estimates for the current and following three financial years, the assumptions underlying the estimates, the sensitivity of the estimates to changes in assumptions and risks that might materially change the fiscal outlook.

3

Projecting long-term fiscal outcomes

Mike Woods

Introduction

Many governments, mainly in developed economies, are adopting the practice of developing projections of their likely fiscal position over the long term. Such projections extend far beyond the three-year 'forward estimates' of expenditure and revenue that some governments produce and also beyond the timeframe of more traditional five-year economic development plans that are still the basis of planning for many governments in East and South-East Asia and elsewhere. While some longer-term reports present projections for at least two decades, others extend to 40 or 50 years.

From a slow start in the reform decade of the 1990s, when the Organisation for Economic Co-operation and Development (OECD) noted that only four countries produced reports of long-term fiscal projections, by 2009, 27 OECD countries were producing such reports (Anderson and Sheppard 2009).

This chapter examines the rationale for producing these reports, surveys international practice, critiques Australia's experience and offers an agenda for further reform.

Rationale for producing reports of long-term fiscal projections

There are at least three broad rationales for governments to prepare and publish long-term fiscal projections:

- to establish a framework for setting short-term fiscal policy within a set of longer-term fiscal objectives that, as a minimum, span the economic cycle
- to understand the sensitivity and vulnerability of budget outcomes to exogenous forces over the longer term
- to demonstrate the sustainability or otherwise of current policies.

The OECD similarly suggests that fiscal projections provide a number of benefits for governments. In their words:

> They raise the profile of fiscal sustainability, provide a framework to discuss the fiscal sustainability of current policies and the possible fiscal impact of reforms, and centralise responsibility for long-term policy analysis. (Anderson and Sheppard 2009: 9)

Underlying the first rationale, a country's economic performance at any particular point is the outcome of a number of forces, both international and domestic, which are interacting with and impacting on the underlying robustness of the economy. International forces include global financial, trade and currency crises. At the national level, governments use their fiscal policy to influence macroeconomic settings and address economic cycles while central banks target inflation through monetary policy.

Fiscal policy is affected, broadly, through governments adjusting their level and allocation of expenditure, as well as their taxation and other revenue-raising. However, fiscal policy is not always readily amenable to significant short-term change. In particular, it has an asymmetric 'stickiness' that has an expansionary bias. During an economic downturn, governments can undertake countercyclical increases in expenditure to ameliorate the reduction in economic activity and employment. That expansion usually coincides with reduced taxation receipts from company profits, personal income taxes and even value-added taxes, thus requiring the expansion to be funded through borrowings. The recent experience of the Global Financial Crisis (GFC) in 2008 provided innumerable examples of governments resorting to fiscal policy—and their central banks providing supportive monetary policy—in an attempt to stave off recessionary outcomes.

In terms of its stickiness, some expenditure, particularly on major capital works, is bound contractually and governments have few options for reducing those outlays over the duration of the contract (and, when they do so, the consequences can be significant). Equally, there can be political lock-in when government expenditure creates a sense of entitlement among its many recipients. Reversal of this expenditure, as the economy levels out and ultimately enters it next growth period, is politically difficult.

Long-term fiscal projections can provide governments with an opportunity to publish evidence of the unsustainability of expansionary fiscal policy settings over the course of the economic cycle and to demonstrate the need to develop surpluses in periods of growth to pay down some of the debt incurred during downturns.

A second rationale for preparing reports of long-term fiscal projections is to be able to test the sensitivity and vulnerability of future budgetary outcomes to a number of plausible, significant exogenous influences on government revenue and expenditures.

A variety of factors largely outside the control of government can have very significant impacts on fiscal outcomes. Whereas many of these are largely the result of domestic and global economic cycles, some have longer-term structural characteristics. As will be discussed below, demographic change—which is inexorably reshaping economies from Japan and Italy to China and Australia—will have very significant fiscal implications for those countries. Another change, only partly related to ageing, is the ongoing increase in the cost of providing health services. A third factor, the fiscal impacts of which are not yet fully understood, is climate change. There are obvious future costs arising from the need to replace infrastructure likely to be stranded or made inoperable by forecast rising sea levels. Other sources of cost include the greater frequency of heatwaves and bushfires that most climate scientists predict. There will be costs and, in some cases, benefits from changes in agricultural practices in various regions in response to changes in temperature, rainfall and rates of evaporation.

The third significant rationale is that projections of long-term fiscal outcomes can be used to model the impact of changes in programs and entitlements on projected future government expenditures and revenue. While some government programs can be adjusted in the short term in response to changing needs or fiscal circumstances, others have longer-term characteristics. In particular, retirement income policies that have defined benefit obligations bring with them accrued liabilities that last over many decades. Other benefit payment schemes are also difficult to radically adjust. Calls for further improvements to benefit levels can be modelled to demonstrate their long-term impact on fiscal balances, and hence their sustainability.

In the hands of a skilful and visionary leader, these reports can create an evidence base on which he or she can develop a narrative that helps to create a public understanding of the benefits of fiscal responsibility and provides support for, or at least acceptance of, any necessary shorter-term budget adjustment measures to achieve long-term prosperity. A recent 12-country survey (Anderson and Sheppard 2009) demonstrated this role of using such policy to justify balancing fiscal pressures and risks over an extended time horizon against political pressures for short-term spending.

International experience

The approaches to adopting legislative frameworks for fiscal responsibility policy settings vary across countries. They can be broadly categorised into two groups: those that set specific fiscal targets, caps or trajectories and those that essentially establish a set of fiscal principles and more transparent reporting standards. In reality, many countries have adopted some combination of both. An early example of the former was the US *Budget Enforcement Act 1990*, the focus of which was very clearly on reducing the budget deficit, to be achieved in large part by targeting discretionary expenditure.

The earliest well-known example of the latter form of legislation was New Zealand's *Fiscal Responsibility Act 1994*. At that time, New Zealand was pursuing a program of extensive economic and fiscal reform, and this had a profound agenda-setting impact, not only on Australia's Commonwealth Government, but also on the governments of many developed countries.

The International Monetary Fund's 2007 update of its *Manual on Fiscal Transparency* observed that New Zealand's legislation is 'a benchmark piece of legislation, which sets legal standards for transparency of fiscal policy and reporting, and holds the government formally responsible to the public for its fiscal performance' (IMF 2007: 95). The New Zealand Act sets out five principles of responsible fiscal management, including limiting public debt to prudent levels and maintaining an operating balance on average over the medium term. Similar legislation has been enacted in the United Kingdom with its Code for Fiscal Stability. Standards of fiscal transparency under such national legislation are generally more demanding than those suggested under the IMF's Code on Fiscal Transparency.

In 2006, the European Union (EU) published its first report on *Long-Term Sustainability of Public Finances in the European Union*, as part of its budgetary surveillance. Critical assumptions included the continuation of current policy, independent population projections and specified macroeconomic projections. Subsequently, demographic change has become an even more pressing issue and the EU has established the Working Group on Ageing Populations and Sustainability (EU EPC 2015). As the website of the working group notes:

> The ageing of the population is becoming a growing challenge to the sustainability of public finances in the EU Member States. The increase of the ratio between the number of retirees and the number of workers will amplify expenditure on public pensions and health and long-term care and thus puts a burden on maintaining a sound balance between future public expenditure and tax revenues. (EU EPC 2015)

Europe is not alone in being impacted by demographic change and, in particular, the ageing of its population. In Asia, Japan is significantly affected, with its dependency ratio (the proportion of its working-age population to those not of working age) declining rapidly. Indeed, Japan's overall population is poised for a long period of absolute decline. As Jones and Fukawa (2015) note, Japan is currently running a level of gross government debt of 226 per cent. Such a high level of debt (described by the authors as 'unchartered territory') leaves the economy highly exposed to economic shocks, with little room to instigate countercyclical fiscal stimulus measures.

The consequences for Japan include ongoing increases in health expenditure, pressure on pension systems and a reducing base of both income taxes and revenue from consumption taxes and other economic activity more generally. The upcoming working-age cohort will be carrying an increasing burden of paying for the publicly funded programs being supplied to the elderly. Jones and Fukawa (2015) suggest that, as a consequence, there is a very real need to promote social cohesion. The clear conclusion is that Japan needs a credible fiscal consolidation plan, on both the revenue and the expenditure sides, to restore some measure of fiscal sustainability.

Even in China, the impact of demographic change is having significant ramifications. The 35 years of the family planning law (somewhat incorrectly referred to as the one-child policy, given that there were exemptions for rural households and ethnic minorities) have led in part to significant issues with workforce availability and social security affordability. Accordingly, there was some relaxation of this policy in 2013 and, following the Fifth Plenum of the Communist Party of China in November 2015, it was announced that, in future, all couples would be able to have two children.

Opportunities to improve long-term fiscal outlooks

A number of multilateral agencies and academics have reviewed the quality of long-term fiscal reporting and identified opportunities for improvement. Three areas are particularly significant: reporting on a whole-of-public-sector basis, improving transparency and reporting on a regular basis.

In relation to the first of these three, the fiscal sustainability of the policy settings of any one level of government is a significant consideration for that government, for its constituents and for financial markets. In particular, the ability of the government's budgetary position to withstand long-term structural change as well as shorter-term economic and financial shocks is important. The principles of fiscal management, adopted by a number of countries, provide guidance on these matters.

However, at an economy-wide and whole-of-society level, there is also great benefit in understanding the projected long-term fiscal outcomes aggregated across all levels of government. Otherwise, a report limited to the national government can say more about the policies of intergovernmental transfers than about the underlying fiscal outlook for governments as a whole.

Transparency is another international concern. A 2008 open budget survey by Carlitz et al. (2009: 1) concluded that 'the state of budget transparency around the world is deplorable'. In a survey of 85 countries (Australia was not included), on average, they provided minimal information on their central government's budget and financial activities. Only five countries, including New Zealand, made extensive information publicly available in accordance with generally accepted good public financial management practices.

Hameed (2005) explored the level of fiscal transparency across many countries, highlighting the importance for the community and financial markets of being able to accurately assess the social and economic implications of a government's activities, not only in present times, but also into the future. Hameed used data from IMF fiscal reports, including on medium-term budgeting, and found that countries with greater fiscal transparency had better fiscal discipline (as well as better access to international financial markets and less corruption).

International agencies have surveyed and analysed the practices of many countries in producing long-term fiscal outlooks. The OECD has produced its *Best Practices for Budget Transparency*, in which it states:

1.7. Long-term report

- The long-term report assesses the long-term sustainability of current government policies. It should be released at least every five years, or when major changes are made in substantive revenue or expenditure programmes.
- The report should assess the budgetary implications of demographic change, such as population ageing and other potential developments over the long-term (10–40 years).
- All key assumptions underlying the projections contained in the report should be made explicit and a range of plausible scenarios presented. (OECD 2002: 11)

Similarly, the IMF *Manual on Fiscal Transparency* states that governments should publish a periodic report on long-term public finances and the focus of the projections should be on more than just demographic changes (IMF 2007: 15).

In an examination of fiscal futures, institutional budget reforms and their effects, Anderson and Sheppard (2009: 9, 10) draw some lessons. They offer six broad areas of reform, an edited version of which is set out below:

- Fiscal projections should be prepared on an annual basis to draw attention to the long-term fiscal consequences of current policies and to eliminate discretion over when projections are produced. Although concerns may exist about the political risks of publishing fiscal projections, attention must focus on the long-term benefits that come from transparency of the government's long-term fiscal position.

- Fiscal projections should incorporate comparisons with previous government assessments to highlight whether the government's fiscal position has improved or deteriorated. Many countries do not provide a comparison with previous projections; Australia and the Netherlands are two notable exceptions.

- Fiscal projections should include sensitivity analysis for changes in demographic, macroeconomic, microeconomic and other assumptions to illustrate the exposure, and general direction of the impact of this exposure, to fiscal risks.

- Fiscal projections should clearly present changes in the methodology, key assumptions and data sources to provide an assurance of their credibility and quality. Disclosure and justification of changes in the underlying assumptions are one means to provide assurance about the quality of the projections and a basis for an independent review of a country's fiscal future.

- Countries should use fiscal projections to illustrate the fiscal consequences of past reforms or general policy options. This has the potential to demonstrate to policymakers that improvements in the country's long-term fiscal position are possible but may not eliminate altogether the long-term fiscal challenge. However, policy options should not be presented as prescriptions or means of circumventing political consultation about the types and specifics of reforms.

- Finally, although fiscal projections should be directly tied to the annual budget process, they also should be linked to other budget practices and procedures to ensure that adequate attention is given to the fiscal consequences of current policies. This may be accomplished through linking the results of fiscal projections to fiscal targets, medium-term budget ceilings or entitlement benefit formulas through either hard or soft budget triggers.

Anderson and Sheppard (2009: 42) conclude by noting:

> The expanding use of fiscal projections in countries with very different governmental and budgetary systems suggests that these recommendations are relevant to a broad range of OECD and non-OECD countries alike.

Australia's early innovations in fiscal reform

In Australia, several state governments were early innovators in introducing fiscal reforms and adopting longer-term fiscal perspectives. One of the principal motivations was to reduce their levels of debt. That the governments found themselves in this situation was the result of a series of events that began in the mid to late 1980s, including revenue reductions from falling asset prices, the national recession of the early 1990s and the failure of several significant state-owned financial institutions.

In 1988, the New South Wales (NSW) Government found itself unable to reliably assess the current and prospective financial position of the state. Accordingly, it appointed a group of prominent businessmen to undertake a commission of audit. In a period of just less than four months, and assisted by a secretariat of officials, this commission produced a seminal report that was to become a blueprint for subsequent inquiries by other Australian governments (NSW Commission of Audit 1988). The headline conclusion was that the state 'has been living beyond its means'.

An important initiative of the NSW Commission of Audit was to attempt to supplement the government's cash accounts with a more commercially focused set of accrual accounts. Essentially, under the cash accounting approach, a government's surplus or deficit position was determined by whether more or less revenue was paid into the Treasury than was paid out in a given period. The NSW Commission of Audit recommended that the preparation of an annual balance sheet and income and expense statement would significantly improve an understanding of the sustainability of the state's fiscal position. This approach more clearly identified the government's longer-term fiscal position by calculating the liabilities and assets of the state.

One of the more substantial liabilities was the employer-funded superannuation that was accruing to the government's public servants. This liability would need to be paid out (i.e. become actual cash expenditures) in future years as those public servants retired and started drawing down their pensions. A second liability, which would equally result in cash expenditure and have a direct future fiscal impact, was the consumption of existing capital assets, which would require their subsequent replacement (in essence, a charge for depreciation).

A third liability worthy of a brief reference at this point is the one associated with government guarantees, memoranda of support, letters of comfort and so on, which are often provided to private businesses under the guise of economic development. These instruments are often (wrongly) perceived, or at least portrayed by both politicians and the business entities in receipt of them, as being essentially 'free' support from governments that have tangible benefits for the recipients, usually in the form of a lower risk premium on the cost of borrowings. Even better, they do not appear under a cash budgeting format and are therefore largely invisible to the general public. However, under the discipline of accrual accounting, such instruments are (correctly) perceived as being liabilities that are contingent on the outcome of specified events, especially the failure of the enterprise that was the recipient of the support. Real and usually very large expenditures can result from such events, and can have major impacts on future fiscal outcomes.

The NSW Commission also developed a framework for its analysis of the activities of government in the economy. The framework set out three fundamental questions:

- Why should the government expenditure be undertaken at all? What would result if the program/activity were abolished?
- What special features of the program/activity mean that the goods cannot be provided more efficiently and cost-effectively by the private sector?
- Why should parliament, ministers and senior public service executives be devoting scarce time to the mechanics of producing these goods?

In 1996, following the election of a new conservative government at the national level, and in accordance with one of the pre-election commitments of that new government, a select group of private sector leaders—mainly from the finance sector, and supported by a secretariat of officials—was tasked with investigating and reporting on, within three months:

The financial position of the Commonwealth Government with a view to advising the Government on the future management of its finances consistent with a medium to long-term goal of improving the Government's fiscal position. (National Commission of Audit 1996: 1)

Within those overall terms of reference, the commission was required to report on six matters, which can be summarised as follows:

1. the actual state of the Commonwealth's finances, including its assets, liabilities and contingent liabilities
2. the compilation of a 'whole-of-government' balance sheet for the Commonwealth Government
3. the impact of demographic change on Commonwealth finances, and how emerging pressures could be provisioned
4. the extent, condition and adequacy of Commonwealth sector infrastructure and possible remedies for any deficiencies
5. a methodology for developing and implementing financial performance targets for Commonwealth departments and agencies
6. current service delivery arrangements between the states/territories and the Commonwealth, and their effectiveness and efficiency.

The commission was also requested to provide advice on additional matters, which were included in another of the incoming government's pre-election commitments: to establish a Charter of Budget Honesty, which would encompass both governmental financial reporting requirements and fiscal policy objectives.

The ensuing analysis adopted a decision framework that was similar to the much earlier NSW Commission of Audit:

• Assess whether or not there is a role for government.
• Where there is, decide which level of government, and assess whether or not government objectives are clearly specified and effectively promoted.
• Assess whether or not effective activities are being conducted on a 'best practice' basis (National Commission of Audit 1996: vii).

The report elaborated on what constituted 'best practice'—the two defining characteristics being that it was input efficient and outcome focused.

One of the major recommendations of the report of the National Commission of Audit (1996: 211) was that the Commonwealth Government should 'adopt accrual accounting principles as the basis for an integrated budgeting, resource management and financial reporting framework both at the agency level and at the aggregate budget sector level'.

The report recommended the Commonwealth introduce legislation that would require the government of the day to set and report against a clear fiscal strategy, which would include setting targets and benchmarks.

The Charter of Budget Honesty

Following the report of the National Commission of Audit in June 1996, the Commonwealth Parliament passed a law to create the Charter of Budget Honesty. As noted in Section 1 of the *Charter of Budget Honesty Act 1998* (Cwlth):

> The purpose of the Charter is to improve fiscal policy outcomes. The Charter provides for this by requiring fiscal strategy to be based on principles of sound fiscal management and by facilitating public scrutiny of fiscal policy and performance.

In similar fashion to the New Zealand Act, Australia's Charter of Budget Honesty sets out the principles of sound fiscal management, including maintaining a prudent level of general government debt, moderating cyclical fluctuations in economic activity and ensuring policy decisions have regard to their financial effects on future generations. In terms of the last, the treasurer is required to publicly release, at least once every five years, an intergenerational report (IGR).

The IGR has had, from its inception in 2002 to its most recent issue, a focus on ageing. This is mandated in the charter, Section 21 of which states:

> An intergenerational report is to assess the long term sustainability of current Government policies over the 40 years following the release of the report, including by taking account of the financial implications of demographic change.

In the foreword to the 2015 IGR, the then treasurer made the following point (Australian Treasury 2015: iii):

> It is fantastic that Australians are living longer and healthier lives but we need to address these demographic changes. If we don't do something, we risk reducing our available workforce, impacting negatively on growth and prosperity, and our income will come under increasing pressure.

The 2015 IGR makes a number of substantive points that have implications for the long-term fiscal outlook (Australian Treasury 2015: vii–xvii).

In terms of basic demographics:

- Australians will live longer and continue to have one of the longest life expectancies in the world. In 2054–55, life expectancy at birth is projected to be 95.1 years for men and 96.6 years for women, which is an increase of around three years for both.
- Both the number and the proportion of Australians aged 85 and over will grow rapidly. In 1974–75, this age group numbered around 80,000 people; however, by 2054–55, nearly two million Australians will be aged 85 and over. While there were 122 centenarians in 1974–75, there are expected to be around 40,000 by 2054–55.

There will be significant fiscal and economic impacts:

- There will be fewer people of traditional working age compared with the very young and the elderly. At present, there are an estimated 4.5 people aged between 15 and 64 for every person aged 65 and over, but, by 2054–55, this is projected to nearly halve to 2.7 people.
- Over the next 40 years, the proportion of the population participating in the workforce is expected to decline as a result of population ageing. A lower proportion of Australians working will mean lower economic growth over the projection period.
- That said, female employment is projected to continue to increase. Today, around 66 per cent of women aged 15 to 64 are employed. By 2054–55, female employment is projected to increase to around 70 per cent.
- During the 1990s, Australia's multifactor productivity (MFP) growth was especially high, with an estimated average of 2.2 per cent growth per year. This has been widely attributed to economic reforms during the 1980s and 1990s. These reforms created more competitive and flexible markets in which businesses became more efficient and

innovative, and new and improved technologies were adopted. More recently, Australia's MFP growth has been relatively flat, as has been the case in many other developed economies.

A limited number of items will drive the expenditure side of the Commonwealth Government's fiscal outlook over the long term:

- The 2015 IGR identifies health as the biggest item of budgetary increase over the next 40 years. Commonwealth Government health expenditure is projected to increase from 4.2 per cent of gross domestic product (GDP) to 5.5 per cent by 2054–55. (In 2013–14, total expenditure on health by all governments, individuals and the non-government sector represented 9.8 per cent of GDP [AIHW 2015].)
- Expenditure by the Australian Government on aged care services is projected to almost double, from the current 0.9 per cent of GDP to 1.7 per cent.
- Expenditure on age and service pensions was projected to stabilise at a little lower than the current 2.9 per cent of GDP, though this was based on government proposals not agreed by the parliament; nonetheless, projections based on current legislation still reveal only modest increases, to around 3.5 per cent of GDP, thanks in part to reforms in the 1990s.

Clearly, the expectation of a long-term rise in health costs (as has already been occurring) will have a major impact on fiscal outcomes. However, while older Australians, per capita, are much greater consumers of health services than younger people, this is not the most significant cause of these escalating health costs. As recognised by the 2015 IGR (Australian Treasury 2015: xvi): 'The report explains how non-demographic factors, including higher incomes, health sector wages growth and technological change, are more significant drivers of the projected increase than demographic changes.'

The Australian Productivity Commission reached a similar conclusion in 2005 (PC 2005: xii): 'In itself, population ageing should not be seen as a problem, but it will give rise to economic and fiscal impacts that pose significant policy challenges.'

The policy response proposed by the Productivity Commission was that '[m]ore cost-effective service provision, especially in health care, would alleviate a major source of fiscal pressure at its source' (PC 2015: xii). There is a rich literature, and many well-researched government-commissioned reports, which sets out constructive agendas for improving the efficiency of health service delivery. It is inevitably the politics of gaining acceptance for reform from the powerful medical and pharmaceutical lobbies that limits the success of these reform initiatives.

The IGR has proved to be a very useful tool for long-term policy analysis at the Commonwealth level. By way of example, Whiteford's (2015) commentary on the 2015 IGR drew attention to the implications of maintaining current welfare policy settings over the long term. He points out that, if current policies for the indexation of working-age payments and family payments are continued, the recipients will be increasingly worse off relative to the average worker. In relation to income support for the unemployed, for example, a single unemployed person currently receives about 19 per cent of the male total average weekly earnings—described by Whiteford (2015) as already being recognised as inadequate—but, in 40 years, this would nearly halve, to only 10.5 per cent of the income of that average worker.

A critique of Australia's 2015 IGR and directions for further reform

The Commonwealth Government's *Intergenerational Report* is one of the world's leading reports on projections of long-term fiscal outcomes. Nonetheless, it does have structural limitations that are, at times, compounded by other detrimental features. On the structural side, there is concern over the potential for politicisation of the report, as well as concern with its limited scope. An operational concern is the limited transparency associated with the preparation and release of supporting assumptions and modelling.

In terms of the possibility of politicisation of the report, the 2015 IGR— the fourth since its inception—received a mixed reception when it was released. Reactions by notable commentators published on an academic current affairs online website, *The Conversation* (theconversation.com/au), provided a sample of views.

John Daley (2015) wrote:

> The Intergenerational Report aims to provide a long-term picture of future Australian prosperity, and the sustainability of government budgets. It should be a serious report. But this year it resembles a Harry Potter movie.

... [M]ost of the report is about the sustainability or otherwise of the Commonwealth Budget.

The Commonwealth abandoned its previous agreement to contribute to the long-term growth in hospital costs paid by the States ... And of course, it simply transfers the deficit problem to State governments to solve.

Perhaps the most worrying issue is that the report glosses over the long-term problems of the real world. Health costs are assumed to grow much more slowly over the next 10 years as a result of specific measures taken by governments. Previous *Intergenerational Reports* have all made the same assumption, and they've all been wrong. Health costs have generally continued to spiral upwards, consuming an increasing share of government budgets.

Stephen Duckett wrote:

The report is an overtly political document—highlighting the wondrous benefits which would accrue if the government's 2014 Budget had passed and the horrendous situation we'll be in if it isn't.

Unlike previous intergenerational reports where the political agenda was less overt and took at least five minutes to discern, the politics of today's report are designed to hit you between the eyes.

... The overall picture painted by the *Intergenerational Report* isn't all bad. Despite the politics, it highlights sensible issues—we can't keep running deficit budgets forever, we need to increase workforce participation rates (for women and older people who can) and we need to increase productivity (which we are doing but we need to go a bit faster). (Pears et al. 2015)

Hal Kendig wrote:

The 2015 *Intergenerational Report* (IGR) is a strong political statement that more than ever places population ageing and older people centre stage in public and political debate. It provides Treasury's technical projections (albeit based on questionable assumptions) wrapped in the Treasurer's political interpretation (aimed at Senate budget debate). (Pears et al. 2015)

As is evident from these reactions to the 2015 IGR, many commentators consider it was a particularly political document. This can be traced back to the enabling legislation, which provides for the treasurer (a minister of the government, not an independent agency) to release the report.

What this means in practice is that the treasurer's department (the Treasury) prepares the report, in consultation with other departments as necessary, but the treasurer has the opportunity to guide its central messaging. In each of the four IGRs published to date, the government of the day has placed emphasis on some matters ahead of others (usually consistent with their underlying ideology). However, the latest report attracted greater criticism on this score.

An alternative approach would be for the report to be prepared by an independent, competent agency, free from opportunity for the government of the day to craft some of its messages. In this respect, Australia has had a history of nearly two decades of benefiting from an agency—the Productivity Commission—which is known for its independence, transparency and broad-based policy analysis and advice. The commission is created, and protected, by its founding legislation, the Commonwealth's *Productivity Commission Act 1998*.

The commission describes itself in the following terms:

> The Productivity Commission is the Australian Government's independent research and advisory body on a range of economic, social and environmental issues affecting the welfare of Australians. Its role, expressed most simply, is to help governments make better policies, in the long term interests of the Australian community.

> The Commission's independence is underpinned by an Act of Parliament. Its processes and outputs are open to public scrutiny and are driven by consideration for the wellbeing of the community as a whole. (PC 2013: ii)

In essence, the three core operating principles of the Productivity Commission are:

- It is independent. The commission is established under its own Act, its independence is exercised by commissioners who are appointed for fixed periods, it has its own budgetary allocation and permanent staff and it operates at arm's length from the government and other agencies. Its findings and recommendations are independently arrived at based on its own analyses and judgments.

- Its processes are transparent. The commission's advice, analysis and modelling are all open to public scrutiny. It holds public hearings and specialist workshops and releases draft reports for public and expert feedback. Its final reports and recommendations to governments are also released to the public.

- It adopts a community-wide perspective. The commission's Act requires it to always be driven by consideration of the best interests of the community as a whole. It takes into account all relevant economic, social, regional and environmental perspectives.

In 2005, an objective analysis of the long-term economic and fiscal outlook for Australia was prepared by the Productivity Commission in response to a request by the state premiers, territory chief ministers and the prime minister through the forum known as the Council of Australian Governments (COAG). The commission's report *Economic Implications of an Ageing Australia* (PC 2005) was prepared on an independent basis. It contained no political interpretation of the results, but laid bare the range of scenarios facing the country, for all to ponder.

A second structural concern with the IGR is its limited scope. Its sole focus is on projections of the fiscal situation of the Commonwealth Government. While there is great value in each government, within their level of responsibility, conducting such an exercise, it nonetheless presents a partial view.

In Australia, where the sovereign states have responsibility for some large budgetary items, there is a need to understand the total public sector fiscal outlook. This is especially so given the states and territories are responsible for expenditure on public hospitals (while recognising that the Commonwealth provides significant financial support for their operation) and public education, as well as community services, policing and many other public goods and services.

The IGR's portrayal of the Commonwealth's future fiscal position therefore reflects, in part, the level of financial support provided by the Commonwealth to the states. A reduction in Commonwealth budgetary support for public hospitals, as proposed by the national government in the 2014 budget, will show up as an improved fiscal outlook for the Commonwealth, but only because it fails to reflect the passing on of the greater fiscal pressures that will be faced by the states.

Australia's experience with long-term fiscal reporting leads to the obvious point that there is a need to supplement such reports with a report that adopts a whole-of-government (national and subnational) focus. The terms of reference for the 2005 report by the Productivity Commission required it to take a 40-year perspective and report on:

1. The likely impact of an ageing population on Australia's overall productivity and economic growth.

2. The potential economic implications of future demographic trends for labour supply and retirement age, and the implications for unpaid work such as caring and volunteering.

3. The potential fiscal impact of the above factors on Commonwealth, State and Territory and, to the extent practicable, local governments. (PC 2005: iv)

The ensuing report encompassed all public expenditure and revenue-raising across the three levels of government. As such, it presented a more comprehensive picture of both the economic and the fiscal outlooks for the Australian economy as a whole. The Productivity Commission's 2013 update followed in similar fashion (PC 2013).

On the issue of transparency, and in contrast to the Commonwealth's IGR, the Productivity Commission's report was prepared in an open and transparent manner, with the commission calling for submissions and holding workshops. The commission also published its extensive databases, laid out its assumptions and released its modelling results and technical papers. New Zealand also makes its model publicly available so that any analyst can test and report on the outcome from other assumptions.

Given the commission's international reputation in terms of its processes (as well as the quality of its reports), it is well placed to produce an objective and transparent report that encompasses all levels of government and that regularly updates the baseline fiscal, economic and social outlooks over the longer term. Such a report can serve as a platform for debating an agenda of productivity reforms that will be required to address the country's looming policy challenges.

References

Anderson, B. and J. Sheppard. 2009. 'Fiscal futures, institutional budget reforms, and their effects: What can be learned?' *OECD Journal on Budgeting* 2009(3). Paris: OECD Publishing.

Australian Institute of Health and Welfare (AIHW). 2015. *Health Expenditure Australia 2013–14*. Canberra: Australian Institute of Health and Welfare.

Australian Treasury. 2015. *2015 Intergenerational Report: Australia in 2055*. Canberra: Australian Government.

Carlitz, R., P. de Renzio, W. Krafchik and V. Ramkumar. 2009. 'Budget transparency around the world: Results from the open budget survey'. *OECD Journal on Budgeting* 9(2): 1–17. Paris: OECD Publishing.

Commonwealth of Australia. 1998a. *Charter of Budget Honesty Act*. Act No. 22 of 1998 as amended. Canberra: Commonwealth of Australia. Available from: www.legislation.gov.au/Details/C2012 C00230 (accessed 11 July 2017).

Commonwealth of Australia. 1998b. *Productivity Commission Act*. No. 14, 1998 as amended. Canberra: Commonwealth of Australia. Available from: www.comlaw.gov.au/Details/C2014C00554 (accessed 11 July 2017).

Daley, J. 2015. 'Intergenerational Report: Joe Hockey and the deathly budget hallows'. *The Conversation*, 5 March. Available from: theconversation.com/intergenerational-report-joe-hockey-and-the-deathly-budget-hallows-38436 (accessed 29 October 2015).

European Union Economic Policy Committee (EU EPC). 2015. 'Working Group on Ageing Populations and Sustainability. Brussels: European Union'. Available from: europa.eu/epc/working-group-ageing-populations-and-sustainability_en (accessed 29 October 2015).

Hameed, F. 2005. *Fiscal Transparency and Economic Outcomes*. IMF Working Paper WP/05/225. Washington, DC: International Monetary Fund.

International Monetary Fund (IMF). 2007. *Manual on Fiscal Transparency*. Washington, DC: International Monetary Fund. Available from: www.imf.org/external/np/fad/trans/manual.htm (accessed 29 October 2015).

Jones, R. and K. Fukawa. 2015. *Achieving Fiscal Consolidation while Promoting Social Cohesion in Japan*. OECD Economics Department Working Papers No. 1262. Paris: OECD Publishing. Available from: www.oecd-ilibrary.org/economics/achieving-fiscal-consolidation-while-promoting-social-cohesion-in-japan_5jrtpbs9fg0v-en (accessed 30 October 2015).

National Commission of Audit. 1996. *Report to the Commonwealth Government*. Canberra: AGPS.

NSW Commission of Audit. 1988. *Focus on Reform: The State's Finances*. Sydney: NSW Commission of Audit.

Organisation for Economic Co-operation and Development (OECD). 2002. *Best Practices for Budget Transparency*. Paris: OECD Publishing.

Pears, A., H. Kendig, I. Lowe, M. O'Brien, R. Norman, R. Viney and S. Duckett. 2015. 'Hockey looks to "armies" in Intergenerational Report: Experts react'. *The Conversation*, 5 March. Available from: theconversation.com/hockey-looks-to-armies-in-intergenerational-report-experts-react-38372 (accessed 29 October 2015).

Productivity Commission (PC). 2005. *Economic implications of an ageing Australia*. Research Report. Canberra: Productivity Commission.

Productivity Commission (PC). 2013. *An ageing Australia: Preparing for the Future*. Research Report. Canberra: Productivity Commission.

Whiteford, P. 2015. 'Intergenerational Report lays uneven path for tough policy choices'. *The Conversation*, 6 March. Available from: theconversation.com/intergenerational-report-lays-uneven-path-for-tough-policy-choices-38295 (accessed 29 October 2015).

4

Budget reform in China: Progress and prospects in the Xi Jinping era

Christine Wong

Introduction

After three decades of remarkable growth and development in the country, the Chinese leadership is confronted with a very different set of challenges to those faced by its predecessors at the outset of its market-oriented reform program. China then was a poor but relatively well-educated and egalitarian country, with an abundance of surplus labour in the rural sector and very little interaction with the global market. A series of measures to increase the scope of the market and facilitate the transfer of labour from agriculture to industry was all it took to launch China's economic lift-off. Now, China is an upper- to middle-income country with emerging shortages of manual labour that dominates the global supply of low to mid-end manufactured goods and global demand for most commodities. The traditional model of extensive growth dependent on exports and investment, however, appears to be running out of steam.

The administration of President Xi Jinping has acknowledged that a major shift is required by announcing a new era of 'comprehensively deepening reforms', which was endorsed at the Third Plenum of the Chinese Communist Party's Eighteenth Congress in November 2013. The 60-point 'Decision of the Chinese Communist Party Central Committee on Several Major Questions about Deepening Reform' (Xinhua 2013) spelled out an ambitious, comprehensive agenda containing 336 reform initiatives under 16 broad headings that cover all parts of the economy, society, the political system and its institutions. Together, the measures are aimed at restructuring the roles of government and the market, with modernising governance the ultimate goal of the program.

The Third Plenum Decisions (TPD) identified fiscal reform as a key priority. Writing in the Communist Party journal *Qiushi*, Finance Minister Lou Jiwei explained that China's fiscal system has not kept up with the needs of the growing and increasingly complex economy:

> [T]he defects have become increasingly apparent: the budget management system is not standardized, transparent, or suited to the requirements of modern governance; the tax system ... is not conducive to supporting the shift to the new development paradigm,[1] social fairness, or market integration. The division of responsibilities between the central and local governments is unclear and unreasonable ... These problems ... affect not only the stability and sustainability of the fiscal system itself, they also [adversely] affect the national development strategy and the effectiveness of macroeconomic policy. (Lou 2014)[2]

Lou (2014) argued that, 'in this round of reform, small patches and fixes will no longer suffice', and fundamental reform of the fiscal system is needed to build the foundation to support the modernisation of governance called for by the TPD.

Fiscal reforms have led the way in the TPD reforms, with many measures and initiatives rolled out in quick order. In June 2014, the Politburo approved the 'Overall Program for Deepening Reform of the Fiscal System', authorising comprehensive reform of that system. In August 2014, the Standing Committee of the National People's Congress approved the revised Budget Law (BL), which sets out provisions mandating numerous changes and, for the first time, authorises local governments to borrow for capital investments (NPC Standing Committee 2014).

Working at the compressed pace set out in the TPD, which called for the entire reform program to be implemented by 2020, Minister Lou announced at a press conference in mid-2014 that the first phase of reform would focus on budget and public financial management (PFM)

---

1   As early as 2002, the government announced its goal of shifting to a development paradigm that promotes services and consumption in place of industry and investment (Wong 2010).
2   Translated by the author.

reforms, phase two would begin in 2015 with a focus on reforms of the tax system and phase three would begin in 2016 and would focus on intergovernmental fiscal reform (Han et al. 2014).

This chapter examines the state of the budget in China today and reviews the proposed reforms of PFM to offer a preliminary assessment of their prospects. The rest of the chapter is organised as follows: section two reviews the fiscal reforms implemented in the 1990s through to the first decade of the current century. Section three discusses the current situation and the proposed reform program for PFM. Section four provides a preliminary assessment of the program's prospects and a brief conclusion.

The fits and starts of fiscal reforms through to 2010

The first major reform of the fiscal system was enacted in 1994, when a new system of taxes was introduced, centring on the value-added tax (VAT), a business tax, a corporate income tax, a personal income tax and several taxes on property, land transactions and land use. These are broad-based taxes with uniform levy rates. They replaced the previous complex system, with its hundreds of product-specific industrial–commercial taxes transplanted from the Soviet economic system, and began to separate government finances from those of state-owned enterprises (SOEs) by introducing an income tax on profits to replace the previous negotiated profit remittances. While the new tax system was far from perfect, it represented a huge improvement in terms of simplifying the tax structure, eliminating distortionary elements and increasing transparency, and it greatly facilitated tax administration and the monitoring of tax capacity across regions. Along with the creation of a new national tax administration, this system restored the government's revenue mechanism and reversed the steep fiscal decline that had characterised the first two decades of market reform (Wong and Bird 2008).[3]

---

3   As in other former planned economies, in China, the budget went into steep decline when market reforms eroded the 'pillars' of the government revenue mechanism: state monopoly over industrial ownership, administratively fixed prices favouring industry and compulsory procurement and delivery of raw materials. At its trough in 1996, China's budget was 11 per cent of gross domestic product (GDP)—one-third the level under the planned economy (Wong and Bird 2008).

Under the planned economy, the budget was not a significant policy instrument. It was simply the financial counterpart to the economic (physical) plan in which the government's allocative decisions were embedded. Budget preparation simply followed the plan, and financial performance was of secondary importance. Even as the budget gained increasing importance when the planned economy and its allocative instruments were gradually phased out in the 1980s and 1990s, the government was slow to recognise the urgent need to install a PFM system to manage its finances, as all attention was focused on finding a way to revive the revenue mechanism.

PFM reform began finally in 1999, when the government introduced a broad package over the following three to four years that included reforms to budget preparation, budget classification, treasury management, government procurement and the installation of new fiscal information systems (Wong 2005). New procedures were introduced for budget preparation and approval, and budget reporting to the National People's Congress was strengthened. Departmental budgets were introduced alongside the traditional functional allocations (e.g. appropriations for 'education' were distributed to all ministries and agencies with responsibility for education and training), aimed at clearly identifying all resources and expenditures for each government department as the first step towards building a system whereby spending units could be held accountable for the public monies they received.

A single treasury account was created to manage the government's cash receipts and payments. To support treasury reform and improved budgeting, the Ministry of Finance began work on a new government financial information management system. A new budget classification system was rolled out in 2006 to improve the tracking of expenditure by functional categories. Standardised procedures for government procurement were introduced to improve cost efficiencies and reduce the scope for corruption, adopting many of the procedures of international organisations for tendering large-scale purchases of equipment and services. With these reforms, China had begun to put in place the basic infrastructure for a modern system of budget management, but the real work was just starting. Many of the reform measures require extensive training and information dissemination so they can be put in place, with full implementation often taking a decade or more. In China, the biggest task was to ensure implementation of the reforms at the subnational level, where 85 per cent of China's public expenditure takes place.

By 2004–05, however, it appeared that these reforms in PFM had stalled across the board. From the outside, it is hard to know exactly why this happened, but a compelling narrative can be put together from the macroeconomic trends over this period to show that reform efforts were likely overwhelmed by the sheer size of the ramp-up in public expenditure.

In economic growth terms, the first decade of the twenty-first century was a golden era for China. Joining the World Trade Organization had opened up wider access to global markets, and China rode the exceptionally buoyant global trade and investment conditions to achieve double-digit growth rates in per capita GDP. Even when the Global Financial Crisis (GFC) hit in 2007, and while much of the world struggled through years of recession and stagnation in its wake, thanks to its massive stimulus program, China continued to race ahead with only a brief slowdown in 2009. As a result, per capita GDP growth averaged an astonishing 13.2 per cent per annum during 2000–12.[4]

During this growth spurt, government revenue grew even faster, at an annual rate of 22 per cent! By mid decade, the government's coffers were overflowing and the government spent lavishly. This fitted well with the populist stance adopted by the government from 2003 onwards, when then president Hu Jintao and premier Wen Jiabao came into office vowing to rebalance public spending to improve services, and, in particular, to 'tilt' in favour of rural areas to reduce their shortfall in provision. Under the banner of a 'harmonious society', adopted at the Fourth Plenum of the Sixteenth Communist Party Central Committee in September 2004, Beijing began to pump resources into expanding the social safety net to include rural citizens and improving the provision of social services (Wong 2010).

Many new programs were introduced with central government subsidies, including reform of rural fees, free rural education, rural cooperative medical schemes, income support for farmers under the rural minimum living stipend scheme (*dibao*) and the universal rural pension (World Bank 2007). Lin and Wong (2012) counted the introduction of no fewer than 12 programs of subsidies that were aimed directly at farming families between 2001 and 2007, from subsidies for seed and farm machinery to subsidies for crop insurance and household appliances.

---

4   Unless otherwise noted, all growth calculations are in real terms after deflating by the consumer price index (CPI).

Typically, the programs began modestly, but were often ratcheted up rapidly as more revenue became available. For example, free rural education began in 2001 as a small program providing subsidies to finance free textbooks and offset school fees and boarding subsidies for children from impoverished households in designated poor counties. It was unexpectedly expanded in 2006 to cover all school fees for all students in rural primary and middle schools (Brock et al. 2008). Likewise, the rural health insurance scheme started in 2003 with an annual subsidy of RMB20 (A$3.75), which grew 15-fold within a decade to RMB300 (A$56) for each of the program's more than 800 million participants.

Many of these 'harmonious society' programs are huge: the provision of free rural education covers some 140 million students; at its peak, the rural cooperative medical scheme had more than 830 million participants; and the universal rural pension scheme has a potential beneficiary pool of more than 800 million people.[5] These programs have made huge additions to budgetary expenditure at the county level, which is the level of government responsible for the provision of rural services, such as agricultural services, education, health care, social welfare and pensions. As a result, the vertical share of total national budgetary expenditures at the county level rose from 26 per cent to 43 per cent during 2000–10, compared with just 18 per cent for the central government. On the ground, this means that an 'average' county has seen its budget grow tenfold within a decade, from RMB200 million (A$37.3 million) to RMB2 billion (A$373 million) by 2010![6]

Sleepwalking into a quagmire

A salient feature of the policies of the Hu–Wen administration was that they were implemented with no adjustment to the central–local government revenue-sharing arrangements. Instead, all the burden of financing was put on the use of transfers. During that decade, central government transfers to local governments grew from 2.4 per cent

---

5   Premier Wen Jiabao cited a figure of 835 million participants in the rural health insurance scheme (new cooperative medical scheme [NCMS]) in his work report to the National People's Congress in 2011. This is much larger than the number of rural residents, but many migrant workers were enrolled in the NCMS as they were ineligible for urban schemes. In recent years, many NCMS programs have been merged with a similar urban basic medical scheme.

6   Figures are in nominal renminbi, based on estimated shares of revenue by tier of government. This was equal to average growth of nearly 24 per cent per annum in nominal terms, or 21 per cent per annum in real terms.

of GDP, in 2000, to 7.7 per cent, even as GDP itself grew fourfold. Moreover, in China's fiscal system, these transfers have to be passed down level by level—from Beijing to the provinces, from provinces to municipalities and from municipalities to counties. The administrative burden of managing the proliferation of new programs and the rapidly growing transfers to fund them must have created an extraordinary strain on the bureaucracy at all levels. Studies such as those by Wong (2010) and Lin and Wong (2012) have pointed to the government's lack of capacity to monitor and evaluate the programs as a constraint on achieving desired policy outcomes, citing problems that ranged from poor program design to coarse financial management and unresponsive services. While many benefits have accrued from the new programs, they were also marred by wastefulness, program capture, cost inflation and even the creation of 'ghost teachers' and 'ghost schools', among other things. Another likely side effect of this onslaught of new programs and new monies raining down from higher levels was that efforts to implement reform were shunted aside as everyone just tried to cope with the flows.

The neglect of institutional reform over the past decade was even more damaging in the cities (Wong 2013a, 2013b). Since market reforms began 35 years ago, people have flocked to China's cities. As the country's urbanisation rate rose from 20 per cent to more than 50 per cent of the total population, more than 500 million new residents have been added to urban areas. During the decade 2000–10 alone, the urban population grew by 210 million.

Around the world, governments struggle with the task of providing infrastructure and public services in the course of urbanisation (Bahl et al. 2013). In China, amid the steep and prolonged fiscal decline in the 1980s and 1990s, the government had few resources to devote to the needs of urbanisation. Instead, political leaders tolerated and indeed encouraged the use of informal, backdoor practices that enabled cities to obtain the resources needed, and China's municipalities therefore came to rely overwhelmingly on extra-budgetary resources (Wong 2009, 2013a). With rapid urbanisation pushing up the price of land, land quickly became the biggest source of extra-budgetary revenue. In recent years, receipts from land sales[7] have accounted for one-third to one-half of all revenue for first- and second-tier cities.[8]

---

7 Strictly speaking, landownership remains with the state, but the right of use can be sold.
8 Estimates from Wong (2013a).

To finance the infrastructure needed to support urban growth (such as schools, public transport and other urban facilities), Chinese cities— like their counterparts around the world—also borrowed money. Since they were, until the recent change, prohibited from direct borrowing, cities borrowed off-budget, through quasi-public financial entities set up as enterprises under government departments. These local investment corporations (LICs)—variously named City X Development Corporation—undertook the coordination and financing of the construction of facilities such as water supply, sewerage, roads and utility hook-ups. Typically, they raised and bundled together bank loans and other financing, using a variety of municipal assets, including budgetary and off-budget revenue, as equity and collateral, with land playing a principal role in providing the financing as well as the collateral (Wong 2013a).

This extra-budgetary financing from land sales and off-budget borrowing developed largely outside the purview of government financial oversight.[9] While it helped greatly to expand the financial resources available and was instrumental in enabling the dynamic urbanisation that took place over the past two decades, it also sowed the seeds for some of the most intractable problems facing Xi Jinping's administration today. The symbiotic relationship between land sales and LICs led inexorably to the overuse of both, resulting in excessive land takings, urban sprawl and the creation of excess capacity in industry as cities competed for job-creating investment to raise land values. And the easy access to money from land sales and LICs also led inexorably to wasteful and inefficient investments and even ghost cities, along with graft and corruption on an unprecedented scale.

The current reform program

Paradoxically, then, even as it appears that China has reached the pinnacle of economic success after a decade in which it claimed a number of world-beating accomplishments—becoming the world's largest manufacturer in 2008, the largest exporter in 2010 and passing Japan in 2012 to become the second-largest economy behind the United States—the view from

---

9   For an early account of how the central government was kept largely in the dark about the development of LICs and the extent of local government borrowing, see Wong (2011).

the top leadership is that the country is facing unprecedented challenges. The program of sweeping reform endorsed by the Communist Party Congress in November 2013 was a manifestation of that view.

Many of the provisions in the revised BL and associated documents are aimed at correcting the problems just described to rein in local government debt, tp rein in extra-budgetary revenue and to regain macroeconomic oversight of fiscal resources, improve budget transparency and strengthen accountability by, among other things, providing better legal foundations and oversight by the National People's Congress. The BL also sought to improve the efficiency and efficacy of intergovernmental transfers by specifying the principles and objectives for their establishment and their budgeting methodology, as well as the timing of provision (BL, Articles 16, 38 and 52). To limit the use of earmarked transfers, the BL emphasises the need to conduct regular appraisals and set exit mechanisms for them.

In a press conference just after passage of the BL, Lou Jiwei (2014) explained that one of the key provisions in the law states that budget management should be *comprehensive*: '[a]ll revenue and expenditures of government should be included in the budget' (Article 4) and government expenditures must include all government activities, including local government debt. Also, this comprehensive budget must be supervised by the People's Congress. To combat corruption, Lou noted, the new BL emphasises budget transparency, to stem the problem at the source. For the first time, the BL makes comprehensive provisions for *budget openness*, with clear rules on the scope, timing and specifics of disclosure requirements for key items such as transfer payments, government debt and departmental budgets for public agencies (Article 14). It also specifies legal liabilities for the breach of these budget disclosure norms (Article 92).

Among the most important provisions in the BL is the authorisation given to provincial governments to borrow—although under tight supervision by the central government as well as the provincial People's Congress. Under a call to 'open the front door, lock the back door and build walls around it', the BL stipulates that local governments must report on the purpose, size and mode of debt, along with specifying the mechanisms of supervision and legal liabilities (Articles 35 and 94). The BL was followed a month later by the issuance of 'State Council Document 43', which laid out an ambitious plan to tackle the stock of existing debt and a structure for managing local government borrowing, starting with separating LICs from local government finance.[10]

In this first phase of reform, all efforts are focused on PFM and regaining control over the budget and allocative processes. It is only in phase three that reforms will turn to addressing issues with the intergovernmental fiscal system. This sequencing makes sense in light of the severity of the problems of local government debt and the extent of extra-budgetary financing. The progress of these reforms, however, may be hindered by some potential sources of resistance. I will note just three below.

The first and most immediate source of resistance is the effort to shut off bank lending to LICs and move it into the more transparent and regulated channel of debt issuance, which is seen as an important step towards bringing local debt under control and regaining fiscal discipline. The dilemma is that, in recent years, local governments have grown reliant on land revenue and LICs to finance public infrastructure at very robust levels, and these investments have been a big part of China's investment-driven growth dynamic. Weaning local governments off these sources of finance will force them to deleverage—a necessary step for rebalancing the economy, but one that risks setting off a fiscal crunch as local governments cut back on investment. The on-again, off-again clampdown on LICs in the past three years has already helped to deflate the housing market and significantly raised the threat of defaults since local governments and LICs are perilously dependent on land sales to service their debt. Unease with the slowing growth has already led to some provisions of the reform being reversed. On 15 May 2015, the State Council ordered banks to continue lending to LICs that have projects under construction, substantially reversing the earlier edict (Anderlini 2015).

Effective PFM requires that the budget is comprehensive and includes all fiscal revenue, expenditures and liabilities. In the past, PFM reform efforts had focused only on the budget execution aspects of financial management—expenditure control, treasury, accounting and procurement—and paid insufficient attention to debt and financial risks, especially at the subnational level. The current reform aims to fix this gap, and the new BL and 'State Council Document No. 63' that followed in December laid down a mandate for governments at all levels to compile

---

10   See Naughton (2015) for a brief discussion of Document 43 and how it is designed to work.

and release to the public a comprehensive government financial report to include not only on-budget revenue, expenditures and direct debts, but also a balance sheet of government assets and liabilities and a statement of cash flows.

The new government financial reporting system (GFRS) is to provide an accurate and comprehensive reflection of government financial outcomes, as a basis for strengthening public resource management, increasing efficiency and guarding against fiscal risks. The new GFRS will be built on modified accrual accounting rules and will have greatly expanded coverage in both reporting entities and contents. It will be far more demanding of the bureaucracy and will require many methodological changes. Some of the changes will likely affect the relationship between government and the reporting entities in fundamental ways, starting with the selection and classification of entities, which moves budget reform into politically contentious territory.

Under the principle that government finance reporting must include all entities that have material impact on the government's fiscal position (IMF 2014), all SOEs—including LICs—must be included. The exclusion of SOEs has long been a blind spot in budget reporting in China given that their financial interaction with government has remained fluid and fuzzy, especially at the local level. The SOE sector is huge. Nationwide, there are hundreds of thousands of SOEs; in 2013, more than 18,000 large ones had annual revenue of more than RMB20 million (A$3.7 million) from their main activity.[11] They had assets totalling RMB34 trillion (A$6.3 trillion) and were distributed across all provinces. In Beijing alone, there were 790 of these large SOEs, with assets of RMB2.3 trillion (A$429 billion) and debts of RMB1.2 trillion (A$224 billion) (NBS 2014: Table 13.1). Given the size and potential impact on government finances of SOEs, reform to include them in government accounting is long overdue. Resistance to letting go of SOEs has made SOE reform among the slowest-moving components of President Xi's reform program, and the effort to incorporate SOEs in budget reporting is more likely to be bogged down than to act as a spur to the much-needed debate on state–market relations.

---

11   These are classified as 'above-scale' enterprises (NBS 2014).

Finally, given the highly decentralised pattern of public expenditure in China, for which the central government accounts for only 15 per cent, PFM reform depends critically on its implementation at the subnational level. As PFM reforms aim to curb extra-budgetary resources and activities, they are seen as depriving local governments of autonomy, and will be met with much foot-dragging. The experience of the 1990s is not encouraging, when the take-up of new PFM processes was slow and uneven at subnational levels. More than 15 years after the first round of PFM reform called for increasing transparency and the adoption of uniform reporting standards, for example, information on local budgets remains spotty and uneven, and few provinces release information on transfers to lower levels (Wong 2013a). In China's hierarchical but delegated system of level-by-level administration, the central government has only attenuated control over subordinates.

In summary, this brief review of the fiscal reform being implemented has found much to praise in the package of proposed reforms; it is ambitious and comprehensive, addresses many of the key problems in the existing system of PFM and the measures are well designed to build the foundation for good governance. The quick rollout of legislation and regulations from the State Council has, to date, provided strong support for implementing PFM reforms in the first phase. At the same time, I have also identified some key obstacles to the implementation of these measures. Building a robust system of PFM is only the first (although critical) step in fiscal reform. The key part is yet to come, which is to realign and rationalise the system of intergovernmental fiscal relations, the linchpin of effective management of a large, multilevel fiscal system that has for so long been missing in the Chinese economy. To push through implementation of these critical PFM reforms against fierce headwinds, Minister Lou will need a forceful intervention from the top, and soon, to maintain the current momentum.

References

Anderlini, J. 2015. 'China orders banks to keep lending to insolvent state projects'. *Financial Times*, 15 May. Available from: www.ft.com/cms/s/0/3ec5fea4-faef-11e4-84f3-00144feab7de.html#ixzz3aw6lymI5 (accessed 11 July 2017).

Bahl, R., J. Linn and D. Wetzel (eds). 2013. *Metropolitan Government Finances in Developing Countries*. Cambridge, MA: Lincoln Institute for Land Policy.

Brock, A., H. Wenbin and C. Wong. 2008. 'Free compulsory education: A natural next step after "Two Exceptions and One Subsidy" (TEOS)'. *Chinese Education and Society* 41(1)(January–February): 87–95.

Han, J., G. Li and H. Yuxin. 2014. 'Deep changes that affect the modernization of the nation's governance system: Minister of Finance Lou Jiwei explains the Overall Program for Deepening Reform of the Fiscal System'. [In Chinese]. *Xinhua*. Available from: www.mof.gov. cn/zhengwuxinxi/caizhengxinwen/201407/t20140704_1108534. html (accessed 25 July 2017).

International Monetary Fund (IMF). 2014. *Government Finance Statistics Manual 2014*. Washington, DC: International Monetary Fund.

Lin, W. and C. Wong. 2012. 'Are Beijing's equalization policies reaching the poor? An analysis of direct subsidies under the "Three Rurals" (Sannong)'. *China Journal* 67(January): 23–46. doi.org/10.1086/665738.

Lou, J. 2014. 'Deepening reform of the fiscal and tax system to build a modern system of public finance'. [In Chinese]. *Qiushi* 2014(20) (13 October).

National Bureau of Statistics of China (NBS). 2014. *China Statistical Yearbook*. Beijing: China Statistics Press.

National People's Congress (NPC) Standing Committee. 2014. Decision on revising the 'People's Republic of China Budget Law'. [In Chinese]. 31 August. Beijing: National People's Congress of the People's Republic of China. Available from: www.npc.gov.cn/npc/xinwen/2014-09/01/content_1877061.htm (accessed 11 July 2017).

Naughton, B. 2015. 'Is there a "Xi model" of economic reform? Acceleration of economic reform since fall 2014'. *China Leadership Monitor* (46)(Winter).

Wong, C. 2005. 'Public sector budgeting issues in China'. In Organisation for Economic Co-operation and Development (OECD) *Governance in China*. Paris: OECD Publishing.

Wong, C. 2009. 'Rebuilding government for the 21st century: Can China incrementally reform the public sector?' *China Quarterly* 200(December): 929–52. doi.org/10.1017/s0305741009990567.

Wong, C. 2010. 'Fiscal reform: Paying for the harmonious society'. *China Economic Quarterly* 14(2): 22–7.

Wong, C. 2011. 'The fiscal stimulus program and public governance issues in China'. *OECD Journal on Budgeting* 11(3): 1–22. Paris: OECD Publishing. doi.org/10.1787/budget-11-5kg3nhljqrjl.

Wong, C. 2013a. 'Paying for urbanization: Challenges for China's municipal finance in the 21st century'. In R. Bahl, J. Linn and D. Wetzel (eds) *Metropolitan Government Finances in Developing Countries*. Cambridge, MA: Lincoln Institute for Land Policy.

Wong, C. 2013b. 'Reforming China's public finances for long-term growth'. In R. Garnaut, C. Fang and L. Song (eds) *China: A new model for growth and development*. Canberra: ANU E Press. Available from: press.anu.edu.au?p=244991 (accessed 11 July 2017).

Wong, C. and R. Bird. 2008. 'China's fiscal system: A work in progress'. In L. Brandt and T. Rawski (eds) *China's Great Transformation: Origins, mechanism and consequences of the post-reform economic boom*. New York: Cambridge University Press. doi.org/10.1017/CBO9780511754234.013.

World Bank. 2007. *China: Public services for building the new socialist countryside*. Report No. 40221-CN. Washington, DC: The World Bank.

Xinhua. 2013. 'Decision of the Chinese Communist Party Central Committee on several major questions about deepening reform'. [In Chinese]. *Xinhua*, 15 November. Available from: news.xinhuanet.com/politics/2013-11/15/c_118164235.htm (accessed 11 July 2017).

5

Public budgeting system in Taiwan: Does it lead to better value for money?

Tsai-tsu Su

One of the major objectives of a public budgeting system—which prescribes and enforces rules for the allocation, expenditure and accounting of fiscal resources—is to maximise the value of taxpayers' money. To achieve this objective, public budgeting systems in industrialised nations have undergone several reforms during the past decades, including the performance budgeting system in the 1950s, the planning–performance– budgeting system in the 1960s, the zero-based budgeting system in the 1970s and the entrepreneurial budgeting system (or new performance budgeting system) in the 1980s. Although each reform employs different budgeting techniques and principles, all aim to safeguard taxpayer dollars in budgetary decision-making.

Similarly, Taiwan has gone through various budgetary reforms in the past decades, most notably the phase of 'democratisation of public budgeting' that began in the mid-1970s and the phase of 'effectiveness of public budgeting' starting in the mid-1990s (Su 2007). The former reform aimed to democratise budgetary decision-making, while the latter—heavily influenced by the ideologies of New Public Management (NPM)—aimed to achieve a 'small and beautiful' government and to increase the value of taxpayers' money.

While these reforms transformed the public budgeting system in Taiwan, it remains unclear whether they met taxpayers' expectations and delivered effective budgetary allocation as promised. This is the central question explored in this chapter. The chapter begins by describing the main characteristics of the four stages in the central government's budget cycle—namely, budget preparation, legislative approval, budget execution, and accounting and audit. Second, it discusses the characteristics of local governments' budget processes. It then introduces the newly adopted budgetary reform measures such as participatory budgeting and performance auditing. The chapter concludes by discussing the prospects of the current public budgeting system achieving better value for public money.

The central government budget process

Budget preparation

The two principle budgeting bodies in Taiwan's central government are the Directorate-General of Budget, Accounting and Statistics (DGBAS) of the Executive Yuan and the Ministry of Finance. The role of the DGBAS resembles that of the Office of Management and Budget in the United States. It is the main authority that assists the country's premier in allocating budgeting resources and preparing the general budget. The MoF is responsible for estimating the revenue for the coming year and providing these estimates to the DGBAS. Based on these estimates, the DGBAS prepares the general budget proposal for the upcoming year, including budget allocations across ministries.

In the budget preparation process, the DGBAS first assigns an annual expenditure cap for each ministry. Each ministry is then required to develop its own budget estimates following the zero-based budgeting approach imposed by the DGBAS. In other words, each ministry should estimate each spending program thoroughly to reflect the latest changes in the macro-environment and respond to emerging public needs, although, in reality, many agencies in the ministries still follow an incremental or decremental budgeting model. In addition, the *Budget Act 1998* stipulates that each ministry should complete a cost–benefit analysis (CBA) before submitting a budget proposal for major projects. In most cases, however, the CBA is a mere formality, and its results are seldom incorporated into the budget preparation process. Meanwhile, whenever a ministry formulates a big spending program exceeding a threshold level,[1] it first submits it to the National Development Council for preliminary review of the demand for, feasibility, economic benefits and social impact of the program. Only when it passes this review will it be included in the ministry's budget estimates.

Each ministry submits its respective budget estimates to the DGBAS for aggregation into the central government's overall general budget proposal. The premier then convenes the Annual Program and Budget Council to review the general budget proposal. While each ministry's budget estimates generally should not exceed the expenditure cap assigned by the DGBAS, it will highlight newly required budget items that exceed the cap for discussion in the council. By law, the DGBAS must submit the central government's general budget proposal to the Legislative Yuan for deliberation before the end of August each year.

The central government's budget preparation has a few key features. First, it is a combination of top-down and bottom-up processes (Su 1996: 25–42). The DGBAS, following a top-down approach, sets an annual expenditure cap for each ministry to plan their respective budgets. But when ministries prepare their own budgets, they take a bottom-up, incremental budgeting approach, and often request additional budget support when needs arise, even if the budget goes beyond the DGBAS's expenditure cap.

Second, when compared with the budget phases described later in this chapter, this budget preparation process is less transparent. The ministry-level budget preparation information and the meeting minutes of the Annual Program and Budget Council are not fully disclosed publicly. This makes it difficult for the public to understand how bureaucrats prepare the budget and the information on which budget allocations rely. Because of this, there is little literature concerning the budget preparation process in Taiwan.

---

1   Take, for example, the preliminary review of the 2017 general budget proposal. Programs that require preliminary review include individual social development programs with a total budget exceeding NT$300 million (A$12.5 million) and scientific development programs with a total budget of more than NT$500 million (A$20.8 million) or an annual budget of at least NT$200 million (A$8.3 million).

Third, it may be argued that the DGBAS is occupied more with controlling the level of total spending and the budget deficit than with focusing on whether each ministry's budget allocation corresponds to the needs of the public and fulfils the principles of efficiency, effectiveness and fairness. This tendency might be attributed to Taiwan's traditional emphasis on containing taxpayers' tax burden, which is usually calculated as the ratio of total tax revenue to gross domestic product (GDP). For example, while the tax burden of the average taxpayer in Taiwan was around 12 per cent between 2010 and 2015,[2] the average for Organisation Economic Co-operation and Development (OECD) countries during the same period was close to 34 per cent.[3] Because of the low tax revenue and the huge gap between tax revenue and spending demands, the DGBAS is forced to devote most its efforts to cutting down on expenditures and reducing the deficit, leaving the issue of cross-ministry or cross-function budget allocation as a secondary concern, which sometimes leads to allocative inefficiency.

Legislative approval

Taiwan's Constitution prescribes a presidential regime, so, like the federal government of the United States, its legislature has final decision-making power regarding the annual budgetary allocation.

However, unlike the United States, where congressional members can add or delete budget items and increase or decrease expenditures in the budget bill proposed by the White House, in Taiwan, the budget decision-making power of legislators is circumscribed by the Constitution. Taiwanese legislators cannot increase the spending in the budgetary bill presented by the Executive Yuan; they can only remove budget items or decrease expenditures.

The budget approval process that takes place in Taiwan's Legislative Yuan has long attracted media attention, especially with the recent increase in competitive party politics. Legislators focus more on gaining publicity during the budget approval process than on exercising professionalism

---

2   The average tax burden for taxpayers in Taiwan for fiscal years 2010–15 were 11.5 per cent, 12.3 per cent, 12.2 per cent, 12 per cent, 12.3 per cent and 12.8 per cent, respectively. The average for these years is 12.12 per cent (Department of Statistics 2017: Table 3.9).
3   The average total tax revenue as a percentage of GDP for OECD countries was 32.4 per cent for 2009, 33.4 per cent for 2012, 34.2 per cent for 2014 and 34.3 per cent for 2015 (OECD 2016: Table 1.1).

(Rigger 1999). This has led to a highly politicised parliamentary approval process, often at the expense of rational dialogue between the ruling and opposition parties. Furthermore, legislative committees fail to fully exercise their budget review functions. When committee members cannot agree to proposed budget cuts for certain spending programs, they resort to cross-caucus negotiations—a process that is not disclosed to the public.[4] Only a few legislators from the ruling and opposition parties have access to these 'secret negotiations' and, as long as one of them refuses to approve a proposal, the negotiation falls apart. In other words, each consultation participant can veto the budget, but they are not held accountable. These 'black-box' negotiations between political parties are the most criticised aspect of the budget approval process in the Legislative Yuan (Hawang 2002; Wang 2002; Chao 2005).

When legislators review the general budget proposal, they can seek professional assistance from the Legislative Budget Center (LBC), which is affiliated with the Legislative Yuan. The LBC is responsible for all research, analysis, evaluation and consultation works related to the central government's budget. In its early years, the LBC's budget assessment reports received little attention. But, since 2000, when the LBC was separated from the Legislative Consulting Office and employed more personnel, its reports have attracted a wider audience among legislators and the media, especially when the LBC issued harsh criticism of the public expenditure efficiency of the executive branch. Meanwhile, given that the core expertise of most LBC staff is in accounting and not in performance evaluation of expenditure programs, there is scope for improving the LBC's role in facilitating the public's understanding of the budgetary process and assisting legislators to play a more effective role.

Despite these issues with the budget approval process in the Legislative Yuan, it has made great strides since the authoritarian era in the budget review phase, as well as in promoting budget transparency and open government. While the party caucus consultation process is still questionable, the proceedings and budget review in all committees are now streamed live online. Through a video-on-demand system, one can also locate the public records of legislators' interpellation in legislative

---

4   According to the Law Governing the Legislative Yuan's Power (Article 70): 'Legislative negotiations, under the support of the Secretary General, should be documented, and voice and video recorded; the proceedings and the negotiation conclusions should be published in the official gazette.' Yet, in practice, only a summarised conclusion is announced, without any negotiation details.

proceedings and committee meetings. This open and transparent broadcast system enhances the public accountability of the Legislative Yuan in its budget decision-making.

Budget execution

Once the general budget proposal goes through three readings in the Legislative Yuan, it is referred to as a 'legal budget' by which all ministries should abide. Many laws in Taiwan govern the budget execution process, including the *Budget Act 1932*, the *Accounting Act 1935* and the *Government Procurement Act 1998*. The purpose of this legislation is to reduce waste and enhance efficiency when executing public expenditures. Throughout the budget execution phase, not only does each ministry conduct internal control, the DGBAS also leverages the accounting system to ensure the legality of all expenses and to monitor the expenditure execution process in all ministries. To eliminate fraud and waste, the DGBAS takes a very stringent approach to budget execution and control, to the extent that many government bureaucrats complain that the internal control and audit procedures have tipped the balance, overemphasising fraud prevention and compromising the public benefits expected from the expenditures involved. Some argue that the system is wasting taxpayer dollars without generating the intended public benefits (Kuo et al. 2013).

Accounting and audit

The accounting and audit phase ensures that the government's actual revenue and expenditures are aligned with the legal budget by detecting any fraud or negligence during budget execution, as well as monitoring the completed and incomplete budget programs. Theoretically, budget decision-makers should adjust the budget proposal for the coming year based on the past performance of budget execution. In reality, however, both government bureaucrats and legislators tend to focus more on budget preparation than on execution. They work very hard to get the annual budget passed in the Legislative Yuan, but, once the money is appropriated, they pay little attention to the performance of budget execution and seldom thoroughly review whether objectives have been met. For instance, according to the *Financial Statement Act 2000*, the auditor-general should submit a final audit report to the Legislative Yuan and, within a year of receipt, the Legislative Yuan should complete deliberation of that report. If deliberation is not completed within this time frame, the report is deemed deliberated and is automatically approved. However, looking back over the past 10 years, the Legislative Yuan failed to complete deliberation nine times.[5] This exemplifies how the performance information collected in the accounting and audit phase fails to provide feedback to budget-makers in a timely manner.

The local government budget process

There are three levels of autonomous local government in Taiwan, with six special municipalities, 13 counties and provincial municipalities and 198 county municipalities and townships. The budgetary process at the local government level mirrors that for the central government, including the budget preparation, budget approval, budget execution and accounting and audit phases. Likewise, the entire procedure is regulated by the *Budget Act*, *Financial Statement Act* and *Audit Act*.

Most local governments in Taiwan face an enormous fiscal burden but enjoy only very limited fiscal autonomy. Taiwan has a unique 'one-whip' budgetary system—a legacy from the authoritarian era—under which the DGBAS holds the authority for appointment of all budgeting and accounting personnel in both central and local governments. Although the people elect local governors, they do not have the authority to appoint their own budgeting and accounting personnel. Furthermore, under this one-whip system, the DGBAS issues annual guidelines on the preparation and execution of public budgets—a binding document that stipulates budgetary preparation and execution for both central and local levels. When local governments prepare and execute their budgets, they have to abide by the DGBAS guidelines. Some scholars criticise this mechanism and argue that local government leaders should try to gain more autonomy in making budgetary decisions so as to better respond to the public's needs (Chen and Lu 2005; Ji 2008).

Meanwhile, some scholars argue that many local governments in Taiwan lack the fiscal discipline to safeguard taxpayer dollars and incentives to expand their revenue sources (Lin and Tsai 2003; Ji 2015). Many politicians continue spending money on large projects to please voters and are oblivious to the accumulated public deficit. Indeed, most voters care more about infrastructure projects and social welfare programs

---

5   Between fiscal years 2005 and 2014, only the audit report for fiscal year 2010 was deliberated and approved by the Legislative Yuan within a year of receipt.

than about controlling public debt. What is even worse is that, when local governments are unable to pay public employees or contractors, the central government simply steps in by increasing intergovernmental grants or general revenue sharing, so that local governments do not go bankrupt. As a result, applying rational political calculations when facing fiscal crises, local governments have figured out that asking the central government for help is a much more convenient approach than increasing tax or cutting expenditures, which might antagonise voters (Jang 2006; Fang 2014). In this political reality, many local governments lack both the capacity and the motivation to properly allocate and manage their fiscal revenue. Some scholars therefore believe that the 'one-whip' regime can at least curtail certain irresponsible or inefficient expenditure items (Chen and Lu 2005). At the very least, the budgeting and accounting officials appointed by the DGBAS, from a more neutral and objective position, might be more capable of looking after the public purse.

In addition to the revenue shortage problem, another challenge facing local governments is the imbalance in revenue distribution. In Taiwan, most local revenue is derived from property taxes. Urban real estate prices are higher than rural prices, which generate greater property tax revenue, while rural and agricultural regions see smaller increases in real estate prices so their local governments collect less revenue. Through intergovernmental fiscal transfers, including general revenue sharing and grants, the central government can shift this balance. Yet, because of the mechanism for such transfers, some local governments become overly reliant on the central government's financial support and fail to establish their own fiscal autonomy. To elaborate further, although real estate prices in certain regions have increased along with local economic development, local governments are often reluctant to adjust their tax base accordingly, so their property tax revenue does not grow in conjunction with economic growth. It is necessary to request local governments to periodically re-examine their property tax structure and to expand revenue sources so they can develop greater fiscal autonomy.

The lack of rational budgetary decision-making is the third challenge in the local budgeting process. Except for a very few governments (such as the Taipei City Government), the overall quality of local budgetary regimes is much poorer than at the central government level. There are two reasons for this disparity. First, local councillors are generally not as qualified as central government legislators, so their budgetary oversight capability requires much improvement. For instance, Miaoli County

Council has not made any modifications to the general budget proposed by the executive branch in the past 23 years, despite having one of the country's heaviest debt burdens (Liberty Times Net 2003). Second, the media and most civic groups tend to pay more attention to budgetary decisions and processes at the central government level and provide less oversight of local government activities. Consequently, the level of fiscal transparency and public accountability in local government budgeting is low (Su et al. 2010).

Continuing budget reforms

Taiwan continues to undertake budget reform, including democratisation of public budgeting following the lifting of martial law in the 1980s and the performance-driven budgeting reform influenced by NPM theory in the 1990s. While these reforms are ongoing, two of the most prominent recent developments in Taiwan are participatory budgeting and performance auditing.

Participatory budgeting

During Taiwan's nationwide nine-in-one election in 2014, many candidates proposed a policy of participatory budgeting, which received wide support and was particularly popular among younger voters. Participatory budgeting was first developed in Brazil in the late 1980s and has since become a global trend. It is a process of democratic deliberation and budget decision-making in which ordinary people decide how to allocate a certain portion of the public budget. Participatory budgeting has the potential to enhance participatory democracy, social inclusion, fairness in allocating social resources and public sector innovation.

The participatory budgeting models adopted in Taiwan can be categorised into three types: the councillors' budget quota model, the executive grant model and the integrative budget process model. Under the councillors' budget quota model, local councillors enjoy the right to propose budgeting bills within a given quota and earmark them for certain local projects or programs. In the early days, such proposals were rarely scrutinised and the executive body simply executed the relevant budget. Yet some of the proposals represented pure 'pork barrelling' and, when investigated, were found to be wasteful and fraudulent (Tang et al. 2002). Some councillors even used the public funds to consolidate personal alliances. Since then, there has been more stringent oversight of these budget quota measures. Generally speaking, however, as long as the spending program proposed by the councillor does not exceed his or her budget quota, the executive branch allocates the budget based on the councillors' proposals. With the shift to participatory budgeting, the so-called councillors' budget quota model requires councillors to take the initiative to refer a part of their budget quota to their constituents to decide how to use the money. With the help of government administrators, citizens propose, discuss and vote for the allocation of the budget quota; the executive branch then executes the chosen programs. This model is similar to the participatory budgeting practices in Chicago and New York.[6]

Taiwan has promoted participatory budgeting since 2015, and a few municipal councillors are developing trial projects in their districts. Although the budget quota is small, all citizens in the community can jointly decide how to spend the public dollars. Compared with the previous situation, when councillors could earmark budget items, this type of participatory budgeting is a great improvement in local governance. Some trial cases have received positive support. While city councillors are initiating these cases, the executive branch also plays a key role, such as through promoting the process, helping citizens evaluate and improve the proposals and enhancing program feasibility. Continued monitoring is required to understand whether this is only for show among councillors or whether councillors are genuinely willing to devolve some budget decision-making to the public in future.

The second model of implementing participatory budgeting is the executive grant model. Each central government ministry or local government department can allocate a budget to grant non-governmental organisations (NGOs) funds to be spent through participatory budgeting. New Taipei City provides an example. Beginning in the second half of 2015, the city's economic development department offered grants

---

6   In 2009, Alderman Joe Moore of Chicago's 49th Ward launched the Participatory Budgeting Project (PBP) by allocating US$1.3 million of his discretionary fund for the residents of his ward. Citizens gathered to discuss, deliberate and vote into implementation projects that were then executed by the administration. This experience was then brought to New York. Harlem-based Community Voices Heard, founded more than 20 years ago, initiated PBPs. So far, more than half of all city council members support the process. City council members commit their discretionary funds, ranging between US$1 million and US$2 million, to PBPs. One provision states that these proposals are limited to the construction or updating of public infrastructure projects that are in use for at least five years.

to two non-profit organisations to advocate, orchestrate and support participatory budgeting in relation to energy conservation.[7] The two selected organisations helped the public formulate, discuss, review and vote for proposals. While it is mainly the government agency that executes the selected projects, the public and NGOs can also take part. Based on this model, both the urban development department of the Taichung City Government and the Research, Development and Evaluation Commission of the Kaohsiung City Government have commissioned university scholars to embark on, respectively, the Taichung Central District Participatory Budgeting Project and the Public Participation and Empowerment for 2017 Hama Star EcoMobility World Festival.

Both the councillors' budget quota and the executive grant models are designed to promote participatory budgeting through individual projects without changing the government's budgetary regime. Taking a more comprehensive approach, the third model integrates participatory budgeting into the government's formal budgetary preparation process, and is therefore the most challenging of the three models. One representative example is the participatory budgeting procedure initiated by the Taipei City Government and led mainly by the Department of Civil Affairs since 2015. Public meetings and training sessions are held in district-level offices and citizens are invited to submit their budget proposals in person at the district offices or through an online platform. Citizens get to vote and rank the proposals, while government officials assist in refining the proposals' content and each bureau prepares the budget estimates. The proposals are then submitted to the Taipei City Government's Public Participation Committee for final reading. Once a proposal is passed, it is incorporated into the city government's general budget proposal, which is then submitted to the city council for approval. The year 2015 was the first year Taipei City had undertaken a participatory budget and only a few hundred participants were involved, so it is too early to fully understand and measure its impact.

No matter which model is applied, participatory budgeting still accounts for only a very small portion of Taiwan's overall budget and the number of participants is but a tiny fraction of the total population. This is similar to the development of participatory budgeting in most other countries (Su et al. 2015). It is fair to say that participatory budgeting plays mainly

---

7   The two non-profit organisations are Yonghe Community College and Ludi Community College.

an educational role for democratic participation and a less substantial role in budget allocation. For participatory budgeting to become more influential in the future, the level of public participation should be further elevated—focusing more on dialogue and engagement throughout the process than on the formality of proposing bills and casting votes. Government agencies should also help to empower people by providing more supportive measures.

Performance auditing

In the past, Taiwan's audit agencies mainly conducted compliance audits, focusing on supervising the legality of budget execution, such as whether there was any financial illegality or delinquency regarding where and how the funds were spent. To enhance the value of audit and to stay abreast of global trends, audit agencies have begun transforming their roles from traditional oversight to providing insight into financial management, key trends and emerging challenges. To become better equipped in playing these new roles, audit agencies in Taiwan are ramping up efforts to develop performance auditing by assessing thoroughly the performance of budget execution.

Performance auditing is much more challenging than compliance auditing. For compliance auditing, auditors only have to be knowledgeable about the regulatory framework, as their work mainly entails reviewing whether an agency is adhering to laws and regulations during the budget execution phase. Performance auditing is about assessing the performance of specific expenditure programs. For example, did a program meet its objectives and is the value of public money maximised? Performance auditing is no longer just about laws and regulations, but also requires interdisciplinary knowledge and expertise, especially when it comes to cross-agency programs. Auditors also have to understand how the work of different agencies relates to one another and to grasp the 'big picture' of how the program should be executed. In other words, auditors in performance auditing must possess in-depth knowledge of policies and have familiarity with the methods of performance or program evaluation. This is a new challenge for auditors, which also implies new auditing risks.

At the same time, performance auditing also presents new challenges for auditors to maintain audit independence—a core value for auditing bodies. In the past, when auditors conducted mainly compliance audits, they could easily come to an objective judgment about legal compliance issues without much involvement by the audited entity. In contrast, in the case of performance auditing, auditors have to actively engage and communicate with audited entities to gain their trust so they can obtain the necessary information for the performance auditing reports. Moreover, the performance auditing reports—unlike the neutral, objective compliance reports—tend to have a degree of subjectivity and hence are more controversial, and can sometimes compromise audit independence. Therefore, in the pursuit of performance auditing, it is important that auditing agencies learn how to interact with audited entities while also maintaining audit independence and impartiality.

Conclusion

Taiwan's current tax burden per taxpayer is low, leaving the government with serious revenue shortages compared with previous years given the increasing demand for government services. The government has to pinch every penny possible to maximise revenue and struggles to meet the needs of the people. Despite decades of reforms, including both budget democratisation and performance-led budgetary reform, the current government's budgetary regime faces challenges. In particular, both the executive and the legislative bodies still undervalue the importance of the assessment stage of major spending programs, such as the practice of CBA. In addition, because of political party confrontation at the budget approval phase, politics overruns rational decision-making, especially among local councillors. As for the budget execution phase, a change in mindset is required for government agencies to move away from the overly conservative, fraud-preventative approach to effective budget control.

The two current budgetary reforms—participatory budgeting and performance auditing—share the objective of maximising the value of taxpayer dollars. Participatory budgeting aims to enhance public accountability and align government expenditure more closely to people's needs by incorporating citizen participation into the budgeting process. Performance auditing aims to transform the role and function of auditing bodies from providing oversight to providing insight and foresight.

This chapter has pointed out a number of problems in Taiwan's public budget system. But, if we look at the overall picture, we see steady improvement in the budgetary institutions over time. As budgetary reform scholars in the United States have commented, wherever we have walked, traces are left behind (Rubin 1990; Posner 2007). When we study budgetary decisions and reforms in Taiwan, the incremental budgeting model is the most common, under which gradual changes are made step by step rather than through radical reforms. Whether it is the democratisation of public budgeting or efficiency-led budgeting reforms in the past, or the current interest in participatory budgeting and performance auditing, each reform has achieved at least some of its objectives and, at the same time, has updated the budget policy reform agenda, identifying more goals to be pursued.

References

Chao, O. H. 2005. 'A study on how to professionalize the committee function and uncover the party coordination in Legislative Yuan'. *Journal of Social Sciences and Philosophy* 13(1): 37–54.

Chen, J.-K. and Y.-C. Lu. 2005. *The Restructuring of One-Whip System under Governmental Reform.* Taipei: Ministry of Civil Service.

Department of Statistics. 2017. *Yearbook of Financial Statistics, 2016.* Taipei: Ministry of Finance.

Fang, K.-H. 2014. 'Mutual consolidation of local fiscal behaviors and institutions: Reinterpreting the fiscal predicament of local government'. In T.-T. Su (ed.) *Challenges and Trends in Local Governance: Taiwan's experiences.* Taipei: Taiwan Foundation for Democracy.

Hawang, S.-D. 2002. 'The improvement of congress: Two waves of reform in the Legislative Yuan'. *New Era Think Tank Forum* 17: 42–56.

Jang, C.-L. 2006. 'Evaluation on the problems of implementing the general law on local taxation: An application of the third generation implementation theory'. *Chinese Local Self-Governance* 59(1): 4–23.

Ji, J.-C. 2008. 'The one-whip system and local government'. *Intergovernmental Relationship Research Newsletter* 1: 5–7.

Ji, J.-C. 2015. 'Financial issues and strategies in Taiwan: Comparison between municipality and county/city'. *Chinese Local Government* 68(4): 3–27.

Kuo, Y.-Y., L.-C. Hung and K.-H. Fang. 2013. *Improving DGBAS's Financial Management System in Taiwan.* Taipei: Research, Development and Evaluation Commission.

Liberty Times Net. 2003. 'Miaoli is not afraid of mounting debt at all; it did not cut its general budgets in 23 consecutive years'. [In Chinese]. *Liberty Times Net*, 3 January. Available from: news.ltn.com.tw/news/politics/paper/1067871 (accessed 3 January 2017).

Lin, J. K.-T. and C.-Y. Tsai. 2003. 'Fiscal discipline of the local governments and the revenues and expenditures classification'. *Journal of Public Administration* 9: 1–33.

Organisation for Economic Co-operation and Development (OECD). 2016. *Revenue Statistics 2016*. Paris: OECD Publishing.

Posner, P. L. 2007. 'The continuity of change: Public budgeting and finance reforms over 70 years'. *Public Administration Review* (November–December): 1018–29. doi.org/10.1111/j.1540-6210.2007.00793.x.

Rigger, S. 1999. *Politics in Taiwan: Voting for democracy*. London: Routledge. doi.org/10.4324/9780203449028.

Rubin, I. S. 1990. 'Budget theory and budget practice: How good the fit?' *Public Administration Review* (March–April): 179–89. doi.org/10.2307/976865.

Su, T.-T. 1996. *The Study of Public Budgeting*. Taipei: Hwa Tai Publishing.

Su, T.-T. 2007. 'Public budgeting reform in Taiwan'. In G. Caiden and T.-T. Su (eds) *The Repositioning of Public Governance: Global experience and challenges*. Taipei: Taiwan Public Affairs Center.

Su, T.-T., W. Sun and H.-F. Tsai. 2015. *The Feasibility of Participatory Budgeting Model in Taiwan*. Taipei: National Development Council.

Su, T.-T., C.-D. Tso and C.-J. Chen. 2010. *The Analytical Framework and Evaluation of Government Transparency*. Taipei: Research, Development and Evaluation Commission.

Tang, C.-P. T., C.-L. Wu and K.-C. Su. 2002. 'Divided government and local democratic administration: Budget for local infrastructure, local factions, and pork-barrel politics in Taichung County'. *The Chinese Public Administration Review* 12(1): 37–76.

Wang, Y.-L. 2002. 'The role of political party and operation of party caucuses in congress'. *The Taiwan Law Review* 86: 82–96.

6

Making 'accountability for results' really work?[1]

Andrew Podger

Introduction

Australia was a pioneer in the 1980s and 1990s in what later became known as New Public Management (NPM) (Pollitt 1990; Osborne and Gaebler 1992). The context was widespread demand for greater efficiency in government in response to global economic pressures and concern that government expenditure may be crowding out private investment and activity. Governments could no longer be exempt from competitive pressures and needed to demonstrate efficiency and effectiveness in the delivery of public services.

The main elements of the agenda in Australia were:

- a focus on results rather than public service processes
- renewed interest in markets, including the use of market-type mechanisms to improve efficiency in the delivery of public services
- devolution of authority from central agencies to line agencies and, within line agencies, towards the front line

---

1   This chapter is based on the author's 2015 Allan Barton Lecture to Australia's Certified Practising Accountants (CPA), which built on a paper presented to the Dialogue workshop in Taipei.

- the use of business management processes including corporate planning and accrual accounting
- a systematic approach to performance budgeting and management.

The Australian approach differed from that in some other countries: it was mostly pragmatic, not ideological, and was largely initiated by the public service itself and strongly endorsed by a reformist Labor government and then extended by a reformist conservative government. While changing the way government operated, the reforms in Australia did not reduce the role of government in any significant way (Keating 2004). The reforms were implemented incrementally over the two decades, with each reform building on previous steps; while some corrections occurred, there were no radical 'U-turns'.

Much of the NPM agenda culminated in financial management and public service legislation in the late 1990s. The legislation replaced previous detailed process requirements with principles to guide public administration and to promote firmer accountability for results. Performance management was embedded in the budget process, reporting arrangements and agency management processes.

Between 2008 and 2013, two major reviews were conducted into Australian government administration: the Moran Review, a largely internal Australian Public Service (APS) review (Moran 2010), and an internal review into Commonwealth financial administration (Commonwealth Financial Accountability Review [CFAR]), managed by the Department of Finance (DoF 2012). Neither identified significant failures requiring fundamental reappraisal of the NPM reforms, but both found weaknesses in how they were being managed, some overreach in devolution, insufficient 'whole-of-government' focus and some loss of strategic capacity and longer-term focus.

Part of the response to these reviews were changes to both the public service legislation (PoA 2013c) and the financial management legislation, the latter involving a new Act, the *Public Governance, Performance and Accountability Act 2013* (*PGPA Act*) (PoA 2013a). The new and revised legislation reaffirms the importance of a focus on results but also places considerable emphasis on 'whole-of-government' coherence and cooperation, recognises a wider range of public sector organisations and governance arrangements, represents a further shift to principles-based management rather than detailed rules, extends the concept of performance management to incorporate 'stewardship' and organisational capability, reflecting increased concern for 'how' and 'why' results are to be achieved as well as for 'what' results are to be achieved, and expands the previous promotion of risk management.

The key question is: will these latest reforms make 'accountability for results' really work? This chapter first describes the journey since 'management for results' first became the catchcry in Australia. It then summarises the new legislation and related policies, exploring three particular aspects: first, broad governance concepts; second, the development and enhancement of Australia's performance management system; and third, the increasing interest in risk management. As these three aspects are explored, the chapter identifies some of the ongoing challenges involved. These are summarised in the concluding comments.

Evolving governance concepts

The shift to principles

An important part of the evolving concept of governance has been the shift away from process controls to principles that not only provide a robust framework for public management, but also allow flexibility to respond to changing environments.

Until the NPM-based legislation in the late 1990s, Australia's financial management was governed by the *Audit Act 1901*, which applied detailed controls on all expenditures, and by a budget process that focused on inputs, with the ensuing Appropriation Acts detailing allocations to individual 'line items' based on different inputs, thereby involving the central financial authority (the Treasury until 1976, then the Department of Finance) in agencies' internal management processes.

The shift towards 'management for results' began with the introduction of program budgeting in 1984, picking up a recommendation in the 1976 Royal Commission on Australian Government Administration (Coombs 1976). The shift to a more principles-based approach was gradual and pursued via a range of strategies. Until the late 1990s, it occurred without any clearly articulated common purpose or principles of public administration and financial management. There was, however, an understanding that the increased focus on results and the reduced emphasis on process controls required better articulation of integrity requirements: means as well as ends still matter.

The new *Financial Management and Accountability Act 1997* (*FMA Act*) (PoA 1997b), which replaced the *Audit Act* for most budget-dependent agencies, specified (s. 44) the responsibility of a chief executive to 'manage the affairs of the Agency in a way that promotes proper use of resources', where 'proper use' meant 'efficient, effective, economical and ethical use that is not inconsistent with the policies of the Commonwealth'. The new *Public Service Act 1999* (*PS Act*) (PoA 1999) went much further, articulating the 'Values of the Australian Public Service' and the associated 'Code of Conduct', replacing a long, process-oriented Act that dated back to 1922. The legislated APS Values were based on versions prepared by the Institute of Public Administration Australia and others during the 1980s and 1990s, and followed negotiations with the unions and in the parliament. They reflected traditional Westminster principles such as nonpartisanship, responsiveness to the elected government, accountability, impartiality, professionalism and the merit principle, and also included a specific reference to achieving results and managing performance.

The *PGPA Act* takes the principles approach further than the former *FMA Act*. It articulates in Section 5 the objectives of the legislation:

    a. To establish a coherent system of governance and accountability across Commonwealth entities;

    b. To establish a performance framework across Commonwealth entities;

    c. To require the Commonwealth and Commonwealth entities:

        i. To meet high standards of governance, performance and accountability;

        ii. To provide meaningful information to the Parliament and the public;

        iii. To use and manage resources properly ('proper' means 'efficient, effective, economic and ethical'); and

        iv. To work cooperatively with others to achieve common objectives, where practicable; and

    d. To require Commonwealth companies to meet high standards of governance, performance and accountability.

For all agencies other than companies, it also sets out the general duties of 'accountable authorities' (the agency head or board) and the general duties of all officials, the latter including duty of care and diligence; the duty to act honestly, in good faith and for a proper purpose; duty in relation to the use of position; duty in relation to the use of information; and duty to disclose interests.

These duties are consistent with the requirements in the *PS Act*, which also apply to about half the people covered by these provisions in the *PGPA Act*.

The 2013 amendments to the *PS Act* simplify the APS Values, reducing the number from 15 to five[2] to promote their wider understanding across the APS. I remain a critic of this new formulation, which may have made the values easier to remember but at the expense of losing sight of important points of substance. 'Merit', which, since the Northcote–Trevelyan Report of 1854 (Northcote and Trevelyan 1854), has been a defining characteristic of Westminster civil services, has been downgraded and the APS Values no longer distinguish the unique role of the public service from that of other parts of government, including the parliamentary service, political advisers and politicians (Podger 2011). Moreover, in 1999, the values were openly debated among the political parties before an agreed formulation was settled. Sadly, in 2013, there was almost no debate and the parliament just went along with what the public service leadership presented without the appreciation of history that one might have expected from the service.

Governance of different types of public sector organisations

The former *Audit Act* applied financial management controls to all Commonwealth organisations. Some organisations, however, were exempt from some of the controls, particularly those that were expected to operate commercially. These exemptions became important during the 1970s as the government then commercialised major services—in particular, what became Telecom (then Telstra) and Australia Post, which had previously

---

2   The APS Commission uses the pneumonic 'I CARE': impartial, committed to service, accountable, respect, ethical (APSC 2014).

been managed within public service departments under direct ministerial control (the former Post Master General's Department held the majority of all Commonwealth public servants until that time).

During the 1980s, the government issued new rules on the management of commercial bodies as part of a rationalisation of accountability arrangements under the more devolved processes emerging under the NPM reforms. The Walsh Rules, as they were known (after then minister for finance, Peter Walsh), exempted commercial bodies from many of the *Audit Act* provisions, making their boards operate under corporate management law principles, accountable to relevant ministers as if they, on behalf of the public as owner, were the shareholders (CoA 1986). Board strategies were subject to ministerial approval and performance was largely in terms of returns to the shareholder ministers to whom the board was accountable, as well as any specified community service obligations. Decisions on dividends and significant investments were matters for the shareholder ministers, but the boards were given very wide authority to manage the companies' resources, including people and finances.

The 1997 legislation reflected this distinction between organisations that were more clearly dependent on government revenue and required close ministerial oversight and more independent organisations. The former came under the new *FMA Act* and the latter under the new *Commonwealth Authorities and Corporations Act 1997* (*CAC Act*) (PoA 1997a), both (together with the new *Auditor-General Act 1997*) replacing the former *Audit Act*. The *CAC Act* covered not only commercial organisations, but also all statutory authorities, whether financially independent or not. This led to some anomalies, as did the rather arbitrary way in which the *PS Act* applied: not all *FMA Act* agencies were subject to the *PS Act* and many *CAC Act* agencies were (the other agencies having their own employment regimes under their own legislation or as companies).

In the early 2000s, the finance department began to publish a list of all Commonwealth organisations identifying which financial management and employment legislation applied to each (DoF 2005a). The list kept growing and the lack of coherence about the coverage of different financial management and employment laws became increasingly obvious. The problem identified was not new or limited to Australia. The New Zealanders had previously referred to the challenge of 'signposting the zoo', highlighting the wide range of government activities, the varying degrees of independence from political control desired and the range of governance structures used.

In 2003, the Australian Government established a review of statutory authorities and statutory officeholders (the Uhrig Review) to examine governance arrangements for these bodies. Led by a prominent businessman, the review had a private sector perspective and recommended the wider use of just two governance templates, with either a single person or an executive board to be held accountable for such an authority (Uhrig 2003). It was a disappointing report because, while the lack of a coherent framework for guiding governance structures was a serious concern, Uhrig did not really appreciate the unique characteristics of the public sector and failed to clarify which organisations should be subject to which legislation.

The Uhrig Review did, however, convince the Department of Finance to issue its own guidelines on agency governance arrangements (DoF 2005b). These encouraged more functions to be managed within government departments under direct ministerial control and, where greater independence from such control was warranted, the use of authorities under a single agency head or an executive board or, in the case of a commercial body, the use of a company structure. The guidelines also clarified the financial management legislation most suited to each type of agency and where the *PS Act* should be expected to apply. The guidance was applied over the following decade, shifting more functions into ministerial departments and leading to more agencies coming under the *FMA Act* rather than the *CAC Act*, and more coming under the *PS Act*. However, there remained concerns that the legislation and the guidance did not 'fit' the wide range of circumstances of different agency types and that a more flexible approach to financial management legislation was needed within common principles.

The *PGPA Act* addresses these concerns more directly by having a single piece of legislation setting out the financial management requirements for all Commonwealth government activities and agencies, based on principles, and allowing a wider range of governance structures. The Act distinguishes between 'Commonwealth entities' and 'Commonwealth companies' and identifies two types of entities: 'corporate Commonwealth entities' and 'non-corporate Commonwealth entities'. Companies are subject to corporations law and financial management is based on private sector principles, with the government acting as shareholder (essentially applying the 1986 Walsh guidelines). Commonwealth entities come under more detailed financial oversight, whether they are departments, statutory authorities or other types of agencies. The distinction between corporate and non-corporate entities relates to whether they are legally separate from the Commonwealth (corporate) as distinct from being part of the Commonwealth (non-corporate), meaning that some features of the legislation may apply in slightly different ways. The legislation does not determine the governance of the entity (e.g. whether it has a single chief executive or a board), but requires consistent standards of accountability regardless of the legal structure.[*]

In presenting the legislation to the parliament, the minister also highlighted the intention to apply the provisions of the Act in a flexible way based on the concept of 'earned autonomy' (PoA 2013b): agencies with proven high performance may be exempt from some of the requirements in finance rules under the Act, while less-effective agencies may be subject to additional disclosure and performance requirements.

The finance department has subsequently issued new guidance, replacing the guidance provided in 2005, to assist the determination of appropriate organisational structures for new activities and any review of existing governance arrangements (DoF 2017). The new guidelines (or 'assessment template') continue to encourage new activities to be managed by existing organisations, but provide more guidance on the factors to be taken into account in determining the appropriate governance structure and whether staff should be employed under the *PS Act* (see Figure 6.1).

Notwithstanding this useful guidance, there remains room for further clarification, particularly over the appropriate structure for service delivery: is this best managed within ministerial departments or would a greater degree of independence facilitate more effective and efficient performance (and, if so, is a statutory authority or an executive agency the more appropriate structure, or should a third party be used—a for-profit or not-for-profit organisation)? There would be advantages in such guidance being subject to wider consultation and deliberation by the parliament.

Three-Stage Governance Gateway Test

Gateway Test 1

    1.   Does the Commonwealth have the constitutional power to undertake the activity?

Gateway Test 2

    2.   Is the government best placed to undertake the activity, in whole or in part, compared with an external body?

         o   Guidance includes: what is the best mechanism to do the activity, examples including grants to state and territory governments, the private sector or the not-for-profit sector.

Gateway Test 3

    3.   Can the activity be conducted by an existing Commonwealth body, in whole or in part?

         o   Guidance includes: what is the most efficient arrangement?

Validation of a (separate) structure

    i.   Does the body require enabling legislation?

         o   Guidance includes: is statutory independence from government required?

    ii.   Will the body exercise coercive or regulatory powers?

         o   Guidance includes: will the body involve regulatory functions under a law of the Commonwealth?

    iii.   Will the body primarily undertake a non-commercial and core government function?

         o   Guidance includes: will the body be primarily budget funded?

    iv.   Does the body need to sue or be sued, or does it need to hold money outside the legal entity of the Commonwealth?

    v.   Does the body have a commercial focus?

         o   Guidance includes: if yes, it may be appropriate to establish it as a company, and to be outside the *Public Service Act.*

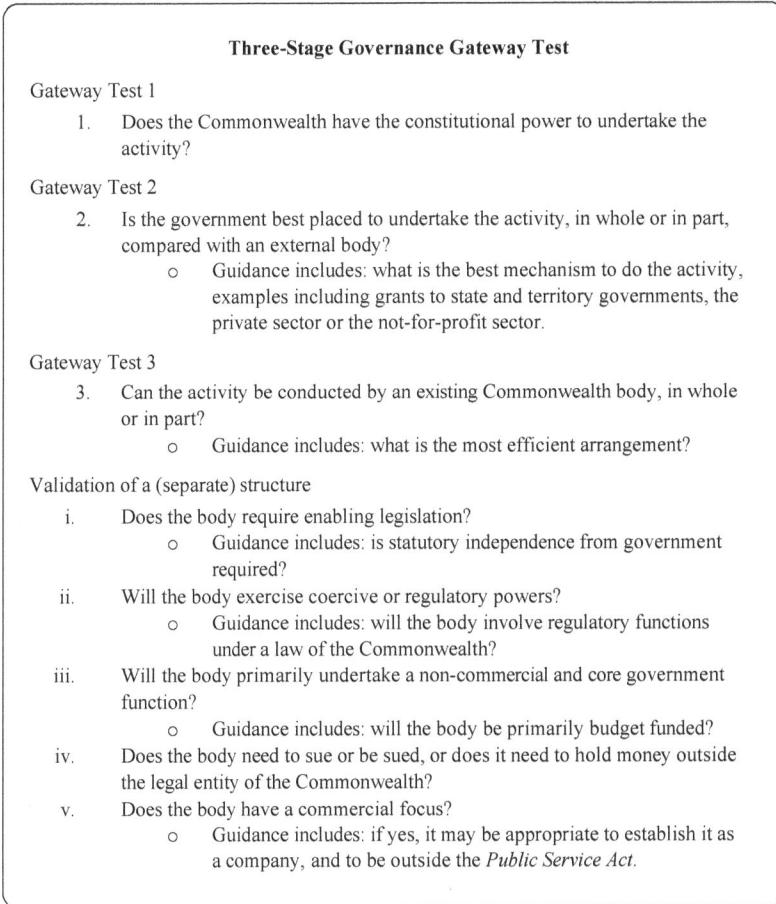

Figure 6.1 Commonwealth governance structures policy assessment template

Source: DoF (2017).

Whole-of-government

The Australian Government has for a very long time had strong coordinating capacity. Its budget processes have been comprehensive, it has had a strong treasury (the Treasury and the Department of Finance since 1976) and, since the 1950s, a strong cabinet process.

Under NPM, considerable authority for financial management and human resource management (HRM) was devolved to agencies, but overall budget control was not weakened; if anything, it increased.

Cabinet government also remained strong. The major restructuring of departments in 1987 introduced 'portfolio' arrangements where each portfolio was represented in cabinet, each portfolio minister had responsibility for a wider range of functions and, with assistant (non-cabinet) ministers and parliamentary secretaries, had more authority to prioritise expenditures within their portfolio allocations, allowing cabinet to focus its attention on the more important policy priorities and cross-government issues. This restructuring strengthened the role of departmental (portfolio) secretaries, complementing the devolution of authority already under way.

The NPM emphasis in agencies was reflected in both the *FMA Act* and the *PS Act*, with the *FMA Act* referring to the responsibilities of agency 'chief executives' and the *PS Act* referring to the responsibilities of 'agency heads'. Substantial authority was devolved to these individual leaders, who were then held accountable through ministers for the performance of their agencies and their agencies' programs.

Despite the strength of the cabinet process and overall budget control, the agency focus increasingly became a matter of concern in the early 2000s, as the 'stovepipes' were seen to inhibit effective responses to a range of complex 'whole-of-government' issues. A report, *Connected Government*, by the Management Advisory Committee (MAC) in 2004 addressed these concerns, promoting various structures and processes to support more collaboration and cooperation across the Commonwealth and also with other jurisdictions and external groups (MAC 2004).

This development in Australia mirrored developments elsewhere, particularly in the United Kingdom, where the Blair Government trumpeted 'joined-up government', and in Canada, where the term used was 'horizontal government'. The broader concept of 'network government' was also receiving attention (Rhodes 1997), involving not just linkages within government, but also partnerships with business and civil society. The term 'governance' itself reflected this idea of interconnectedness and shared responsibility and has widely replaced the term 'government' in academia and the public service.

CFAR and the Moran Review also highlighted whole-of-government concerns and recommended legislative change: CFAR recommended new financial management legislation and the Moran Reveiw recommended changes to the *PS Act*. The ensuing legislation, passed in 2013, gives explicit encouragement to cooperation across government and, indeed, beyond government.

The *PGPA Act* requires Commonwealth entities to 'work cooperatively with others to achieve common objectives, where practicable' (s. 5), and the duties of accountable authorities include the 'duty to encourage cooperation with others' (s. 17). The Act also allows the government to identify key priorities and objectives (s. 34) that would then be taken into account in agencies' own corporate plans (s. 35[3]). The rule for corporate plans issued under the Act also requires that plans include the purposes of the entity, with guidance from the finance department clarifying that this must include any relevant whole-of-government priorities or objectives identified under Section 34 of the Act.

A few cautionary comments, however, need to be made about these calls for more whole-of-government cooperation. The 2004 MAC report contained an important warning about 'group think': the risk that pressure to cooperate might discourage healthy professional debate and clarification of different perspectives. There is also the danger of excessive political control constraining advice that does not reflect prevailing political orthodoxy: 'whole-of-government' can become a euphemism for everyone to be 'on message'. The 2004 report also warned against trying to link everything to everything else all of the time, noting the costs involved and the proven benefits of devolved administration.

Performance management

Australia's performance management system drew heavily on the program budgeting experience in the United States in the 1970s, but applied in Australia's parliamentary democracy framework.

The central elements of the system that emerged in the mid-1980s and largely continued until 2015 were:

- A comprehensive budget and three-year forward estimates system based on identified programs for each government agency, with the system being managed by the Department of Finance.
- Annual budgets developed primarily through the Expenditure Review Committee (ERC) of cabinet after consideration of portfolio budget submissions from portfolio ministers that had been subject to scrutiny by the Departments of Finance and Treasury.

- Tabling in the parliament with the overall budget statements and appropriation bills of a 'portfolio budget statement' (PBS) for each portfolio, setting out the detailed budget and forward estimates of expenditure by program and agency in the portfolio along with the new policy measures proposed by the government, with specified program objectives, performance indicators and targets.

- Annual reports by each agency in each portfolio tabled in the parliament after the end of the financial year with the audited accounts for the year and performance reports for each program using the indicators and targets set out in the relevant PBS.

Pre-budget year
- November/December: Senior ministers set broad fiscal targets for budget and priority framework for portfolio ministers' budget submissions.
- February: Portfolio ministers' budget submissions lodged.
- February/March/April: ERC and cabinet deliberations.
- May: Budget presented to parliament, appropriation bills introduced, portfolio budget statements tabled.
- June: Appropriation bills passed.

Budget year
- From July: Implementation of budget measures, management of programs in line with appropriations and budget estimates.
- November/December: Mid-Year Economic and Fiscal Outlook, identification of any 'additional estimates' required and associated appropriation bills introduced.
- March/April: Additional appropriation bills passed.

Budget reporting year
- September: Final budget outcome presented to parliament.
- October: Agency annual reports for budget year tabled, linked to relevant portfolio budget statement performance targets.
- November: Consolidated financial statements for the general government sector released, audited by the Australian National Audit Office (ANAO).

Figure 6.2 The budget and performance management cycle until 2015
Source: Author's personal knowledge and correspondence with the Department of Finance.

The parliamentary processes have responded to this cycle by holding regular senate committee hearings to scrutinise the budgets and performance of each agency in each portfolio based largely on the PBS in May and June of the pre-budget year (directly after the budget is announced and before the appropriation bills are passed) and the annual reports in November and December (after the reports have been tabled and usually in association with the 'additional estimates' process).

Around the central elements there is an elaborate process of government decision-making at the whole-of-government level and within each portfolio and agency. At the whole-of-government level, the ERC of cabinet plays the central role, but it is also guided by a group of senior ministers, usually comprising the prime minister, the treasurer, the minister for finance and the deputy prime minister. These senior ministers set the broad fiscal parameters for the coming budget in light of the most recent data available to Treasury and the Department of Finance on the economy and revenue and expenditure trends; they also set high-level political priorities to guide portfolio ministers on what they may bring forward to the ERC in their budget submissions. The central agencies (the Departments of the Prime Minister and Cabinet, Treasury and Finance) also exercise considerable influence over the content of the portfolio budget cabinet submissions and control the integrity of the estimates and the provision of evidence in support of new policy proposals; they also comment on all submissions, with the finance department's guidance (its 'green briefs') often becoming the central focus of ERC discussion. The finance department is also frequently asked to identify options for expenditure savings.

At portfolio and agency levels, the development of budget submissions begins well before any guidance from the senior ministers, drawing on both external political input and internal analysis of program performance. The portfolio department coordinates the process for the portfolio minister and advises on the package of proposals to be included in the submission consistent with the requirements of the senior ministers and their departments. After the budget is presented and any legislation is enacted, each agency manages its program responsibilities and any new policy measures bearing in mind the objectives and performance targets set.

Strategic or corporate planning by each agency with supporting business plans by each business unit in the agency has been encouraged since the 1980s, complementing the PBS by focusing on the management strategies needed to meet performance targets. In addition, individual performance appraisal processes managed by each agency have been encouraged, linked to the agency's corporate and business planning and hence to the PBS and the broader performance management system.

The legislation that emerged in the late 1990s refers specifically to performance management and accountability. The 1999 *PS Act* included among the APS Values that '[t]he APS focuses on achieving results and managing performance'. The 1997 *FMA Act* required the 'efficient, effective, economical and ethical' management of resources, emphasising accountability for performance through ministers. The 1997 *CAC Act* required boards to be accountable for performance.

The ideal relationship between the performance budgeting process and agency planning and performance management was identified in a MAC report on performance management (MAC 2001).

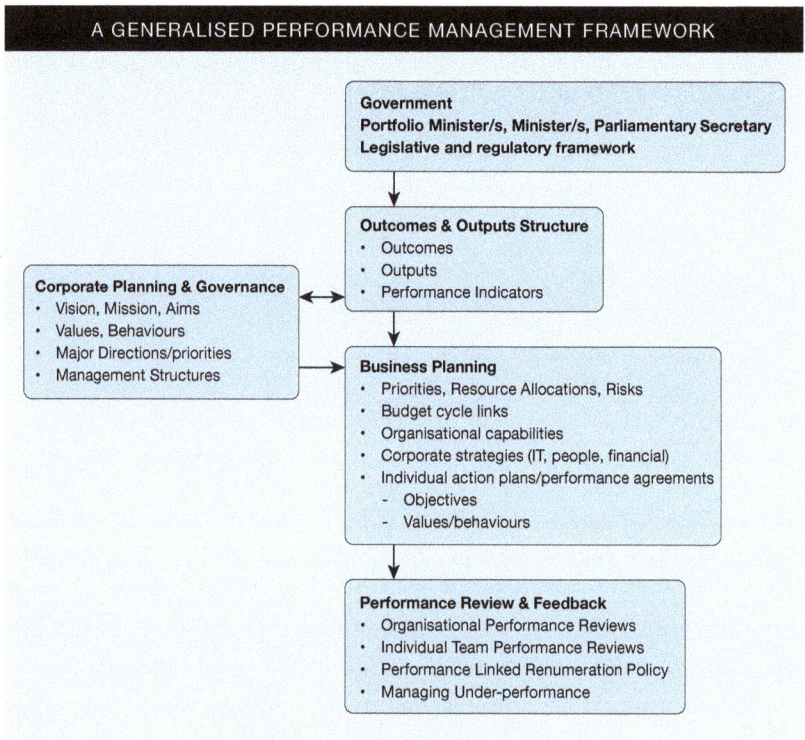

Figure 6.3 The performance management framework
Source: MAC (2001).

This had the government determining the outcomes, outputs and performance indicators ('what' is to be achieved) in the PBSs and each agency's corporate planning and governance determining the vision and mission, strategies and behaviours to achieve these results ('how' and 'why'). Business plans and individual performance appraisal were expected to draw on both. This relationship was not prescribed in any legislation or other formal requirements and each agency was left to design and manage its own corporate planning and governance arrangements, and its own performance appraisal system, consistent with the general principles of accountability for results that were eventually set out in legislation.

As the performance management system has developed and evolved, a number of challenges have emerged, not all of which have been met as successfully as the advocates of the system had hoped.

A continuing challenge has been how best to link inputs, outputs and outcomes. In the 1980s, the system focused on individual programs within agencies with reasonably easily identified inputs and outputs, but with narrowly defined objectives and measures of effectiveness. There were, however, complementary requirements for regular evaluations of programs and all new policy proposals put to the ERC were required to identify how and when they would be evaluated if agreed. This latter requirement was dropped in the late 1990s to streamline the ERC process, and the narrowness of the program approach was addressed instead by way of a new 'outputs and outcomes' framework that allowed related programs to be aggregated with the intention of giving more emphasis to the overall impact—and effectiveness—of government activity in that field.

The outcomes framework, however, presented its own problems, partly because the associated appropriation items were very broadly expressed. The parliament was concerned that it allowed ministers and agencies too much flexibility with insufficient accountability (one case went to the High Court, which, while finding the relevant spending lawful, accentuated the dangers involved; HCA 2005). The language used in outcome statements was also not as publicly recognisable as the names of programs, and the gap between 'outputs' and 'outcomes' made it difficult at times to be confident of cause and effect. A study led by former senator Andrew Murray, 'Operation Sunlight' (Murray 2008), led to a compromise 'outcomes–programs framework' with a renewed focus on programs within outcomes and related 'suboutcome' objectives and the use of 'intermediate outcomes' as indicators of likely overall outcome performance.

A related concern was the constant reframing of the outcomes and the performance indicators used, making more difficult the monitoring of performance over time and the assessment of performance across government activities at a point in time (Australian National Audit Office [ANAO] 2007).

The limited success of the outcomes framework also came at the expense of the less systematic approach to evaluation after the framework was introduced, and it seems evaluation was not given the priority it had attracted previously.

Another ongoing challenge has been the quality and integrity of performance measures. Associated with this has been the incidence of 'gaming' to report better performance than was really achieved, which has been particularly significant when financial rewards for organisations are directly linked to particular measures of performance such as hospital waiting lists and times and university research rankings.

Managing individual performance has also raised challenges. During the late 1980s, the idea of performance pay took hold, initially for senior executives and later extended more widely. Practice varied widely under Australia's devolved financial and human resources arrangements, but, for a while, performance pay was applied to all chief executives and to almost all senior executives and middle managers. Staff surveys consistently reported unhappiness among the majority of the public service, not only about the fairness of the system, but also about whether it was in fact supporting teamwork and organisational performance or was instead undermining morale and public service motivation (e.g. APSC 2004, 2005). I also expressed concern in 2007 that performance pay for departmental secretaries was placing undue political pressure to be responsive (Podger 2007). While performance pay still operates in some agencies, the practice is becoming less common (and no longer applies to departmental secretaries), and more emphasis is now placed on appraisal and feedback to promote alignment with organisational goals and staff development.

A particular issue identified in the Moran Review related to organisational capability and concerns about strategic policy capacity and aspects of people management, in particular. This led to the inclusion in the amended *PS Act* of references to the 'stewardship' responsibility of secretaries and the introduction of a capability review program by the Australian Public Service Commission (APSC); it also contributed to CFAR's focus on corporate planning. It seems that, despite the encouragement of corporate planning since the 1980s, practice had waned by the late 2000s and the quality and usefulness of plans varied widely.

The *PGPA Act* builds into the performance management system specific new requirements about corporate planning. A statutory rule under the *PGPA Act* was issued in early 2015 spelling out the nature of the corporate plans that must be prepared and the matters that must be included (PoA 2015). The plans must cover at least four years, starting with the immediate budget year (or 'reporting period'), and must be published. The matters that must be included are:

1. Introduction: A statement that the plan is prepared for the *PGPA Act*, the budget year for which it is prepared and the years covered by the plan.
2. Purposes: The purposes of the entity.
3. Environment: The environment in which the entity will operate for each year covered by the plan.
4. Performance: For each year covered by the plan, a summary of how the entity will achieve its purpose and how the entity's performance will be measured and assessed (including any measures, targets and assessments that will be used in annual performance statements).
5. Capability: The key strategies and plans the entity will implement to achieve the entity's purposes.
6. Risk oversight and management: A summary of the entity's risk oversight and management systems.

The *PGPA Act* and the rule are also firmer than the previous legislation about reporting on performance. Annual performance statements must be included in entities' annual reports tabled in the parliament, setting out the results of the measurement and assessment of performance set out in the corporate plan for the relevant budget year (reporting period). The annual performance statements must include the following matters:

1. Statements: That it is prepared for the *PGPA Act*, the reporting period concerned and that, in the opinion of the accountable authority of the entity, the performance statement accurately presents the entity's performance and complies with the legislation.
2. Results: The results of the measurement and assessment.
3. Analysis: An analysis of the factors that may have contributed to the entity's performance, including any changes to the entity's purposes, activities or organisational capability, or its environment, that may have had a significant impact.

These provisions address some of the key findings of both CFAR and the Moran Review about the importance of a longer-term view and the need to pay more attention to organisational capability and 'how' and 'why' agencies go about trying to achieve 'what' results the government is seeking. They also reinforce the stewardship responsibility of agency heads ('accountable authorities') for organisational capability as well as results and, by implication, the capability to achieve future results that may be different under different governments or in different circumstances.

The minimum requirements for corporate plans are not intended to impose a standard template, but there is a danger that they will be interpreted as a prescription for all plans. There is an extensive literature on corporate planning processes and content, which emphasises the importance of organisations clarifying their particular role or 'mission', the overall strategic direction they are determined to pursue, the particular circumstances in which they are operating, the challenges they face and the particular strategies they need to follow. As the legislation provides, agencies will need to consider any whole-of-government priorities and objectives and must work cooperatively to achieve common objectives, but each agency will need to develop its own plan to meet its particular purpose, taking into account its particular circumstances.

A common theme in the literature is that the process of corporate planning is almost as important as the content—for example, Senge (1990) emphasises the development of a 'shared vision'. Plans need to be owned by agency staff and accepted by the agency's stakeholders. They need explicit endorsement by the agency's ministers. They must be based on sound and frank analysis, including of organisational strengths and weaknesses and of the likely impact of social, economic, environmental, technological and political developments. On occasions, corporate plans require fundamental reappraisal of the agency's *raison d'être* and its relationships with other organisations as well as its internal management structures and processes.

This has been my own experience as a departmental secretary. On taking charge of the new Department of Housing and Regional Development in 1994, which the Keating Government established to lead renewed Commonwealth involvement in cities and regions, I embarked on a major corporate planning process that included time reflecting on the failures of the former, short-lived Department of Urban and Regional Development under the Whitlam Government (1972–75). We recognised the need to build better partnerships with the states and territories and to have clearer alignment with the government's broader economic policies if we were to succeed. The process therefore included extensive engagement with state and territory officials and leaders of Commonwealth central agencies.

When appointed secretary of the Department of Health and Family Services by the newly elected Howard Government in 1996, I used corporate planning to gain the new ministers' confidence, to engage with a wide range of stakeholders and to reset the organisation consistent with the new government's policy priorities. The final document (DHFS 1996) contained a wide range of specific measures that guided management action over the following three years, aimed at an agreed vision that the department should become the accepted leader of Australia's national health system. The plan was endorsed by ministers and became, in effect, an agreement between the portfolio minister, Michael Wooldridge, and me as secretary of the department. Measures included new portfolio consultation arrangements, improved processes for engaging with the states and territories and other external stakeholders, the commercialisation and outsourcing of various activities under a dedicated project team, a new information strategy, a two-year leadership development program for all Senior Executive Service and Executive Level staff and significant downsizing to achieve efficiency targets.

The current health department's corporate plan (2015), prepared in line with the requirements of the *PGPA Act*, is also a substantial document that should guide the organisation for several years and help it play a leadership role in strengthening the national health and health insurance systems (DoH 2015). But the requirement to publish plans by a particular date and to include specific matters may impede some agencies from pursuing the most valuable planning processes and may constrain plan content. The requirements may not appear onerous, but more value is likely from simply encouraging agencies to compare practices and to draw on the considerable literature available, including by having corporate planning in top management training programs, with chief executive officers and their top executives applying their learning to their agencies' particular circumstances.

There was some debate within the parliament during 2015 after the finance department suggested that the performance measures be in the corporate plans and not in the PBSs. The auditor-general rightly advised the Joint Committee of Public Accounts and Audit (JCPAA) that the PBSs tabled in parliament with the budget must contain the expected performance measures and targets because the corporate plans would only become available after the parliament approved the appropriation bills (McPhee 2015). This was an important matter going to the heart of the performance management system: the system is not just about the public service managers, but also about the way the legislature considers executive budget allocations and measures and subsequently holds the executive to account. Program objectives and performance indicators are fundamentally political: they require political authority and form the basis of political accountability. The suggestion by the finance department would also have reduced the emphasis of corporate planning on capability-building, muddying the water about the respective roles of the PBSs and corporate plans and the associated roles of ministers and senior administrators. The capability of organisations is related not just to delivering the results set out by the government at that time, but also to positioning the organisation to deliver results a future government may want in the years to come.

The JCPAA accepted the auditor-general's advice, so that the PBSs remain as government documents owned by ministers and informing the parliament when approving appropriations, while corporate plans are owned by the officials, who are the 'accountable authorities'.

Finance now presents the PBSs, corporate plans and annual reports as forming a continuous performance and budget cycle (Figure 6.4). This is a helpful presentation but might be improved if it made clearer that the PBS remains the key document setting out 'what' results the government is seeking, the corporate plan is the key document on 'how' and 'why' and annual reports should report achievements against both.

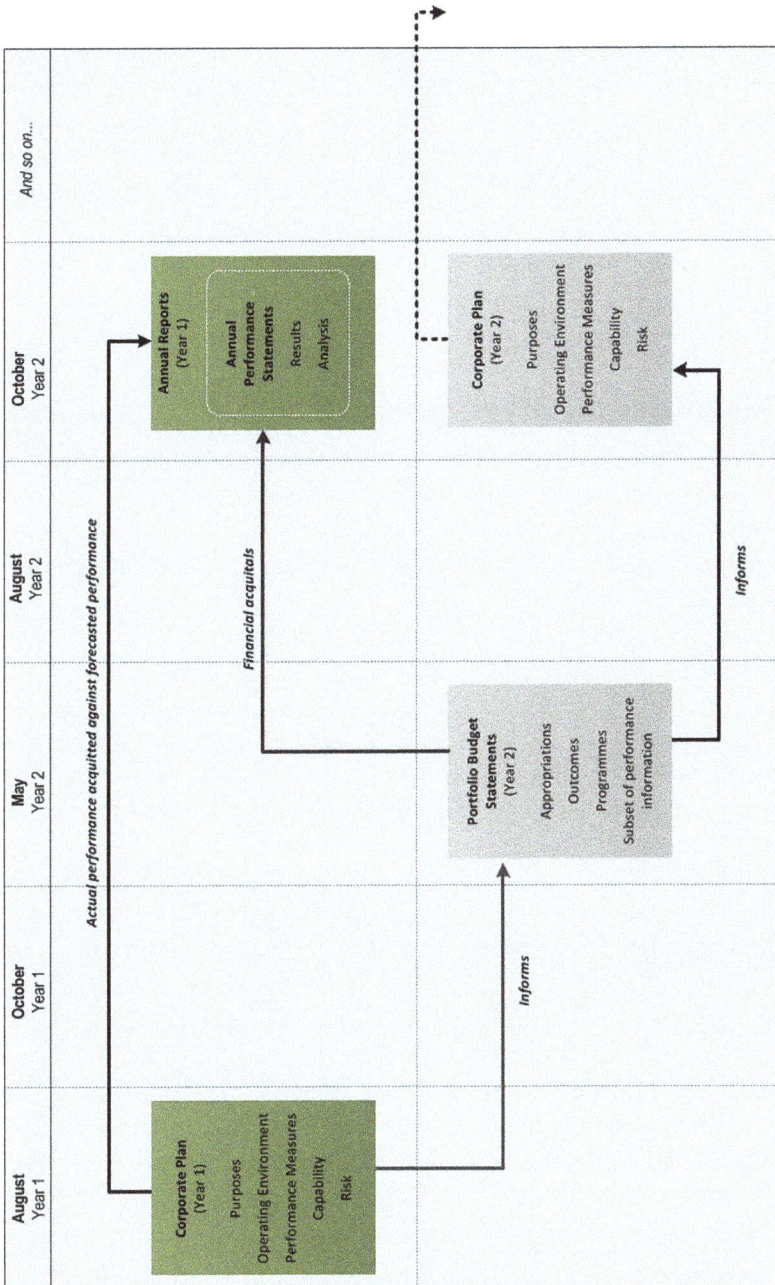

Figure 6.4 Enhanced Commonwealth performance and budget cycle

Source: Correspondence with the Department of Finance, 2015.

More generally, a difference in perspectives on performance and performance management between politicians and administrators has been apparent from the beginning of the NPM journey in the 1980s and remains today, typified by the limited use of performance information by senate estimates committees. In part, this is driven by our strongly adversarial two-party approach to politics, in which parliamentary scrutiny is dominated by party-political considerations. But it is also partly to do with a misunderstanding of the political process by some administrators (and of administration by some politicians) and of insufficient appreciation that program objectives and associated performance indicators are not just technical issues, but also reflect political judgments and require political input.

This is not something the *PGPA Act* can or should resolve on its own, but it highlights the importance of a good understanding of the respective roles of the legislature and the executive and of the different worlds of politics and administration. There remains a great deal of room for improved deliberation and debate in the legislature, drawing on the improved information that should result from the *PGPA Act*. This could motivate ministers also to have more regard for performance information and to be more involved in determining the performance indicators used. Administrators also need to accept the legitimate interest of politicians in information that is not directly related to program results and their demands for information about events as they occur outside the formal budget and performance cycle.

Risk management

Managing risk was not identified as relevant to public administration in Australia until the late 1980s, as NPM embraced a number of private sector practices such as corporate and business planning and the use of accrual accounting in commercialised government activities. Risk management also had synergy with the general shift under way from a focus on process controls to a focus on performance for results that required more proactive and innovative management.

Risk management was explained and promoted during the 1990s by the Department of Finance and the ANAO and led to an influential report, *Guidelines for Managing Risk in the Australian Public Service*, by the Management Advisory Board's Management Improvement Advisory Council (MAB-MIAC 1996). The concept was not identified in the 1997 financial management legislation, however, which touched only obliquely on the issue with its requirement for agencies to have fraud control plans.

Action was nonetheless being taken—in particular, through an increased role by internal audit committees, strengthened by requirements for independent chairs and members and a clearer focus on agency risk assessments and management strategies. The ANAO also referred to the issue in a number of its audits and in speeches by the auditor-general, providing a strong impetus with the implied threat of adverse ANAO findings presented to the parliament if risk management was inadequate.

Concerns about the poor implementation of some policy decisions also led the government in the early 2000s to strengthen senior management accountability for implementation as well as policy advice (Shergold 2007). A new implementation unit was established in the Department of the Prime Minister and Cabinet to ensure cabinet was informed of implementation risks when considering new policy proposals, and to monitor implementation through a 'traffic signals' approach; major projects were also subject to a 'gateways' monitoring system based on risk assessments. The stated intent of these measures was not to introduce second-guessing or centralised control, but to ensure early risk assessment and light-touch monitoring by the centre to promote active risk management by the responsible agencies.

The growing interest in 'innovation' in the 2000s added weight to the importance of risk management, reflected in both the CFAR and the Moran Review.

The *PGPA Act* now includes a specific duty of accountable authorities 'to establish and maintain systems relating to risk and control' (s. 16) and a further duty that requirements imposed on others (such as grant recipients) in relation to 'the use or management of public resources must take account of the risks associated with that use or management, and the effects of imposing the requirements' (s. 18). The rule issued under the Act about corporate plans also requires plans to include risk oversight and management—this being seen as an essential component of agencies' core planning and relevant to their day-to-day operations. The minister for finance has also issued the Commonwealth Risk Management Policy that non-corporate entities must follow and corporate entities should use as a guide to better practice (DoF 2014). This policy sets out nine elements to which agencies should adhere:

1. establishing a risk management policy
2. establishing a risk management framework
3. defining responsibility for managing risk
4. embedding systematic risk management in business processes
5. developing a positive risk culture
6. communicating and consulting about risk
7. understanding and managing shared risk
8. maintaining risk management capability
9. reviewing and continuously improving the management of risk.

Notwithstanding the profile now given to risk management, there is an ongoing challenge for the public sector because of the very nature of its role, which includes providing a secure and stable environment in which people can go about their lives, and organisations can go about their business, with confidence (Podger 2015). Innovation in the public sector is not the same as the concept used in economics to describe the process of 'creative disruption' in the market. Innovation in government administration requires a degree of public support and must be managed fairly and in accordance with administrative law. These factors help to explain the political environment and the tendency to highlight mistakes and to promote a risk-averse culture, and the limited extent of political acceptance of the principles of risk management. Countering these institutional factors by mandating specific processes for risk management may, however, cause agencies simply to comply with the new rules without genuinely improving management or promoting innovation.

The challenge is to gain a genuine understanding of how good risk management can support a forward-looking approach to performance management rather than a focus on measuring the past and holding people to account. This requires applying the idea to the way new policy is developed and the way new ideas for program management are encouraged and reviewed, without necessarily imposing a new set of processes on top of the old ones.

One area that deserves particular attention is whether and how to work across government, with other jurisdictions or with external organisations. As mentioned earlier, both the *PGPA Act* and the amended *PS Act* explicitly encourage working cooperatively. There are risks in agencies managing programs exclusively on their own: inadequate skills and information, insufficient pressure to be efficient and limited effectiveness because of the failure to take advantage of the capacity of other agencies and organisations. But there are also risks in working with others.

Competition through outsourcing and public–private partnerships (PPPs) has often delivered greater efficiency over the past 30 years, but care is needed to ensure the services being purchased are effective in delivering the outcomes the responsible agency is seeking through its program responsibilities. Information technology (IT) outsourcing in the late 1990s largely failed because the policy was imposed politically with no regard for risk and because agencies' specific requirements were treated as secondary considerations.

Ongoing efficiency from outsourcing also requires agencies to retain sufficient skills to continue to be informed purchasers, retain strategic management capacity and carefully balance the need for regular competition with the benefits of long-term agreements—for example, limited disruption and the capacity for both providers and purchasers to learn on the job. There are too many cases over the years where these have gone wrong: IT outsourcing that has led to excessive costs because of overreliance on contractors to advise on future requirements and procurement processes; HRM outsourcing that has left the agency with insufficient people management expertise, which is a corporate priority for any organisation; and PPPs that have provided a monopoly deal to a company despite all the risks remaining with the government as if it were still the owner and manager of the infrastructure (airports and some road contracts come to mind).

Among the lessons I would draw from Australia's recent experience in both intra-agency management and management through others are the importance of a forward-looking approach to risk management, that an appropriate mindset is far more important than a list of prescribed processes, the need to ensure a learning environment and to have the capacity to adjust in light of experience and the importance of values and of recognising differences in values and objectives when working with external organisations.

Conclusion: Challenges and lessons

The Australian approach to financial management, and performance management, in particular, is rightly referred to by external observers as one of the most successful models (e.g. Hawke 2007; Bouckaert and Halligan 2008), partly because of its comprehensive and systemic nature. But it is important to note from the experience of more than 30 years the following points:

- It has evolved on the back of highly sophisticated systems of civil service and financial management that, while previously focused on detailed rules and processes rather than results, ensured integrity in the use of public resources.

- Means and ends both matter, with appropriate means ensuring both integrity in government and concern for capability to achieve results into the future.

- Performance management encourages a disciplined results-based approach but has never been (and can never be) the only way in which decision-making in government occurs; much government decision-making is inherently political, requiring judgments on priorities, and also often involves reaction to events where performance information is lacking.

- It has proven to be a constant 'work-in-progress', particularly in the development of performance measures, in learning to use new techniques such as risk management and in responding to new policy agendas and events.

The latest iteration of the system reflected in the *PGPA Act* responds to concerns that devolution had gone too far, fragmenting government, that a more whole-of-government approach was needed and that too little effort was being directed to organisational capability to meet current and future needs and too much was directed towards short-term and tactical issues with an inevitably risk-averse attitude.

Some of the challenges officials face in responding to the new legislation are:

- Recognising the importance of ethical standards—of means as well as ends—and appreciating how public service values differ from those in the private and not-for-profit sectors.

- Getting the balance right between whole-of-government coherence and agency flexibility and agility to maximise efficiency and effectiveness.

- Promoting better management and enhanced organisational capability without introducing unnecessarily prescriptive processes that merely demand compliance.

- Relating inputs, outputs and outcomes in a meaningful way, and ensuring individual performance appraisal promotes better organisational performance.

- Presenting documentation to ministers and the parliament (and the public) that is easily read and understood, is relevant to their concerns and promotes informed discussion and debate.

- Gaining public and political acceptance for public officials to 'engage' with risk rather than having their attitudes consciously or unconsciously promoting a risk-averse culture in government administration.

Several of these challenges go to the underlying relationships between the legislature and the executive and between politics and administration that define Australia's accountability process. Better understanding of these relationships and mutual respect would go a long way to achieving a more results-based approach to both management and political decision-making, while recognising the limits involved.

The *PGPA Act* improves on the groundbreaking legislation that came out of the NPM reforms and, rightly, does not represent any fundamental change in direction. It draws on a further decade and a half of experience, with the aim this time of making 'accountability for results' really work. Whether this can ever be fully achieved is uncertain, but, if the *PGPA Act* is to deliver significant improvement, it needs to influence both politicians and administrators, and it needs to promote genuine learning and leadership about good management and capability-building.

References

Australian National Audit Office (ANAO). 2007. *Application of the outcomes and outputs framework*. Audit Report No. 23 2006-07 Performance Audit. Canberra: ANAO.

Australian Public Service Commission (APSC). 2004. *State of the Service Report 2003–04*. Canberra: APSC.

Australian Public Service Commission (APSC). 2005. *State of the Service Report 2004–05*. Canberra: APSC.

Australian Public Service Commission (APSC). 2014. *Strengthening A Values-Based Culture: A plan for integrating the APS Values into the way we work*. Canberra: APSC.

Bouckaert, G. and J. Halligan. 2008. *Managing Performance: International comparisons*. London: Routledge.

Commonwealth of Australia (CoA). 1986. 'Policy guidelines for statutory authorities and government business enterprises'. Tabling Statement by the Minister for Finance and Minister Assisting the Prime Minister on Public Service Matters, Senator the Hon. Peter Walsh. Parliament House, Canberra.

Coombs, H. C. 1976. *Royal Commission on Australian Government Administration: Report*. [Coombs Report]. Canberra: AGPS.

Department of Finance (DoF). 2005a. *Commonwealth Entities and Companies Flipchart*. Canberra: Australian Government.

Department of Finance (DoF). 2005b. *Governance Arrangements for Australian Government Bodies*. Canberra: Australian Government.

Department of Finance (DoF). 2012. *Sharpening the Focus: A framework for improving Commonwealth performance*. Commonwealth Financial Accountability Review Position Paper, November. Canberra: Australian Government.

Department of Finance (DoF). 2014. *Commonwealth Risk Management Policy*. Canberra: Australian Government.

Department of Finance (DoF). 2017. *Commonwealth Governance Structures Policy Assessment Template: Review of new and existing bodies*. Canberra: Australian Government. Available from: finance.gov. au/sites/default/files/governance-assessment-template.docx (accessed 14 July 2017).

Department of Health (DoH). 2015. *Corporate Plan 2015–16*. Canberra: Australian Government. Available from: www.health.gov. au/internet/main/publishing.nsf/Content/corporate-plan-archive (accessed 1 November 2015).

Department of Health and Family Services (DHFS). 1996. *Commonwealth Department of Health and Family Services Corporate Plan 1996–97*. Canberra: Australian Government.

Hawke, L. 2007. 'Performance budgeting in Australia'. *OECD Journal on Budgeting* 7(3). Paris: OECD Publishing.

High Court of Australia (HCA). 2005. *Combet v Commonwealth*, HCA 61. Canberra.

Jarvie, W. and T. Mercer. 2015. 'Improving value for money in Australia's employment services through performance monitoring and evaluation'. Paper presented to Greater China Australia Dialogue on Public Administration 2015 workshop, Taiwan University, Taipei, November.

Keating, M. 2004. *Who Rules? How government retains control in a privatised economy*. Sydney: The Federation Press.

McPhee, I. 2015. 'Opening statement'. Joint Committee of Public Accounts and Audit Hearing on the Commonwealth Performance Framework, 19 March. Parliament House, Canberra.

Management Advisory Board Management Improvement Advisory Committee (MAB-MIAC). 1996. *Guidelines for managing risk in the Australian Public Service*. Report No. 22. Canberra: Australian Government.

Management Advisory Committee (MAC). 2001. *Performance Management in the APS*. Canberra: Public Service and Merit Protection Commission.

Management Advisory Committee (MAC). 2004. *Connecting Government*. Canberra: APSC.

Moran, T. 2010. *Ahead of the Game: Blueprint for the reform of Australian Government administration/Advisory Group on Reform of Australian Government Administration*. [Moran Review]. Canberra: Department of the Prime Minister and Cabinet.

Murray, A. 2008. *Review of Operation Sunlight: Overhauling budget transparency*. Canberra: Department of Finance.

Northcote, S. H. and C. E. Trevelyan. 1854. *Report on the organisation of the permanent civil service, together with a letter from the Rev. B. Jowett.* House of Commons, London.

Osborne, D. and T. Gaebler. 1992. *Reinventing Government: How the entrepreneurial spirit is transforming the public sector.* Reading, MA: Addison-Wesley.

Parliament of Australia (PoA). 1997a. *Commonwealth Authorities and Companies Act 1997.* Parliament of Australia, Canberra.

Parliament of Australia (PoA). 1997b. *Financial Management and Accountability Act 1997.* Parliament of Australia, Canberra.

Parliament of Australia (PoA). 1999. *Public Service Act 1999.* Parliament of Australia, Canberra.

Parliament of Australia (PoA). 2013a. *Public Governance, Performance and Accountability Act 2013.* Parliament of Australia, Canberra.

Parliament of Australia (PoA). 2013b. *Public Governance, Performance and Accountability Bill 2013 Explanatory Memorandum.* Parliament of Australia, Canberra.

Parliament of Australia (PoA). 2013c. *Public Service Amendment Act 2013.* Parliament of Australia, Canberra.

Parliament of Australia (PoA). 2015. *Public Governance, Performance and Accountability Amendment (Corporate Plans and Annual Performance Statements) Rule 2015.* Parliament of Australia, Canberra.

Podger, A. 2007. 'What really happens: Departmental secretary appointments, contracts and performance pay in the Australian Public Service'. *Australian Journal of Public Administration* 66(2): 131–47. doi.org/10.1111/j.1467-8500.2007.00524.x.

Podger, A. 2011. 'New APS Values: Still time for another go'. *The Canberra Times Public Sector Informant,* 6 December.

Podger, A. 2015. 'Innovation in the public sector: Beyond the rhetoric to a genuine "learning culture"'. In J. Wanna, H.-A. Lee and S. Yates (eds) *Managing under Austerity, Delivering under Pressure.* Canberra: ANU Press.

Pollitt, C. 1990. *Managerialism and the Public Services: The Anglo-American experience*. Oxford: Blackwell.

Rhodes, R. A. W. 1997. *Understanding Governance: Policy networks, governance, reflexivity, and accountability*. Philadelphia: Open University Press.

Senge, P. 1990. *The Fifth Discipline: The art and practice of the learning organization*. New York: Currency Doubleday.

Shergold, P. 2007. 'Driving change to bring about better implementation and delivery'. In J. Wanna (ed.) *Improving Implementation: Organisational change and project management*. Canberra: ANU E Press.

Uhrig, J. 2003. *Review of the corporate governance of statutory authorities and office holders*. Parliamentary Paper 2004/352. Canberra: Parliament of Australia.

7

Adoption or implementation? Performance measurement in the City of Guangzhou's Department of Education

Meili Niu

Introduction

Over the past few decades, performance budgeting has become a widely used management instrument to improve budgeting accountability in both developed and developing countries (Economic Commission for Africa 2003; ADB 2006; Hatry 2006; OECD 2007; Bouckaert and Halligan 2008; Wescott et al. 2009; Niu and Ho 2014). China is no exception to this trend.

In 2003, Guangdong province launched six pilot programs to measure the performance of government programs after they had been fully implemented (Niu et al. 2006). Since then, many Chinese local governments—including provinces, prefectures, counties and districts—have measured the performance of government programs.

Performance budgeting reform in China is a unique budgeting innovation and has been used now for more than 10 years. This makes it one of the longest lasting budgetary reforms in China, even though it was debatable whether China was ready for performance-based budgeting (PBB) (Ma 2005; Wu and Niu 2010).

Despite its wide application globally, the PBB process in developed countries varies considerably and is always challenging, especially when it comes to improving budget decision-making (de Lancer Julnes and Holzer 2001; Andrews 2005; Curristine 2005; Shah and Shen 2007; Wanna 2010; Ho and Im 2015; Lu et al. 2015).

Performance measurement is a crucial technique to promote PBB (Martin 1997). Based on the extent to which performance information is used for budget allocations, Shah and Shen (2007) classified PBB into four types: performance-reported budgeting (PRB), performance-informed budgeting (PIB), performance-based budgeting (PBB) and performance-determined budgeting (PDB). Very few countries have adopted PBB or PDB.

Apart from technical difficulties, organisational, cultural and political contexts also make performance evaluation a very challenging reform in the public sector (Shah and Shen 2007; Bouckaert and Halligan 2008; Ho and Im 2015). Therefore, an examination of PBB requires a deep understanding of the governance context (Niu and Ho 2014; Ho and Im 2015). De Lancer Julnes and Holzer (2001) find that rational and political factors have different impacts on the utilisation of performance measurement.

Inspired by Cronbach et al. (1981) and Beyer and Trice (1982), de Lancer Julnes and Holzer (2001) argue that, to understand the use of performance measurement in the public sector, there is a need to separate the two stages of utilisation into an adoption stage and an implementation stage.

Adoption refers to 'the development of measures of outputs, outcomes, and efficiency' and implementation represents 'the actual use of performance measures for strategic planning, resources allocation, program management, monitoring, evaluation, and reporting to internal management, elected officials, and citizens or the media' (de Lancer Julnes and Holzer 2001: 695).

This distinction is particularly useful when researching China's PBB reforms. Due to the fragmentation of the Chinese budgeting system, the primary concern in budget accountability is controlling the line agency's spending behaviour (Ma and Niu 2007). Since the late 1990s, when China launched its departmental budget reform (DBR), line agencies have been the focus of budgetary reform. Making line agencies more accountable is the key to improving the accountability of the whole Chinese budgeting system.

PBB reform in China is also fragmented. Accountability in many developed countries, such as the United States, Australia and New Zealand, can be achieved through legislative measures that promote PBB and related financial management reforms. But China's PBB reform followed a bottom-up process. Finance departments at the local government level took the lead, investing a considerable amount of resources in developing performance indicators and designing the evaluation procedures through administrative orders (Niu 2012).

The bottom-up approach does have limitations. As the central budgeting office, the finance department has the authority to review departmental budget requests and monitor budget implementation, but it does not have any formal power to make line agencies accountable for following the administrative orders it issues. It is an open question whether a line agency merely adopts performance measures or actually uses the performance information to improve its departmental budget management.

Despite this lack of formal power, most of the existing literature on China's PBB uses the finance department as the unit of analysis. Scholars concentrate on the finance department's strategies and instruments and their impacts on budget management. What is not examined is how the line agency perceives PBB and actually uses performance measurement.

Current performance measurement, as observed by the reporting finance departments, relies on self-evaluation reports (SERs) prepared by line agencies. If the report is well written, the agency's performance is usually given high marks regardless of how the program actually performs. A better-performing program that is represented by a poorly written SER may not be given a high score.

To understand how a line agency actually uses performance measurement, more detailed case analysis is required, particularly to determine the line agency's adoption or implementation level.

This is a single case study. The author selected the education department of the City of Guangzhou for several reasons:

1. Although Guangzhou is not the first city to use PBB, it is one of the more successful cases in China, and its education department is one of the best experimental cases in Guangzhou.

2. While the education department's budget is not representative of line agencies in terms of its size, it has a number of unique characteristics that demonstrate the impact of technical, organisational, cultural and political factors on budget management.

   - First, China's education system has a long tradition of performance management; from preschools to universities, teachers are paid, in part, according to performance. For example, student testing results, academic publications and so on are used to measure teacher performance. This makes the concept of performance evaluation easier to accept at the program level.

   - Second, the education department has a large budget compared with most other line agencies, and its financial office must deal with a variety of programs, making it a challenge to evaluate them all.

   - Finally, education services in China are always in the public eye and receive extensive media coverage, making them a political priority. For example, when Guangzhou published all 114 line agencies' budgets in 2009, the education department's budget received the most attention from the media. This puts more pressure on the department to improve its services.

3. The author has been collaborating with the education department since 2009 on training staff, designing performance procedures and developing indicators. As a third party, the author has also created a research team to evaluate the performance of a preschool program in 2012. Over the past few years, the author has also worked as an expert at the request of the city's finance department and the city's congress to examine the education department's program management. Therefore, the author has access to program information and is able to observe the evolution of the education department's efforts to install performance management into its budgeting system.

In the next section, this chapter describes China's PBB reform, followed by a description of the education department in Guangzhou and why it uses performance measurement. The chapter then explores the extent to which the department has adopted and/or implemented performance measurement and budgeting, including how its approaches have evolved over time. The final section sets out some conclusions about the key factors affecting the utilisation of performance measurement by line agencies.

PBB reform in China

PBB reform in China is regarded as a continuing innovation, following DBR. DBR was launched in the late 1990s as a way to improve line agencies' budget management through a more transparent and rule-based process.

DBR required line agencies to share information on employees, facilities and programs with the finance department so its oversight would be based on complete information (Niu 2010). Before the DBR reform, the finance department did not have timely access to such information.

DBR also enhanced budget control over line agencies by separating departmental spending into three components: employee payments, operational expenses and program expenditure (Niu 2010). This division is aligned with the way China's government divides areas of responsibility:

1. Employee payments in the public sector are fully regulated by the human resources department. Both the size of a line agency's workforce and each position within it (and its pay level) are decided by the Commission of Public Sector Reform, so there is no discretion over the funds.

2. Operational expenses are difficult to estimate because they include many miscellaneous items. To control total spending, DBR assigns each agency an operational quota per capita. For example, for an agency with 200 employees, if the operational quota is RMB30,000 (A$5,700), the operational budget will be RMB6 million (A$1.1 million) (= 30,000 x 200).

3. Program spending is the largest component of a department's budget. DBR required line agencies to rank the priority of programs based on their importance; however, it did not develop a particular approach to priority setting. Performance—the commonly used concept in a public budgeting system—was not the major concern in China during DBR. This resulted in legitimacy problems for program budgeting.

One problem for program budgeting was that program information was not transparent. The finance department did not have complete information with which to examine an agency's budget requests. Another problem was that most program budget proposals were very simple and lacked details about cost and performance. Cost–benefit analysis was also absent in the departmental budgeting system. Difficulties in program management also led to problems with regard to resource allocation. For example, many approved programs were unable to proceed due to poor planning, so a large amount of allocated money went unspent (Ma and Yu 2012).

To solve the problems related to program budgets, performance measurement was introduced into the Chinese local budgeting system in the early 2000s. As with many other budgetary reforms, this was initiated by the finance department. As Niu (2012) explained, although there were differences in the application of performance measurement by local governments, some similar instruments were used:

1. To avoid an increased workload and to provide credibility, finance departments contracted third parties to evaluate their programs. These outside contractors were usually university research teams, accounting firms or consulting companies, hired to evaluate program performance.

2. Because PBB involves very complicated, technical and political concerns, PBB reform in China started with post-program evaluations. The purpose of the reform was primarily to improve program implementation rather than allocation efficiency.

3. As mentioned above, line agencies have no discretion when it comes to employee payments and operational spending. Therefore, measurement focuses on programs only. Neither employee payments nor operational expenses are evaluated. Usually, programs with a budget up to RMB5 million (A$950,000) at the provincial level and up to RMB500,000 (A$95,000) at the city or county level were selected for evaluation.

4. Although the indicators used for evaluation are quite different, four dimensions are commonly used: inputs, implementation, outputs and results.

5. Because performance measurement was a new concept for the Chinese public budgeting system, both finance departments and line agencies received intensive training in how to develop performance indicators and write SERs.

After years of experiments at the local government level, beginning in 2011, the Ministry of Finance (MoF) passed several administrative orders to promote PBB in both central and local governments,[1] such as the 'Interim Approaches on Evaluating the Performance of Fiscal Expenditures' (2011) and 'Guidelines on Advancing Performance Budgeting Management' (2011).

To put more pressure on central agencies and provincial governments, the MoF promulgated the 'Methods on Assessing Performance Budgeting Management' (2011), which create an index for the assessment of PBB reforms. Within this index, only 30 per cent of the total score is about program evaluation. The remaining 70 per cent is given to the implementation of the reform. Implementation includes whether the governor has given a public speech on PBB reform, whether the province established clear rules for using PBB, the percentage of the budget applying PBB, staff training on PBB, and so on.

In 2011, the MoF also issued the 'Work Plan on Performance Budgeting Management' (2012–15) to set out the medium-term goals of the reform. Because the development of performance indicators has been a daunting challenge, the MoF issued the 'Framework on Common Indicators of Budgeting Performance Evaluation' in 2013. The framework was not new to those localities that had used performance measurement for many years, but most local governments had not started PBB by 2013. Nevertheless, issuing this framework became the signal that PBB was the major reform the MoF wanted to promote.

In 2014, China amended its Budget Law. As the highest level of legislation on public budgeting, the amendment requires that both line agencies and each level of government consider the previous year's performance when making budgeting decisions.

---

1   According to the formal rules, in the Chinese departmental budget system, employee and operational expenses are together called basic spending, which is supposed to maintain the organisation's daily operations. All other expenses are program spending for achieving specific policy goals. However, in practice, because the quota for operational expenses is usually not sufficient for funding daily operations, the finance department allows line agencies to include some operational expenses in the program budget under 'operational programs' (Niu 2010).

In China, the executive arm of government usually initiates public sector reform, with the legislature (people's congresses) having a much more limited role. Therefore, the tradition is to use administrative orders instead of legislation to launch reform and establish its rules.

Even though performance measurement has become a quite popular practice over the past decade in China, generally speaking, the evaluation results seem to have had very limited impact on budgeting allocation (Niu 2012)—for two reasons. First, line agencies are reluctant to use the instrument because it takes a lot of effort to evaluate programs, and there is almost no connection between the performance result and the next year's departmental budget. Second, the development of performance indicators is very complicated and information on program implementation is not completely transparent in China. Therefore, both line agencies and finance departments are very cautious about relying on the performance result when making budget allocation decisions (Niu 2012).

To understand whether China has fully implemented PBB or merely adopted PBB mechanisms, and the factors that lead to that choice, the key is to examine what the line agency actually does.

The purpose of PBB reform, as the continuing budgetary innovation after DBR, is to improve program planning and implementation to control line agencies' budgeting behaviour. For post-program evaluation, a line agency's SER is the fundamental document used for performance measurement, regardless of which third party conducts the evaluation.

As for pre-program evaluations, the finance department still relies heavily on the information provided by the line agency to review the program budget request. Therefore, how line agencies respond to the reform and how they utilise performance measurement tools will shed the most light on whether PBB is merely adopted (and largely ignored) or fully implemented in the Chinese local budgeting system.

The education department of Guangzhou

The education department is one of the 105 line agencies in the City of Guangzhou. In 2016, there were 65 subordinate units within the education department (see Table 7.1) and 25,108 employees, including 10,133 retirees (40.36 per cent of total employees).[2]

---

2   In China, public sector retirees' pensions and social benefits are not paid through a unified social security system, but are still part of the line agency's departmental budget.

Table 7.1 Subordinate units of the education department (departmental budget 2015)

Types	Numbers
Head administration office	1
Elementary schools	1
Preschools	12
Middle and high schools	11
Special schools	3
Vocational high schools	2
Vocational middle schools	13
Vocational colleges	4
Universities	3
University-affiliated hospitals	7
Others	8
Total	65

Source: Bureau of Education of Guangzhou Municipality (various years).

Figure 7.1 shows that the education department's budget was balanced in most years and both revenue and spending grew quickly over the past seven years. In 2016, total revenue was RMB1.4 million (A$264,000), with 98.62 per cent growth compared with 2010 (RMB696.61 million (A$133 million)). Total spending was RMB1.4 billion (A$267 million), with 100.91 per cent growth compared with 2010. And basic spending (on employees and operational expenses) increased from RMB532 million (A$101 million) in 2010 to RMB1.1 billion (A$209 million) in 2016, an increase of 106.66 per cent.

The proportion of program spending decreased from 38.54 per cent in 2012 to 21.5 per cent in 2016. This was primarily due to the growth in the number of retirees and performance pay to employees (Niu and Song 2015a). Another major reason for the smaller proportion devoted to program spending is the reduction in basic construction projects. Guangzhou, as a municipal government, has built many educational facilities and its schools are well equipped. However, the one-child policy has had a shrinking effect on the number of schoolchildren using those facilities and the demand for new infrastructure projects is now low.

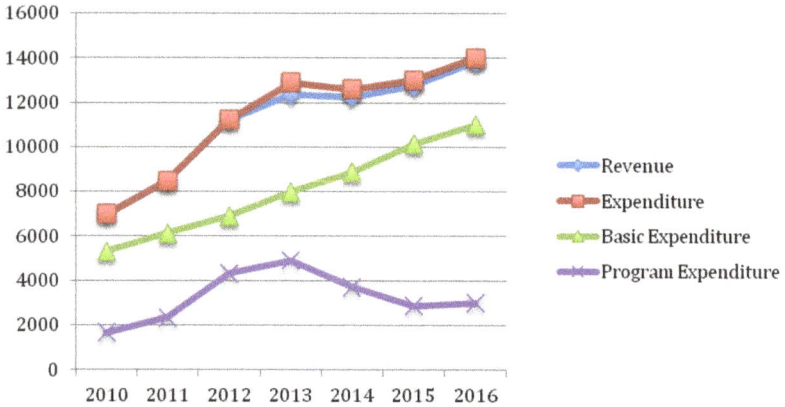

Figure 7.1 Education department's budget, 2010–16 (RMB million)
Source: Bureau of Education of Guangzhou Municipality (various years).

Why did the education department use performance measurement?

Guangzhou's finance department required the education department to use performance measurement and it has done so since 2005, when Guangzhou launched its pilot program.

In 2004, the finance department established its Performance Evaluation Office (PEO) and, in 2005, it issued the 'Methods for Public Spending Performance Evaluation of Guangzhou (Trial)'. In the same year, the PEO selected two pilot programs: 'sparrow school' upgrading[3] and construction of water and road infrastructure for rural areas.

In 2006, the filing of SERs was required for a total of RMB17.5 billion (A$3.3 billion) in program funds across 48 line agencies. The finance department evaluated program performance based on those reports. In 2007, all 400 programs with a budget up to RMB5 million (A$953,000) were evaluated.

---

3   'Sparrow schools' are schools that are relatively small and have poor facilities and low-quality instruction. From 2000 to 2004, Guangzhou invested RMB1.1 billion (A$209 million) to upgrade these schools.

A leadership change in the education department greatly contributed to the use of performance evaluation. From 2005 to 2008, the department was not very interested in developing its own instruments to evaluate program performance. That changed in 2008 when the Ministry of Education in Beijing appointed one of its senior directors, who happened to have a PhD, as the deputy head of the Guangzhou education department. At the same time, the department also appointed to its finance office a key person who happened to have a Masters of Public Administration.

Both these leaders favoured the idea of performance evaluation to improve program management. The deputy head sold the idea to the departmental head and other deputy heads to win the support of the whole leadership team. He also attended all meetings related to performance measurement. This was very important to build the confidence of the financial office and reduce conflicts with subordinate organisations.

External pressure also played a crucial role. Because education services are always in the public eye and education is one of the largest areas of public spending in China, both the media and the legislature like to bring up issues related to education programs.

In 2008, the City Congress of Guangzhou began examining select departmental budgets during its annual plenary session. The education department was one of the first to be examined. Subsequently, it has been one of the departments selected by the congress's deliberation seminar almost every year. Besides the congress, the Mayor of Guangzhou also required more education spending, which further increased the external pressure on budget allocation and program management.

Adoption versus implementation

De Lancer Julnes and Holzer (2001) argue that, to better conceive the use of performance measurement, the two stages of utilisation—adoption and implementation—should be examined separately. Adoption is influenced more heavily by rational factors, while implementation is more heavily influenced by political factors (de Lancer Julnes and Holzer 2001). This distinction helps in the development of a framework to assess the education department's experiment. The two stages are not necessarily part of an evolutionary process. Instead, even though an organisation enters the implementation stage, it could step back to the adoption stage if the context changes (de Lancer Julnes and Holzer 2001).

The adoption stage: 2005–08

In 2005, as one of two departments selected by the finance department for the pilot evaluation, the education department did not develop any specific approaches for its adoption of performance measurement. Instead, it just followed the requirements listed in the 'Methods for Public Spending Performance Evaluation of Guangzhou (Trial)' to begin its performance measurement. These included:

1. Establishing a self-evaluation work group, chaired by the departmental head. The secretary of the Commission for Discipline Inspection and the deputy head responsible for financial affairs served as vice-chairmen. The other 13 group members were all senior managers of different offices within the education department.

2. Forming a self-evaluation work plan for the department and submitting it to the city's Performance Evaluation Work Group[4] as a record.

3. Collecting, justifying and analysing the data to evaluate the programs.

4. Calculating the evaluation score and preparing the SER.

One unique feature of China's performance measurement is that it uses not only the outputs and outcomes but also the input and program management to assess program performance. Until 2014, Guangzhou had been evaluating inputs, program management, outputs and outcomes of program spending. And, because the major reason for Guangzhou using performance evaluation was to reduce the proportion of the budget that remained unspent, the rate of use of budget funds was one of the major performance indicators.

In 2006 and 2007, over 60 per cent of the indicators were input measures. The weights given to input measures were about 30 to 40 per cent at the beginning of the reform. Output and outcome indicators made up about 30 per cent of the total number of indicators, and the remaining 30–40 per cent were program management indicators. Efficiency measures, such as per capita cost, were never indicators of program performance.

---

4   The Performance Evaluation Work Group was established in 2006 to enhance the authority of performance measurement. As well as the finance department, the audit department, the statistics department and the Commission of Discipline Inspection also serve in the group.

Input indicators are financial measures that include the disbursement rate as well as the appropriation arrival rate,[5] the investment multiplier effect, and so on. Program management indicators were developed based on the following procedures: program application and approval, implementation, budget adjustment, program operation and fulfilment. However, due to the diversity of public programs, program management varies across the different types of programs. The finance department required more detailed indicators based on three types of programs: basic construction/renovation, facility purchases and others. Following the finance department's guidelines, the education department did not develop any other specific approaches to improve performance measurement.

SERs are very important documents for a line agency to demonstrate the results of its programs and the challenges of program operation. In 2006, the finance department required line agencies to submit SERs, including information on line agencies' responsibilities and organisation, strategic planning, performance goals in the annual work plan, performance achievements, annual program budgets, actual expenses and financial management. Along with the SER, the line agency also had to submit all supporting documents, such as files identifying the establishment of the Performance Evaluation Work Group, the completion document, the audit report for basic construction projects and regulations on financial and program management.

In terms of the completion of the required document and the timeliness of its submission, the education department has always been one of the best-performing departments. One reason for this is that schools usually keep better-quality program records than other public agencies, so it is easier to collect the program data.

However, as with all other agencies, the education department, in the SER section dealing with the challenges for program implementation, stated that shortage of money was the big issue. There was, however, no detailed analysis of why the budget was inadequate and how much more would be needed.

---

5   In China, it was very common for the line agency or the program to receive less than its full appropriation during the budget year. This was true even though the budget was approved by the legislature. In fact, the finance department is responsible for transferring the money to the line agency's account and this indicator is meant to evaluate the finance department rather than the line agency. Therefore, it was later removed in some programs.

The implementation stage: 2009–12

The 2009 fiscal year was a watershed for the education department's performance measurement. Due to the leadership change and the external pressure for transparency and effectiveness of education spending, the department decided to use performance measurement to improve its budgeting management, instead of just fulfilling the finance department's requirements.

First, the education department extended the scope of its program evaluation. In addition to the programs demanded by the finance department, it also evaluated the performance of selected programs of the subordinate organisations not requiring evaluation by the finance department. And, for those programs evaluated by the finance department, the education department first conducted internal assessments, by inviting experts to comment on its SERs and program operation. The procedures for the two types of evaluations are described in Figure 7.2.

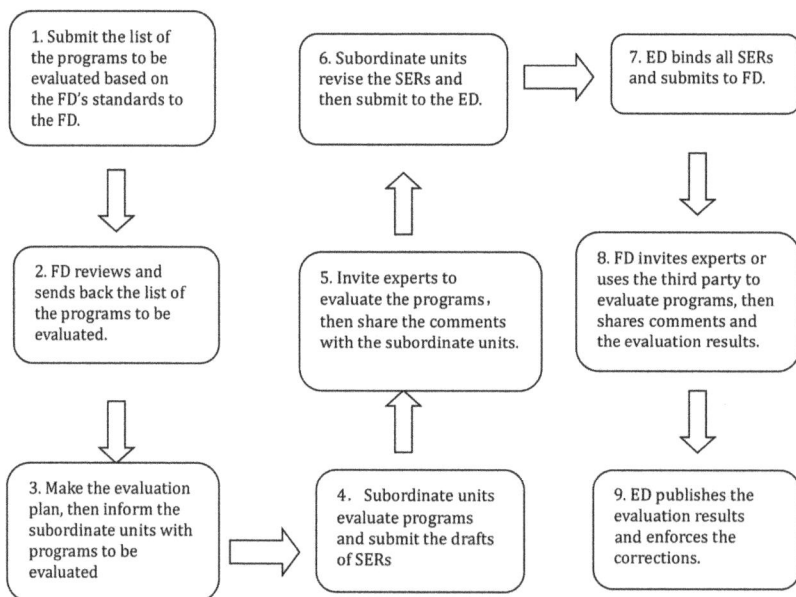

Figure 7.2 Evaluation procedure for the programs assessed by the finance department

Notes: FD refers to the finance department and ED refers to the education department.

Source: Based on interviews with civil servants at the Education Bureau of Guangzhou.

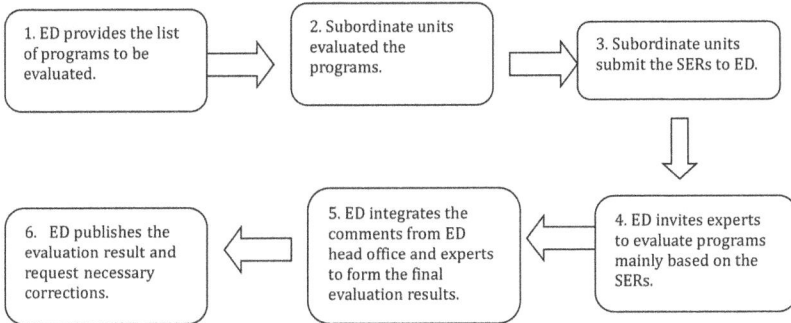

Figure 7.3 Evaluation procedure for selected programs assessed by the education department

Source: Based on interviews with civil servants at the Education Bureau of Guangzhou.

Figure 7.2 shows that the education department put a lot of effort into improving its program evaluations. This raises the question of whether the external experts were just window dressing for the post-program evaluation or whether they were there to actually help improve the budgeting and program management.

Bischoff and Blaeschke (2015) argued that window dressing is a common reason for imperfect performance management. China is no exception in this. Because performance evaluation relies heavily on SERs and because program information is still not transparent, as long as the SERs are written well, the performance results will look good, whether they are positive or negative. Line agencies invest a lot of time in polishing SERs, and the education department used experts for this purpose as well.

However, the evidence strongly suggests that the education department's efforts were much more than window dressing. First, the experts also met with program managers, financial officers and school managers and discussed how to improve program and budgeting management.

Second, the education department used experts from universities and the finance department to train staff every year. The training was separated into two components. The first component was about developing performance indicators. Because the programs were classified into three categories— basic construction and renovation, facility purchases and others—the training was separated into three lectures. The second component of training was how to write SERs. This included topics such as how to cite government documents as supporting evidence for a program, how to explain incomplete budget disbursement and how to analyse problems related to program operation or financial management. The training was a signal to its subordinate units that the education department wished to use performance measurement tools as substantive instruments to improve budgeting management. The training also helped staff and school managers to understand the implications of performance measurement and improve their organisational capacity for performance management.

Third, to strengthen the impact of performance measurement on budget allocation, the education department had a trial pre-program evaluation and introduced competitive allocation and citizen participation into budget decision-making.

In 2012, the education department selected the Private Affordable Preschools (PAP)[6] program as a pilot for pre-program evaluation. In Guangzhou, the city has been investing in private schools to improve the quality of education services and now over 70 per cent of preschools are privately run. In 2012, the education department received special funding of up to RMB100 million (A$19 million) to improve the PAP facilities. After consulting with external experts, the department decided to allocate RMB65 million (A$12.4 million) to 12 districts based on the size of the student population and fairness concerns about fiscal capacity. The remaining RMB35 million (A$6.7 million) was allocated based on each district's proposed performance.

On 29 May 2012, directors (or deputy directors) of the education departments from the city's 12 districts made a presentation on existing conditions, challenges, vision and strategic goals for their PAP. They also proposed operational plans, detailed budget plans and expected results, in front of a 30-member jury. The jury comprised parents, schoolteachers, officials from the education and finance departments, members of the city's congress and its People's Political Consultative Conference and experts, such as university professors. They were also required to address any concerns raised by the jury members.

The jury evaluated the program plans and ranked all 12 proposals. The budget allocations among the 12 districts were based on the jury's assessment. After the program was finished in March 2013, third-party consultants evaluated the results for each district. Instead of another round

6   Private Affordable Preschools are those that provide decent-quality service, but are underequipped. The city requests that such preschools charge a rate that is slightly lower than the market price and promises to subsidise them to upgrade their facilities.

of competitive allocation through on-site presentations, the performance rankings were used for the next year's budget allocation for the PAP program.

Back to the adoption stage: From late 2012

Due to its efforts, the education department was viewed as the best example of the use of performance measurement in the budgeting system in Guangzhou. The department's financial officer was invited by the finance department to present some civil servants' training programs to share the education department's experience.

Unfortunately, the education department's passion for PBB did not last long and, since late 2012, it has switched its focus to other budgeting innovations. There are several possible explanations for the change in dynamics.

First, due to a leadership change in the finance department, PBB was no longer prioritised. The director of the department's PEO also transferred to another agency. In three years, the director of the PEO has changed twice, which is very discouraging.

The education department was not convinced by the new proposals the PEO developed. For an agency that had won the support of top leaders, the education department considered some technical challenges—such as upgrading performance indicators and benchmark analysis—more urgent than the PEO's proposals at that time. With disappointment, the education department decided to switch its focus to other reforms, such as internal control.

Second, performance evaluation can cause an accountability deadlock, which can discourage line agencies from stepping forward. A key prerequisite for good performance is the ability to spend money. However, in practice, the significantly increased controls on budgeting and the tediously long review and approval process—which is often beyond the control of the line department, especially for basic construction and government purchases—often result in delays or cancellation of programs.

For education services, summer and winter breaks are the best times for construction projects. But, with approval delays, it is impossible for such programs to be fully implemented. Therefore, the agency is stuck with perceptions of poor performance. According to Niu and Song (2015b), the average implementation period was 504 days for 299 year-long construction and renovation projects—much longer than a fiscal year (365 days). That is, the current performance evaluation saddles the line agencies with responsibility for a burden that is not of their making.

Third, PBB reforms were promoted through administrative orders by the finance department, but it has no legal power over line agencies. And, in any case, budgeting and financial management usually account for only 5 per cent of the total score in the evaluation of departmental performance.

In addition, apart from PBB, the finance department also initiated other reforms, such as internal control and government accounting. The competition for attention among reform programs is fierce. In such circumstances, it is rational for the education department to temper its efforts in adopting performance evaluation. That is not to say that the department disrespects performance measurement. In fact, it still follows the finance department's guidelines for PBB, such as creating a program inventory and enhancing real-time monitoring of program operation. It is, however, no longer a pioneer. The impact of performance evaluation results on budget allocations and program management has thereby reduced in recent times.

Conclusion

This study uses the education department in Guangzhou as a case study to explore how a line agency in China can use performance evaluation. Inspired by de Lancer Julnes and Holzer's (2001) argument about the two stages of performance measurement, this chapter finds that both stages—adoption and implementation—existed in the education department's case.

From 2006 to 2008, the department mainly followed the guidelines developed by the finance department, as did other agencies, without further innovation to improve result-oriented budgeting reform. However, from 2009, due to a leadership change and external pressure, the education department became ambitious and actually implemented, not just adopted, the PBB instrument. It did this by extending the scope of evaluation, inviting experts to help build organisational capacity, launching pre-program evaluations and welcoming citizen involvement. All these endeavours made the education department the pioneer of line agencies in Guangzhou in promoting performance measurement.

Surprisingly, however, after three years' hard work, the education department stopped taking the lead and went back to the adoption level, involved only in those activities required by the finance department. This case analysis finds that disagreement between the finance department and the education department about reform strategies was the major reason for the latter making performance measurement less of a priority. The approach to promoting PBB reform and the administrative processes involved (with long time frames) caused conflicts between the existing program management system and the accountability mechanism under PBB, discouraging the education department from continuing its pioneering innovation. It is evident that a shared understanding between the finance department and line agencies is essential for successful implementation of PBB. This includes the finance department acknowledging the expertise and administrative experience of the line agencies. Moreover, it seems to take time for China to incorporate the PBB instruments into the existing accountability system, which is the fundamental challenge and explains why the performance results have a very limited impact on decision-making.

De Lancer Julnes and Holzer (2001) discovered that rational factors have a preponderance of influence on the adoption stage and political factors have a preponderance of impacts on the implementation stage. This does not seem to be an inevitable conclusion in China. The swing between adoption and implementation of PBB in the education department shows that, although the rationale for performance measurement was appreciated, the contextual factors, including both political and organisational variants, are vital for making the reform sustainable.

Ho and Im (2015) argue that applicability and appropriateness should be carefully examined when a Western-oriented reform is borrowed for use in a developing country. Although it is debatable whether China is a developing country, the key point is that the Western-style reform established on a technical rationale will have to adapt into non-Western contexts to achieve the dynamics of the reform. This case study suggests that the next design for PBB reform must not only take the technical upgrading into account, but also develop strategies to deal with institutional barriers.

References

Andrews, M. 2005. 'Performance-based budgeting reform'. In A. Shah (ed.) *Fiscal Management*. Public Sector Governance and Accountability Series. Washington, DC: The World Bank.

Andrews, M. 2006. 'Beyond "best practice" and "basic first" in adopting performance budgeting reform'. *Public Administration and Development* 26(2): 147–61. doi.org/10.1002/pad.401.

Asian Development Bank (ADB). 2006. *Capacity for Results Management: A Guide for conducting a rapid assessment of the capacity of developing member countries to manage for results*. Manila: ADB.

Beyer, J. M. and H. M. Trice. 1982. 'The utilization process: A conceptual framework and synthesis of empirical findings'. *Administrative Science Quarterly* 27(4): 591–622. doi.org/10.2307/2392533.

Bischoff, I. and F. Blaeschke. 2015. 'Performance budgeting: Incentives and social waste from window dressing'. *Journal of Public Administration Research and Theory* 26(2): 344–58. doi.org/10.1093/jopart/muv013.

Bouckaert, G. and J. Halligan. 2008. *Managing Performance: International comparisons*. New York: Routledge.

Bureau of Education of Guangzhou Municipality. Various years. *Departmental Budget*. Available from: www.gzedu.gov.cn/gov/index2. htm?classInfoId=991 [in Chinese] (accessed 20 March 2016).

Cronbach, L. J., S. R. Ambron, S. M. Dornbusch, R. D. Hess, R. C. Hornik, D. C. Phillips, D. F. Walker and S. S. Weiner. 1981. *Toward Reform of Program Evaluation*. San Francisco: Jossey-Bass.

Curristine, T. 2005. 'Government performance: Lessons and challenges'. *OECD Journal on Budgeting* 5(1): 127–51. Paris: OECD Publishing.

de Lancer Julnes, P. and M. Holzer. 2001. 'Promoting the utilization of performance measures in public organizations: An empirical study of factors affecting adoption and implementation'. *Public Administration Review* 61(6): 693–708. doi.org/10.1111/0033-3352.00140.

Economic Commission for Africa. 2003. *Public Sector Management Reforms in Africa: Lessons learned.* Addis Ababa: Economic Commission for Africa.

Hatry, H. 2006. *Performance Measurement: Getting results.* Washington, DC: Urban Institute.

Ho, A. T. 2010. 'Budget reforms in the United States: A perfect storm for a new wave of deficit-reduction reforms'. In J. Wanna, L. Jensen and J. de Vries (eds) *The Aftermath of Reform: The impact and consequences of budget reform in OECD nations.* Cheltenham, UK: Edward Elgar. doi.org/10.4337/9781849805636.00008.

Ho, A. T. and T. Im. 2015. 'Challenges in building effective and competitive government in developing countries: An institutional logics perspective'. *American Review of Public Administration* 45(3): 263–80. doi.org/10.1177/0275074013501856.

Lu, Y., Z. Mohr and A. T. Ho. 2015. 'Taking stock: Assessing and improving performance budgeting theory and practice'. *Public Performance and Management Review* 38(3): 426–58. doi.org/10.1080 /15309576.2015.1006470.

Ma, J. 2005. 'Goal setting of China's budgetary reform: Short-term goal and long-term goal'. *Journal of Central University of Economics and Finance* 10: 1–15.

Ma, J. and M. Niu. 2007. 'Restructuring China's budgeting systems: Power and relations'. *China Development Observations* 1: 13–16.

Ma, J. and L. Yu. 2012. 'Why money cannot be spent as budgeted? Lessons from China's recent budget reform'. *Journal of Public Budgeting, Accounting & Financial Management* 24(1): 83–113.

Martin, L. 1997. 'Outcome budgeting: A new entrepreneurial approach to budgeting'. *Journal of Public Budgeting, Accounting and Financial Management* 10: 108–26.

Niu, M. 2010. *Zero-Based Budgeting Reform in China.* Beijing: Central Compilation & Translation Press.

Niu, M. 2012. 'Achievements and challenges: Ten years of performance-based budgeting reform in the Chinese local government'. *Journal of Wuhan University (Philosophy and Social Science Version)* 6: 85–91.

Niu, M. and A. R. Ho. 2014. 'Evaluating the conceptual and methodological challenges in results-oriented management and budgetary reform'. [In Chinese]. *Journal of Public Administration* 3: 55–70.

Niu, M. and X. Song. 2015a. 'Restructuring municipal education spending in China: A case study of Guangzhou'. Paper presented at Accountability and Control in the Xi Jinping Era, Centre for Contemporary Chinese Studies, University of Melbourne, Melbourne, 21–22 August.

Niu, M. and X. Song. 2015b. 'Why can't the budget be spent? A re-examination'. Paper presented at the Third National Conference of Public Finance and Policy, Fudan University, Shanghai, 5–6 December.

Niu, M., A. T. Ho and J. Ma. 2006. 'Performance-based budgeting in China: A case study of Guangdong'. In R. Ahmad (ed.) *The Role of Public Administration in Building a Harmonious Society*. Manila: Asian Development Bank.

Organisation for Economic Co-operation and Development (OECD). 1997. *In Search of Results: Public management practices*. Paris: OECD Publishing.

Organisation for Economic Co-operation and Development (OECD). 2007. *Performance Budgeting in OECD Countries*. Paris: OECD Publishing.

Shah, A. and C. Shen. 2007. 'A primer on performance budgeting'. *Budgeting and Budgetary Institutions*: 137–78.

Wanna, J. 2010. 'Investigating the reality of reform in modern budgeting'. In J. Wanna, L. Jensen and J. de Vries (eds) *The Reality of Budgetary Reform in OECD Nations: Trajectories and consequences*. Cheltenham, UK: Edward Elgar Publishing.

Wescott, C. G., B. Bowornwathana and L. Jones. 2009. *The Many Faces of Public Management Reform in the Asia-Pacific Region*. Oxford: Emerald Group Publishing. doi.org/10.1108/S0732-1317(2009)18.

Wu, S. and M. Niu. 2010. 'Understanding China's budgetary reform'. *Wuhan University Journal (Philosophy and Social Science Version)* 63(6): 1–9.

8

Public financial management and the campaign against extravagant position-related consumption in China

Hanyu Xiao[1]

Introduction

China has been plagued by pervasive corruption in multiple and complex forms since the 1980s, and especially in recent years, posing a serious challenge to governance and the government's legitimacy. Among various forms of corruption and misconduct, extravagant position-related consumption (*san gong xiao fei* in Chinese) attracts the general public's attention, generating a widespread belief that position-related consumption is closely related to corruption and misconduct among officials. Such extravagant consumption, if not effectively controlled, may affect the public's trust in the government and its legitimacy. Accordingly, President Xi Jinping, with his colleague Wang Qishang, the General Secretary of the Central Discipline Inspection Commission (CDIC), launched an anti-extravagance campaign in late 2012.

---

1   An early version of this chapter was presented at the Fifth Greater China–Australia Dialogue held at National Taiwan University in November 2015. I am grateful to Professor Andrew Podger, Professor Hon S. Chan and other participants for their comments.

This study does not aim to examine the current campaign comprehensively. Instead, it argues that the campaign has provided a unique opportunity to examine the dynamics and effectiveness of an anticorruption process, and it may provide solid evidence-based policy suggestions for decision-makers. The lack of an evidence base to date seems clear. Over the past three decades, the Chinese Government has made intensive endeavours to fight against official extravagance, so the reoccurrence of anti-extravagance campaigns itself indicates the ineffectiveness of the pre-2012 efforts. The current campaign has achieved an effective short-term goal: seriously disciplining government officials who violate rules and regulations. According to the monthly reports from the CDIC (2016b), 81,049 government officials were reported and sanctioned for violation of rules against extravagant position-related consumption by May 2016. The revenue of high-end restaurants and sales of luxury wine have also dropped dramatically since the current anti-extravagance campaign began. Nevertheless, extravagant position-related consumption seems to continue, with about 3,000 government officials reported and sanctioned every month (CDIC 2016a). More importantly, it is apparent that the institutional incentives that lead to extravagant position-related consumption largely remain in place, which casts doubt on the long-term effectiveness of this latest campaign (Gong and Xiao 2017).

This chapter explores the persistence of extravagant position-related consumption by emphasising the role of formal and informal rules as well as their interactions and focusing on public financial management (PFM). Over the past two decades, the government has strengthened its financial management framework. This includes the formation of formal financial rules to regulate governmental activities. As a result, corruption related to public money has been reduced over the past decade. However, the growth of formal rules does not necessarily lead to a decline in the role of informal rules within the public sector. The informal rules evolve and continue to play a significant role in influencing position-related consumption. The empirical analysis identifies three forms of interactions where informal rules override formal ones.

Empirical evidence for this research consists of three sources. First, 65 interviews were conducted at different administrative levels in different cities, including Beijing, Shanghai, Guangzhou, Zhanjiang and Changsha, from 2012 to 2014.[2] Second, more than 150 official documents on

---

2   For details of the interviewees' information (such as administrative levels, posts and organisation types), refer to Gong and Xiao (2017).

position-related consumption were collected. As demonstrated below, this study analyses the content of these rules and regulations to understand how the government fights official extravagance. Finally, this research is supported by media reports. Collecting data from these different sources helps to ensure the validity of the empirical evidence and reduces any potential bias.

The next section introduces the concept of position-related consumption. This is followed by a discussion of the theoretical concepts behind the forces that guide position-related consumption—the formal and informal rules. Section four discusses how the rules of PFM have developed to regulate position-related consumption. Section five goes a step further to analyse how informal rules override formal financial rules and lead to extravagant position-related consumption, and the final section discusses the theoretical and practical implications.

Position-related consumption in China

Position-related consumption in China manifests itself in three forms of public expenditure (*sangong zhichu*): official hospitality, government vehicles and official trips. According to the Ministry of Finance (MoF 2012: 224):

> [The] three public expenditures, which are included in the central-level budgeting and auditing management [*yujuesuan guanli*], refer to expenditures on official overseas trips; the purchase, operation and maintenance of government vehicles; and official hospitality.

Several points should be elaborated. First, the actual spending items of position-related consumption are more complex than they appear. For example, official hospitality consists of all kinds of official banquets, accommodation and other expenditure (such as conference costs and transportation fares). Second, the government lacks accurate information about the magnitude of position-related consumption because such consumption happens in all government organisations and each unit holds the actual consumption information. Third, the government defines only official activities funded by budgetary appropriation (*caizheng bokuan*) as position-related consumption, whereas similar consumption supported by small amounts of off-budget revenue held in separate accounts or made by non–budget funded organisations such as state-owned enterprises (SOEs) is not recognised in the official definition.

As distinct from the official definition, this study defines position-related consumption as *public expenditure on official hospitality, government vehicles and official trips (both overseas and domestic) regardless of funding sources.* This definition is broader than the official one because all relevant activities involving government officials as recipients are considered as position-related consumption. For example, lavish official banquets for superiors provided by other government departments are seen as position-related consumption, although the spending is not reimbursed in the superior department. Public service units and SOEs other than government departments also experience position-related consumption because they either receive public money from the government or are affiliated with and supervised by the government.

Admittedly, position-related consumption is necessary for the daily operation of government departments. However, few countries have position-related consumption as lavish as China. Extravagant position-related consumption has been widely discussed by the public and Chinese scholars. First, the overall magnitude of position-related consumption is extremely high. Second, Chinese people widely believe that lavish position-related consumption is a form of corruption. Finally, lavish consumption is a nationwide phenomenon rather than a local practice confined to a few regions. Those in both rich eastern and poor middle and western regions have been found to consume lavishly.

The Chinese central government has intensified its efforts to curb and stop lavish position-related consumption since the 1980s. The central government or central-level departments stipulated over 150 official circulars during this period, among which three types of efforts can be identified. The first is ad hoc policy, which is a short-term response to lavish position-related consumption, especially when the problem catches the attention of central authorities. Ad hoc policies include special rectifications that target a particular phenomenon and official circulars that reiterate the disciplinary rules with which government officials must comply. Second, the central government has made intensive efforts to establish legal rules and guidelines through various official circulars and provisions. Compared with ad hoc policies, this type of measure usually adopts a long-term perspective and seeks to provide basic behavioural guidelines for government officials. Formal regulations are usually derived from provisional regulations following several years of trial and error. Finally, the government employs various fiscal instruments to regulate and control extravagant position-related consumption. Section four will discuss this in detail.

Nevertheless, extravagant consumption continues. Regarding official banquets, an often-cited estimation offered by a scholar from the Central Party School in 2006 suggested that the annual expenditure on official banquets had reached RMB200 billion (A$38 billion) (Study Times 2004). In 2012, the *People's Daily*, the mouthpiece of the central authorities, reported that hundreds of billions of dollars of public money were spent annually on official hospitality, and that this expenditure made up two- or three-tenths of the administrative fund (*xingzheng jinfei*) (People's Daily 2012). Reports on the attitude of the public towards lavish official hospitality also echo the likely scale of the problem. Based on an online survey of 10,844 people in early 2012, *China Youth Daily* found that 85.5 per cent perceived official hospitality as a very serious phenomenon and 63.8 per cent of the respondents were concerned about the reforms. Regarding the effectiveness of official circulars in reducing lavish hospitality, only 22.2 per cent of the respondents believed that these measures were 'very good', while 40.6 per cent thought they were ineffective (China Youth Daily 2012). Another online survey, in 2011, involving 10,275 respondents, revealed more striking results: as many as 99.1 per cent of the respondents considered official hospitality expenditure a serious phenomenon (China Economic Times 2011).

Evidence shows that government vehicles are still being mismanaged and misused to this day, including both their purchase and their use. Purchases need to be analysed in terms of two factors: who is eligible to purchase a vehicle and the price of the vehicle. Although some rules specify that only officials at or above the deputy ministerial/provincial level can purchase designated government vehicles, many low-ranking officials are using such vehicles. In fact, one deputy chief of a district department advised that even the officials at the section level (*keji ganbu*) could have designated vehicles.[3] Former governor of Guangdong province Huang Huahua held a similar view:

> We have too many government vehicles. In the old days, only those officials at or above deputy-provincial level could be given designated government vehicles. Nowadays, even the chiefs of units [*gu zhang*][4] may have their own government vehicles. (Yin 2011: 25)

---

3   Interview with an official at the district level, Shenzhen, May 2012.
4   The unit chief is the lowest administrative rank within the bureaucratic system.

In addition, the prices paid for government vehicles were often far beyond the price spectrum set by the rules and regulations, thus contributing to excessive expenditure in this area. According to a news report, one SOE spent as much as RMB9.21 million (A\$1.8 million) to purchase 16 vehicles, indicating the average cost of each vehicle was RMB576,000 (A\$110,000) (Guangzhou Daily 2011)—far beyond the allowable purchase price set by the central government. Most strikingly, the party secretary of one very poor county (based on its gross domestic product [GDP] per capita) used a government vehicle valued at more than RMB1 million (A\$190,000) (China News Service 2013). The rules and regulations for monitoring and controlling the number and price ceiling of government vehicles have thus often failed and work only on paper.

As a result, extravagance was found in the management of government vehicles. There were approximately four million government vehicles in 2004, with a total annual cost of RMB408.5 billion (A\$77.8 billion), which accounted for 13 per cent of the fiscal revenue for that year (Study Times 2004). A proposal submitted by a representative of the national congress estimated that the government had approximately 3.5 million vehicles in the mid-1990s, and spent about RMB300 billion (A\$57 billion) every year (Nanfang Metropolis Daily 2003). Although the aforementioned figures are estimates, they suggest that the amount of money wasted on government vehicles is sizeable and the management of government vehicles has largely been ineffective.

Finally, expenditure on official trips has been considerable in recent years. An often-cited estimation reported that the expenditure on overseas trips reached RMB300 billion (A\$57 billion) in 1999.[5] Another source reported that overseas trips cost RMB200 billion (A\$38 billion) in 2004 (People.com 2005). These estimations are of a similar order to those for spending on official hospitality and government vehicles. The former president of Xinhua News Agency Tian Congming expressed the view that spending on overseas trips remained rampant because of a loophole in off-budget revenue (Beijing News 2012).

---

5   For more details, see Phoenix (2013); Study Times (2004).

A theoretical concept

The existing literature has provided several perspectives with which to understand extravagant position-related consumption. Various scholars argue that extravagance is caused by Chinese culture (or *mianzi*) (Ho 1976; Guo 2010), the greed of individual government officials (Cope 2000; Hindmoor 2006) or poor policy implementation (Dong et al. 2014).[6] These perspectives provide useful insights for explaining extravagant position-related consumption. Yet, few studies have explored the process, dynamics and mechanisms of such consumption and how different rules and values interact with one another in this area.

This chapter argues that a PFM perspective provides an opportunity to investigate the dynamics of extravagant consumption, for the following reasons. PFM plays a key role in good governance because it 'stands at the heart of resource management in all governments and has broad influence on the ability of government to provide services, manage transparently, and ensure stability' (Andrews 2010: 11). Conducting an interim assessment, Ma and Ni (2008) find that a control-oriented reform of the budget system in China has reduced fund misuse at local levels. An effective financial management system is also vital for the control of position-related consumption because, essentially, all such consumption involves public money.

Currently, Gong and Xiao (2017) employ institutional isomorphism theory to explain why extravagant position-related consumption has circumvented the government's anti-extravagance endeavours over the past three decades. According to this study, extravagant position-related consumption is embedded in the Chinese bureaucracy and driven by substantial institutional incentives: vertical, horizontal and normative pressures. However, their study does not pay sufficient attention to particular rules and regulations of PFM. This chapter will focus on PFM, employing institutional analysis and drawing on the literature on formal and informal rules as well as their interactions.

Scholars have long emphasised the role of rules and regulations in understanding the behaviour of individuals, organisations and societies (North 1990; Knight 1992; Greenwood and Hinings 1996; Hall and

---

6   For more detailed discussion, refer to Gong and Xiao (2017).

Taylor 1996). There are two types of rules: formal and informal. While formal rules are generally officially written and endorsed by the formal power governing organisations, informal rules are often thought to be socially shared, unwritten and enforced outside the official power of organisations (Helmke and Levitsky 2004).

The existing literature has examined various organisational phenomena from the perspective of formal and informal rules. Dittmer (1995) argues that informal politics is an important way to understand real politics in contemporary China. Tsai and Dean (2015) examine the *mishu* system in authoritarian China, which has influence and power beyond the formal rules.[7] Similarly, Liu and Lin (2014) find intensive interactions between formal and informal rules when they investigate the decision-making process for a project earmarked for enterprise listing involving different departments in a Chinese province. Following the approach of these studies, this chapter identifies the formal and informal rules affecting position-related consumption and examines how their interactions lead to extravagant consumption.

The next section explores how the PFM framework regulates position-related consumption.

Attempts to strengthen public financial management

Since the 1990s, China's central government has been strengthening the PFM framework, which is helpful for controlling lavish position-related consumption. In recent years, the Chinese Government has introduced several important budget reforms to tighten the control of public money.

---

7   The *mishu* (secretary) system in China consists of institutional *mishu* and personal *mishu*—support staff employed mainly in party committee general offices. Since *mishu* work closely with leading cadres and are involved in the decision-making and implementation processes, they often have higher informal power than their formal positions and levels suggest.

Development of public financial management in China

First, laws and regulations pertaining to PFM have been introduced and updated. China's Budget Law, government accounting law and auditing regulations (*shenji tiaoli*) took effect from the 1980s, providing basic guidelines for PFM. Second, budget reforms have been introduced since the 1990s. Departmental budget reform demands that government departments include all revenue and expenditure when compiling departmental budgets. A centralised treasury management system and a centralised procurement system were introduced as well, replacing the old decentralised management methods in respective fiscal areas (Ma 2009). According to recent studies, budget reforms since 1999 have increased budget control capacity and reduced fiscal misconduct (Ma and Ni 2008; Ma 2009).

Third, the central government gradually increased its control and management of revenue and expenditures. The Chinese fiscal system has traditionally consisted of official budgets, extra-budgets and even illegal money (Wedeman 2000). While rules and regulations for official budgets were comprehensive, the use of extra budgets and illegal money was rife among local governments. Such activity periodically becomes public and the central government has to take action against it. An important initiative has been separating revenue and spending (*shouzhi liangtiaoxian*). For example, a circular promulgated by the General Office of the State Council (2001) requires departments to include all extra-budget revenue in their official budget and to hand over all revenue to the government. The central government has also moved to rectify the malpractice regarding small off-budget accounts in recent years. With weak regulation from superiors, small off-budget accounts often led to malpractice and became a major source of lavish position-related consumption.

To sum up, China has made great endeavours to strengthen its PFM and establish a control-oriented fiscal system.

Detailed financial regulations on position-related consumption

The central government has introduced various fiscal methods to regulate position-related consumption. More than 67 circulars relevant to the PFM of position-related consumption have been issued over the past three decades. These circulars cover all the important components of position-related consumption—namely, the cost of domestic and overseas trips, official hospitality and government vehicles. The central government has issued as many as 10 circulars focusing on official trips (domestic and overseas) in recent years. Four specify major expenditure items pertaining to domestic trips, including accommodation, intra- and inter-city transportation fares and meal subsidies. The MoF has adopted lump-sum management for these expenditure items for officials below the level of division chief (*si zhang*), indicating that fixed standards are applied to these items. In 2006, the MoF also identified designated hotels and restaurants that should be used to enhance the management of official meetings and domestic trips. In particular, government officials who make a local visit have to stay at hotels on the official list and the sites for official meetings should be chosen from the list of designated restaurants (MoF 2006). Six circulars have been issued regulating overseas trips, according to which expenditure consists of costs for international travel, inter-city transportation, accommodation, meal subsidies and minor charges (*zafei*). The central government makes clear the required standards for these items and updates these standards according to price changes in the market. The MoF has also required improvements to the financial management of overseas trips with respect to budgeting plans, verification of relevant receipts and audit and investigation. A circular issued in 2013 requires that relevant central departments inspect the details of official overseas trips in either a regular or a more random manner (MoF and Ministry of Foreign Affairs 2013).

Two circulars focus on particular aspects of official hospitality (General Office of the CCPCC and General Office of the State Council 1994a; MoF 1998). The 1994 circular emphasised that, when central government officials visit, the accommodation and banquet standards should not exceed the rates set for local governments. The MoF in 1998 issued the *Regulations of the Fiscal Management of Official Hospitality Items in Administrative Organs and Public Service Units* (*xingzheng shiyu danwei yuwu zhaodaifei liezhi guanli guiding*) (MoF 1998), which remain the most important fiscal guidelines for official hospitality. This guideline specifies the maximum share of official reception costs in departmental operation costs (*gongwu feiyong*), with 2 per cent for local government entities and 1 per cent for central government departments.

Regarding the financial management of government vehicles, the *Fiscal Management Methods of Budget and Final Reports of Government Vehicles in the Party and Government Organs* (*dangzheng jiguan gongwuyongche yusuan juesuan guanli banfa*) was promulgated in 2011 (MoF 2011). This circular was the first decree authorised by central authorities targeting the fiscal management of government vehicles. This measure was also an extension of the *Regulations on the Purchase and Use of Government Vehicles in the Party and Government Organs* (General Office of the CCPCC and General Office of the State Council 1994b). The 2011 measure included the administrative procedures for managing government vehicles, the identification in budgets of vehicle purchase and operational costs, the implementation process for purchasing vehicles and the compilation of final reports on the purchase and use of vehicles.

In addition to these circulars specifically concerning position-related consumption, others have been introduced to regulate activities that may breed extravagant spending. Two main efforts have been made in recent years. First, the central government has sought to disclose budgetary information to the public. The 'Regulations on Opening Government Information', which took effect in May 2008, require the government to disclose governmental information to the public. Later, information about position-related consumption was required, including detailed explanations (General Office of the State Council 2012). Second, the State Council has frozen budgets for position-related consumption since the 2010 fiscal year. This followed the MoF and the National Audit Office (NAO) jointly promulgating a circular in 2009 calling for a reduction in expenditure on position-related consumption. Specifically, departmental budgets for official overseas trips were limited to 80 per cent of the average spending over the previous three-year period (2006–08). The spending on government vehicles was limited to 85 per cent of the respective average, while the cost of official receptions was required to be reduced by 10 per cent below that of 2008 (MoF and NAO 2009).

To conclude, the central government has made intensive efforts and has established strict fiscal management measures trying to curb extravagant position-related consumption. There would be few opportunities for lavish consumption if the government strictly followed these financial rules. The next section analyses how government officials circumvent the formal financial rules and why extravagant consumption continues.

How do informal rules circumvent formal rules of financial management?

This section examines how government officials sidestep the formal financial rules and consume lavishly. There are several types of circumstances by which informal rules circumvent the formal ones.

Informal rules promoting organisational interests override formal financial rules

When informal rules are closely tied to organisational interest, formal financial rules often become weak in regulating consumption. Government organisations often emphasise their own organisational interests at the cost of other socially desirable goals; in other words, some activities may enrich the organisation at the cost of a whole sector or society. Lu (2000: 275) revealed that a common pattern of corruption in the Chinese Government is 'organisational corruption', which is department-based and conducted in the name of an official unit.

A closer analysis of lavish consumption reveals that organisational interest is considered the most important rationale for government officials to try to ethically justify governmental malpractice. Even though engaging in lavish consumption may bring ethical anxiety for government officials, especially those who tend to follow the formal rules, moral concerns would be significantly reduced if such behaviour was justified in the name of organisational interests:

> In many cases, good official hospitality arrangements for upper officials can yield organizational benefits. The provincial governor approached Beijing to obtain approval for the large programs for the province … The governor was personally reluctant to participate in drinking and dining because it is not helpful and healthy for him. However, the governor had to offer extravagant hospitality because he must get approval from Beijing so he could begin implementing his projects in the province.[8]

> In reality, our work entails official hospitality. For the problems that cannot be solved on the table, we can easily tackle them in private places (in restaurants for official hospitality). To be honest, none of us is willing

---

8   Interview with the departmental official of a provincial Beijing liaison office, Beijing, May 2013.

to eat and drink in that manner. In fact, I prefer to eat at home after work. Official hospitality is exhausting. However, such hospitality is part of our work, and we cannot escape from it.[9]

In the fieldwork for this chapter, many other interviewees presented the author with similar views. Organisational interest became the main reason for lavish consumption. In this situation, government officials usually follow the informal practice—engaging in lavish consumption—because they envisage that it will yield higher organisational benefits. Therefore, following the financial rules pertaining to position-related consumption becomes less important.

'Invite' other government departments to pay for the consumption

It is nonetheless risky to explicitly violate the formal rules and consume lavishly, especially when the government has launched such a severe anticorruption campaign. An alternative is to mobilise additional sources of funds while the government departments initiating the consumption still follow the formal rules. It is common for upper-level government departments to 'invite' lower-level ones to pay for their additional position-related expenditure. Therefore, such expenditure does not appear in the accounts of the upper-level departments. The following interviews demonstrate how officials respond to the strict formal rules:

If a bureau has limited money, then it is reasonable to purchase government vehicles by forced apportionment funds collected from other units. Otherwise, the bureau should find someone who can offer financial support.[10]

It is hard to imagine that I cannot use government vehicles. I will immediately call someone and borrow a vehicle in that case.[11]

Forced apportionment funds possibly exist for overseas trips. Upper governments sometimes assign travel expenses to our bureau when they cannot assign them to their own departments.[12]

Official trips also have forced apportionment of funds. For instance, senior officials from the People's Congress or the People's Political Consultative Committee in my county have few things to do. To kill time,

---

9   Interview with a departmental official, Guangzhou, July 2012.
10   Interview with the deputy chief of a county bureau, Zhanjiang, July 2013.
11   Interview with the deputy chief of a county bureau, Zhanjiang, July 2013.
12   Interview with an official in a district finance bureau, Guangzhou, July 2012.

they sometimes call me and demand that I accompany them to conduct fieldwork in local places. For me, this 'invitation' means that I should pay part of the travel costs. They may have the travel budget from the Bureau of Finance. Generally speaking, an official trip costs RMB3,000 [A$570], but my bureau often pays RMB5,000 [A$950] for the trip.[13]

The above evidence demonstrates that forced apportionment is often used by upper-level units to shift additional consumption. This finding is also supported by the NAO's report. The NAO launched an audit of 58 central departments in 2013 and the results revealed that, among these departments, 31 (or 53.4 per cent) had forced apportionment pertaining to lavish consumption to lower-level departments or units. The total amount of forced apportionment was more than RMB34.7 million (A$6.6 million).[14] The forced apportionment related to two forms of lavish consumption, the first of which were overseas trips. In many cases, central government departments demanded subordinate units cover their costs on overseas trips, while sometimes subordinates actively provided funds to support the overseas trips of their supervisors. Among 58 central departments, 18 were found to have conducted forced apportionment for overseas trips. Second, some lavish consumption was reimbursed under the name of conference expenditure by subordinate units. Audit reports showed that 22 ministries apportioned conference expenditures to other units, including affiliated units, subordinates and other organisations (*qita danwei*).[15] Nine ministries had forced apportionment on both official conferences and overseas trips.

Manipulating the auditing

When the first two options are not available, government officials may seek to hide extravagant consumption by colluding with auditors and accountants within the government department. Accountants in the public sector must obey the financial rules and monitor possible financial flaws, thereby securing the proper spending of public money. By contrast, fieldwork by the author indicates that, in reality, public accountants' first priority was to follow the instructions of departmental leaders, regardless of their professional values and formal rules. The following interview was illustrative:

---

13   Interview with the deputy chief of a county bureau, Zhanjiang, July 2013.
14   This figure is based on the author's calculations. In some cases, accurate figures related to this malpractice were not given in audit reports.
15   No further explanation on other organisations exists in official reports; however, those organisations are usually subject to the supervision of ministries.

Our accountants are supposed to serve the department. However, they mainly serve the leaders. Although there are professional guidelines for their work, they have to obey the instructions of the leaders in the first place. Why? If you refuse to follow the leaders because their directions violate professional rules, then the leaders will fire you immediately.[16]

Although departmental leaders may not dare to ask the accountants directly to engage in corruption, leaders could ask them to hide some extravagant position-related expenditure in departmental accounts. Another interviewee from a district-level department told this story:

Now it is demanded that departments should disclose their position-related consumption to the public. We will submit the 'real expenditures' to the department head for their approval before the disclosure. Since the real expenditures are very high, it is impossible to disclose them to the public. Therefore, before the disclosure, accountants have to revise the information so that it seems to follow the fiscal rules.[17]

The above evidence indicates that accountants within government departments play a very weak role in correcting fiscal flaws. They believe they have to follow their leaders' instructions.

In addition, PFM focuses only on activities funded by public money, while much position-related consumption is supported by small off-budget accounts that are subject to weak financial rules. Simply put, the accounting system does not provide comprehensive guidelines to clearly identify specific position-related consumption items. The blurred definition of position-related consumption has resulted in high levels of discretion for government departments, allowing them to easily hide such consumption. For example, the definition of an official banquet by the local audit office was problematic:

The audit office only recognises the expenditure as official hospitality with banquet receipts, which is ridiculous. In this case, we do not go to restaurants that can only issue banquet receipts. Instead, we go to restaurants that can offer meeting receipts. Nowadays, we are making a list of restaurants that cannot provide meeting receipts, so that we won't go there anymore.[18]

To escape auditing, government departments hide real expenditure on official banquets under meeting expenditure.

---

16   Interview with the deputy chief of a county bureau, Zhanjiang, July 2012.
17   Interview with an official in a district finance bureau, Guangzhou, July 2012.
18   Interview with a departmental official, Guangzhou, July 2012.

Do formal financial rules go too far and inadvertently foster informal rules?

According to the fieldwork, financial rules dominated by frugality may have inadvertently generated incentives for government officials to consume lavishly. The standards set for consumption items may sometimes be too low for government officials to fulfil their official duties. In other words, the central government emphasises frugality too much and does not adjust spending ceilings for position-related consumption sufficiently or in a timely way:

> The spending standard for domestic official trips is believed to be too low [such] that government officials who pay a local visit could not arrive [at] the destination at all, if officials strictly follow the train fare standard. However, all officials make it.[19]

This quotation illustrates that the reimbursement allowed for domestic trips is too low. Thus, government officials have to evade fiscal rules. Other interviewees have similar views. An official who works at a provincial department told the author:

> Government officials should not stay in cheap chain hotels for domestic official trips. These hotels are not appropriate for officials. We have to find more comfortable restaurants. However, rules and regulations do not allow us to do that.[20]

Low salaries for government officials at the local level may also be an important cause of lavish position-related consumption. The effectiveness of PFM entails some necessary conditions, including competitive salaries for government officials. Studies have revealed that government officials are more prone to corruption if their salaries are low (Wu 2014). This may hold true for lavish position-related consumption. Government officials with lower salaries may have higher incentives to engage in lavish position-related consumption. Several government officials complained about their low salaries when they talked about position-related consumption.[21]

---

19 Interview with a senior official of the MoF, Beijing, May 2013.
20 Interview with an official in a provincial office, Changsha, March 2014.
21 Interview with a departmental official, Guangzhou, July 2012; interview with an official in a provincial office, Changsha, March 2014.

The problems with formal financial rules have therefore provided opportunities for government officials to think about violating these specific rules about position-related consumption.

Discussion and conclusion

The above analysis focuses on consumption before 2012. Given the notable effects of the current anti-extravagance campaign, it is worthwhile discussing position-related consumption since 2012 in more detail. The current campaign was launched in late 2012, starting with the enforcement of an official circular—the 'Eight Regulations'—by the Chinese Communist Party (CCP) on 4 December. The new regulation tightened control over official extravagance and bureaucracy. Several ad hoc circulars were issued immediately after the start of the campaign. The CDIC, for example, issued circulars in 2013 to ban New Year's cards and New Year shopping using public money (CDIC 2013), gift-giving during the Mid-Autumn Festival and on National Day (CDIC and The Mass Line Education Small Leading Group 2013a) and forbidding government officials from participating in private club activities (*hui suo*) (CDIC and The Mass Line Education Small Leading Group 2013b). The central government issued long-term guidelines providing detailed instructions in line with the 'Eight Regulations'. In October 2013, the CCP and the State Council jointly stipulated the 'Regulations on Guiding the Party and Government Organs in Practising Frugality and Rejecting Extravagance'. This circular tightened the management of expenditure on management, overseas and domestic trips, official hospitality, government vehicles, official conferences, use of official houses and resource saving. The CDIC promptly prioritised the reduction of lavish official extravagance, which was the first time it had taken severe disciplinary action over official extravagance. The discipline inspection system increasingly mobilised resources to detect and penalise behaviour that violated the guidelines in the Eight Regulations. Wang Qishang said the implementation of the Eight Regulations should be reported to the Nineteenth CCP National Congress (People.com 2014), which indicates that the enforcement of the Eight Regulations was an important agenda item for the CDIC at least until 2017.

The sanction against government officials who violate the Eight Regulations was increasingly severe: they were demoted or dismissed. A provincial official noted that a deputy minister was demoted because he was caught receiving lavish official hospitality in a locality.[22] This sanction was particularly heavy, given that few officials at such an administrative rank have been demoted for such activity.

The current anti-extravagance campaign has yielded mixed results. On the one hand, evidence shows it has had a significant effect on the level of spending on official hospitality. In early 2014, the chief executive officer of the New Century Tourism Group (*kaiyuan lvye jituan*), which has more than 40 five-star restaurants, said the average turnover of its catering sector was reduced by 20 per cent in 2013 and revenue from catering and conferences dramatically decreased (Xinhua 2014). Government officials also commented that they seldom hosted guests in high-end restaurants since the current campaign began and superiors at high levels refused official banquets offered by low-level officials.[23]

On the other hand, more complex forms of lavish position-related consumption were reported. Malfeasance was organised in the name of plausible activities, such as inviting superiors to luxurious food tasting events, whereas others held luxurious banquets at remote or hidden places (Wangyi 2013). One report observed that the enforcement of the Eight Regulations led to the emergence of private clubs and internal canteens, which were difficult to detect.[24] As high-end restaurants are no longer 'safe' for government officials, private clubs, *nongjiale*[25] and internal canteens are more popular for lavish banquets.

The following interviewee explained how local officials responded passively to the current anti-extravagance campaign:

---

22 Interview with the chief of the general office of a provincial department, Changsha, March 2014.

23 Interviews with several officials of a prefectural discipline inspection commission, Zhuhai, May 2014.

24 For more details, see Nanjing Daily (2013); Beijing News (2014).

25 *Nongjiale* is a Chinese version of rural tourism and it literally means 'delights in farm guesthouses'. Government officials like to use *nongjiale* as a way to have lavish official banquets because it is difficult to detect.

Officials now dare not consume luxuriously since the Eight Regulations. However, the crux is not solved. Everyone now behaves in a low-key manner, being quiet and waiting. The problem remains. Officials now passively respond to the directives of the central government. How to solve the crux remains an open question.[26]

In spite of the significant achievements of the campaign, eliminating official extravagance will be a protracted war. According to Helmke and Levitsky (2004), the interaction between formal and informal rules has two dimensions: convergent/divergent outcomes and effective/ineffective formal rules. Convergent outcomes indicate that informal rules produce similar results to those of the formal ones; otherwise, the outcome is divergent. The second dimension considers the effectiveness of formal rules. Table 8.1 summarises these four types of interactions between formal and informal rules. According to Helmke and Levitsky's (2004) analysis, the relationship between formal and informal rules relating to position-related consumption is too often *competing*, where formal rules are weak in curbing extravagant consumption and informal rules tend to circumvent the frugality goal of formal rules. The competing relationship significantly hampers the governance of position-related consumption. When formal rules (such as the enforcement of sanctions against official extravagance) are severe, the effectiveness of formal rules increases, at least in the short term. This may lead to a decline in extravagant consumption. When the enforcement becomes weak, however, official extravagance led by informal rules proliferates again.

Table 8.1 Four types of interaction between formal and informal rules

		Formal rules	
		Ineffective	Effective
Informal rules	Convergent	Substitutive	Complementary
	Divergent	Competing	Accommodating

Source: Helmke and Levitsky (2004: 728).

The question, therefore, is how to change their relationship so both types of rules are able to curb lavish position-related consumption. The desirable type of interactions would be *complementary*, where both formal and informal rules produce similar outcomes and formal rules are effective in curbing official extravagance (Helmke and Levitsky 2004).

---

26   Interview with a departmental official, Shanghai, October 2013.

The current anti-extravagance campaign may increase the effectiveness of formal rules, as we can see from its significant short-term effects. Given the outcomes, frugality is apparently the main goal of formal financial management. The CCP has a long tradition of emphasising the need for government officials to exercise frugality in official activities. Frugality is further embodied in various official circulars that regulate and constrain position-related consumption. The frugality standards may contribute to the legitimacy of the CCP. However, those standards for position-related consumption are often too low,[27] reinforcing informal rules and allowing the formal ones to be ignored.

Convergent outcomes are key to shifting the rules relationship from competing to complementary. According to this research, the proliferation of some informal rules is caused by frugality-oriented formal rules that go too far. Following this logic, accepting the more reasonable aspects of informal rules and reflecting them in the formal rules may be helpful to foster a complementary relationship. However, some of the informal rules are unreasonable and need to be addressed if they are to complement the formal rules. These include a culture of excessive deference to authority and excessive emphasis on personal material gain.

More broadly, the financial management framework and the stronger rules on position-related consumption represent an essential discipline promoting the efficient and effective use of public resources and, in the long run, internalising ethical behaviour and shifting the culture away from personal gain or excessive deference to superiors. With a control-oriented fiscal system, the Chinese Government will be able to effectively control position-related consumption. Meanwhile, our research finds that informal rules are persistent and have a competing relationship with formal fiscal rules. While the financial management framework will eliminate some informal rules closely related to official extravagance, it needs to consider the reasonable part of some informal rules and perhaps include them in the framework. That inclusion may help shift the competing relationship to a complementary one.

---

27   Interview with a senior official of the MoF, Beijing, May 2013; interview with an official in a provincial office, Changsha, March 2014.

References

Andrews, M. 2010. 'Good government means different things in different countries'. *Governance: An International Journal of Policy, Administration, and Institutions* 23(1): 7–35. doi.org/10.1111/j.1468-0491.2009.01465.x.

Beijing News. 2012. 'How to manage off-budget?' [In Chinese]. *The Beijing News*, 8 March. Available from: epaper.bjnews.com.cn/html/2012-03/08/content_322631.htm?div=0 (accessed 13 May 2015).

Beijing News. 2014. 'Media exposed official banquets'. [In Chinese]. *The Beijing News*, 14 May. Available from: www.chinanews.com/gn/2014/05-14/6166667.shtml (accessed 2 June 2015).

Central Discipline Inspection Commission (CDIC). 2013. *Notice on Forbidding the Purchase, Printing, and Shipping of Greeting Cards and Related Items using Public Funds*. 31 October. Beijing: CDIC.

Central Discipline Inspection Commission (CDIC). 2016a. 'China reported 4785 cases against eight regulations in December 2015'. 12 January. Beijing: CDIC. Available from: www.ccdi.gov.cn/xwtt/201601/t20160112_72579.html (accessed 29 July 2016).

Central Discipline Inspection Commission (CDIC). 2016b. 'China reported 3215 cases against eight regulations in May 2016'. 21 June. Beijing: CDIC. Available from: www.ccdi.gov.cn/xwtt/201606/t20160620_80637.html (accessed 29 July 2016).

Central Discipline Inspection Commission (CDIC) and The Mass Line Education Small Leading Group. 2013a. *Notice on the Implementation of the Eight Regulations and Strictly Stopping Unhealthy Tendencies, Such As Giving Gifts Bought using Public Funds During Mid-Autumn Day and National Day*. 3 September. Beijing: CDIC.

Central Discipline Inspection Commission (CDIC) and The Mass Line Education Small Leading Group. 2013b. *Notice on Severely Rectifying the Unhealthy Tendencies of Club Activities in the Party's Mass Line Educational Practice*. 22 December. Beijing: CDIC.

China Economic Times. 2011. '99 per cent of the public questioned the official banquet'. [In Chinese]. *China Economic Times*, 18 October. Available from: lib.cet.com.cn/paper/szb_con/125324.html (accessed 4 August 2017).

China News Service. 2013. 'The party secretary of Baihe County of Shanxi Province was reported to use high-end vehicles'. [In Chinese]. *China News Service*, 16 January. Available from: www.chinanews.com/fz/2013/01-16/4493858.shtml (accessed 13 May 2015).

China Youth Daily. 2012. '87.4 per cent respondents advocated the state to promulgate the standard of official banquets as soon as possible'. [In Chinese]. *China Youth Daily*, 27 March. Available from: zqb.cyol.com/html/2012-03/27/nw.D110000zgqnb_20120327_1-07.htm (accessed 13 May 2015).

Cope, S. 2000. 'Assessing rational-choice models of budgeting—from budget-maximising to bureau-shaping: A case study of British local government'. *Journal of Public Budgeting, Accounting & Financial Management* 12(4): 598–624.

Dittmer, L. 1995. 'Chinese informal politics'. *The China Journal* 34: 1–34. doi.org/10.2307/2950131.

Dong, L., T. Christensen and M. Painter. 2014. 'Health care reform in China: An analysis of development trends and lack of implementation'. *International Public Management Journal* 17(4): 493–514. doi.org/10.1080/10967494.2014.958802.

General Office of the Chinese Communist Party Central Committee (CCPCC) and General Office of the State Council. 1994a. *Notice on Abandoning Central-Level Officials' Official Banquets and Accommodation at Domestic Official Visits Over Local Standards.* 28 April. Beijing: General Office of the CCPCC.

General Office of the Chinese Communist Party Central Committee (CCPCC) and General Office of the State Council. 1994b. *Regulations on the Purchase and Use of Government Vehicles in the Party and Government Organs.* 5 September. Beijing: General Office of the CCPCC.

General Office of the State Council. 2001. *Notice on Forwarding the MOF's Suggestions on Deepening the Reform of Two Lines in Revenue and Expenditure, and Strengthening Fiscal Management.* 10 December. Beijing: General Office of the State Council.

General Office of the State Council. 2012. *The Major Work Plan of Government Information Disclosure in 2012.* [In Chinese]. Beijing: General Office of the State Council. Available from: www.gov.cn/ zwgk/2012-05/17/content_2139583.htm (accessed 10 October 2015).

Gong, T. and H. Xiao. 2017. 'The formation and impact of isomorphic pressures: Extravagant position-related consumption in China'. *Governance: An International Journal of Policy, Administration, and Institutions* 30(3)(July): 387–405. doi.org/10.1111/gove.12242.

Greenwood, R. and C. R. Hinings. 1996. 'Understanding radical organizational change: Bringing together the old and the new institutionalism'. *The Academy of Management Review* 21(4): 1022–54.

Guangzhou Daily. 2011. 'Who has borrowed these 16 high-end official vehicles?' [In Chinese]. *Guangzhou Daily*, 20 August. Available from: opinion.hexun.com/2011-08-20/132643169.html (accessed 4 August 2017).

Guo, Y. 2010. 'Political culture, administrative system reform and anticorruption in China: Taking the official car management institution reform as an example'. *Crime Law and Social Change* 53(5): 493–508. doi.org/10.1007/s10611-010-9238-5.

Hall, P. A. and R. C. R. Taylor. 1996. 'Political science and the three new institutionalisms'. *Political Studies* XLIV: 936–57. doi.org/10.1111/ j.1467-9248.1996.tb00343.x.

Helmke, G. and S. Levitsky. 2004. 'Informal institutions and comparative politics: A research agenda'. *Perspectives on Politics* 2(4): 725–40. doi.org/10.1017/S1537592704040472.

Hindmoor, A. M. 2006. *Rational Choice.* London: Palgrave Macmillan. doi.org/10.1007/978-0-230-20997-8.

Ho, D. Y. 1976. 'On the concept of face'. *American Journal of Sociology* 81(4): 867–84.

Knight, J. 1992. *Institutions and Social Conflict*. Cambridge: Cambridge University Press. doi.org/10.1017/CBO9780511528170.

Liu, Y. and M. Lin. 2014. 'Formal and informal politics in the budgeting process: A case study of a provincial earmarked fund'. [In Chinese]. *Journal of Public Administration* 4: 112–32.

Lu, X. B. 2000. 'Booty socialism, bureau-preneurs, and the state in transition: Organizational corruption in China'. *Comparative Politics* 32(3): 273–94. doi.org/10.2307/422367.

Ma, J. 2009. 'If you can't budget, how can you govern? A case study of China's state capacity'. *Public Administration and Development* 29: 9–20. doi.org/10.1002/pad.509.

Ma, J. and X. Ni. 2008. 'Toward a clean government in China: Does the budget reform provide a hope?' *Crime, Law and Social Change* 49(2): 119–38. doi.org/10.1007/s10611-008-9101-0.

Ministry of Finance (MoF). 1998. *Regulations of the Fiscal Management of Official Hospitality Items in Administrative Organs and Public Service Units*. 14 May. Beijing: MoF.

Ministry of Finance (MoF). 2006. *The (Trial) Management Method of Official Trips and Official Meetings at Designated Restaurants by Central Government Departments*. November. Beijing: MoF.

Ministry of Finance (MoF). 2011. *Fiscal Management Methods of Budget and Final Reports of Government Vehicles in the Party and Government Organs*. 4 March. Beijing: MoF.

Ministry of Finance (MoF). 2012. 'On strengthening the fiscal management of three public expenditures and administration cost'. Internal document. Beijing: MoF.

Ministry of Finance (MoF) and Ministry of Foreign Affairs. 2013. *Fiscal Management Methods of Temporary Official Overseas Trips*. 20 December. Beijing: MoF & Ministry of Foreign Affairs.

Ministry of Finance (MoF) and National Audit Office (NAO). 2009. *Notice on Reducing Expenditures on Three Public Expenditures in the 2009 Fiscal Year*. 10 March. Beijing: MoF & NAO.

Nanfang Metropolis Daily. 2003. 'To reduce administration cost from the details'. [In Chinese]. Nanfang *Metropolis Daily*, 10 June. Available from: www.southcn.com/news/gdnews/chuanmei/200306100198.htm (accessed 13 May 2015).

Nanjing Daily. 2013. 'Media reported SOEs' canteens hold banquets for government officials'. [In Chinese]. *Nanjing Daily*, 27 March. Available from: native.cnr.cn/society/201303/t20130327_51224 0041.shtml (accessed 16 August 2017).

North, D. C. 1990. *Institutions, Institutional Change, and Economic Performance*. Cambridge: Cambridge University Press. doi.org/ 10.1017/CBO9780511808678.

Peiffer, C. and L. Alvarez. 2015. 'Who will be the "principled-principals"? Perceptions of corruption and willingness to engage in anticorruption activism'. *Governance: An International Journal of Policy, Administration, and Institutions* 29(3): 351–69. doi.org/10.1111/gove.12172.

People.com. 2005. '700 billion for official banquets'. [In Chinese]. *People.com.cn*, 27 May. Available from: cppcc.people.com.cn/GB/ 34957/3422068.html (accessed 13 May 2015).

People.com. 2014. 'Wang Qishang's report at the People's Political Consultative Conference has five important messages'. [In Chinese]. *People.com.cn*, 7 September. Available from: politics.people.com.cn/ n/2014/0907/c1001-25619012.html (accessed 2 June 2015).

People's Daily. 2012. 'Luxurious banquets should be penalised as soon as possible'. [In Chinese]. *People's Daily*, 31 January. Available from: society.people.com.cn/GB/1062/16973737.html (accessed 13 May 2015).

Persson, A., B. Rothstein and J. Teorell. 2013. 'Why anticorruption reforms fail: Systemic corruption as a collective action problem'. *Governance: An International Journal of Policy, Administration, and Institutions* 26(3): 449–71. doi.org/10.1111/j.1468-0491.2012.01604.x.

Phoenix. 2013. 'It is sure that position-related consumption is not as high as 900 billion every year'. [In Chinese]. *Phoenix*, 26 March. Available from: finance.ifeng.com/news/macro/20130326/7822778. shtml (accessed 16 August 2017).

Study Times. 2004. 'Several starting points of government's administration reform'. [In Chinese]. *Study Times*. Available from: big5.china.com. cn/chinese/zhuanti/xxsb/1154431.htm (accessed 13 May 2015).

Tsai, W. H. and N. Dean. 2015. 'Lifting the veil of the CCP's mishu system: Unrestricted informal politics within an authoritarian regime'. *China Journal* 73: 158–85. doi.org/10.1086/679273.

Wangyi. 2013. 'Eight Regulations has no effect because too many government officials come here'. [In Chinese]. *Wangyi*, 10 December. Available from: news.163.com/13/1210/03/9FN08TGJ0001124J_ all.html#p1 (accessed 2 June 2015).

Wedeman, A. 2000. 'Budgets, extra-budgets, and small treasuries: Illegal monies and local autonomy in China'. *Journal of Contemporary China* 9(25): 489–511. doi.org/10.1080/713675947.

Wedeman, A. 2012. *Double Paradox: Rapid Growth and Rising Corruption in China*. Ithaca, NY: Cornell University Press. doi.org/10.7591/ cornell/9780801450464.001.0001.

Wu, A. M. 2014. *Governing Civil Service Pay in China*. Copenhagen: Nordic Institute of Asian Studies.

Xinhua. 2014. 'Over 50 star hotels want to downgrade or remove stars'. [In Chinese]. *Xinhua*, 19 January. Available from: news.xinhuanet. com/politics/2014-01/19/c_119033709.htm (accessed 2 June 2015).

Yin, H. 2011. 'When will three public expenditures not be a hot topic?' [In Chinese]. *Nanfengchuang* 5: 24–6.

9

Accountability reform, parliamentary oversight and the role of performance audit in Australia

Zahirul Hoque and Des Pearson[1]

Introduction

In its *Budget Paper No. 4, 2015–16: Agency Resourcing*, the Australian Government sets out a 'smaller government' reform agenda aimed at transforming and modernising the public service while eliminating waste and duplication (Commonwealth of Australia 2015: 1). The government is methodically examining all aspects of the public sector, from the functions of agencies to how they operate and are structured. Further, specific reforms in the 2015–16 budget are making a material contribution to budget repair while improving the responsiveness and effectiveness of government. Key elements of the smaller government reforms include: 1) reducing the size of the Commonwealth public service; 2) public sector wage restraint; 3) functional and efficiency reviews; and 4) streamlining government bodies.

1   An earlier version of this chapter was presented at the 2015 Greater China–Australia Dialogue on Public Administration Workshop on 'Value for Money' in Taipei (14–15 November). The authors would like to thank Andrew Podger and Tanja Porter for their constructive advice on an earlier draft of this chapter. Research assistance by Thiru Thiagarajah is also acknowledged.

These changes create a greater demand for reform of organisational strategic priorities and involve related issues such as organisational structure, accounting and accountability systems, strategic planning, performance management and reporting and value for money in public sector organisations (Lapsley and Pettigrew 1994; Hood 1995; Hoque and Moll 2001; Hoque 2015). This chapter focuses on the relationships between performance management, parliamentary oversight and performance (or value-for-money) auditing in the context of the Australian Government's reform agendas for the past two decades. It describes how the audit role has expanded from compliance to performance and the changing nature of the relationship between the audit office, the executive and the legislature.

The remainder of the chapter is organised in the following manner. Section two discusses the nature of accountability and the structure of government, section three presents a discussion on the state of audit roles in Australia and section four presents the research evidence on the challenges involved in performance auditing. This is followed by a discussion on the performance of the auditor-general. The final section concludes by outlining some lessons that can be learned from Australia's experience by other nations across the globe.

The nature of accountability and the structure of government

Public accountability exposes the choices of decision-makers to public scrutiny, to being discussed and criticised in public (Steffek 2010). If one is accountable then one is answerable for one's decisions and actions. Various forms of accountability have been developed by academics consistent with these ideas (Hood 1995; Pollitt et al. 1999; Jones et al. 2010; Hoque 2015).

Broadbent and Laughlin (2003) draw a distinction between two forms of government accountability structures—namely, political accountability and managerial accountability. Political accountability is when governments are accountable to their electors for the authority granted to them; managerial accountability is when they are made accountable for the responsibilities delegated to them. The literature discusses the separation of politics from administration, suggesting that politicians are responsible for policies and professional administrators are responsible for administration through politicians to the legislature.

In Western democracies, governments exercise control over society, which, in turn, votes to elect them into power. However, although the voting public has the power to elect these bodies, it does not have the power to dictate practical action, which leaves governments in a powerful position. Parliaments are a complex nexus of relationships and authority and, as this grows, it becomes even more difficult to manage them. This has encouraged the burgeoning of parliamentary committees in many jurisdictions.

The Public Accounts Committee (PAC) is one such parliamentary committee. It was established to review the expenditure of government and ensure public funds are spent in an effective, efficient, economical and ethical manner (James 2009; Jones and Jacobs 2009; Khan and Hoque 2016). The PAC scrutinises the reports on government entities tabled by the auditor-general and holds the executive responsible for acting on them. Broadbent and Laughlin (2003) argue that increasing public pressure on governments has broadened the scope of political accountability to encompass managerial accountability. Although this has not bestowed direct control of administration, governments can be held accountable for the legitimacy and implementation of their decisions and be pressured to 'steer' societal institutions and organisations. In this context, Pelizzo and Stapenhurst (2013) distinguish between vertical accountability; horizontal accountability as existing forms of government accountability. Vertical accountability is where citizens, mass media and civil society seek to enforce standards of good performance on officials and horizontal accountability is where state institutions (particularly supreme audit institutions) play the vital role of oversight of other public institutions, agencies and branches of government.

Legislatures legislate, but it is also the responsibility of the legislature to oversee the actions of the executive, to ensure what is executed is in line with what is legislated (Pelizzo and Stapenhurst 2013). Indeed, the legislature takes on the role of watchdog for all government activities. In the next two paragraphs, the role of this oversight function under the parliamentary and presidential systems of government is discussed. The differences between them serve to highlight the different conceptions of the auditing function.

Under the Westminster parliamentary system, the executive is formed from within the legislative branch of government. The head of the government (the prime minister or chancellor) and the cabinet (or executives made up of members of the government) sit together in the legislature, which makes the executive dependent on the legislature's confidence. The executive is responsible to the legislature, which may remove it with a vote of no confidence. The legislature holds the government to account on behalf of the citizens.

In contrast, the presidential system is characterised by the separation of powers, meaning the president and the cabinet (executive) are not and cannot be Members of Parliament (MPs) and do not require the legislature's confidence. According to the separation-of-powers doctrine, the legislature in a presidential system is considered an independent and coequal branch of government, along with both the judiciary and the executive. In presidential systems, both the legislature and the government are accountable directly to the public; the legislature's role is more that of an oversight institution (Pelizzo and Stapenhurst 2013).

In both systems, the legislature has an oversight function and an enforceability function. To implement the oversight function, there are parliamentary committees, question time and review and approval of certain government appointments. To carry out this function effectively, the legislature asks the government to provide information on policy proposals to be approved by the legislature and on programs and policies implemented by the government. They assess what the expected results are and whether they were achieved, and whether implementing a policy was consistent with the funds that were appropriated. This makes governments accountable for their actions, and each and every aspect of a government's activity can be scrutinised (Pelizzo and Stapenhurst 2013; Khan and Hoque 2016).

In the parliamentary system, PACs and the supreme audit institutions play a vital role in enabling the legislature to carry out the legislative oversight function effectively, making governments accountable. The very first PAC in Australia came into existence as early as the nineteenth century and, since then, it has remained in existence under various names. More recently, specialised audit and public accounts committees have been adopted in presidential systems, suggesting a dynamic approach to the accountability function (Pelizzo and Stapenhurst 2013; Khan and Hoque 2016).

As mentioned, the legislature is responsible for making the elected government responsible for its actions. Thus, the prime minister and ministers (the executive) are answerable to the legislature and accountable for implementing policy decisions effectively, efficiently, economically and ethically. Public sector accounting and accountability in Australia are products of the constitutional requirements of representative government (Funnell et al. 2012). The broad framework of financial accountability, including the mechanisms of accountability for the Commonwealth Government, comprises the *Constitution Act 1901*, the *Auditor-General Act 1997* and the *Public Governance Performance and Accountability Act 2013* (which recently replaced the *Financial Management and Accountability Act 1997* and the *Commonwealth Authorities and Corporations Act 1997*). The PAC was originally established under the *Public Accounts and Audit Committee Act 1951*. It reviews the reports tabled by the auditor-general's office on behalf of the parliament to assist it to hold the executive accountable for outcomes.

The Commonwealth of Australia's PAC is known as the Commonwealth Joint Committee of Public Accounts and Audit (JCPAA). In addition, because Australia is a federation of self-governed states and territories, each state and territory has its own PAC or an equivalent. Each is a parliamentary committee that scrutinises the activities of government, including the performance of government agencies. The purpose of the committee remains unchanged from its earliest days—namely, to hold government agencies accountable for the legality, efficiency and effectiveness of their operations. Although internationally it seems unusual for the chair of such a committee to be a member of the government, it is the norm across Australian jurisdictions. According to Funnell et al. (2012: 100):

> Since its resurrection, the Public Accounts Committee's operations have been carried out with a very high level of co-operation between the different sides of politics. The committee has endeavoured to direct its investigations away from matters which could reduce the discussion to political point-scoring and emphasise issues which will enhance the Parliament's oversight of the Executive.

Amendments to the *Public Accounts and Audit Committee Act 1951* strengthened the Commonwealth PAC's relationship with the auditor-general and made the committee the auditor-general's financial guardian, hence the name: Commonwealth Joint Committee of Public Accounts and Audit. While nominally part of the executive arm of government (and subject to the *Public Service Act 1999*), the auditor-general is also 'an officer of the parliament' under the *Auditor-General Act*. As Funnell et al. (2012: 101) comment:

> A significant innovation [was] the Committee's right to approve or reject any candidates for the post of Auditor-General. The Auditor-General is similar to the JCPAA in that both, theoretically, carry out their functions on behalf of the Parliament. Both, in other words, are answerable to the Parliament and only to the Parliament. From each of the investigations carried out by the Australian National Audit Office (ANAO) reports will emerge which will be transmitted to the Parliament through the JCPAA. The JCPAA may not examine each report in great detail, however, preferring instead to be prompted by the Auditor-General towards potentially significant areas of investigation. During its investigations, the JCPAA is assisted by representatives from the ANAO and the Department of Finance and Deregulation.

Audit role: The shift from compliance to performance

The report of the Royal Commission on Australian Government Administration (Coombs 1976; also known as the Coombs Report) proposed program budgeting and more emphasis on effectiveness and efficiency. This was not pursued until 1983, when John Dawkins, who was both the minister for finance and the minister for the public service, pushed public sector reform. Another key initiative that year was the publishing of the forward estimates, which had a profound effect on political debates that still applies. But, ahead of the Dawkins reforms, there were the first moves to 'efficiency audits' under the Fraser Government in the late 1970s. The finance department's subsequent push (including through the Financial Management Improvement Program) for wider reforms that focused on results influenced the ANAO to go further in the 1980s. Pat Barrett, as a senior officer in the Department of Finance at the time (and later to become the auditor-general), was very influential in this process. Research evidence suggests that the performance audit was strongly influenced by what is now known as New Public Management (NPM). The International Organization of Supreme Audit Institutions (INTOSAI 2004: 11) defined performance auditing as: 'An independent examination of the efficiency and effectiveness of government undertakings, programs or organisations, with due regard to economy, and the aim of leading to improvements.'

This definition highlights the fact that performance auditing is an evaluating activity and is concerned with the merit, worth or value of something or a product of a process. It is not just about compliance, which concerns the legal authority and proper reporting of finances and management activity. Performance audits have been criticised as potentially compromising the ability of the auditor-general to provide independent and effective oversight of the implementation of government policies, as they are influenced by the auditor-general and are lacking in objectivity, hence presenting the risk of legitimising or criticising government policies (Gendron et al. 2001, 2007).

In 1989, Peter Hamburger studied the evolution of 'efficiency' audits from an Australian perspective. He said:

> Efficiency audit was proposed as part of an ambitious set of changes designed to increase the accountability and responsiveness of public sector agencies to their political masters and their clients. It was implemented in isolation with a justification that had shifted to value-for-money. (Hamburger 1989: 3)

He went on to argue that, from its humble beginnings:

> The audit office had evolved by the 1970s into a modern audit agency staffed by professional accountants. The systems-based audit was on the horizon and Auditor-General [Duncan] Craik had nudged the Office some way towards a performance orientation with his project audits. In 1979 legislation marked a much larger shift from the certainty of compliance audit to the difficult and subjective evaluation of performance. (Hamburger 1989: 8)

In June 1999, then Commonwealth auditor-general Pat Barrett highlighted the nature of contemporary public administration and his office's role in auditing the contemporary public sector as follows:

> ANAO's role is to provide assurance to the Parliament and the Australian community on these two aspects, that is, public sector performance and accountability for that performance. While the public sector reforms demand a greater focus on achieving efficient and effective outcomes for citizens, we also need to recognise that such outcomes also depend importantly on robust and credible administrative and management processes. In short, good processes should ensure good outcomes. They are complements, not alternatives. (Barrett 1999: 56)

Barrett (1999) addresses the issue of whether performance audits risk involving the auditor-general in politics by distinguishing the auditor-general's performance audit functions from auditing the performance of ministers and from examining or reporting on the appropriateness of government policy. However, he says the performance audits can, and do, evaluate how effectively and efficiently government policy has been implemented. He identifies four areas of interest in contemporary public administration audits: contract management, corporate governance, risk management and control and privatisation. These areas are a result of growing private sector participation in public sector activity, resulting from the NPM emphasis on competition. Under the NPM reforms, the public sector is subject to increased levels of scrutiny of its performance and effectiveness and, in many areas, it is subject to competitive processes. Performance assessment covers a range of measures, both qualitative and quantitative, and meeting legislative, community service and international obligations for equity in service delivery and for high standards of ethical behaviour.

The ANAO (2008: 3) defines performance audit as 'an independent, objective and systematic assessment of public sector entities' programs, resources, information systems, performance measures, monitoring systems and legal and policy compliance'. Barrett (2012) identified maintaining parliamentary and public confidence in the coverage, timeliness and outcomes of performance audits as a major issue, followed by successful implementation of the recommendations and conclusions. This requires the confidence, cooperation, involvement and commitment of the organisation and the people being audited—important ingredients for the success of the performance audit. There can be an expectations gap in this area. The organisation/people at the strategic planning and programming stages of performance auditing can provide favourable results for both the auditor and the auditee.

McKay (2003) explores two generations of performance evaluation in the public sector in Australia: pre-1997 and post-1997 reforms. The principle behind the pre-1997 reforms was to 'let the managers manage' (McKay 2003: 9). It focused on the devolution of powers and responsibilities, encouraging better performance and providing much greater autonomy. The government promoted program management and budgeting, focusing on the efficiency and effectiveness of government programs through sound management practices, collection of performance information and the regular conduct of program evaluations. The Department of Finance and the then Public Service Board were responsible for guidance material on these principles. Central departments also participated in measuring program effectiveness and joint management reviews of programs. However, the Department of Finance formed the view that the progress made was insufficient and proposed a firmer top-down evaluation strategy to improve program performance. The program evaluation strategy put in place involved evaluating every program every three to five years and requiring all new policy proposals to refer to evaluation evidence and to describe how future evaluation was to be conducted. According to McKay (2003), the new program evaluation strategy had one serious limitation, in that it paid insufficient attention to the regular collection, use and reporting of performance information and did not use tools such as management information systems and performance indicators effectively, making it difficult to enforce.

The ANAO played a crucial role in program evaluation in this first generation with 'efficiency audits' and publishing two 'better practice guides', reminding departments about the importance of systematically planning their evaluation activity. This strong support for evaluation by the ANAO continues today with its 'performance audit' providing invaluable support for Australia's performance evaluation and management system (McKay 2003).

The second generation of reforms (post-1997) focused on the introduction of accrual accounting in the federal budget and a new 'outcomes and outputs' framework replacing program budgeting. This led to benchmarking of the unit cost of government outputs (service delivery), which facilitated further market testing and contracting out. Budget appropriations were based on stated 'outcomes' and moved away from a traditional focus on spending (inputs). The formal evaluation system of the first generation disappeared, although, from 2004–05 onwards, ministers who wished to acquire new program funding (via a submission to cabinet) for fixed-term programs were still required to review the program's performance to ensure it was achieving its objectives. The Department of Finance and Administration (previously known as the Department of Finance) prepared terms of reference to guide such reviews but with no requirement for review of ongoing programs. The Department of Finance and Administration described this new-generation performance evaluation and management system as a devolved approach

(Russell 2003, cited in McKay 2003). The then Australian auditor-general characterised these reforms as deregulation of evaluation (Barrett 2001, cited in McKay 2003).

When the ANAO conducted performance audits of a sample of departments' and agencies' annual reports to the parliament, this new generation of 'outcomes and outputs' framework was considered inadequate. The 2001 ANAO audit found:

> while the performance reporting of agencies did focus on outcome indicators, these indicators were inadequate to measure actual outcomes of government activities because reported indicators are often influenced by factors beyond the agencies' control and which mask any direct effects of the agencies themselves. (McKay 2003: 15)

It concluded:

> there was a strong argument for conducting evaluations and reviews as a complement to performance indicators so that the relative importance of the agencies' performance vis-a-vis external factors can be assessed. The ANAO also noted that the performance information did not always include targets, and where it did they were often vague or ambiguous. (McKay 2003: 15)

In summary, the ANAO found that annual reports do define outcomes clearly, but the provision of accurate information to assess performance was not supported by adequate data quality and coherence due to lack of standards and procedures. As McKay argues:

> ANAO concluded that 'Performance information' had not been presented and analysed in annual reports in a way that would allow Parliamentarians and other stakeholders to interpret and fully understand results. (McKay 2003: 15)

There is also dissatisfaction from parliamentary committees, particularly in relation to definitional changes from year to year on the performance information provided (McKay 2003). ANAO performance audits revealed that, in spite of the second-generation (outcomes-and-outputs) framework having been in place for over five years, the information base was inadequate for the necessary achievement of the strategic objectives of that framework (McKay 2003)

It has now been over a decade since McKay's article on the performance evaluation history and there have been many further developments. However, in a recent article, Lewis (2012: 312), quoting the ANAO's 2011 annual report, notes that, in 2011, the ANAO completed a performance audit of the quality of performance information in portfolio budget statements (PBSs). The report found that weaknesses observed by the ANAO and others in earlier assessments remain stubbornly persistent, particularly in relation to the lack of consistency and quality of performance information.

The auditor-general is responsible under the *Auditor-General Act 1997* for the provision of audit services to the parliament and public sector entities. The two significant functions of the auditor-general are the performance audits and the financial statement audits. Performance audits by the ANAO highlight the need to continue to strengthen program performance measurement and reporting. This has resulted in establishing frameworks within entities to guide performance measurement activity. The key performance indicators (KPIs) set appropriate baselines and benchmarks for program implementation, and reporting on appropriate KPIs informs stakeholders of the progress of those programs. There were amendments to the *Auditor-General Act 1997* in December 2011 that provided the auditor-general with the explicit authority to audit the suitability of entities' KPIs and the completeness and accuracy of their reporting (ANAO 2012–13)

The ANAO follows continuous improvement practices to enhance the quality of performance audits, and state and territory offices follow suit. The most recent performance audit (2012) by the Victorian Auditor-General's Office (VAGO) outlines the extent to which VAGO performance audit recommendations were adopted and monitored. The Victorian Auditor-General does not have powers to enforce recommendations made to government agencies; however, findings indicate:

> Agencies reported significant acceptance of—and activity in response to—our 2012–13 performance audit recommendations. This demonstrates the relevance and value of these recommendations and shows that agencies are working to address audit issues. However, some agencies can improve the clarity and completeness of their responses, and could address delays in commencing and completing actions. This will help agencies to rectify the issues raised by audits in a thorough and timely way. (VAGO 2014–15: 5)

Another observation by the Victorian Auditor-General is that local government councils' performance reporting remains inadequate. Inadequate quality and availability of performance information have reduced councils' accountability for performance and have impeded their capacity to address the issues (VAGO 2012). The VAGO report (2012: 7) identifies the following recurring themes:

- Poor financial and asset management practices were identified repeatedly, offering little assurance that councils' long-term financial management is robust.

- A lack of effective policies, planning, monitoring and evaluation, including data quality assurance was identified in multiple audits, reducing assurance that councils are operating efficiently and in compliance with relevant obligations.

- Inadequate oversight of procurement processes was an ongoing issue, despite similar issues being identified 10 years earlier.

According to the VAGO report (2012: 7), 'these issues are due in part to deficiencies in the quality and availability of performance information to managers and councillors. This impedes their capacity to take corrective action'. The report argues:

> performance weaknesses also reflect resource constraints at councils, the administrative burden of compliance with state and Commonwealth requirements, and the difficulty of attracting and retaining skilled staff, particularly in regional and rural areas. (VAGO 2012: 7)

In conclusion, Australia is now well experienced in performance auditing complementing broader performance management reforms and is at least comparable with other developed countries in their use. It has largely avoided the risks identified by some scholars of entering into the political field. Recent changes to legislation, the high adoption rate of audit recommendations and other developments in the arena of performance audit will continue to strengthen the overall impact of performance audit in meeting the strategic objectives of government program evaluation, which are transparency, efficiency, effectiveness, economy and ethical administration. The audit activity has helped to improve performance management in Australia, identifying weaknesses in various public sector reform developments since the 1980s and highlighting directions for further improvement.

Challenges for the new role for audit under performance-based accountability

This section discusses the challenges of performance-based auditing for the public sector. In so doing, the findings of researchers are highlighted in relation to the shift in the role of audit such as the capacity of MPs to undertake new oversight roles, success factors for performance accountability and the independence of the auditor-general, among others.

Coghill et al. (2014) add to the literature of accountability by recommending formal induction and development programs for MPs to enhance their capacity to undertake new oversight responsibilities. As many parliamentary oversight functions occur through parliamentary committees, the capacity of committees to perform these functions is effectively largely contingent on the knowledge, skills and abilities of individual committee members. They recognise that parliament, the legal infrastructure and parliamentary culture are important; however, they recommend developing parliament's oversight capacity through MPs' professional development programs.

O'Dea (2012, 2015), in his study of PACs across Australia, identified six key success factors. He refers to the PAC as one arm of government (parliament) competing against another (the executive). This, he says, is not surprising in the context of Australia's adversarial political system, however, both the executive and the parliament can operate well together through the PAC in a balanced way so that, ultimately, the public wins. The six success factors for the PAC he identifies are impartiality, the stage in the political cycle, the resources available, parliament's level of interest, the level of media involvement and a healthy relationship with the audit office.

Clark and De Martinis (2003) compare the enabling legislation of four officers of the Victorian state parliament in terms of their powers, independence, funding and mandate, as well as the accountability mechanisms available to parliament in terms of their appointment, tenure and oversight. Their study used a two-part independence and accountability framework as a basis to examine the enabling legislation. The four officers studied are the auditor-general, the ombudsman, the regulator-general and the director of public prosecutions. The role of auditor-general is of particular relevance to the PAC. This analysis revealed ways in which the relationship between these officers and the parliament may be further strengthened, including through amendments to the enabling legislation—for example, requiring the auditor-general to submit an annual work plan to parliament. Arguably, this requirement could be seen to inhibit the scope and independence of the auditor-general—for example, if parliament tried to constrain the auditor-general either away from what the executive is concerned about politically (noting the executive has command of the lower house of parliament) or towards narrow political concerns of the opposition or minor parties, and not where the auditor-general considers the serious risks are.

Jones and Jacobs (2009) explored the impact of NPM on the PAC of the State of Victoria, Australia. They ask the question: what makes public accounts committees work? Among several other findings, they reiterate the need for political will to be applied to overseeing the government. Trenordan (2001) describes the issues for public servants who are questioned during committee hearings. The PAC is a vital accountability mechanism and it is not unusual for the committee to have questions regarding reports submitted by the auditor-general. There has been an increasing demand for public servants to appear before parliamentary committees to answer questions and explain or justify their own and their department's actions. Although lower house ministers do not usually appear before senate committees, there is always a government senator to represent the minister; however, most questions are answered by public servants. This is consistent with English and Guthrie's (2000) argument that there has been a shift to public servants being held accountable rather than ministers. However, the process of questioning public servants leads to much political gaming to get the public servants to embarrass their ministers, rather than to pursue genuine performance matters. Trenordan (2001) concludes there is a need to find some balance between the accountability of public servants for administration and the political responsibility of ministers.

Crawford et al. (2006) focus on reforms to ministerial responsibilities and conclude that ministers must make all reasonable efforts to meet any request made by the committee for information that is relevant to their inquiry, including facilitating the presence of public servants. Laing (2007) draws attention to various legal and technical aspects of public accounting and their relevance to accountability, including for performance. Departmental appropriations authorise spending from what is called the Consolidated Revenue Fund (CRF). The CRF is a notional fund where all government revenue is accumulated for appropriation towards government expenditure; this provides important discipline both for comprehensive oversight of revenue and for promoting prioritisation of all expenditure allocations. The rules of appropriations are that monies appropriated for specific services must be spent for that particular service, and accounted for. This provides additional discipline and the basis for proper accountability. In the past, there have been cases where a mismatch has occurred between the formal appropriations and the actual purpose for which funds were spent. These variations may be dismissed as technicalities of accounting; however, their impact may have far-reaching consequences for accountability, revealing poorly administered or inappropriate expenditure on programs, which rightly attracts public and media review. Laing (2007) concludes that accounting and accountability are not synonymous: while technical aspects of accounting are based on a set of rules, overall accountability is based on broader criteria of appropriate, effective, efficient, economical and ethical allocation of resources. Andrew Podger (Chapter 6, this volume) picks up on other important technical issues here, such as MPs' concerns that the outcomes framework gives too great a licence to ministers (allowing very broad interpretations of the purpose of appropriations), particularly when the wording is vague, leading to the return to program appropriation arrangements.

James (2009) investigated the requirement that governments respond to parliamentary committee reports and considered to what extent government responses are important in evaluating the effectiveness of committees. In Australia, the federal government formally responds to committee reports by way of a statement presented to one or both houses of parliament. James (2009) refers to media releases that state millions of dollars have been wasted on reviewing and making recommendations for better response mechanisms for parliamentary committee inquiries, including the PAC. Owing to this lack of response, committees have been deemed ineffective and wasteful. However, it is a misnomer to state that the government response to a parliamentary committee inquiry is the only factor determinative of the effectiveness of a committee, even if it certainly remains an important measure. In the Commonwealth, auditors-general reports are almost always the focus of senate estimates hearings, whether or not the government agrees with the auditor-general or the PAC. For a while, the government used to report regularly to the parliament on the progress of its agreed actions after the auditor-general's reports, but that practice has now disappeared. It is possible that the government policy may still change as a result of a committee inquiry irrespective of the lack of formal government response. James (2009) concludes that responding to recommendations made by the committee in the subsequent annual report may be an effective way of dealing with the issue.

Pearson (2012), the former auditor-general of the State of Victoria, sheds light on the changing nature of the auditor-general's role. He argues that Victoria's audit legislation across the 1970s, 1980s and 1990s gave rise to the kinds of modern audit reports that parliament now uses—the distillation of targeted audits of systemic issues and the provision of opinions on the reliability and accuracy of agencies' own financial reports—and that '[f]or the first time, Parliaments could ask their auditor to report to them not just "how much"—but "how well"' (Pearson 2012: 175). This went beyond the realm of traditional financial audit and bestowed a more contentious role on the auditor-general. The executive became answerable to a critic (the auditor-general) who is able to probe into operational matters and report directly to the elected legislature. This shift to a more active, and more controversial, role for auditors-general made necessary the next phase of public sector audit legislation in Victoria: the 'independence reforms' (Pearson 2012). Victoria's *Constitution Act 1975* introduced special protection for the independence of the auditor-general, including complete discretion in his or her functions or powers, with new accountability requirements for the auditor-general and his or her office, notably in the area of performance audits and the requirement for the auditor-general to consult extensively with a committee of the parliament in determining his or her audit program (Pearson 2012).

Ojiha (2012) studied the effectiveness of parliamentary committees in Queensland. A total of 235 committee reports were consulted and interviews were conducted with parliamentarians. Specifically, in relation to the PAC, Ojiha (2012) analysed the various reports and ministerial responses to committee reports and found that 81 per cent of the recommendations were fully accepted, 13 per cent were partly accepted and 4 per cent were not accepted by the executive during the study period. However, he cautions that this result should not be interpreted as the executive's willingness to adopt recommendations, because the more difficult recommendations that impact on the executive were not adopted or only partially adopted.

Performance of the auditor-general

Academic research (Hoque and Adams 2011; Hoque 2015; Sutheewasinnon and Saikaew 2015; Khan and Hoque 2016) has shown that the reform process in the public sector may not be driven solely by economic rationality, but rather could also involve 'window dressing' by organisations. Within such an environment, public sector entities may be undergoing reforms not to achieve managerial efficiency but to legitimise themselves to the electorate and other constituents, such as government and the media.

Based on the authors' observation of several government agencies' performance reporting to the VAGO, the advent of performance audits has undoubtedly contributed, along with other public sector reform and improvement initiatives, to improved government performance in Australia. Overall standards of program delivery have steadily improved even as the size of the task (as indicated by the growth in population) has grown. Nevertheless, given the lack of maturity and cohesiveness of performance reporting in the public sector, it is not possible to reliably quantify or otherwise reliably measure this improvement or to attribute responsibility.

In this context, it is also important to again recognise that the audit role has no executive authority to impose a penalty or demand particular action: the role of the auditor-general, as established by legislation, is to undertake audits and express an audit opinion. The role of the auditor is therefore to provide assurance and to inform the parliament so the parliament can hold the executive to account. The persuasive effect of the 'sanction' of a publicly expressed authoritative opinion or report, however, cannot be underestimated.

Auditors-general nevertheless are on the record as seeking to leverage their assurance role, to provide adequate audit coverage of the highest risk and most material areas of administration. In other words, their audit planning and reports can be used as a catalyst for improvements in the standard of public administration, both in the immediate areas subject to audit and more broadly across the public sector. This approach can be illustrated with two examples.

First, the Victorian Auditor-General, in his 2014–15 *Annual Report* (VAGO 2014–15: 6), refers to '[d]oing the right topics at the right time' and explains that the *Annual Plan 2015–16* was developed with a particular emphasis on providing a nimble and well-targeted program of audits. Reference was also made to a key factor in addressing the audit task: increased engagement with agencies, MPs and the general public. This approach indicates a strong alignment of audit activity with topic areas warranting priority attention. Exceptions reported are then followed up by responsible management, oversight within the executive by central agencies such as the departments of treasury or finance and by parliament via the PAC. This provides a strong process to ensure appropriate remedial action is taken that will lead to improvement in program delivery.

Second, the ANAO reports on its own performance, using the standard outcome and programs framework. According to its 2014–15 annual report, the ANAO's Outcome 1 is to improve public sector performance and accountability through independent reporting on Australian government administration to the parliament, the executive and the public. Program 1.2: Performance Audit Services has three objectives:

- To report objectively on the performance of Australian government programs and activities, including opportunities for improvement, by undertaking a program of independent performance audits and related reports for the information of parliament, the executive and the public.
- To contribute to improvements in Australian government administration by identifying and promoting better practice.
- To contribute to the auditing profession and public sector developments nationally and internationally.

The performance criteria applied by the ANAO (2014–15: 7) are stated as the potential benefits to public administration, reducing risks to reputation and service delivery and the extent of previous audit and review coverage. These all point to leveraging the assurance role to achieve improvements in the performance of government programs.

In terms of seeking to influence improved program management more broadly, in addition, auditors-general are required to table their reports in parliament, where they are on the public record, debated in parliament and commented on in the media, and also to make presentations on their work at conferences and seminars. This leads to the broader public sector being alerted to shortcomings identified by the audit—importantly, for attention by the management of comparable programs.

A scorecard is implemented that outlines the performance of the ANAO in areas relating to the satisfaction of parliamentarians with ANAO activity, measured by a survey and the percentage of audit recommendations accepted by the JCPAA. The indicators of satisfaction are coverage, timeliness and quality of activity measured by a survey of the JCPAA. The value added to the auditee is measured by the percentage of audits that add value to the public sector, as acknowledged by the public sector body audited. The financial impact of the ANAO's work is highlighted in three reports from 2004 to 2006, which indicate an annual saving of about $21–$32 million could be realised if ANAO audit recommendations were implemented (ANAO 2004, 2006, cited in Colin and Jay 2010). Table 9.1 presents an extract of the ANAO's outputs–outcome framework.

Table 9.1 The ANAO output–outcome framework

Outcome 1. Improvement in public administration: Independent assessment of the performance of Commonwealth public sector activities, the scope for improving efficiency and administrative effectiveness.		
Outcome 2. Assurance: Independent assurance of Commonwealth public sector financial reporting, administration, control and accountability.		
Output group 1	Output group 2	Output group 3
Performance audit services	Information support services	Assurance audit services
Performance audit reports	Assistance to the parliament, national and international	Financial statement audit reports
Other audit and related reports	Representation Client seminars Better practice guides	Other assurance reports Business support Process audit reports Protective security audit reports

Source: Adapted from ANAO (2005–06).

Colin and Jay (2010) explore the performance audit practices across the United Kingdom, Australia, Canada, the United States and New Zealand. Of particular relevance are their findings of the impact of performance reports in Australia. They state the ANAO demonstrates an obligation to systematically record and measure value through the capture of key information of its activity, referring to the above reporting by the ANAO of its own performance.

Each year, the ANAO submits a PBS to parliament setting out the outcomes to be achieved and outputs to be delivered in that year. An outputs–outcome framework guides the ANAO and the PBS scorecard, which provides a breakdown of performance against the framework. Both quantitative and qualitative measures are used to ascertain the performance of the ANAO against its objectives; these include surveys of activity with clients, reviews of audit quality, feedback from participants in ANAO seminar activity and the number of reports produced (Colin and Jay 2010: 58).

A recent initiative developed in the VAGO has been to more formally distil and promulgate key audit themes. This has now developed into volume two of its annual report (VAGO 2014–15). The VAGO's program of financial and performance audits has covered hundreds of agencies, with each audit leading to recommendations for improvements specific to that agency. Audits are designed to be tools for improvement and VAGO has sought to help agencies learn from the experience of others; VAGO analyses their reports and develops a summary of the most frequent and significant audit findings. While this has been done since 2009, it is now at the stage where the themes are being included in volume two of the annual report and include self-assessment questions for each theme, developed from the criteria applied to agencies during the audit process. Collectively, these approaches and initiatives strongly indicate that performance audit has contributed to improved government performance.

Conclusions

Using evidence primarily from Australia, this chapter has shown how government reforms over the past two decades have changed the nature of performance audits undertaken in government agencies.

There are a number of lessons from the Australian context that may be transferable, including to developing nations. First and foremost is the strong foundation provided by the financial audit. Since colonisation, jurisdictions in Australia have had a strong emphasis on probity and regularity. This has served the nation well and enabled a progression from, first, a labour-intensive, transaction-based approach to auditing to, second, a systems-based approach that established the reliability of systems and processes that encouraged a sampling approach to auditing, and, third, to a risk-based audit approach guided by the principles of risk and materiality of transactions and systems, which enables more focused and cost-effective audit coverage. This final approach provides a higher level of assurance of the regularity of financial reports. From this strong financial auditing base, Australia has added a performance audit role. By focusing on the policies as articulated by the executive and exploring the efficiency and effectiveness (and propriety) of administration in achieving these policy objectives, this has largely kept audits from entering into the political field.

Second, complementing this progression in the auditing approach has been the adoption, more recently, of accrual-based accounting across the public sector. This more comprehensive and integrated approach to accounting for public sector resources has provided more informative and reliable financial reporting. Through the use of traditional financial ratios—such as current and asset replacement ratios—it has also made more transparent whether revenues are covering all (both cash and non-cash) costs and provides a basis for determining the financial sustainability of entities and the sector as a whole.

Finally, developing nations can also benefit from the experience of Australian auditors-general developing a mutually respectful and productive relationship with their public accounts committees. These initiatives generally build on the basic legislative requirements to cooperate for the mutual benefit of the auditor and the committee. Initiatives such as consulting with the PAC during the development of the audit program can have significant benefits to the planning process. Similarly, auditors-general and PACs can benefit from the auditor-general providing tailored briefings to the committee on key matters raised in reports to parliament and by the auditor-general and senior audit staff making themselves available as observers when PACs inquire into reports. This has the advantage of being able to contribute timely observations and advice in relation to matters being contemplated in preparation for an inquiry and those arising in the course of an inquiry. This facilitates more informed and timely deliberations for the PAC while also contributing to more focused follow-up of audit reports and initiation of remedial action by audited entities.

References

Australian National Audit Office (ANAO). 2004. *Corporate Plan.* Canberra: ANAO. Available from: www.anao.gov.au/uploads/documents/ANAO%20Corp%20Plan%.pdf

Australian National Audit Office (ANAO). 2005–06. *Performance Audit Report No. 52.* Canberra: ANAO.

Australian National Audit Office (ANAO). 2006. *The Auditor-General Annual Report 2005–06.* Canberra: ANAO. Available from: www.anao.gov.au/work/annual-report/auditor-general-annual-report-2005-06 (accessed 22 December 2017).

Australian National Audit Office (ANAO). 2008. *Performance Auditing in the Australian National Audit Office.* Canberra: ANAO.

Australian National Audit Office (ANAO). 2011. *Development and implementation of key performance indicators to support the outcomes and programmes framework.* Audit Report No. 5, 2011–12. Canberra: ANAO.

Australian National Audit Office (ANAO). 2012–13. *The Australian Government performance measurement and reporting framework.* Report No. 28 2012–2013. Canberra: ANAO.

Australian National Audit Office (ANAO). 2014–15. *Performance Audit Report No. 52.* Canberra: ANAO.

Barrett, P. 1999. 'Auditing in contemporary public administration'. *Canberra Bulletin of Public Administration* 94: 53–72.

Barrett, P. 2001. 'Evaluation and performance auditing: Sharing the common ground—A review of developments'. Address to the Australasian Evaluation Society, Canberra, 10 October.

Barrett, P. 2012. 'Performance auditing: Addressing real or perceived expectation gaps in the public sector'. *Public Money & Management* 32: 129–36. doi.org/10.1080/09540962.2012.656019.

Broadbent, J. and R. Laughlin. 2003. 'Control and legitimation in government accountability processes: The private finance initiative in the UK'. *Critical Perspectives on Accounting* 14: 23–48. doi.org/10.1006/cpac.2001.0525.

Clark, C. and M. De Martinis. 2003. 'A framework for reforming the independence and accountability of statutory officers of parliament: A case study of Victoria'. *Australian Journal of Public Administration* 62: 32–42. doi.org/10.1111/1467-8500.00312.

Coghill, K., R. Donohue and C. Lewis. 2014. 'Developing parliament's oversight capacity through MPs' professional development'. *Australasian Parliamentary Review* 29(1): 43–53.

Colin, T. and W. Jay. 2010. 'The public value of the National Audit Office'. *International Journal of Public Sector Management* 23: 54–70. doi.org/10.1108/09513551011012321.

Commonwealth of Australia, 2015. *Budget Paper No. 4, 2015–16: Agency Resourcing.* Canberra: Commonwealth of Australia. Available from: budget.gov.au/2015-16/content/bp4/html/index.htm (accessed 22 December 2016).

Coombs, H. C. 1976. *Royal Commission on Australian Government Administration: Report.* [Coombs Report]. Canberra: AGPS.

Crawford, D., O. Hughes, G. Hodge, B. Grant, A. Hunt, R. Mathews, K. Coghill, I. Cunliffe, S. Zifcak, A. Mancini and K. Rozzoli. 2006. 'Why accountability must be renewed: A discussion paper on reform of Government accountability in Australia'. *Australasian Parliamentary Review* 21(2): 10–48.

English, L. and J. Guthrie. 2000. 'Mandate, independence and funding: Resolution of a protracted struggle between parliament and the executive over the powers of the Australian Auditor-General'. *Australian Journal of Public Administration* 59: 98. doi.org/10.1111/1467-8500.00143.

Funnell, W., K. Cooper and L. Lee. 2012. *Public Sector Accounting and Accountability in Australia.* Sydney: UNSW Press.

Gendron, Y., D. J. Cooper and B. Townley. 2001. 'In the name of accountability: State auditing, independence and new public management'. *Accounting, Auditing and Accountability Journal* 14(3): 278–310. doi.org/10.1108/EUM0000000005518.

Gendron, Y., D. J. Cooper and B. Townley. 2007. 'The construction of auditing expertise in measuring government performance'. *Accounting, Organization and Society* 32: 101–29. doi.org/10.1016/j. aos.2006.03.005.

Hamburger, P. 1989. 'Efficiency auditing by the Australian Audit Office: Reform and reaction under three auditors-general'. *Accounting, Auditing & Accountability Journal* 2(3): 1–21. doi.org/10.1108/ EUM0000000001927.

Hood, C. 1995. 'The "new public management" in the 1980s: Variations on a theme'. *Accounting, Organizations and Society* 20: 93–109. doi.org/10.1016/0361-3682(93)E0001-W.

Hoque, Z. (ed.). 2015. *Making Governments Accountable: The role of public accounts committees and national audit offices*. London: Routledge.

Hoque, Z. and C. Adams. 2011. 'The rise and use of balanced scorecard measures in Australian government departments'. *Financial Accountability & Management* 27(3): 308–32. doi.org/10.1111/j. 1468-0408.2011.00527.x.

Hoque, Z. and J. Moll. 2001. 'Public sector reform: Implications for accounting, accountability and performance of state-owned entities— An Australian perspective'. *International Journal of Public Sector Management* 14(4): 304–26. doi.org/10.1108/09513550110395256.

Hoque, Z. and T. Thiagarajah. 2015. 'Public accountability: The role of the auditor-general in legislative oversight'. In Z. Hoque (ed.) *Making Governments Accountable: The role of public accounts committees and national audit offices*. London: Routledge.

International Organization of Supreme Audit Institutions (INTOSAI). 2004. *Implementing Guidelines for Performance Auditing*. Stockholm: INTOSAI Auditing Standards Committee. Available from: www. intosai.org (accessed 22 November 2004).

Jacobs, K. and K. Jones. 2009. 'Legitimacy and parliamentary oversight in Australia: The rise and fall of two public accounts committees'. *Accounting, Auditing & Accountability Journal* 22(1): 3–34. doi.org/10.1108/09513570910922999.

James, C. 2009. 'Government responses to parliamentary committee enquiries'. *Australasian Parliamentary Review* 24(2): 182–96.

Jones, K. and K. Jacobs. 2009. 'Public accounts committees, new public management, and institutionalism: A case study'. *Politics & Policy* 37: 1023. doi.org/10.1111/j.1747-1346.2009.00209.x.

Jones, K., D. Smith and K. Jacobs. 2010. 'An analysis of the source of public accounts committee inquiries: The Australian experience'. *Australasian Parliamentary Review* 25(1): 17–31.

Khan, S. J. and Z. Hoque. 2016. 'Changes in public accounts committee in a less developed democratic country: A field study'. *Financial Accountability and Management* 32(1): 80–103. doi.org/10.1111/faam.12082.

Laing, R. 2007. 'Accounting and accountability'. *Australasian Parliamentary Review* 22(1): 19–27.

Lapsley, I. and A. Pettigrew. 1994. 'Meeting the challenge: Accounting for change'. *Financial Accountability and Management* 10(2): 79–92. doi.org/10.1111/j.1468-0408.1994.tb00146.x.

Lewis, H. 2012. 'Australian public sector performance management: Success or stagnation?' *International Journal of Productivity and Performance Management* 61: 310–28. doi.org/10.1108/17410401211205669.

McKay, K. 2003. 'Two generations of performance evaluation and management system in Australia'. *Canberra Bulletin of Public Administration* (December): 9–20.

O'Dea, J. 2012. 'The role of public accounts committees'. *Australasian Parliamentary Review* 27(1): 191–5.

O'Dea, J. 2015. 'Making a public accounts committee effective: A chair's perspective from the State of New South Wales, Australia'. In Z. Hoque (ed.) *Making Governments Accountable: The role of public accounts committees and national audit offices*. London: Routledge.

Ojiha, S. 2012. 'The effectiveness of parliamentary committees in Queensland: 1996–2001'. *Australasian Parliamentary Review* 27(2): 71–87.

Pearson, D. 2012. 'Trends in public sector audit legislation: From federation to follow-the-dollar'. *Australasian Parliamentary Review* 27(1): 174–6.

Pelizzo, R. and F. Stapenhurst. 2013. *Government Accountability and Legislative Oversight*. Hoboken, NJ: Taylor & Francis.

Pollitt, C., X. Girre, J. Lonsdale, R. Mul, H. Summa and M. Waerness. 1999. *Performance or Compliance? Performance audit and public management in five countries*. Oxford: Oxford University Press. doi. org/10.1093/acprof:oso/9780198296003.001.0001.

Russell, D. 2003. 'Performance management and evaluation: The Australian experience'. In J.-H. Kim (ed.) *Developing a Performance Evaluation System in Korea*. Seoul: Korea Development Institute.

Sutheewasinnon, P. and S. Saikaew. 2015. 'The public accounts committees in Thailand: A short note'. In Z. Hoque (ed.) *Making Governments Accountable, The role of public accounts committees and national audit offices*. London: Routledge.

Steffek, J. 2010. 'Public accountability and the public sphere of international governance'. *Ethics & International Affairs* 24: 45–68. doi.org/10.1111/j.1747-7093.2010.00243.x.

Trenorden, M. 2001. 'Public sector attitudes to parliamentary committees: A chairman's view'. *Australasian Parliamentary Review* 16(2): 97–100.

Victorian Auditor-General's Office (VAGO). 2012. *Performance reporting by local government*. PP No. 126, Session 2010–12. Melbourne: VAGO.

Victorian Auditor-General's Office (VAGO). 2014–15. *Responses to 2012–2013 performance audit recommendations*. PP No. 4, Session 2014–2015. Melbourne: VAGO.

10

The development of performance auditing in Taiwan

Kai-Hung Fang and Tsai-tsu Su

Performance auditing in Taiwan is at an early stage of development. Although the idea of doing an audit based on economy, efficiency and effectiveness criteria has been a feature of the audit law since 1972, the approach did not materialise until 2007, when Auditor-General Ching-Long Lin took office. Since then, the National Audit Office (NAO) has made great efforts to promote performance auditing in Taiwan. For instance, the *Guideline for the NAO on Performance Audit* was published in 2009. It began the process of transferring more financial and human resources from traditional financial audits to performance audits (Lin 2012: 6–7).

However, the transition to performance audits is not an easy task. It involves not only training existing personnel and hiring new personnel with different professional backgrounds, but also fostering a new organisational culture in which NAO staff are open-minded and willing to adopt a new style of auditing. This is inevitably a slowly evolving process. This chapter describes this process. It begins by describing the context in which the NAO makes performance auditing an organisational priority, the efforts taken by the NAO to promote performance audits and its initial achievements. The chapter also discusses feedback from both NAO personnel and auditees. Finally, general discussion and conclusions about the development of performance auditing in Taiwan are presented.

The National Audit Office in transition

The NAO is an independent government agency in Taiwan. As a branch of the Control Yuan,[1] the Office of the Auditor-General, the head of the NAO, shall complete audits and submit annual audit reports to the Legislative Yuan after receiving the annual financial statements of the central government from the Executive Yuan. Due to the constitutional requirement to audit the central government's financial statements, the focus of the auditing has traditionally been placed on financial audits to ensure government agencies spend public funds in accordance with applicable laws and regulations.

The roots of performance auditing can be traced back to 1972, when the *Audit Act 1925* was amended to add two new chapters that required the NAO to evaluate the efficiency and effectiveness of government agencies' budget execution and determine their financial accountabilities accordingly. However, it was not until 2007, when Lin became the auditor-general, that performance auditing became a priority. Lin (2012: 6) proclaimed that strengthening the evaluation of government performance and improving the efficiency and quality of public service provision should be core duties of the NAO (Xu 2009: 28). In 2012, he reaffirmed that the continuous improvement of performance auditing to enhance the value of public funds would be one of the primary objectives of his second term.[2]

The effort of the NAO to place more emphasis on performance auditing is further supported by trends in the international audit community. In the past decade, performance auditing has become increasingly common among supreme audit institutions (SAIs) (Colin and Wiggan 2010), which are the national authorities responsible for scrutinising budget execution and providing independent opinions on how government agencies use public funds. One of the drivers of this trend is the philosophy behind the 'maturity model of SAIs' suggested by the US Government Accountability Office (GAO) (see Figure 10.1).

---

1   The central government in Taiwan has five branches: the Executive Yuan, Legislative Yuan, Judiciary Yuan, Examination Yuan and Control Yuan. According to Article 104 of the Constitution, in the Control Yuan, there shall be an auditor-general who shall be nominated and, with the consent of the Legislative Yuan, appointed by the President of Taiwan. Article 105 states that the auditor-general shall, within three months of presentation by the Executive Yuan of the final accounts of revenue and expenditure, complete the auditing thereof in accordance with law and submit an audit report to the Legislative Yuan.
2   See the NAO's website: www.audit.gov.tw/files/11-1000-138.php (accessed 20 December 2016).

The GAO (2007) argues that SAIs in industrialised countries have traditionally focused on oversight, as indicated at the bottom of the pyramid in Figure 10.1. This concentrates on the purchase of agency inputs and its legality and therefore is important for checks on waste, fraud and abuse. Nevertheless, although this oversight function can enhance financial transparency, combat corruption and ensure accountability, it is not sufficient on its own to help the government fulfil its policy objectives or take more timely and informed actions in an ever-changing society. By adopting performance auditing, SAIs may identify areas of waste and mismanagement that, if eliminated, would permit the same policy or program objectives to be achieved at less expense and areas where the same resources, if used differently, would produce greater value for the same cost (Allen and Tommasi 2001: 352). This type of value-added audit work makes up the middle layer of the pyramid in Figure 10.1 and is designed to provide insights to improve the efficiency and effectiveness of public expenditure.

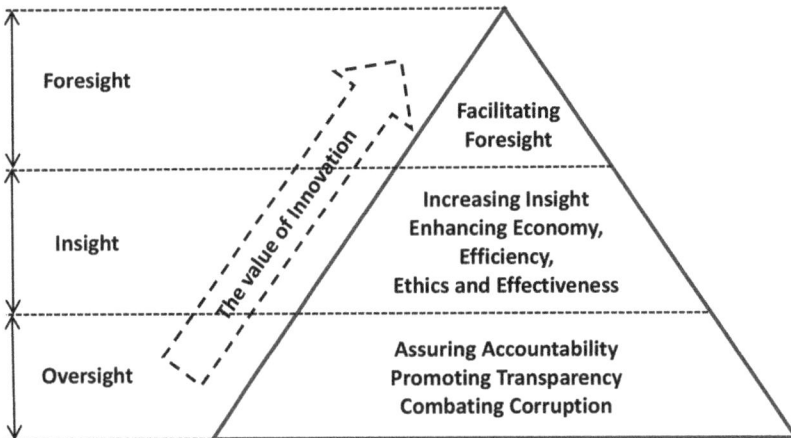

Figure 10.1 The maturity model of SAIs
Sources: GAO (2007); NAO (various years(b): 7).

At the top of the pyramid, according to the GAO (2007), is a foresight function that more mature SAIs should be undertaking. A mature SAI is able to provide policymakers with foresight about emerging trends and help them grasp the long-term implications of current policy paths in a professional, evidence-based and nonpartisan manner.

In summary, under the influence of the maturity model for SAIs, the goal of the NAO in the twenty-first century is to climb up the hierarchy of audit functions. The traditional financial audit concentrates on the basic audit function; its oversight activities deal with aspects of legality and aim to minimise corruption. The newly emphasised performance audits are aimed at both insight and foresight functions to further identify which spending programs or policies are effective and help government agencies take more timely and informed actions to maximise the value of public funds.

Capacity-building in human resources

Table 10.1 demonstrates that the NAO of Taiwan is a relatively stable organisation in terms of the number and average age of staff. From 2001 to 2015, the total number of staff grew by only 2 per cent and the average age increased by less than one year. The NAO employed a group of well-educated professionals. According to the statistics released at the end of 2015, the majority of NAO staff were equipped with professional licences and 92 per cent had a bachelor's degree or above. However, most staff specialised in accounting or procurement regulation and, while familiar with financial audits, they had little experience in performance audits.

In addition, the total number of NAO staff has grown very slowly over the past decade (from 834 in 2001 to 853 in 2015) and, given restrictions on new recruitment imposed on the public sector,[3] it is not expected to increase drastically in the coming years to cope with the additional workload derived from conducting performance audits. Hence, the only way to handle an increased workload is to initiate a capacity-building process so auditors are able to perform their jobs in a smarter and more productive way.

Table 10.1 Total number of NAO staff and their average age

Year	Total number of staff	Average age of staff (years)
2001	834	42.9
2010	823	43.3
2011	836	43.2
2012	815	43.3
2013	855	42.9

---

3   To control the number of government employees, the Legislative Yuan passed the 'Basic Law for Central Government Agency Manpower Allocation' in 2010. It imposes an upper limit on the number of civil servants in the executive branch.

Year	Total number of staff	Average age of staff (years)
2014	859	43.2
2015	853	43.7

Sources: Data collected from NAO (various years(a)).

Table 10.2 Educational level of NAO staff

Year	Education level				Number of licensed staff
	High school	Junior college	Bachelor's degree	Graduate degree	
2001	32 (4%)	208 (25%)	516 (62%)	78 (9%)	113
2010	13 (2%)	107 (13%)	398 (48%)	305 (37%)	462
2011	12 (2%)	93 (11%)	394 (47%)	337 (40%)	484
2012	9 (1%)	84 (10%)	370 (46%)	352 (43%)	501
2013	9 (1%)	77 (9%)	377 (44%)	392 (46%)	531
2014	9 (1%)	70 (8%)	377 (44%)	403 (47%)	640
2015	7 (1%)	62 (7%)	369 (43%)	415 (49%)	828

Sources: Data collected from NAO (various years(a)).

To meet the challenge of evolving from financial to performance auditing, the NAO needs to build up its organisational capacity. One basic requirement is to have sufficient personnel with the knowledge and skills necessary to conduct performance audits. The NAO amended its *Organic Act 1939* in 2010 to allow the recruitment of new auditors with policy analysis, public administration and management expertise. By the end of 2016, the NAO had recruited 52 auditors who were equipped to conduct performance audits to replace retirees and those who had left the NAO. This has brought greater diversity to the specialisation of employees in the NAO.

Furthermore, existing employees are encouraged to acquire performance auditing knowledge and skills through training and attending conferences. To this end, the NAO established a taskforce consisting of auditors skilled in quantitative analysis and social research methods. They introduced program evaluation techniques such as social surveys, in-depth interviews and focus groups for auditors who are in search of new analytical tools with which to evaluate the effectiveness and efficiency of policy programs (Liu 2014: 104). The NAO's training institute also devotes more resources to performance auditing, such as sending staff to the training programs held by the National Academy of Civil Service and to conferences held by professional auditing associations and academia (Lin 2012: 19). Approximately three-quarters of the training hours received by each NAO employee from 2011 to 2015 were related to performance auditing (see Table 10.3). It is evident that the NAO is working hard to provide opportunities for its staff to become more acquainted with performance auditing.

Table 10.3 Performance auditing–related training received

Fiscal year	Numbers attending training	Number of training hours	Training hours per employee	Percentage of performance auditing–related training hours per employee in overall training hours per employee
2011	2,260	36,767	53.83	74.00%
2012	2,087	35,486	53.12	72.26%
2013	2,130	38,118	74.27	72.37%
2014	2,684	46,762	65.77	82.70%
2015	3,618	47,750	67.54	79.51%

Sources: Data collected from NAO (various years(b)).

Redirecting budgets to performance audits

Along with improving human capital to build up organisational capacity, the NAO also triggered a process of allocating more budgetary resources to performance auditing–related activities. While spending related to performance auditing made up 45 per cent of the NAO's total budget in 2009, the remaining 55 per cent comprised spending related to financial auditing. The percentage of performance auditing–related budgets grew slowly but steadily from 2009 to 2015 (NAO various years(a)). In 2015, the budget allocated to performance audits exceeded the budget for financial audits for the first time at the NAO.

Developing audit guidelines and manuals

In the process of capacity-building to carry out more performance audits, the NAO developed several guidelines and manuals to assist frontline auditors. For instance, it released the 'Guideline for the NAO on Performance Audit' in 2009, and amended it several times to ensure it was at the cutting edge of development in the field of performance audit. The guideline is mostly based on the *Performance Audit Guidelines: Key principles* published by the International Organization of Supreme Audit Institutions (INTOSAI 2010). It highlights the values and rules of performance auditing, the importance of better communication between auditors and auditee agencies, the techniques for conducting interviews and social surveys, the requirement to summarise audit evidence and findings, provide background information in audit reports and the need for public access to performance audit reports (Lin 2013: 68). The 'Guideline for the NAO on Performance Audit' is the cornerstone of performance audit activities.

Based on the guideline, the NAO also published a series of manuals and best practices to further expand the knowledge base of its auditors, including a manual for selecting suitable performance audit targets using a risk-assessment approach (Lin 2012: 7; 2013: 66). Another guideline, titled *Basics of Program Evaluation*, was published, in 2014, to assist auditors to understand the complexity of public policy, to pay attention to the diversified needs of internal and external stakeholders and to facilitate more public debate on policy issues (Su and Wang 2015: 93–5).

Outputs of performance auditing

Although the transition from financial auditing to performance auditing is not an easy task, the NAO has steadily moved forward and made some achievements.

The NAO uses various indicators to measure its own annual performance (NAO 2016b). Among them, two indicators are closely related to performance auditing and are worth mentioning: the number of performance audit reports and the number of cases reported to the Control Yuan.

The number of performance audit reports

Following the adage 'what gets measured, gets done', the NAO designates the number of performance audit reports as one of its major indicators in its performance management system. This has introduced strong incentives for NAO employees to strive to reach their performance targets. As shown in Table 10.4, between 2010 and 2015, the actual number of performance reports completed by the NAO exceeded the performance objective each year, with the achievement rates ranging from 107 per cent to 124 per cent for the period examined.

Table 10.4 Number of performance audit reports

Fiscal year	Expected number/actual number	Total	Achievement rate
2010	Expected number	153	107%
	Actual number	163	
2011	Expected number	140	114%
	Actual number	159	
2012	Expected number	142	111%
	Actual number	157	
2013	Expected number	121	114%
	Actual number	138	
2014	Expected number	118	124%
	Actual number	146	
2015	Expected number	119	111%
	Actual number	132	

Source: NAO (various years(b)).

The number of cases reported to the Control Yuan

The number of performance audit reports discussed above is mostly a quantitative measure, which does not deliver much information about the quality of performance auditing. The indicator concerning the number of cases reported to the Control Yuan reveals relatively more information on the quality of performance audits conducted by the NAO.

According to Article 69 of the *Audit Act*, if the NAO considers an audited agency negligent of duty or suffering from major inefficiencies or ineffectiveness, it should report the case to the Control Yuan. The Control Yuan will then conduct further investigation to decide whether to exercise its power of censure on the audited agency. Because it may involve the exercise of censure power by the Control Yuan whenever an audited case is reported, the NAO, before making a decision to report to the Control Yuan, usually dedicates more effort to fully understand the operation of the audited agency, to communicate thoroughly with various stakeholders and to collect hard evidence in an objective manner. So, Article 69 of the *Audit Act* provides an effective tool for enhancing accountability in public governance.

As a result, the NAO assumes that the better the overall quality of performance audit, the higher is the number of cases of negligence of duty or poor performance reported to the Control Yuan, and vice versa.

Figure 10.2 reveals the number of cases reported to the Control Yuan due to dereliction of duty or poor performance as specified in Article 69 of the *Audit Act*. It is striking to see that the number of cases reported increased drastically after the NAO began to focus more on performance audits in 2009. There were 36 reported cases in 2008, jumping to 95 cases in 2009—an increase of 163 per cent. During the years without performance auditing (i.e. 1997–2008), the average number of cases reported to the Control Yuan due to dereliction of duty or poor performance each year was 21.6; the average increased to 80.3 cases for the period 2009–15, when the NAO was actively engaged in performance audits.

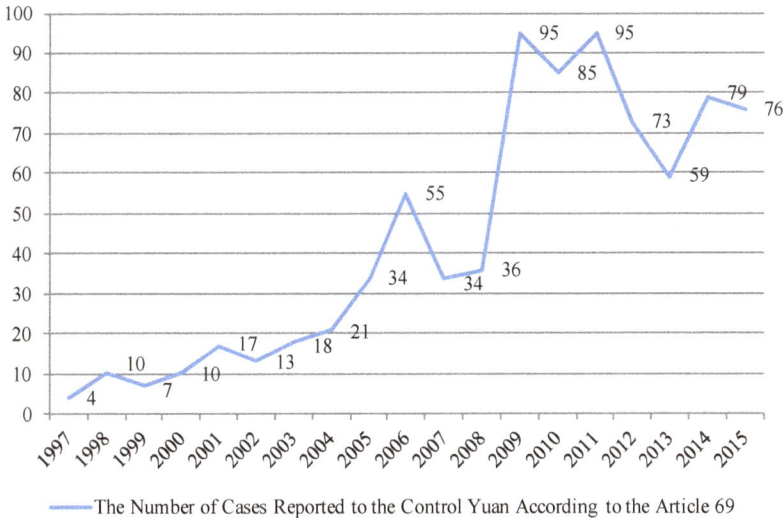

The Number of Cases Reported to the Control Yuan According to the Article 69

Figure 10.2 Number of cases reported to the Control Yuan due to negligence of duty or poor performance

Source: NAO (various years(a)).

Feedback from NAO employees and auditees[4]

Solid financial audits may keep government honest, yet they do little to encourage government agencies to fulfil their mission (Lee and Johnson 1998: 341). This is one of the reasons the NAO of Taiwan subscribes

---

4   The feedback described in this section is mostly based on the study by Su and Wang (2015) and five in-depth interviews by the authors with NAO employees in 2016.

to the international trend in recent years towards focusing on performance audits. Nevertheless, conducting performance audits in the public sector is complex and challenging. Even though the NAO has a stable and well-educated taskforce, its conservative organisational culture (Su and Fang 2009, 2011) and ways of conducting audits are not easy to change.

Auditors' opinions

A study by Su and Wang (2015) finds that initial evaluations and feedback from NAO employees are generally positive. The majority of the auditors interviewed in the study are supportive of the NAO's transition towards performance auditing. Taiwanese auditors believe that performance auditing is an international trend that cannot be reversed. The auditors also believe that the publication of performance audit reports plays a vital role in the communication of essential information to public authorities and the general public, thus reducing the asymmetry of information in government performance. In fact, the performance audit reports released by the NAO have received more attention and publicity than the traditional financial audit reports, particularly during the election season. Legislators, electoral candidates and the media often use findings in audit reports to criticise incumbent candidates and the ruling party. To a certain extent, these performance audit reports have increased the influence of the NAO.

Many auditors point out that performance auditing applies new techniques and methodologies and is much more time-consuming (Su and Wang 2015). Unlike performance auditing, the traditional financial auditing process is conducted using a prescribed checklist of steps to establish uniformity. While many auditors find performance auditing conceptually elusive and difficult to undertake, most agree that one of its unexpected benefits is that it expands the boundaries of their comfort zone and helps them gain a sense of greater self-achievement at work.

Apart from the benefits of performance auditing for the NAO and its auditors, the auditors interviewed in the study also highlighted limitations and challenges that need to be addressed (Su and Wang 2015). First, most junior auditors complained that the time allowed for the audit team to complete a performance audit is usually insufficient to ensure the quality of their work. That is, in addition to conducting the performance audits assigned to the audit team, auditors are required to manage other duties as well. These duties may include conducting financial audits regularly, collecting data or preparing written reports for legislators when requested and investigating cases assigned by the Control Yuan. Moreover, the application of performance audit techniques and methodologies is new to most of the auditors and the scope of the performance audit is broader and more diversified compared with financial auditing, so they need more time to undertake this type of audit. Given the tight time frame imposed on completing an audit case at the NAO, auditors are under considerable pressure. Consequently, many of them fail to collect all the information and evidence needed to support their statements in the final report— for example, external stakeholders' opinions relevant to the audited case are often ignored. In other words, the quality of audit results may be compromised due to the time constraints.

Several auditors perceive that the performance evaluation system inside the NAO may further compound the situation of 'quality versus quantity'. One of the implications of linking auditors' individual performance indicators to the production of performance audits is that there is an increase in competition at both the divisional level and the individual level at the NAO for the quantity of performance audits. It drives auditors towards short-term performance outputs rather than long-term performance results, such as improving the quality of performance audits or getting action-oriented audit recommendations, and this may be inconsistent with divisional goals.

The biggest concern for the NAO's auditors is how to avoid an infringement of executive power when conducting a performance audit. A traditional financial audit usually occurs after the government budget is executed. It then checks to ensure that the operations did not violate the budget plan or applicable laws and regulations. The main focus is on aspects of legality, and the major audit activities are to detect operational errors and abuses after the government program is implemented. This is the oversight function that lies at the base of the maturity model of SAIs (Figure 10.1), and the NAO's auditors feel comfortable in the exercise of their oversight duties. However, with regard to performance audits, the NAO aims to provide the executive with insightful advice and foresight to prevent inefficiency or ineffectiveness before it happens. Hence, it is likely that the policy recommendations written in a performance report will involve advice to the executive to alter the design or management of an audited program. Sometimes, it may even recommend the executive terminate an ineffective program while it is still at the implementation stage. On the surface, this is only 'advice' or a 'recommendation', yet audited agencies are obliged to explain to the NAO in a written report if they fail to follow the advice or recommendations. With this kind of power at hand, the auditors are worried about being accused of overstepping their authority (Su and Wang 2015). Moreover, they are afraid that, if the audited agency modifies the policy program as suggested by the NAO and it turns out to be a bad move, the auditors will have to share the blame with the agency, which may blur the accountability relationship.

Auditees' opinions

The feedback from public officials in the audited agencies is mixed. Some recognise that experienced auditors can provide insightful information to improve the execution of spending programs, particularly those that are jointly administered by several agencies. Because it is easy to miss seeing the wood for the trees when interagency coordination and planning are involved, boundary-spanning management is often a source of poor performance in the public sector. Several interviewees stated that experienced auditors without selfish parochialism might see the big picture better and help explain why some interagency programs and policies work, while others do not. This is why a holistic audit recommendation is regarded as helpful and is welcomed by the audited agency (Su and Wang 2015: 101). This is also why the emphasis is increasingly placed on interagency programs in the implementation of performance auditing. For instance, in the selection of major performance audit targets in 2015, the NAO selected 25 policy programs. Among them, 19 were interagency programs (Su and Wang 2015: 94).

A less positive feeling towards performance auditing is related to the increased workload for the audited agencies. Although it is well known that performance audits use economy, efficiency and effectiveness criteria to assess the value and impact of government spending (Power 1997), there is no general agreement on a distinct and operational definition of a performance audit (English 2007; Gronlund et al. 2011). Hence, when the NAO extends its role from conducting financial audits to conducting performance audits in Taiwan, it expands the scope of audit from financial documents to agencies' policy planning processes, administrative procedures and performance results. As a result, the administrative burden of an audited agency to collect data and prepare summaries has increased tremendously (Su and Wang 2015: 101–2).

This may be justified if the extra workload resulting from performance audits brings in useful policy recommendations for the audited agencies. However, it is not unusual for the audited agencies to receive audit recommendations that are too vague to be truly useful. There are several reasons a performance audit report may have vague or infeasible policy recommendations. One reason is the lack of competence of the audit team, which creates an obstacle to producing quality recommendations. Another possible reason is a deliberate choice by the audit team to avoid the infringement of executive power and the responsibility that may come with it. As explained earlier, many auditors at the NAO are concerned about overstepping the NAO's authority with their audit recommendations. The best way for them to avoid this risk is to issue vague policy recommendations that cannot go wrong in any circumstances, which nevertheless may be perceived by auditees as a waste of their time.

Research for this study found that many auditees find the auditors' mindset and expectations disturbing. Theoretically, the ultimate goal for performance auditing is to provide insights and foresight for the executive to help them improve the economy, efficiency and effectiveness of government services. So a partnership, not an adversarial relationship, should exist between the auditors and the audited agencies. They share the same objective and should work together as a team to improve the delivery of government services. However, auditees complained that auditors often focused exclusively on finding problems. This is because an auditor is encouraged and expected by the NAO's incentive structure to detect inefficiency, ineffectiveness or misconduct in the service provision process. If an audit team fails to detect any 'faults' in the audited program, the audit operation is considered a 'failure' (Su and Wang 2015: 104–5). When an audit team conducts performance audits with this mindset, it is not difficult to imagine that audited agencies and auditors would develop an adversarial relationship, not a partnership. Hence, the auditees would not cooperate fully to provide all the necessary information for the purposes of program evaluation. As a result, the goal of enhancing the performance of audited agencies' spending programs will be compromised.

Discussion and conclusions

While financial audits focus on the purchase of agency inputs and their legality, performance audits evaluate the result of government programs and services based on their economy, efficiency and effectiveness. Performance audits are therefore often perceived to be synonymous with value for money (Power 1997).

The Taiwanese Government today is facing a rapidly ageing population, rising public pension and healthcare costs and relatively low public revenue as a percentage of gross domestic product (GDP).[5] Therefore, there is increased pressure on the financing and performance of government services and, as a consequence, expectations of the NAO's contribution are formidable. Thus, it is essential for the NAO to perform both financial audits and performance audits well if it wants to prove to the public that its audit work maximises value for public money and mitigates risks for society. Yet, while the NAO is experienced with financial audits, and some progress is being made on performance auditing, there is still a long way to go before it wins strong credibility in performance auditing. As a new approach for both auditors and audited agencies, performance audit activities at the NAO must cope with the following challenges.

First, it needs to overcome the problem of 'soft' or vulnerable evidence in the audit outcome. Compared with financial audits, which can usually objectively identify illegal conduct or irregularities in audit reports, performance audits present evidence that is more vulnerable to interpretation. That is, audited agencies may argue that evidence in audit reports is subjective or inconclusive since it is often derived from research methods such as in-depth interviews, opinion surveys or quantitative analyses. Unfortunately, these social science methods may lead to incorrect conclusions or inconclusiveness if used improperly. For instance, the audited agency may question the scientific rigour of evidence obtained through a social survey or it may question the opinions collected from stakeholders who are not 'representative' of all those who are involved. As a result, auditors at the NAO may find themselves devoting a lot of time and energy to learning new skills and improving the quality of evidence in a performance audit, yet being frustrated when the evidence obtained is questioned by the audited agency or the media.

The best solution to enhance the robustness of evidence presented and hence the credibility of audit reports is to improve the research design and to employ techniques and methodologies appropriately. For example,

---

5   The tax burden of taxpayers is usually evaluated by the ratio of total tax revenue to GDP. The ratios released by the Ministry of Finance of Taiwan for the years 2013–15 are 12 per cent, 12.3 per cent and 12.8 per cent, respectively. In comparison with other countries, Taiwan's taxpayers have a relatively low tax burden. For instance, in 2013, the tax burdens for Japan, Korea, France, Germany and the United States were between 17.9 per cent and 28.3 per cent. See the Ministry of Finance eTax Portal: www.etax.nat.gov.tw/etwmain/front/ETW118W/CON/417/5792586571079918315?tagCode= (accessed 1 January 2017).

one approach is to increase the representation of stakeholders involved in the spending program in the performance audit process. The stakeholders of a policy program include policy decision-makers, program managers, target groups and other related individuals or groups. According to the INTOSAI (2016), maintaining good relationships with external stakeholders is important not only in the short-term perspective of getting access to information and achieving a good understanding of the audited program; it is equally important in the long-term perspective for the NAO to gain trust and credibility with stakeholders. Currently, due to the tight time constraints given to completing a performance audit, stakeholders outside the public sector are seldom invited to voice their opinions. Most opinions or evidence presented in the audit reports are obtained from staff working within the audited agencies. When evidence is not collected from all stakeholders involved in the design and implementation of a program, the findings can be biased and of little reference value. For instance, if external stakeholders are not consulted, it is difficult to assess rigorously and holistically the extent to which government programs reach their intended targets.

Another challenge that needs to be addressed is the insufficient incentive for interdivisional cooperation inside the NAO (Su and Wang 2015). More and more government spending programs are being implemented across organisational boundaries. To evaluate this type of policy program, the NAO must set up an interdivisional audit team to provide various types of domain knowledge and technical expertise needed to complete the audit. However, each division inside the NAO has its own turf and its own performance target. So, the organisational norm is that each division devotes most resources, including the best personnel, to its own audit cases, while dispatching fewer resources and less-experienced auditors to audit activities that involve interdivisional cooperation. Nevertheless, given the fact that more and more policy programs nowadays are of a cross-boundary nature and are also more vulnerable to poor coordination and inefficiency, it is suggested that the NAO restructure its incentive system to effectively motivate individual auditors and each division to commit themselves more to interdivisional audit activities.

One more challenge for the NAO is to improve its communication with the public and the media, including to gradually increase the number of performance reports that are available for free download from its website and to publicise audit results in a more user-friendly format. To be fair, this is exactly what the NAO has been trying to do in recent years, although it is taking place slowly. For instance, the NAO completed 895 performance audits between 2010 and 2015 (see Table 10.4), but not all the results are available on the NAO's website. Only those audit reports that passed internal screening processes appear on the website. Only one performance audit report was released on the website in 2010 and no reports in 2011. The number gradually grew as time went by. Specifically, the number of performance audit reports appearing on the website increased from three in 2012, to 18 in 2013, 25 in 2014 and to 27 reports in 2015. The total number of performance reports available online by the end of 2015 was 74, accounting for 8 per cent of the total number of reports completed (895 reports). It is expected that the number of reports posted to the NAO's website will continue to grow in the future.

In addition to posting more performance audit reports to its website, the NAO has also started to use social media such as YouTube and Facebook to publicise its audit results in a more user-friendly manner.[6] Its efforts to communicate effectively with the public not only help to correct information asymmetry whereby the executive branch dominates the information available about government service provision, it also addresses the important accountability issue of 'who audits the auditors' (Porter et al. 2012). Taxpayers can look through audit reports and results to determine whether the NAO has done a good job in promoting maximum value for public funds.

Finally, the biggest challenge facing the NAO is how to change the mindset of auditors and build up mutual trust between the audit team and audited agencies. In retrospect, monitoring and holding audited agencies accountable have been the primary roles played by the NAO. However, if the purpose of conducting performance audits continues to be aligned with this traditional role (i.e. a focus on finding faults and holding the agencies accountable) then it is likely that the audit environment will not foster effective communication and mutual trust and thereby a culture of partnership between auditors and auditees. The audited agencies will not then cooperate willingly during the audit process and the information collected will likely be insufficient to produce credible or useful conclusions and recommendations for the auditee agencies to improve their efficiency and effectiveness. To help create an audit environment with relationships of trust, the auditor should follow two principles. One is to stick to the

---

6   For audit results on YouTube, see: www.audit.gov.tw/files/40-1000-15.php?Lang=zh-tw (accessed 1 February 2017).

fundamental principle that quality should come first—that is, the focus of promoting performance audits should continue to be placed on quality instead of quantity. A large number of performance audits without robust findings or quality recommendations add little value to government service provision, and could even reduce administrative efficiency by diverting resources from implementing policies that meet citizens' needs to assisting audit activities.

The second principle for building trust is to pay more respect to executive power. For example, the audit team should frame the wording of their audit opinions in a way that provides helpful suggestions or advice, rather than instructions. The audited agencies should also be given the opportunity to comment, not only on the material facts of the performance audit report, but also on the conclusions and recommendations therein. In addition, unless required by law or regulation, the executive agency that is responsible for the final results of its government programs should have the discretion to determine whether or not to adopt audit recommendations. This is the case in many industrialised countries such as Australia and the United States.

In other words, it is suggested that, with respect to its performance audit activities, the NAO of Taiwan should take on the role of an independent management consultant to give advice to help the executive branch improve public services, and leave the role of public accountant or judge to the field of traditional financial audit.[7] As public accountants, auditors must produce reports aimed at enhancing the transparency and accountability of executive agencies, while, as a judge or magistrate, the audit organisation has the authority to pronounce on the legality of the actions of executive agencies and give decisions on how well they conform to requirements (Pollitt 2003: 164). Both roles are consistent with the oversight duties and meet the stringent requirement of government accountability. Conversely, when confining the institutional role of the NAO as a management consultant during the process of performance auditing, its main objective is to provide insights and foresight for the

---

7   According to Pollitt (2003: 164), performance auditing involves four alternative roles, which are not perfectly reconcilable with one another. They are: '(a) As a public accountant, producing reports aimed principally at enhancing the accountability and transparency of public bodies. (b) As a management consultant, giving help and advice to public bodies to help them improve themselves. (c) As a scientific or research-based organization, unearthing, creating and disseminating new, scientifically tested knowledge about how public programs and projects are working. (d) As a judge or magistrate, pronouncing on the legality of the actions of public bodies and giving decisions on how far they conform to formal procedures and requirements.'

executive branch as an equal partner; therefore, the influence of the NAO hinges not on formal authority or law, but on the technical capacity of its staff and effective communication with its clients and stakeholders.

References

Allen, R. and D. Tommasi. 2001. *Managing Public Expenditure: A reference book for transition countries.* Paris: OECD Publishing.

Colin, T. and J. Wiggan. 2010. 'The public value of the National Audit Office'. *International Journal of Public Sector Management* 23(1): 54–70. doi.org/10.1108/09513551011012321.

English, L. M. 2007. 'Performance audit of Australian public private partnerships: Legitimizing government policies or providing independent oversight?' *Financial Accountability and Management* 23(3): 313–36. doi.org/10.1111/j.1468-0408.2007.00431.x.

Government Accountability Office (GAO). 2007. *Enhancing Performance, Accountability, and Foresight.* GAO-07-165CG. Washington, DC: GAO.

Gronlund, A., F. Svardsten and P. Ohman. 2011. 'Value for money and the rule of law: The (new) performance audit in Sweden'. *International Journal of Public Sector Management* 24(2): 107–23. doi.org/10.1108/09513551111109026.

International Organization of Supreme Audit Institutions (INTOSAI). 2010. *Performance Audit Guidelines: Key principles.* ISSAI 3100. Vienna: INTOSAI.

International Organization of Supreme Audit Institutions (INTOSAI). 2016. *Guidelines on Central Concepts for Performance Auditing.* ISSAI 3100. Vienna: INTOSAI.

Kuo, T.-J. and Z.-Y. Xu. 2013. 'The study on establishing performance management system at auditing offices'. *Government Audit Journal* 33(2): 92–100.

Lee, R. D., jr, and R. W. Johnson. 1998. *Public Budgeting System.* 6th edn. Frederick, MD: Aspen Publishers.

Lin, C.-L. 2012. 'The status and prospects of promoting government performance auditing'. *Internal Auditor* 78: 5–13.

Lin, C.-L. 2013. 'The role and function of government audit in public governance'. *Public Governance Quarterly* 3: 58–73.

Liu, Y.-C. 2014. 'The development of government performance auditing in Taiwan'. *Government Audit Journal* 35(1): 95–107.

National Audit Office of Taiwan (NAO). Various years(a). *Government Annual Audit Report*. Taipei: NAO.

National Audit Office of Taiwan (NAO). Various years(b). *NAO's Annual Performance Report*. Taipei: NAO.

National Audit Office (NAO). 2009. *Guideline for the NAO on Performance Audit*. Taipei: National Audit Office.

National Audit Office (NAO). 2014. *Basics of Program Evaluation*. Taipei: National Audit Office.

Pollitt, C. 2003. 'Performance audit in Western Europe: Trends and choices'. *Critical Perspectives on Accounting* 14(1): 157–70. doi.org/10.1006/cpac.2002.0521.

Porter, B., C. Ó hÓgartaigh and R. Baskerville. 2012. 'Audit expectation–performance gap revisited: Evidence from New Zealand and the United Kingdom'. *International Journal of Auditing* 16(2): 101–29. doi.org/10.1111/j.1099-1123.2011.00443.x.

Power, M. 1997. *The Audit Society: Rituals of verification*. Oxford: Oxford University Press.

Su, T.-T. and K.-H. Fang. 2009. *Strategies for Restructuring Audit Organizations in Taiwan*. Taipei: NAO.

Su, T.-T. and K.-H. Fang. 2011. *Strategic Management and Performance Evaluation System in Audit Organization*. Taipei: NAO.

Su, T.-T. and H.-W. Wang. 2015. *Strategies to Promote Program Evaluation in Audit Organizations*. Taipei: NAO.

Wang, Y.-S. 2002. 'The study on enhancing government audit functions'. *Audit Journal* 22(4): 7–21.

Xu, Z.-Y. 2009. 'The status and prospects of performance auditing'. *Government Audit Journal* 29(4): 25–35.

11

Budgeting and financial management of public infrastructure: The experience of Taiwan

Yu-Ying Kuo and Ming Huei Cheng

Public–private partnerships (PPPs) for public infrastructure have been the dominant model to create new job opportunities, expand domestic demand, stimulate the economy and deliver on infrastructure needs more efficiently in Taiwan. The Ministry of Finance (MoF) has endeavoured to promote private participation in infrastructure projects, improve the quality of public services, accelerate social and economic development and control government financial expenditure.

Private investors can participate through build–operate–transfer (BOT), build–operate–own (BOO), rehabilitate–operate–transfer (ROT) and operate–transfer (OT) in accordance with the *Promotion of Private Participation in Infrastructure Projects Act 2000* (*PPIP Act*). The *Urban Renewal Act 2010* provides joint development and creates special rights to make use of government-owned land, while tax incentives provide some exemptions from business tax and customs duties. In terms of Taiwan's experience with PPPs, the key factors in public infrastructure funding are the financial feasibility of meeting the interests of all parties involved in PPP projects and ensuring public infrastructure investment plans focus on long-term effects.

Introduction

In line with New Public Management (NPM) and governance, privatisation, contracting out and outsourcing are among the strategies that have been used in many countries to make greater use of private sector capacities in public sector management. In the face of fiscal difficulties and economic stagnation, several countries have also attempted to finance government infrastructure projects by incorporating private investment. This is to create new job opportunities, expand domestic demand and stimulate the economy, as well as to deliver on infrastructure needs more efficiently. This chapter analyses the budgeting and financial management of public infrastructure in Taiwan in terms of the government's objectives for promoting private participation.

PPPs for public infrastructure have been the dominant model in Taiwan. Key issues involved in promoting this model in Taiwan, as elsewhere, include the criteria for success (what the government is seeking), the allocation of risk and the criteria for selecting qualified private partners.

Such investment typically includes infrastructure such as energy (power generation and supply), transport (roads, rail systems, bridges and tunnels), water (sewerage, wastewater treatment and water supply), telecommunications (telephone and internet connections) and social infrastructure (hospitals, prisons, courts, museums, schools and government accommodation) (Grimsey and Lewis 2002: 108). PPPs are prevalent internationally—for instance, the United Kingdom issued its renewed 'PF2' (private finance) policy in late 2012 (HM Treasury 2012), while the Organisation for Economic Co-operation and Development (OECD 2012) has issued guidelines on how governments should proceed with PPPs. Likewise, member countries of the Association of Southeast Asian Nations (ASEAN 2014), with assistance from the OECD, have developed a new framework for PPPs. The European Commission (EC 2014) has launched an ambitious *Investment Plan for Europe*, which entails encouraging private financing of public infrastructure programs on a grand scale. US President Donald Trump's plan to spend US$550 billion (A$695 billion) over the next decade to upgrade the nation's crumbling roads, bridges and waterways has been celebrated as a key driver of the stock market's post-election rally and a potential jolt to a listless economy (Davidson 2016). According to Trump's economic adviser, the President's plan would depend heavily on private investors, which the federal government will encourage by providing very generous federal tax credits (Pianin 2016).

PPPs—in which the government contracts a private partner to variously finance, design, build and operate infrastructure assets for a fixed period—are growing in use. Government cooperation with the private sector via PPPs, which allows for the joint completion of public infrastructure and provision of services, has become a significant method to facilitate investment in public infrastructure as well as to stimulate the economy. This growth is due in large part to the scope of benefits PPPs offer to bring in terms of private sector management skills, the opportunities that bundling design, construction and operation provide to improve efficiency and the ability to bring forward the provision of infrastructure services. There can also be less scrutiny from off-budget financing.

While some governments focus on a particular type of long-term PPP contract—'design, build, finance, operate and maintain' (DBFOM)—the reality is there are many possible contractual arrangements. Contracts may differ in terms of which of the different tasks and activities the public or private sector is held responsible for (from initial planning through to the final maintenance and operations), the extent of finance from each sector, the specific nature of the project to be delivered, which party bears which risks, the strength of incentives for performance as well as issues of transparency (Hodge and Greve 2013).

A PPP is a way of funding and delivering public infrastructure projects where project risks are shared between the public and the private sectors. Chan et al. (2009) argued that PPPs may assist in transferring construction and operational risks to private partners, while governments retain regulatory and demand risks with a commitment to underwrite minimum revenue from user charges. Therefore, the effectiveness of the alignment depends on a sufficient and appropriate transfer of risk to the private partner. But the complexities and risk transfers associated with the financing arrangements have also led to failures of the PPP model, particularly if the private investment involves indirect government borrowing (exacerbating problems with budget bottom lines).

In the international literature, PPPs remain both widely praised and loudly criticised. For instance, Ross and Yan (2015) compare PPPs with traditional public procurement using economic theory. They acknowledge that one of the longstanding potential problems with PPPs is:

> the loss of flexibility that comes with the long lived contractual obligations governments must respect when changing circumstances may require significant change in the way the public service is provided. (Ross and Yan 2015: 443)

Ross and Yan argue that PPPs will be superior to government provision (in terms of value for money or social surplus) when their potential efficiencies are large, the probability that there will need to be changes to the project is small, the gains to project redesign are small and when the government's bargaining power in renegotiation is greater. They suggest that PPPs ought to be more attractive for road or bridge projects, where there is little chance that a redesign will be needed, and less attractive for more dynamic projects such as healthcare or information technology projects.

Some scholars suggest PPPs offer more speedy investment in the economy, but warn against the dangers of poor regulation that leave excessive risks with government. Reeves (2015) draws attention to the fundamental shift in the Irish Government's motives for PPPs following the Global Financial Crisis (GFC) towards levering private funds for investment and job creation. He describes the origins of the policy prior to the GFC and points to the government's desire to alleviate capacity constraints on infrastructure delivery, to effect 'speedy delivery' of infrastructure and to achieve value for money. He concludes that PPPs did make a contribution to infrastructure investments over and above those that would have occurred anyway.

Albalate et al. (2015) compare the transfer of different types of risk in transport-related PPPs in many South American and European countries and highlight the importance of risk-mitigation strategies and of institutional quality and stability. For instance, they report that Spain suffered because of instability in PPP regulation, which led to the government bearing most of the financial risks. More recently, in a stable regulatory environment, the French Government was able to successfully allocate risks to its private partners. Financing challenges along with weak legal protections have inhibited private participation in PPPs. Albalate et al. concluded:

countries with higher institutional quality and stability are able to engage in PPPs with fewer guarantees or less need for sharing the risks associated with demand, cost overrun and maintenance and operation. (2015: 496)

Care in risk allocation is emphasised, particularly for social-investment PPPs. Acerete et al. (2015) examine healthcare PPPs in Spain, which pioneered the 'Alzira model' to provide clinical services, with potentially attractive revenue streams, as well as physical infrastructure. They conclude that 'care is needed to avoid unwarranted inferences about claimed benefits of lower costs while maintaining sustainable quality' (Acerete et al. 2015: 503). Hellowell (2015) compared the agency problems that led to budgetary problems with PPP hospitals in the United Kingdom and Spain. He noted that, while PPPs have long been advocated on the grounds of efficiency, 'strategic misrepresentation' often occurs with public projects, with costs being deliberately underestimated and benefits deliberately overestimated to ensure favoured projects gain approval for funding (Hellowell 2015: 45).

Eldrup and Schütze (2013) point out that the apparent advantage of PPPs' access to private funding comes at a cost, as the PPP model leads to higher costs of finance compared with public funding and potentially costly changes subsequent to contract signature. In addition, the private partner may be tasked with the design, construction, financing, operation and management of the infrastructure asset and the delivery of a service to the government or to the public using that asset but most of the risk remains with the government. In many cases, failures of PPP projects are attributed to poor project preparation or financial shortages, where the advantages of private sector expertise and competitive processes do not outweigh the risks to government, including the cost of private sector financing. For PPPs with high involvement of state-owned enterprises, contingent liabilities may increase as a result of implicit or explicit government guarantees. Hansakul and Levinger (2016) argued that PPPs could add to explicit debt and could lead to higher financing costs. As a result, large-scale PPP programs risk being halted or terminated due to a change in political leadership or adverse economic circumstances.

Taiwan's experience

Whether a government should invest in infrastructure projects to stimulate the economy or reduce investment to save government expenditure has long been debated in Taiwan. To some degree, private participation in public infrastructure projects can open up new opportunities for infrastructure investment ventures. The MoF is in charge of the *PPIP Act*. The *PPIP Act* is one of the MoF's most important policies, aimed at improving the quality of public services, accelerating social and economic development and containing government financial expenditure.

In addition to private sector participation in infrastructure projects through BOT, BOO, ROT and OT, in accordance with the *PPIP Act*, investors can also participate through the *Urban Renewal Act 2010*, via joint development and creation of special rights to make use of government-owned land. By building on the different strengths of the public and private sectors, partnerships between the two can result in appropriate allocation and sharing of risks in each project's design, implementation, logistics, legal changes and ongoing operational management, and can contribute to the success of a project by making use of the private sector's capital, operational efficiency and professional talent and by using competition to get maximum value for money. By attracting private participation, the MoF hopes to revitalise Taiwan's economy and better the lives of its people. With the long-term, steady revenue brought by PPP projects and the tax and land acquisition incentives provided by the *PPIP Act*, private investors can enjoy better profit margins, business expansion opportunities and enhance their corporate image. The MoF invites private investors to participate in quality PPP projects to create triple-win situations: higher revenues for investors, lower expenditure for government and better public services (MoF 2013).

Incentives under the *PPIP Act* are set out in Table 11.1. First, 'regulatory relaxation' refers to the elimination or relaxation of restrictions on government-owned land, such as leases longer than 10 years, and allowing the private sector to gain benefits from the land and from the issuance of corporate bonds by private institutions. Second, 'fundraising' means the authority in charge may subsidise part of the interest accrued from the loan needed by the private institution, invest in part of the construction or coordinate with financial institutions or special funds to provide medium- or long-term financing to the private institution. Third, 'preferential land rentals' are situations where the land required for the infrastructure project is government-owned but is rented in connection with a lease and superficies may be extended on favourable terms. For major infrastructure projects, the authority in charge may expropriate the land and provide it for use to a private institution. Moreover, tax incentives can include exemption from business income tax for five years, investment tax credits for capital expenditure, preferential customer duties on imported machinery and equipment, reduction of or exemption from building tax, land value tax and deeds tax and investment tax credits for subscriptions of shares issued by the private institution. For major transportation projects, relaxation of restrictions on lines of credit for loans is provided to private institutions.

Table 11.1 Incentives for promotion of private participation in public infrastructure projects

Regulatory relaxation	Elimination of restrictions under Article 25 of the *Land Act*: Relaxes restrictions on disposition of government-owned land, creation of encumbrances or leases longer than 10 years. Elimination of restrictions under Article 28 of the *National Property Act* and *Local Government Property Management Act*: Relaxation of restrictions on the disposition of government-owned property or the collection of benefits from it. Elimination of restrictions under Article 270, Subparagraph 1, of the *Company Act*: Relaxes restrictions on the issuance of new shares by private institutions. Elimination of restrictions under Article 247, Article 249, Subparagraph 2, and Article 250, Subparagraph 2, of the *Company Act*: Relaxes restrictions on the issuance of corporate bonds by private institutions.
Fundraising	The authority in charge may, in the case of incapacity to cover the portion of costs for self-financing, subsidise part of the interest accrued from the loan needed by the private institution or to invest in part of the construction. The authority in charge may coordinate with financial institutions or special funds to provide medium- or long-term financing to the private institution.
Preferential land rentals	Where the land required for the infrastructure project is government-owned, rentals in connection with the lease and the creation of superficies may be extended on favourable terms.
Major infrastructure projects[1]	
Expropriation of privately owned land	The authority in charge may expropriate the land and provide it for use by the private institution.

Tax incentives	Exemption from business income tax for five years. Investment tax credit for capital expenditure. Preferential customer duties on imported machinery and equipment. Reduction of or exemption from building tax, land value tax and deeds tax. Investment tax credits for subscriptions of shares issued by the private institution.
Loan credits	Relaxation of restrictions on lines of credit for loans provided to private institutions (only for major transportation projects).

[1] Major infrastructure projects are those that are important and of a certain scale, the scope of which will be determined by the competent authority in conjunction with other relevant authorities.

Source: MoF (2013).

The Statute for Encouragement of Private Participation in Transportation Infrastructure Projects also provides tax incentives, including exemptions from business tax and customs duties (for details, see Appendix 11.1). The tax incentives create tax expenditure ranging from NT$195.2 million (A$8.2 million) to NT$997.05 million (A$42 million), but evaluations by the MoF and the Ministry of Transportation and Communications claim the benefits of PPPs outweigh the costs from tax expenditure.

Each project is subject to a strict approval process. Based on Article 34 of the *Budget Act*—covering major public construction projects and major policy implementation plans—before the budget estimates and budget proposals are compiled, a cost-efficiency analysis report that canvasses alternative measures must be drawn up, with a full description of the financing arrangements proposed. This report must be forwarded to the Legislative Yuan (DGBAS 2015). As shown in Figure 11.1, for each PPP project, the government conducts a social cost–benefit analysis (CBA) on the legal, market, environmental and financial aspects, including opportunity costs and indirect costs/benefits. Only project proposals deemed feasible will be publicly released for private investment.

Table 11.2 Tax expenditure on tax incentives for infrastructure projects (NT$ million)

	2002	2003	2004	2005	2006	2007	2008	2009	2010	2011	2012	2013	2014
Exemption from business income tax for five years	129.5	77.1	1.5	1.2	6.3	8.00	14.07	3.23	72.3	121.71	156.85	81.01	1.38
Investment tax credit for capital expenditure	24.9	18.1	20.0	19.0	13.6	0.78	9.87	128.00	92.0	30.00	50.20	21.70	61.00
Investment tax credit for subscriptions of shares issued by the private institution	451.2	407.0	274.0	203.0	175.3	205.00	384.00	268.00	377.0	526.00	790.00	299.00	449.00
Total	605.6	502.2	295.5	223.2	195.2	213.78	407.94	399.23	541.3	677.71	997.05	401.71	511.38

Source: DGBAS (2015).

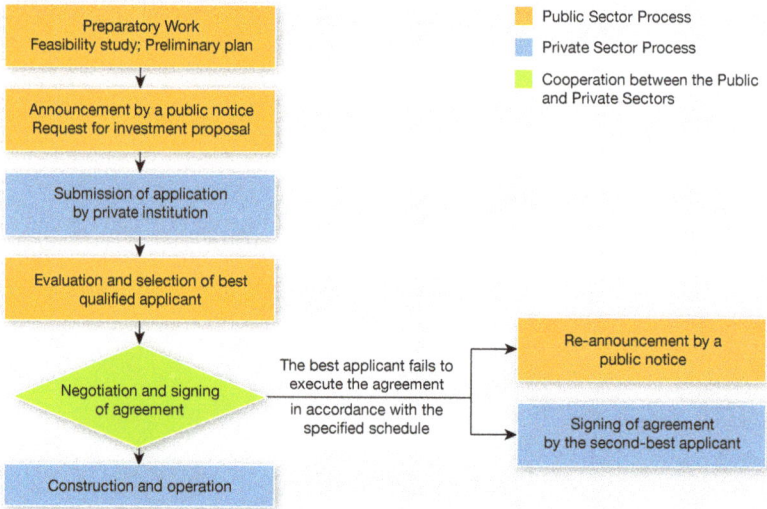

Figure 11.1 Application and evaluation procedure for government planned projects
Source: MoF (2013).

Furthermore, each private sector applicant must include their financial institution's evaluation opinion on the investment proposal when submitting a letter of intent. The principal condition for providing private financing may be stated in the evaluation opinion. Before inviting private participation through a public notice, the authority in charge may, depending on the character of the infrastructure project, provide general information to private investors about the project or conduct an information meeting, finalising the contents of public notices and tender documents after consulting with private investors. The public notice includes the following content:

1. the character, basic requirements, concession period and scope of the infrastructure project
2. qualification requirements for the applicant
3. items and standards of application review
4. items awaiting negotiation
5. the date of announcement, deadline for application, the application procedure and the deposit required
6. the scope for ancillary enterprises allowed for private investment and the concession period for the land needed
7. the matters authorised or commissioned by the authority in charge.

The tender documents need to cover the following items:

1. the main content and format of the investment proposal
2. the measure and schedule of application review
3. commitment and cooperation matters required of the government
4. items and procedures for negotiation once negotiations are allowed
5. the deadline for contract negotiation and execution
6. a draft of the proposed concession agreement.

Where an infrastructure project in which a private institution participates is for a public utility enterprise, according to Article 49, the private institution may set the user charge and schedule and method for the adjustment of user charges in the financial plan submitted in its application. The financial plan is to include: 1) the cost expenditure for planning, construction, operation and other financial matters; 2) the income derived from operations and ancillary enterprises; 3) the operation period; 4) payment of any royalties; and 5) the price index used.

The user charge and the schedule and method for the adjustment of the user charge must be approved by the relevant authority in charge of the public utilities concerned before the execution of the concession agreement by the authority and the private institution in accordance with applicable laws. If, after the operation of the infrastructure project, it is necessary to make any adjustment to the user charge and/or the schedule and method for the adjustment of the approved user charge, this must first be approved by the competent authority in charge of the public utilities in accordance with applicable laws. The competitive assessment of user charges is part of the CBA to ensure reasonable costs to consumers. Afterwards, the authority in charge shall have the concession agreement modified accordingly and announced via a public notice.

The Statute for Encouragement of Private Participation in Transportation Infrastructure Projects has similar provisions. For public infrastructure in Taiwan, the central government adheres to the policy implementation principle of 'putting Taiwan first for the benefit of the people', proposed by former president Ma Ying-jeou in 2008. To map out a vision for national development, and set clear macroeconomic targets, Taiwan has introduced a plan built on six 'main axial policies': undertaking spatial remodelling, promoting industrial renovation, pursuing global linkages, cultivating innovative manpower, establishing a just society and achieving a sustainable environment. The ultimate goal is to develop Taiwan into an advanced country marked by vitality, innovation, equitable spread of wealth, social justice, sustainability and energy conservation.

Under the title 'i-Taiwan', 12 projects constitute an important economic development blueprint for Taiwan, designed to boost dynamism in the country's economic growth, which, in recent years, has been losing momentum against the headwinds of globalisation and intensifying international competition. The purpose of the projects is to expand domestic demand, improve the investment environment and boost the health of the economy and quality of life. The i-Taiwan 12 projects cover four dimensions: transportation networks, industrial innovation, urban and rural development and environmental protection. The 12 projects are detailed in Appendix 11.2 and summarised in Table 11.3.

Table 11.3 i-Taiwan 12 projects

Transportation Network	Industrial Innovation
• A fast and convenient transportation network • Kaohsiung Port–City regeneration • Taoyuan International Airport City	• Central Region New High-Tech Industrial Clusters Program • Intelligent Taiwan • Industrial innovation corridors
Urban and Rural Development	Environmental Protection
• Urban and industrial park regeneration • Farm village regeneration	• Coastal regeneration • Green forestation • Flood prevention and water management • Sewer construction

Source: Invest Taiwan (2015).

With regard to transportation, the i-Taiwan projects constitute the main means for integrating Taiwan's high-speed rail, Taiwan Railways and the metropolitan Taipei Mass Rapid Transit (MRT) networks, and improving the integration of freeways and other roads to build a fast and convenient island-wide transportation network. They will also enhance Kaohsiung Port's geographic advantage as a shipping hub, speed up the regeneration of the port and Kaohsiung City and improve airport links, speed up airport operations and peripheral construction and develop Taoyuan International Air City.

The second-largest dimension of the projects—industrial innovation— includes major investments in education, a nationwide wireless broadband system, intelligent transport systems as well as new industrial clusters, corridors and parks. Construction mechanisms for effectively attracting private investment include quality-control mechanisms for the life cycle of public works, strengthening the competitiveness of the engineering industry and comprehensively raising the quality of public construction and services.

The Taiwanese Government has been eager to strengthen investment in public construction and has endeavoured to encourage private participation in public construction projects. These projects are expected to deliver economic benefits by bolstering public infrastructure, revitalising the domestic economy, promoting investment, increasing income and employment opportunities, upgrading the quality of life and improving the equitable distribution of income. The Taiwanese Government will carry out its 'Strategic Plan for the Spatial Development of National Land' to achieve a new vision for the country's spatial development through such strategies as hazard prevention and land restoration, sustainable urban and rural development and green and intelligent transportation. Overall, the government believes that the 12 prioritised public construction projects can regenerate Taiwan's economy.

Table 11.4 indicates total investment in i-Taiwan projects will be almost NT$4 trillion (A$169 billion), with private investment comprising about 30 per cent, or NT$1.3 trillion (A$53.6 billion). Among the 12 projects, the fast, convenient transportation network is the biggest investment project, involving NT$1.2 trillion (A$51.3 billion), or more than 30 per cent of the total investment. The second-largest investment is 'Intelligent Taiwan' and the third-largest is 'Urban and Industrial Park Regeneration'. It is estimated about 120,000 direct employment opportunities were created each year over the period of the project (2008–16).

Table 11.4 Total investment and private investment in i-Taiwan 12 projects

Item	Total investment (NT$ billion)	Private investment (NT$ billion)	Private investment (%)
A fast convenient transportation network	1,215.70	76.30	6.28
Kaohsiung Port–City reconstruction	38.80	16.10	41.45
Taoyuan International Airport City	293.70	64.4	21.93
Transportation Network	1,548.20	156.80	69.66
Central Region New High-Tech Industrial Cluster Program	323.00	217.1	67.21

Item	Total investment (NT$ billion)	Private investment (NT$ billion)	Private investment (%)
Intelligent Taiwan	775.20	357.60	46.13
Industrial innovation corridors	147.50	76.10	51.60
Industrial Innovation	1,245.70	650.80	164.94
Urban and industrial park regeneration	458.20	373.30	81.48
Farm village regeneration	208.40	10.20	4.92
Urban and Rural Development	666.60	383.50	86.40
Coastal regeneration	39.40	1.80	4.45
Green forestation	59.80	0.60	0.95
Flood prevention and water management	273.00	0.00	0.00
Sewer construction	162.90	77.10	4.73
Environmental Protection	535.10	79.50	10.13
Total	3,995.60	1,270.60	31.80

Source: Invest Taiwan (2015).

Table 11.5 shows that, in terms of private investment, the top three projects are the Central Region New High-Tech Industrial Cluster Program, Intelligent Taiwan and the urban and industrial park regeneration (comprising nearly 80 per cent of the total private investment). The specific projects within these include Taichung Science Park, advanced research parks, central regional machine-driven industry development, Taichung Harbour logistics district, construction of wireless broadband, digital content and design industry, radio-frequency identification construction, urban regeneration, industrial park regeneration and high-speed rail station district development.

Table 11.5 Major private investment projects

Item	Private investment (NT$ million)/ percentage of total investment	Major private investment projects
A fast convenient transportation network	76.3/6.4%	Constructions of MRT systems in three metropolitan areas, grade separation and rapid transit systematisation of city railways.
Kaohsiung Port–City reconstruction	16.1/1.3%	Construction of international container terminal.

Item	Private investment (NT$ million)/ percentage of total investment	Major private investment projects
Taoyuan International Airport City	64.4/5.4%	Airport city development, construction of Terminal 3
Transportation Network	156.8/13%	
Central Region New High-Tech Industrial Cluster Program	217.1/18.1%	Taichung Science Park, advanced research park, central region machine-driven industry development, Taichung Harbour logistics district
Intelligent Taiwan	357.6/29.8%	Construction of wireless broadband, digital content and design industry, radio-frequency identification construction
Industrial Innovation Corridors	76.1/6.3%	Science/technology parks, Hsinchu Biomedical, Agriculture Technology Park, Kaohsiung Software Technology Park
Industrial Innovation	650.8/54.2%	
Urban and industrial park regeneration	373.3/31.1%	Urban regeneration of 30 locations, industrial park regeneration, high-speed rail station district development
Farm village regeneration	10.2/0.9%	Farm Village Regeneration Plan, 'Small landowner, big farmer'
Urban and Rural Development	383.5/32%	
Coastal regeneration	1.8/0.1%	Diversified economic development of fishing ports and villages
Green forestation	0.6/0.1%	Lowland forest recreation areas
Flood prevention and water management	0/0%	
Sewer construction	77.1/0.6%	Sewer construction
Environmental Protection	79.5/0.8%	
Total	1,270.6/100%	

Source: Invest Taiwan (2015).

The Taiwanese Government is giving priority to public infrastructure and expects it to raise the economic growth rate. While most i-Taiwan projects are ongoing, after President Tsai Ing-wen took office in 2017, they no longer appeared in the budget. To take fiscal year 2017, for example, the public infrastructure budget amounted to NT$186.9 billion

(A\$7.9 billion), shown in Table 11.6, which accounted for 9.4 per cent of total government expenditure (NT\$2 trillion [A\$84.3 billion]). If coupled with special budget, enterprise and non-enterprise funds, the annual amount of public infrastructure projects in 2017 will add up to NT\$326.6 billion (A\$13.8 billion). This budget funding excludes private investment and tax expenditures. Parts of the projects under the headings Transportation Network, Urban and Rural Development and Environmental Protection are included in the 2017 budget, but the projects have been reassembled so it is hard to determine what is going on.

Table 11.6 Public infrastructure projects, 2017 (NT\$ billion)

Item		Budget	Special budget	Enterprise funds	Non-enterprise funds	Total	Percentage
Total		186.9	15.7	93.1	30.9	326.6	100.0
1. Transportation		96.2	-	13.1	12.4	121.7	37.3
	Road	44.7	-	-	3.8	48.5	14.9
	Railway	44.8	-	1.2	0.7	46.7	14.3
	Air	-	-	7.1	0.5	7.6	2.3
	Harbour	2.5	-	4.8	6.3	13.6	4.2
	Tourism	4.2	-	-	1.1	5.3	1.6
2. Environment		28.7	13.0	13.0	2.8	57.5	17.6
	Protection	2.8	-	-	0.7	3.5	1.1
	Water	12.2	11.0	13.0	2.1	38.3	11.7
	Sewer	12.0	2.0	-	-	14.0	4.3
	National parks	1.7	-	-	-	1.7	0.5
3. Economy and energy		4.6	-	67.0	3.3	74.9	22.9
	Facility	4.6	-	6.9	3.3	1.48	4.5
	Electricity	-	-	60.1	-	60.1	18.4
4. Urban regeneration		5.4	-	-	8.6	14.0	4.3
5. Cultural facility		8.7	-	-	0.3	9.0	2.8
6. Education		12.1	-	-	0.1	12.2	3.7
	Education	7.4	-	-	0.1	7.5	2.3
	Sports	4.7	-	-	-	47.0	1.4
7. Agriculture		30.2	2.7	-	0.9	338.0	10.4
8. Health and welfare		1.0	-	-	2.5	35.0	1.0

\- no data.

Source: Directorate-General of Budgeting, Accounting and Statistics (www.dgbas.gov.tw/mp.asp?mp=1).

Some strengths and weaknesses of Taiwan's approach

Under fiscal constraints, effective use of models encouraging private participation in public development projects, such as BOT, will help ease some of the financial pressure on government infrastructure programs. There are numerous laws governing private participation in infrastructure projects, including, since 2000, the *PPIP Act* and, since 1994, the Statute for Encouragement of Private Participation in Transportation Infrastructure Projects. The different objectives and operating guidelines of each law together make up a sound legal environment that has contributed to many successful cases over the past decades. To stimulate economic development, in 2012, the Executive Yuan passed the Economic Power-Up Plan. It designated using private investment to spur public works and expand investor solicitation. Whenever there is an infrastructure project, the feasibility of private participation will be assessed as a priority.

Since 2003, more than 1,000 contracts have been signed, totalling over NT$1 trillion (A$42.2 billion) in value. Over their lifetime, these agreements were estimated to save the government NT$930 billion (A$39.2 billion) in expenditure, add NT$670 billion (A$28.3 billion) in revenue and create more than 180,000 employment opportunities— all while allowing the government to provide excellent public services. To continue promoting such achievements, the MoF gathered proposals from government agencies to offer an estimated NT$150 billion (A$6.3 billion) in investment opportunities to the private sector in 2015 (MoF 2015).

Notwithstanding the claimed benefits, infrastructure development in Taiwan in the past few years has experienced significant problems. First, an excessive number of infrastructure programs have distracted the public from the essence of the overall infrastructure strategy. Many infrastructure programs have been wrapped up in package deals, which appear to have become must-do tasks for each cabinet rather than changing in response to the ever-changing environment. In retrospect, many of the programs have not fulfilled their purpose. As it is often impossible to see the effect of infrastructure programs right away, people have, in general, felt the frustration of expecting too much and not being able to feel the actual benefits (Huang 2008).

Second, there has been a lack of reasonable evaluation methods to assess the achievement of each program. Despite the MoF's requirement for social CBAs before projects are approved, evaluations are not always valid, resulting in poor investments that cause Taiwanese people to lose faith in the necessity of various infrastructure programs. Moreover, there is no systematic evaluation of completed projects to check whether the costs and benefits originally expected have been generated. The Council for Economic Planning and Development and the Public Construction Commission have attempted to develop a model suitable for application in Taiwan. Their efforts, however, have often been thwarted by political interference. Resources, as a result, are often assigned to the wrong places, leaving worthy sectors constantly in want of capital (Huang 2008).

The third weakness lies with the fact that the attention placed on the potential for financial leverage has long overwhelmed the attention given to financial efficiency. In recent years, Taiwan's finances have been in poor shape, and most local governments have run out of resources for capital investment. The job of scrutinising investment often falls to the media. Media reports can be biased and journalists may be unfamiliar with the legal requirements and professional assessments. Taken together, these three issues mean that development resources are likely to have been misplaced, with implications for the next stage of development in Taiwan (Huang 2008).

The new Taiwanese Government would do well to fund a more efficient procurement model that addresses these three weaknesses. As different countries are at different stages of development and face diverse macroeconomic backdrops and endowments, suitable financing options for infrastructure development will vary. Governments and multilateral agencies will remain important providers of funding, but the role of private financing looks set to grow. This underscores the need to put more effort into improving transparency and governance as well as enhancing cooperation in harmonising capital market standards and facilitating cross-border flows (Hansakul and Levinger 2016).

Although financing preferences will differ according to the macroeconomic and capital market conditions of each country, successful fundraising as well as project completion will depend on factors such as fiscal discipline and governance standards. Private investors, eager to benefit from long-term investment, can be enticed to take a greater role in infrastructure financing, but, as with public sector investment, this requires greater transparency, assessments of value for money and a more solid institutional framework—areas in which the government could improve its processes.

Discussion and conclusion

Private participation in infrastructure development is often promoted as it provides a popular option for public service delivery under fiscal constraint, offers opportunities for greater efficiency and innovation through competition and provides stable and long-term investment opportunities for the private sector. Governments have played the dominant role in owning and operating infrastructure facilities such as schools, hospitals, roads, bridges, railways, ports, telecommunications networks and water and electricity supply facilities. Their investment in infrastructure has been justified as a response to natural monopolies, and where the infrastructure services are seen as essential to the public good. Despite facing financial difficulty, governments are looking to expand investments in infrastructure projects as a source of fiscal stimulus, with the twin objectives of job creation and improving economic performance.

While these features may justify some public funding for infrastructure services, on their own they do not require public provision of infrastructure. Efficient financing is one element of efficient investment. The costs of financing large and complex infrastructure projects are substantial, so the savings from getting it right can be significant. The financing vehicle may provide information and create incentives that improve other aspects of an efficient investment decision. It may facilitate a better and narrower definition of any natural monopolies and thereby allow greater use of market competition to improve efficiency and promote innovation. Such vehicles should minimise the lifetime financing costs of a project. While the major financing task is meeting upfront investment costs in a timely manner, the central efficiency issue is which financing vehicle best manages project risk. Financing vehicles that assign risk to the partner best placed to manage each type of risk are more efficient, reducing the overall cost of the project. There may also be scope for the financing vehicle to influence allocative efficiency by imposing greater discipline on investment and funding decisions.

Investment in infrastructure development is the cornerstone of regional competition for efficiency and sustainability. Due to the participation of emerging developing countries in this competition and ever-changing domestic production elements and trade conditions, Taiwan's overall economic environment, which originally relied on exports as its chief growth engine, is being challenged. Therefore, effective use of the local market to boost the national economy becomes a feasible policy option, while continuous development of infrastructure is an important component of local demand. More importantly, it takes qualitative and quantitative enhancement of infrastructure to facilitate investment and improve living environments. In the midst of global competition, this can attract foreign investment and can play an instrumental role in keeping local capital in Taiwan for domestic development. At the turning point of industrial transformation, Taiwan's next phase of development will be dependent on whether its infrastructure development projects are more attractive than those of its competitors, whether it is more appealing to domestic/foreign investors and attracts international intelligence to help Taiwan become a better location for industrial activities and in which to live.

In terms of Taiwan's experience with PPPs, the key factor in public infrastructure funding is the financial feasibility of meeting the interests of all parties involved in such projects. During the tendering stages, the issues of transparent bidding and concrete concession agreements are most evident when unanimity exists between the government and interest groups. Also, project financing, efficient structuring of PPPs and negotiation focused on achieving win–win outcomes are the important factors during the project development phase, while experienced construction contractors and appropriate cost and quality control are the most significant factors during the construction phase. The use of the PPP concept in a well-defined legal environment offers the advantages of stimulating investment and promoting private participation in infrastructure development. To achieve best results when applying this concept, the critical factors identified in this chapter need to be addressed before the project's model is adopted.

Lessons from Taiwan's experience can be summed up as follows: 1) a public infrastructure investment plan must focus on long-term effects; 2) the expansion of public investment helps to stimulate the economy in the short term; 3) the widespread use of (flexible) financing tailored to the specific needs of each project offers the opportunity for increased efficiency and returns on investment; and 4) cost–benefit calculations help in the decision of whether to engage in a PPP. The budgeting and financial management of private participation in Taiwan's infrastructure encourage efficient financing and efficient investment through a bottom-up approach. Important lessons include the design of incentives to induce private investment and a careful review system to incorporate CBA. The enhancement of public–private infrastructure management, creation of win–win incentives, the promotion of a self-liquidating mechanism and the establishment of local government fiscal systems are essential for improving public–private partnerships.

References

Acerete, B., M. Gasca, A. Stafford and P. Stapleton. 2015. 'A comparative policy analysis of healthcare PPPs: Examining evidence from two Spanish regions from an international perspective'. *Journal of Comparative Policy Analysis: Research and Practice* 17(5): 502–18. doi.org/10.1080/13876988.2015.1010789.

Albalate, D., G. Bel, P. Bel-Piñana and R. R. Geddes. 2015. 'Risk mitigation and sharing in motorway PPPs: A comparative policy analysis of alternative approaches'. *Journal of Comparative Policy Analysis: Research and Practice* 17(5): 481–501. doi.org/10.1080/1387 6988.2015.1010788.

Association of Southeast Asian Nations (ASEAN). 2014. *ASEAN Principles for PPP Frameworks*. Jakarta: ASEAN Secretariat.

Boardman, A. E., C. Greve and G. A. Hodge. 2015. 'Comparative analyses of infrastructure public–private partnerships'. *Journal of Comparative Policy Analysis: Research and Practice* 17(5): 441–7. doi.org/10.1080/1 3876988.2015.1052611.

Chan, C., D. Forwood, H. Roper and C. Sayers. 2009. *Public infrastructure financing: An international perspective*. Staff Working Paper, 31 March. Melbourne: Productivity Commission.

Davidson, P. 2016. 'Trump's infrastructure plan: Potholes or a smooth ride?' *USA Today*, 16 November. Available from: www.usatoday.com/story/money/2016/11/16/trumps-infrastructure-plan-potholes-smooth-ride/93890402/ (accessed 17 July 2017).

Directorate-General of Budget, Accounting and Statistics (DGBAS). 2015. *Global Reach: Achieving quality*. Taipei City: DGBAS. Available from: www.dgbas.gov.tw/ (accessed 17 July 2017).

Eldrup, A. and P. Schütze. 2013. *Organisation and financing of public infrastructure projects: A path to economic development of the Danish Welfare Model*. Main report. Copenhagen: Offentligt-Privat Partnerskab.

European Commission (EC). 2014. *An Investment Plan for Europe*. Brussels: European Commission.

Grimsey, D. and M. K. Lewis. 2002. 'Evaluating the risks of public private partnerships for infrastructure projects'. *International Journal of Project Management* 20: 107–18. doi.org/10.1016/S0263-7863(00)00040-5.

Hansakul, S. and H. Levinger. 2016. 'Asia infrastructure financing: Getting it right would lift medium-term growth'. *DB Research Management* (January): 1–14.

Hellowell, M. 2015. 'Public investment as a driver of economic development and growth: What is the appropriate role of public–private partnerships?' In S. Caselli, V. Vecchi and G. Corbetta (eds) *Public–Private Partnerships for Infrastructure and Business Development: Principles, practices, and perspectives*. London: Palgrave Macmillan. doi.org/10.1057/9781137541482_3.

Her Majesty's (HM) Treasury. 2012. *A New Approach to Public–Private Partnerships*. London: HM Treasury.

Hodge, G. A. and C. Greve. 2013. 'Introduction: Public–private partnerships in turbulent times'. In C. Greve and G. Hodge (eds) *Rethinking Public–Private Partnerships: Strategies for turbulent times*. London: Routledge. doi.org/10.1016/b978-0-7020-4356-7.00001-x.

Hodge, G. A., C. Greve and A. E. Boardman (eds). 2010. *International Handbook on Public–Private Partnerships*. Cheltenham, UK: Edward Elgar.

Huang, H. 2008. *Challenges and opportunities for infrastructure development in Taiwan*. Economic Analysis Paper, June. Taipei: Taiwan Institute of Economic Research. Available from: english.tier.org.tw/eng_analysis/ EA200806_6.asp (accessed 17 July 2017).

Huang, Y. L. 1995. 'Project and policy analysis of build–operate–transfer infrastructure development'. PhD dissertation. Department of Civil Engineering, University of California at Berkeley.

Invest Taiwan. 2015. 'Taipei: Invest Taiwan'. Available from: investintaiwan. nat.gov.tw/homePage?lang=eng (accessed 17 July 2017).

Marris, S. 2008. 'Infrastructure fund to help development'. *The Australian*, 13 May. Available from: www.theaustralian.com.au/archive/national-affairs/infrastructure-fund-to-help-development/news-story/5ae0351 7d92d2a3f14c95218c85b7ca2 (accessed 28 August 2017).

Ministry of Finance (MoF). 2013. *Promotion of Private Participation.* Taipei: MoF. Available from: ppp.mof.gov.tw/PPP.Website/English/ Default.aspx (accessed 17 July 2017).

Ministry of Finance (MoF). 2015. *Private Participation in Infrastructure Projects: Investor's manual projects.* Taipei: MoF. Available from: ppp. mof.gov.tw (accessed 17 July 2017).

Ministry of Justice (MoJ). 2015. *Laws and Regulations Database of the Republic of China.* Taipei: MoJ. Available from: law.moj.gov.tw/Eng/ (accessed 17 July 2017).

National Development Council (NDC). 2015. 'Taipei City: NDC'. Available from: www.ndc.gov.tw/en/ (accessed 17 July 2017).

Organisation for Economic Co-operation and Development (OECD). 2012. *Recommendations of the Council on Principles for Public Governance of Public–Private Partnerships.* Paris: OECD Publishing.

Pianin, E. 2016. 'Trump's $1 trillion infrastructure plan raises a red flag for Dems'. *The Fiscal Times*, 21 November. Available from: www.the fiscaltimes.com/2016/11/21/Trump-s-1Trillion-Infrastructure-Plan-Raises-Red-Flag-Dems (accessed 17 July 2017).

Reeves, E. 2015. 'A review of the PPP experience in Ireland: Lessons for comparative policy analysis'. *Journal of Comparative Policy Analysis: Research and Practice* 17(5): 467–80. doi.org/10.1080/13876988.20 15.1023018.

Ross, T. W. and J. Yan. 2015. 'Comparing public–private partnerships and traditional public procurement: Efficiency vs. flexibility'. *Journal of Comparative Policy Analysis: Research and Practice* 17(5): 448–66. doi.org/10.1080/13876988.2015.1029333.

Wu, L. 2014. 'A study on the water infrastructure investment efficiency in the western rural areas of China: From the perspective of public service capacity'. Presentation to 2014 International Conference on Public Administration, University of Electronic Science and Technology of China, Chengdu, China, 24–26 October.

Wu, W. 1999. 'Reforming China's institutional environment for urban infrastructure provision'. *Urban Studies* 36(13): 2263–82. doi.org/ 10.1080/0042098992412.

Wu, W. 2008. 'Urban infrastructure financing and regional economic performance under China's fiscal decentralization'. Presentation to Symposium on Local Public Finance and Property Taxation in China, Lincoln Institute of Land Policy, Cambridge, MA, 12 May.

Wu, W. and L. Wang. 2011. 'Study on the current situation, problems and countermeasures of the water infrastructure in China'. [In Chinese]. *Macroeconomic Management* 11: 36–8.

Zhao, Z. and C. Cao. 2011. 'Funding China's urban infrastructure: Revenue structure and financing approaches'. *Public Finance and Management* 11(3): 284–305.

Appendix 11.1 Sections of the Statute for Encouragement of Private Participation in Transportation Infrastructure Projects

Article 28 states: A private entity encouraged under this Statute may be exempted from the business income tax for a maximum period of five (5) years from the year in which taxable income is derived after the commencement of operation of the transportation infrastructure project concerned.

Article 29 indicates: A private entity encouraged under this Statute may credit 5 per cent to 20 per cent of the amount of the following expenditures against the business income tax payable for the current year:

V.   Capital expenditures invested in building, operation equipment or technology.

VI.   Capital expenditures invested in procurement of pollution control equipment or technology.

VII.   Capital expenditures invested in research and development (R&D), and personnel training.

VIII.   Other investment expenditures as approved by the Executive Yuan.

Article 30 provides that: The machinery, equipment, special transporting vehicles, training apparatus and the required parts/components thereof which are imported by a private entity encouraged under this Statute for use in building the transportation infrastructure projects concerned shall be exempted from customs duties; provided that the purpose of use of such items is confirmed by Ministry of Transportation and Communications, and it is certified by Ministry of Economic Affairs that such items have not yet been manufactured and supplied domestically.

Appendix 11.2 i-Taiwan 12 projects

1. Island-wide Transportation Network

- MRT networks in northern, central and southern metropolitan areas.
  - Northern metropolitan MRT network: Linking of Taipei MRT with Tucheng, Sanxia, Yingge, Wanhua, Zhonghe, Shulin, Ankeng, Xizhi and Danhai; Keelung–Taoyuan–Taipei rail links; regional light-rail transit network linking Shezi, Shilin and Beitou.
  - Central metropolitan MRT network: Linking Taichung, Wuri, Changhua, Fengyuan, Wuqi, Dali, Wufeng, Caotun and Nantou.
  - Southern metropolitan MRT network: Chiayi High-Speed Rail Station to the urban area; Tainan MRT; extension of Kaohsiung MRT to Gangshan, Luzhu and Pingtung and continued construction of latter-stage network.
- Elimination of railway level crossings and transformation of rail lines into rapid transit systems, in northern, central and southern metropolitan areas.
- Electrification and double-tracking of the eastern railway.

- Purchase of passenger cars for the Neiwan Branch Line of the Taiwan Railway in Hsinchu, the Shalun Branch Line in Tainan and the East Coast Line.
- Integration of the freeway and highway systems.

2. Kaohsiung Free Trade and Ecology Harbour

- Construction of international container centre at Kaohsiung Harbour.
- Construction of a harbour eco-park and establishment of a marine technology and cultural centre.
- Transformation of the Qijin area into an international-class marine recreation area.
- Transformation of old harbour areas at Hamaxing, Gushan and Lingya.
- Expansion of warehousing and logistics facilities at Kaohsiung International Airport and improvement of peripheral transportation.

3. Taichung Asia-Pacific Sea–Air Logistics Centre

- Construction of a shipping network linking Taichung Harbour, Taichung Airport, the Central Taiwan Science Park and Changhua coast to provide an Asia-Pacific sea–air logistics centre.
- Expansion of the Central Taiwan International Airport and development of an air cargo terminal.
- Establishment of a warehousing, logistics and value-added processing zone.

4. Taoyuan International Aviation City

- Promotion of the enactment of the *Special Act for the Taoyuan Aviation City*, aimed at transforming Taoyuan International Airport into a 6,150-hectare Asia-Pacific international aviation city.
- Completion of the third terminal in 2018, followed by the fourth terminal and third runway.
- Renovation of Terminal 1.
- Construction of a comprehensive access network for the aviation city.

5. Intelligent Taiwan

Personnel development

- Strengthening of education in language and information, elimination of the urban–rural gap and the digital divide and encouragement of lifetime learning investment, the implementation of tuition-free high and vocational schools and the improvement of teachers, facilities and curricula in technical and vocational schools. Implementation of the eight-year, NT$80 billion (A$3.4 billion) Advance Toward Elite Universities and Educational Excellence plans with the goal of bringing research results up to world standards.

Cultural and creative industries

- Promotion of the *Cultural and Creative Industries Development Act*; establishment of cultural, creative and digital industrial parks; allocation of NT$10 billion (A$421.8 million) from the National Development Fund for start-up investment in enterprises related to cultural and creative industries; earmarking of a budget to provide incentives for operators in the cultural, creative and digital content industries to engage in international marketing and participate in international exhibitions.
- Development of Taiwan as a 'World No. 1 Wireless Broadband Country'.
- Extension of Taipei's 'Wireless City' experience to all major metropolitan areas throughout the country, with the installation of citywide wireless internet connectivity, and the building of a 'wireless freeway' that allows remote areas to enjoy the same wireless services as the cities.
- Development of an intelligent transportation system and intelligent living environment.
- Development of intelligent transportation management; intelligent integrated land, sea and air transportation; intelligent logistics and customs clearances; integrated and intelligent ticketing; and intelligent medical care, safety, funds flows and e-trading.

6. Industrial innovation corridors

- Taipei–Keelung–Yilan Industrial Innovation Corridor: In addition to the existing Neihu Technology Park and Nangang Software Park, construction of a new Beitou–Shilin Technology Park, Keelung Taipei Consolidated Technology Park, Taipei County Game Industry and Cultural Industrial Park and Yilan Science Park.

- Taoyuan–Hsinchu–Miaoli Industrial Innovation Corridor: Accelerated development of the Taoyuan Aviation Technology Park, Longtan base of the Hsinchu Science Park, fourth-stage expansion of the Zhunan base and Tonglo Defence Technology Park; establishment of 'international villages' to attract high-level professionals from overseas.

- Taichung–Changhua–Nantou Industrial Innovation Corridor: Establishment of a Changhua base of the Central Taiwan Science Park and a central Taiwan branch of the Industrial Technology Research Institute.

- Yunlin–Chiayi–Tainan Industrial Innovation Corridor: Development of agricultural biotechnology industries southwards from the central west coast.

- Kaohsiung–Pingtung–Penghu Industrial Innovation Corridor: Expansion of the Kaohsiung Software Park into an innovative technological R&D park, with residents such as branches of major central government research institutions, including the Industrial Technology Research Institute and the Institute for Information Industry.

- Hualien–Taitung Industrial Innovation Corridor: Provision of assistance to Hualien County in the establishment of a Stone Art Innovation Park, assistance for the development of the deep-ocean industry on the east coast and help for Taitung County in the establishment of a deep-water industrial park.

7. Urban and industrial park renewal

- Northern Taiwan: Implementation of the Capital Centre Historical Preservation and Redevelopment Plan and revitalisation of the positioning function and the Keelung Railway Station and Harbour Shore Renewal Plan.

- Central Taiwan: Renewal of Zhongxing New Village as a cultural, creative and high-level R&D park, and redevelopment of the former Shuinan Airport site.

- Southern Taiwan: Harbour Shore Redevelopment Plan for the mouth of the Love River in Kaohsiung City.
- Renewal and development of former industrial zones in northern, central and southern Taiwan.
- Development of new high-speed rail stations (in Nangang, Miaoli, Changhua and Yunlin) and special station zones.

8. Agricultural village revival

- Promotion of the enactment of the *Agricultural Village Revival Act 2010*, providing care for 600,000 farm families in 4,000 rural communities; establishment of a retirement mechanism for farmers (with the government providing NT$30 billion [A$1.3 billion] in interest subsidies); implementation of the 'Small Landlord, Large Tenant' system; encouragement of professional farmers to expand and industrialise their operations; and large-scale release of unsuitable farmland under a graded area management and rational payback mechanism to enhance the efficiency of utilisation of national land.

9. Seashore regeneration

- Removal of sediment from fishing harbours throughout Taiwan on a regular basis, re-engineering of traditional fishing harbours into modern dual-purpose fishing and tourist harbours and relaxation of restrictions on coastal yachting activities.
- Promotion of international investment in the development of coastal scenic spots and the building of coastal living and travel areas; development of cruise-ship tourism and promotion of Kaohsiung, Keelung and Hualien harbours as ports of call on international cruise routes; and review of forest protection and release of those areas that present no national security or ecological concerns, to enliven the use of coastal land.

10. Greening afforestation

- Afforestation of 60,000 hectares of flatland within eight years and development of three 1,000-hectare flatland forest recreation areas in central and southern Taiwan.

11. Flood control and river rectification

- Overall review of flood control plans, strengthening implementation and evaluation and increasing budgets where necessary.

- Implementation of the *Special Act for Gaoping River Rectification 2010* and use of a special fund to control flooding and pollution of the river.

- Strengthened injection of groundwater to improve the land subsidence situation; implementation of a general forest fire prevention plan; delineation of areas of mudflow danger and environmental sensitivity; and establishment of a mudflow monitoring and early warning system.

- Allocation of a four-year budget of NT$50 billion (A$2.1 billion) for the rebuilding of aboriginal homelands and the promotion of land conservation.

12. Sewer construction

- Construction of sewer lines to raise the sewerage connection ratio by 3 per cent per year, and strengthened construction of small-scale sewerage systems in remote and mountain areas to ensure the quality of water sources.

12

Municipal financial strategy responses to fiscal austerity: The case of Taiwan

Hsin-Fang Tsai

Introduction

Sima Guang, a historian of the Northern Song Dynasty, once admonished his son: 'It is easy for the frugal to become extravagant, but very difficult to reverse the process.' Centuries later, the context for considering the virtues of frugality has grown from 'regulating the family' to 'governing the country'. In the interests of providing social security and income redistribution, welfare spending—for example, on social assistance, unemployment insurance and medical insurance—has increased exponentially and has substantially extended the role of governments. The beginnings of local government autonomy in Taiwan could be characterised as a type of state guardianship, because local governments lacked independent authority and money. Since 1999, the central government has launched a series of financial system reforms to enhance the role of local government. The *Local Government Act 1999* provided a substantial increase in power for local governments and the *Act Governing the Allocation of Government Revenues and Expenditures* was revised in the same year to improve the financial resources of local government. A series of institutional reforms was launched, including increasing general grants and empowering local governments to levy new taxes. However, these failed to significantly increase local revenue or allow revenue to keep pace with expenditure. Local finances have been constantly in deficit in Taiwan, with little sign of improvement over the past decade (Table 12.1).

The challenge for municipalities has been how to address a surge in expenditure at a time of revenue stagnation. The response has involved an excessive dependence on the centralised system of taxes and grants. Of the five municipalities in Taiwan studied here—New Taipei, Taipei, Taichung, Tainan and Kaohsiung—Tainan City has the highest financial dependence on the centralised system, receiving 38.88 per cent of its average annual expenditure from grants (Table 12.2). Over the years, personnel expenses have absorbed an increasing proportion of revenue, which, combined with substantial growth in welfare spending, has led to structural rigidities in local fiscal expenditure and increasing local debt. In summary, the large gap between revenue and expenditure has resulted in a major debt burden. Municipalities have had to deliver public services to meet citizen demands despite this continuing fiscal imbalance.

Table 12.1 Revenue, expenses and balance at all levels of government (NT$100 million)

Year	Central government			Local government		
	Revenue	Expense	Balance	Revenue	Expense	Balance
2005	16,164	14,542	1,622	6,017	8,378	−2,361
2006	15,909	13,930	1,979	5,861	8,212	−2,351
2007	16,361	14,425	1,936	6,087	8,477	−2,390
2008	16,488	14,368	2,120	5,828	9,068	−3,240
2009	15,666	16,911	−1,245	5,470	9,798	−4,328
2010	15,005	15,799	−794	6,150	9,869	−3,719
2011	16,729	15,575	1,154	6,333	10,555	−4,222
2012	16,617	16,228	389	6,595	10,551	−3,956
2013	17,451	16,246	1,205	7,125	10,406	−3,281
2014	17,069	16,048	1,021	7,606	11,766	−4,160

Note: The numbers for 2005–13 are actual (settlement) amounts for those years; the numbers for 2014 are from the budget.

Source: Ministry of Finance (MoF 2014: 18–20).

Table 12.2 Ratio of five municipalities' revenue and dependence on grants (per cent)

Year	New Taipei		Taipei		Taichung		Tainan		Kaohsiung	
	A[1]	B[2]	A	B	A	B	A	B	A	B
2005	63.91	25.76	62.19	3.93	53.44	29.53	45.48	34.33	39.79	37.19
2006	59.81	24.71	62.02	3.26	55.82	28.91	42.84	37.67	42.40	30.95
2007	60.57	23.38	61.79	3.20	55.13	29.54	42.11	38.42	46.68	20.39
2008	44.37	20.36	57.76	17.15	47.90	37.38	33.61	46.09	44.49	30.34
2009	43.85	24.02	59.75	15.88	50.75	33.53	35.62	43.18	38.78	39.26
2010	53.22	14.98	62.37	16.59	50.97	36.45	35.84	44.80	41.57	36.46
2011	51.88	31.44	59.45	19.58	48.37	29.25	33.35	41.54	43.28	33.98
2012	58.01	21.05	58.88	18.45	54.01	23.75	42.01	34.42	48.10	24.98
2013	62.47	17.98	62.59	15.26	58.46	20.40	46.25	29.51	53.25	21.41
Average	55.34	22.63	60.76	12.59	52.76	29.86	39.68	38.88	44.26	30.55

[1] Ratio of municipality's revenue (A): (revenue – grants – allocation of income)/revenue × 100.

[2] Ratio of dependence on grants (B): (grants/revenue) × 100.

Source: DGBAS (2014).

In 2014, Taiwan's Ministry of Finance (MoF) announced its Local Fiscal Consolidation Project to promote local fiscal autonomy and control debt. Its practical strategies for local government included increasing resources for self-financing, reducing expenditure and debt and providing financial counselling. Local governments were encouraged to accept greater autonomy despite still being highly dependent on central government fiscal resources. To understand the strategies and measures the five Taiwanese municipalities under study adopted in response to fiscal austerity, this research addresses the following questions: 1) How did the municipalities respond to the Local Fiscal Consolidation Project? 2) What types of strategies and measures did the municipalities adopt to increase their revenue? 3) How did they control their expenditure? 4) How did they manage their debt?

The following sections consist of a brief literature review of local government strategies when facing financial difficulties, a discussion of the MoF's strategies in its Local Fiscal Consolidation Project, a description of the design and methodology of this research, a discussion of local governments' financial management strategies in response to fiscal austerity and a conclusion.

Municipal financial strategies in fiscal retrenchment

Pollitt (2010: 17–18) noted that many governments worldwide are facing a new era of 'public spending cutbacks and austerity'. In other words, governments are facing an unprecedented challenge generated by a conflict between public spending cutbacks in light of revenue limitations and increasing demands for public services (Pandey 2010; Overmans and Noordegraaf 2014: 99).

During times of fiscal austerity, when revenue is under severe pressure and governments face significant debt, a government's financial management strategy may be called 'cutback management' or 'austerity management'. In the field of public administration, Levine (1978) pioneered the study of cutback management, which he defined as 'managing organizational change toward lower levels of resource consumption and organizational activity' (Levine 1979: 180). It is difficult to determine which programs should be terminated during the process of cutback management, as there can be many problems that are difficult to solve and the people affected might not accept such changes. The public sector might also face challenges from professional norms and procedures, veterans' needs, affirmative action commitments and collective bargaining agreements. In addition, there could be problems related to morale and job satisfaction.

Raudla et al. (2013) conducted a systematic review of the literature on cutback management, noting the diversity of recent research. They found that some researchers have focused on the long-term relationship between cuts, reforms and some responsibilities of governments during periods of fiscal austerity (e.g. Dabrowski 2009; Thynne 2011; Gieve and Provost 2012). Other studies have focused on citizens' declining trust in government coupled with heightened expectations (e.g. Massey 2011; Posner and Blöndal 2012; Van de Walle and Jilke 2012; Kattel and Raudla 2013). Some have argued that the diversity of researchers' conclusions demonstrates a lack of consensus and also reflects the fact that various countries have pursued different strategies in response to financial difficulties (e.g. Pollitt 2010; Verick and Islam 2010; Bideleux 2011; Peters 2011; Peters et al. 2011; Kickert 2012; Lodge and Hood 2012; Raudla et al. 2013: 4).

Cutback management strategies differ by country, and the question of their effectiveness is highly controversial. Whether cutback management succeeds depends on the specific strategy utilised: expenditure cutting, revenue enhancement or management improvement. Each category has a range of specific measures and tactics often associated with it (Table 12.3).

Expenditure cutting strategies include curbing public services or access to them, deferral of maintenance and capital improvements, reduction in administrative expenses, suspension of public service projects, wage reductions and hiring freezes. Walzer et al. (1992) observed that there are two main characteristics of expenditure cutting strategies. One is that governments always cut the least important service programs. The other is that the effectiveness of the cutbacks depends on the nature of the cut. For example, if governments cut capital investment projects, the effect will be short term (Krueathep 2013).

Table 12.3 Strategies for cutback management

Expenditure cutting strategies	Revenue enhancement strategies	Management improvement strategies
1. Reduction in miscellaneous administrative expenses – e.g. overtime, travel, supplies 2. Hiring freeze 3. Across-the-board cuts in service programs 4. Cuts in least important service programs 5. Reductions in core services 6. Deferral of maintenance and capital improvement 7. Cuts in capital investment projects	1. Increasing tax rates or bases 2. Levying additional user fees or charges 3. Spending control through stringent tax and revenue targets 4. Drawing down fiscal reserves	1. Undertaking public expenditure reviews 2. Work process redesign 3. Medium-term spending cut and budgetary balance targets 4. Delegating services to other organisations (e.g. contracting out)

Source: Krueathep (2013: 455).

Revenue enhancement strategies include levying additional user fees, increasing tax rates or bases and drawing down fiscal reserves. According to empirical research, governments in the United States and Europe prefer to levy additional user fees because the concept of 'user pays' is readily accepted by their citizens (Pammer 1990; Walzer et al. 1992). Increasing tax rates or bases is an option for increasing revenue, but the political costs are very high and citizens have a strong antipathy towards taxation increases. More politically palatable are indirect increases in taxes by not adjusting thresholds for movements in prices and incomes. Drawing down fiscal reserves is another option, but it can only be used when governments have a budget surplus. Generally, government officials prefer to use revenue enhancement strategies, as these raise the most revenue with ongoing desirable effects. However, such strategies are very often not politically palatable.

Finally, governments can implement management improvement strategies to provide sufficient or improved public services with limited resources. This type of strategy includes delegating services to other organisations, redesigning work processes, medium-term spending cuts, setting targets to balance budgets and undertaking public expenditure reviews. Some researchers have noted that contracting out might enhance efficiency through competition and motivating the private sector to pursue profit maximisation (Borcherding et al. 1982; Daft 2007). Redesigning work processes can enhance efficiency and reduce the cost of public services. Setting medium-term targets to balance budgets and performing expenditure reviews can enable reallocation of public resources over time, promoting increased productivity, economic growth and stability (Schick 1998).

In Taiwan, many scholars have expressed concern about the financial difficulties faced by local governments. Since the 1990s, they have analysed the revenue structure of local governments and problems of insufficient financial resources, and have provided practical advice such as to increase taxes, broaden the concept of user pays and examine other options aimed at increasing revenue (Shan 1996). Some scholars have found that many local governments in Taiwan rely on a single source of revenue, which might adversely affect revenue stability. They have suggested that local governments should increase self-financing resources and enhance revenue diversification (Liu and Kuo 2012). Additionally, some scholars have emphasised the importance of oversight by, and the coordination mechanisms of, the central government. They have been concerned about the capacity of local government, in the absence of central government support, to handle increased fiscal responsibilities, promote fiscal autonomy, develop and use local financial information, impose local financial discipline and enhance cooperation with other local governments (Liao and Wu 2005; Hsu and Zheng 2011).

To address the fact that local governments in Taiwan are still facing fiscal imbalances, in February 2014, the MoF proposed its Local Fiscal Consolidation Project. This reform was aimed at integrating central and local governments' efforts to address fiscal imbalances. As the reform has been implemented for more than a year, the following section briefly reviews the initial results.

The Local Fiscal Consolidation Project in Taiwan

According to the MoF's National Treasury Administration, local governments in Taiwan now face four main fiscal challenges: insufficient self-financing resources, rigid revenue structures, fiscal imbalances and heavy debt burdens, and deficient financial discipline. The basic objectives of the reform package were promoting local governments' fiscal autonomy and controlling their debt, the target outcomes of which were to reduce their dependence on centrally allocated taxes and grants and to enhance their financial discipline and fiscal responsibility.

The Local Fiscal Consolidation Project has three main strategies for assisting local governments: increasing their self-financing resources, reducing their debt and providing them with financial counselling. The practical measures, each discussed below, can be divided into four main aspects: income source diversification, expenditure reduction, debt management and financial counselling (NTA 2014). The structure of the Local Fiscal Consolidation Project is presented in Table 12.4.

Table 12.4 Structure of the Local Fiscal Consolidation Project

Status quo	1. Insufficient self-financing resources 2. Rigid revenue structures 3. Fiscal imbalances and heavy debt burdens 4. Deficiency of financial discipline	
Objectives	1. Promote local governments' fiscal autonomy 2. Control local government debt	
Strategies	1. Increase local governments' self-financing resources 2. Reduce local government debt 3. Provide local governments with financial counselling	
Practical measures	Income source diversification	1. Revenue from tax 2. Non-tax revenue 3. Promotion of private participation in infrastructure projects
	Expenditure reduction	1. Change the use of land reserved for public infrastructure 2. Manage the number of personnel in municipalities 3. Organisational re-engineering 4. Review non-legal financial obligations 5. Reduce educational and personnel expenditure
	Debt management	1. Prepare debt repayment budget 2. Debt early warning system 3. Establish public debt administration committee
	Financial counselling	1. Strengthen the assessment of fiscal balance and debt 2. Benchmarking 3. Establish local financial appraisal index

Source: NTA (2014).

Income source diversification

To avoid excessive dependency on the central government, local governments need to increase their self-financing resources. The central government suggests this can be done from three sources: tax revenue, non-tax revenue and the promotion of private participation in infrastructure projects.

First, to increase tax revenue, local governments should review existing local tax credits and enhance the assessment of real estate values. Local tax credits include land value tax, housing tax exemptions and vehicle licensing tax exemptions for people with disabilities, and so on. Local governments could also review house and land valuations and, in particular, raise the tax rate on houses used for non-residential purposes.

Second, non-tax revenue could be increased by two methods: applying the user-pays model more widely and developing and activating public assets. Central and local governments could sign contracts with the private sector to activate real estate that is publicly owned but not required for public use. With private funding, such developments could be very successful. For instance, local governments could implement transit-oriented development initiatives, integrating transportation construction (e.g. mass rapid transit and railway systems) with land development. Local governments could benefit from such projects because the value of publicly owned real estate would likely increase (Chen 2012: 74).

The final measure to broaden sources of income is the promotion of private participation in infrastructure projects. Local governments could try different ways to attract private funds, such as build–operate–transfer (BOT) or operate–transfer (OT) project financing, relaxing investment barriers and holding investment conferences. Local governments could also encourage private finance initiatives.

Expenditure reduction

The means for reducing expenditure include changing the use of land reserved for public infrastructure, organisational re-engineering, managing the number of personnel, reviewing non-legal financial obligations and reducing expenditure on education and personnel. For instance, the Ministry of the Interior has offered subsidies to local governments to review and change the use of reserved land, the aim of which is to solve inefficiencies in the use of public land. Further, the central government assembled the Re-engineering Task Group to advise local governments on limiting their personnel expenses, promote downsizing measures, redesign the structure of organisations, and so on. Additionally, due to the falling birth rate in Taiwan, the number of new students has declined, providing an opportunity to review the distribution of education resources. According to the central government, local governments could also examine non-legal financial obligations to identify any unnecessary expenditure on social welfare.

Debt management

There are three practical measures in the MoF project concerning debt management. The first is budget control. Article 12 of the *Public Debt Act* (amended in 2013) states:

> For the purpose of stepping up debt management, the central government and municipalities shall prepare their budgets with at least 5 percent of tax revenues of the current fiscal year, and the counties (and county-level cities) and townships (and township-level cities) shall allocate at least 1 percent of the forecasted amount of outstanding public debt for the preceding fiscal year, for repayment of principal on debt.

Thus, governments at all levels are required to not only meet the debt interest costs, but also take action to reduce debt. The second measure is the establishment by the central government and each municipality of a public debt administration committee, regulated by the MoF, to supervise debt management and schedule repayments. The final measure is to establish an early warning mechanism for debt. If the forecast amount of public debt with a maturity of one year or more reaches 90 per cent of the loan cap, the local government should propose a repayment plan. Furthermore, local governments should publish an overview of their annual debt online.

Strengthening financial counselling to local governments

To strengthen financial counselling, local governments could improve their assessment of their fiscal balance and debt by benchmarking as well as by establishing local financial appraisal indices. Initially, governments could assess their debts and then identify means to broaden sources of income, reduce expenditure and make new tax-raising efforts (particularly in the taxation of housing). Benchmarking enables local governments to share governing experiences with each other, enabling them to continue enhancing financial management. The MoF has provided support for benchmarking by identifying financial performance indicators to guide action to reduce expenditure and control the deficit, broaden sources of income and/or manage debt (see Table 12.5). The central government should, however, go further and help to establish an impartial local appraisal index. The establishment of such an index would enhance the fiscal transparency of local governments, provide valid comparisons of performance and motivate local governments to make progress.

Table 12.5 Local financial appraisal index indicators

Aspects	Indicators
Expenditure reduction and deficit control	1. **Annual revenue and annual expenditure:** Comparing the rate of increase of annual revenue and annual expenditure 2. **Size of annual expenditure:** Last year's final determined expenditure minus the year before last year's final determined expenditure 3. **Surplus or deficit change:** Last year's final determined surplus or deficit minus the year before last year's final determined surplus or deficit
Income source diversification	1. **Increase or decrease in tax revenue:** Last year's final determined tax revenue minus the year before last year's final determined tax revenue (centrally allocated tax and tobacco and alcohol tax excluded) 2. **Increase or decrease in fee income:** Last year's final determined fee income minus the year before last year's final determined fee income 3. **Increase or decrease in self-financing resources:** Last year's final determined self-financing resources minus the year before last year's final determined self-financing resources 4. **The ratio of self-financing resources to annual revenue**
Debt management	1. **The assessment of debt** a) The ratio of debts to the loan cap b) Increase or decrease in the ratio of debts to the loan cap 2. **The assessment of interest payments burden** a) The ratio of interest payments to self-financing resources b) Increase or decrease in the ratio of interest payments to self-financing resources

Source: NTA (2014).

Research design and method

This research analyses municipalities' financial management strategies and explores their response to the Local Fiscal Consolidation Project. It addresses the likelihood that local fiscal action will be affected by each governor's concept of governance and fiscal responsibility and by the local political ecology. There are also differences and similarities among local governments—they may have differing degrees of self-responsibility, different business development situations and different sources of revenue, while facing similar rigid revenue structures and budget deficits. These differences and similarities may affect the influence the central government has in coordinating and consolidating local financial management.

The research used established statistical and qualitative analysis methods. The source of statistical data was the National Treasury Administration's local financial appraisal (NTA 2014). The research is also based on related acts, regulations and news reports. In addition, the differences and similarities among municipalities' strategies for managing financial distress were explored. In-depth interviews were conducted to collect qualitative data from respondents selected through a purposive sampling approach. Two accounting officers and seven financial officers were selected from across the five municipalities. The basic information provided by the respondents is presented in Table 12.6.

Table 12.6 In-depth interview respondents

Number	ID	Interview date	Title/institution
1	A	21 July 2014	Secretary-general/Finance Bureau
2	B	31 July 2014	Section chief/Finance Bureau
3	C	9 July 2014	Secretary-general/Budget, Accounting and Statistics Office
4	D	9 July 2014	Secretary-general/Finance Bureau
5	E	9 July 2014	Section chief/Finance Bureau
6	F	17 July 2014	Section chief/Finance Bureau
7	G	17 July 2014	Senior executive officer/Finance Bureau
8	H	16 July 2014	Section chief/Finance Bureau
9	I	16 July 2014	Section chief/Budget, Accounting and Statistics Office

Source: Author's work.

The in-depth interviews aimed to collect information about how bureaucrats in local governments respond to fiscal stress and the Local Fiscal Consolidation Project. Although local politicians might play a role, this research focused on administrative responsiveness and influences, so responses were invited from bureaucrats rather than politicians.

The interview outline is as follows:

1. The municipality you belong to uses what type of strategies or measures to increase revenue?

2. The municipality you belong to uses what type of strategies or measures to control expenditure?

3. The municipality you belong to uses what type of strategies or measures to manage debt?

4. What do you think of the Local Fiscal Consolidation Project? What is its impact on local finances?

Municipal financial strategies and responsiveness in Taiwan

The following section discusses income source diversification, expenditure reduction and debt management separately. In each instance, the manner in which municipalities have responded to the Local Fiscal Consolidation Project is discussed as well as their strategies and practical measures.

Income source diversification

To broaden sources of income, local governments could increase both tax revenue and non-tax revenue. Practical measures to increase tax revenue include reviewing credits for local taxes and enhancing the assessment of real estate values. Reviewing credits for local tax involves considering low tax rates for houses used for non-residential purposes, limiting landowners' eligibility for land tax exemptions, and so on. Real estate is valued regularly for the purposes of housing, land and land value increment taxes. In 2012, the Taiwanese Government introduced a requirement for registration of the sale price of real estate and, in 2014, it found that the average ratio of assessed land value to the trading price was 86.25 per cent. In May 2014, the *House Tax Act 2014* was amended so that land value assessments could more closely match the true market value (Department of Land Administration 2015). In 2015, every municipality and county adjusted its valuations[1] so that current assessed property values could match the true value, thereby enlarging the tax base for property taxes.

Practical measures for increasing non-tax revenue include user pays and developing and activating public assets. The concept of user pays may be accepted by most Taiwanese people and, according to the *Charges and Fees Act 2002*, local governments can charge fees that are affordable for citizens, but they should review the fees every three years. This offers considerable opportunity to increase charges to cover more of the costs of services. Furthermore, local governments could develop and activate real estate that is publicly owned but not required for public use. With the private sector's expertise and capital funds, local governments could create new

---

1   According to the Ministry of the Interior, in 2015 the ratio of assessed land value to trading price in municipalities and counties rose by: Penghu, 24.94 per cent; Kinmen, 17.91 per cent; Yilan, 16.57 per cent; New Taipei City and Kaohsiung, 15.17 per cent; Hsinchu City, 13.21 per cent; Pingtung, 12.92 per cent; Taoyuan, 12.56 per cent; Tainan City, 12.49 per cent; Taichung City, 11.06 per cent; and Taipei City, 10.63 per cent.

business opportunities and increase local revenue. Since 1997, Taipei City has used the BOT model for project financing, signing contracts with the private sector to develop and activate real estate that is publicly owned but not required for public use. In 2012, BOT projects in Xinyi and Shilin districts were successfully executed, generating NT$27.1 billion (A$1.14 billion) for the Taipei City Government (Lin 2012). Currently, Taipei City has the most BOT cases of the five municipalities considered in this study and its local government is seeking additional opportunities for generating income.

As identified in Table 12.5, indicators of local government income diversification include the change rates of tax revenue, fee income and self-financing resources and the ratio of self-financing resources to annual revenue. The results for 2013 are shown in Table 12.7. In that year, every municipality's tax revenue increased (the maximum was New Taipei City's, at 18.89 per cent, and the minimum was Taipei City's, at 5.17 per cent). Kaohsiung City and Taichung City exhibited a significant increase in self-financing resources (19.51 per cent and 16.58 per cent, respectively). Their ratios of self-financing resources to annual revenue were over 50 per cent. On this score, Taipei City and New Taipei City outperformed the other municipalities, with over 60 per cent of self-financing resources, whereas Tainan City lagged behind all other municipalities.

Table 12.7 Municipalities' performance in broadening sources of income, 2013 (per cent)

Items Municipality	Change in tax revenue[1]	Change in fee income[2]	Change in self-financing resources[3]	Ratio of self-financing resources to annual revenue
Taipei City	5.17	−1.19	5.67	62.59
New Taipei City	18.89	12.42	9.71	62.47
Taichung City	13.93	9.62	16.58	58.46
Tainan City	7.81	14.80	4.23	46.25
Kaohsiung City	10.59	6.34	19.51	53.25

[1] Change in tax revenue: The final determined tax revenue for 2013 minus that for 2012 (centrally allocated tax and tobacco and alcohol tax excluded).

[2] Change in fee income: The final determined fee income for 2013 minus that for 2012.

[3] Change in self-financing resources: The final determined self-financing resources for 2013 minus those for 2012.

Source: NTA (2014).

Expenditure reduction

Although local governments need to control personnel expenses by themselves, the central government should respect local government autonomy and help them to find the means to do so. Direct supervision by the central government might not receive a positive response from local governments, which might undermine the goal of reducing expenditure. To help control social welfare expenditure, the central government provides general grants to local governments for specific items and decides future funding on the basis of local governments' previous performance. Therefore, local governments are encouraged to cooperate with the central government through their access to more grants.

It is common for local governments to change the use of land reserved for public infrastructure to reduce expenditure. Through zone expropriation and urban land consolidation, local governments can maximise revenue from their land. Furthermore, by changing the use of some of the land reserved for public infrastructure, local governments can reduce maintenance costs while keeping sufficient land for public infrastructure. Moreover, after urban land consolidation, current land values tend to rise, in which case local tax revenue increases. Taking Taichung City as an example, in the past 10 years, zone expropriation has created more than NT$10.2 billion (A$420.5 million) in revenue and the Phase VII Urban Land Consolidation program has created more than NT$25.3 billion (A$1.06 billion) in revenue and related expenditure savings. According to the Land Administration Bureau of Taichung City, this tactic saved the public almost NT$14.6 billion (A$614 million). Further, the ongoing Phases XIII and XIV of the Urban Land Consolidation Program could save NT$57.7 billion (A$2.4 billion) for the Taichung City Government.

As set out in Table 12.5, indicators of expenditure reduction include comparisons of annual revenue and expenditure growth, the size of annual expenditure relative to the previous year and the level of the surplus or deficit. These indicators for the five municipalities are set out in Table 12.8. In Taichung City and Tainan City, the increases in annual expenditure budgets are much higher than the increases in annual revenue (in Taichung City, it is about 12.7 per cent higher). Of the five municipalities studied here, all except Taichung City successfully controlled their expenditure (Tainan achieving actual expenditure savings despite budgeting for more growth in expenditure than in revenue). Generally, in 2013, New Taipei City and Kaohsiung City performed comparatively well, whereas Taichung City was the only municipality to exhibit a deficit increase.

Table 12.8 Municipalities' performance in reducing expenditure, 2013 (per cent)

Items Municipality	Annual expenditure budget growth rate compared with revenue budget growth rate[1]	Size of annual expenditure increase[2]	Surplus or deficit[3]	
			Change in surplus	Change in deficit
Taipei City	−6.15	−3.69	-	−2.96
New Taipei City	−0.25	−2.08	-	−3.62
Taichung City	12.70	9.67	-	1.70
Tainan City	7.82	−5.65	-	−0.33
Kaohsiung City	−1.39	−2.26	-	−8.68

[1] Annual revenue and annual expenditure budget growth rate: Annual expenditure budget increase compared with annual revenue budget increase in 2014.

[2] Relative size of annual expenditure increase: Final determined expenditure for 2013 minus that for 2012.

[3] Surplus or deficit: Final determined surplus or deficit for 2013 minus that for 2012.

Source: NTA (2014).

Debt management

Because local governments could not balance their budgets, the Local Fiscal Consolidation Project established a mechanism for controlling debt. For example, the rules for forced budget repayment required every municipality to allocate at least 5 per cent of the current fiscal year's tax revenue for debt repayment and to establish a public debt administration committee before 2014; according to the National Treasury Administration, this requirement was met. The committees were established to supervise debt management and make repayment schedules.

Another mechanism for debt management is based on information transparency. With a debt early warning and control system, local governments can be held more responsible for debt management. If a local government's forecast amount of public debt with a maturity of one year or more reaches 90 per cent of the loan cap, the central government issues a public warning and forces it to make plans for repayment. Moreover, without public debt administration committee approval, a local government with poor debt management may not be able to borrow more money.

Local governments' performance in debt management is shown in Table 12.9. For 2013, the Tainan City Government tried to reduce its debt-to-loan cap ratio but still reached 94.5 per cent of its loan cap, which activated the early warning mechanism, requiring it to propose a debt management plan and schedule to repay the debt. It is worth mentioning that New Taipei City increased its debt-to-loan cap significantly (by 19.72 per cent), to 72.91 per cent, suggesting it could be heading for a quite high debt-to-loan cap ratio. At the same time, its ratio of interest payments to self-financing resources increased about 22.29 per cent, which is relatively high among the five municipalities.

Table 12.9 Municipalities' debt management performance, 2013 (per cent)

Items Municipality	Assessment of debt amount[1]		Assessment of interest payment burden[2]	
	Ratio of debt amount to loan cap	Change in ratio of debt to loan cap	Ratio of interest payments to self-financing resources	Change in ratio of interest payments to self-financing resources
Taipei City	40.13	3.95	2.75	26.59
New Taipei City	72.91	19.72	0.65	22.29
Taichung City	71.43	−4.86	0.73	−3.95
Tainan City	94.50	−2.53	1.88	14.89
Kaohsiung City	70.64	2.21	1.89	−39.04

[1] The assessment of debt amount: a) The ratio of debt to loan cap in 2013; b) Change in ratio of debt amount to loan cap—the ratio of debt amount to loan cap for 2013 minus that for 2012.

[2] The assessment of interest payment burden: a) The ratio of interest payments to self-financing resources in 2013; b) Change in the ratio of interest payments to self-financing resources—the ratio of interest payments to self-financing resources for 2013 minus that for 2012.

Source: NTA (2014).

The aim of the central government's establishment of these local financial appraisal indices was to strengthen financial counselling of local governments to enhance their financial discipline and fiscal responsibility. But do these municipalities really follow the Local Fiscal Consolidation Project? How are they responding in practice?

Some interviews with local officials indicate that local governments have a negative attitude towards the Local Fiscal Consolidation Project and have little respect for it. In their view, it is a recycled initiative and has limited ability to improve their local financial situation. The problem is that most of the central government's remedies are ways to take money from citizens; consequently, local government leaders cannot or do not want to accept these remedies, primarily because of the effect they believe such measures would have on election outcomes. It is unsurprising, then, that local governments have demonstrated little interest in the Local Fiscal Consolidation Project.

> Basically, I think the Local Fiscal Consolidation Project is not a novel idea. It could not solve any financial problem. It's just a matter of form, and it is no help on local finance. I think the most important thing is supervision and maybe there is the effect of benchmarking. (Respondent B)

> I think it is of no use because the Local Fiscal Consolidation Project is just like a poor combination of old ideas. Most of the ideas already exist. (Respondent A)

Subjectively, local governments prefer approaches that do not adversely affect citizens, but, rather, attract their notice and support. In particular, local governments with land sites to develop prefer zone expropriation and urban land consolidation strategies. These measures can both reduce expenditure and broaden sources of income. Many local governments promote this idea and some have achieved significant fiscal outcomes.

> I think zone expropriation and urban land consolidation contribute a lot to government revenue. It has great outcomes. (Respondent D)

> The most successful policy is the urban land consolidation. After the urban land consolidation, our government could earn approximately NT\$30 billion [A\$1.3 billion]. Moreover, the land value would rise and the tax base of land value tax, house tax, and land value increment tax would also rise. (Respondent C)

> Through zone expropriation and urban land consolidation, the city government does not need to spend money. It can make ends meet and even earn some more money. (Respondent F)

> The process of urban land consolidation goes very fast. It can generate tax revenue from house tax or land value tax and enrich the city government. (Respondent H)

Local governments also favour private participation in infrastructure projects. In the case of financial difficulties, local governments have no choice but to cooperate with the private sector. The central government does help local governments find investors, decide what infrastructure to build and remove investment barriers. Local governments use different methods, such as BOT or OT, to finance infrastructure. Even if the public and private sectors could benefit from public–private partnerships (PPPs), governments need to strike a balance between public and private interests when they develop such partnerships.

> Promotion of private participation in infrastructure projects could save money for governments. It is the government's responsibility to provide infrastructure. However, with the private sector's assistance local governments could save money and enhance efficiency. Take our city as an example, we develop 22 public–private partnerships and the private sector has invested more than NT$20 billion [A$842 million]. (Respondent F)

When local governments try to solve debt issues through the promotion of private participation, they need to consider carefully whether they are replacing direct loans (or debt) with indirect loans, particularly if the PPP deal involves the private partner being paid a fee by users. From a political perspective, there are likely to be limits to the extent to which new capital developments, whether through land consolidations or PPPs, can solve local financial problems. While local governments might not like the pressure from the central government to live within their means, it is understandable that the central government does not want to provide more grants and revenue transfers when local governments could accept more of the financial burden.

Conclusion

In a new era of governance, the role of local governments in Taiwan is changing. They face a dilemma in the need to make cutbacks as well as an expectation to provide more public services. After 2000, there was a series of fiscal decentralisation reforms aimed at responding to the call for fiscal autonomy. Unfortunately, these reforms seemed neither to increase local governments' revenue significantly nor to diminish their financial dependence on the central government. In the past 10 years, most local governments in Taiwan have had to fight for funding from higher levels of government, while also looking to broaden revenue and reduce expenditure; local government politicians, however, have made commitments during election campaigns causing expenditure increases.

In 2014, the MoF launched the Local Fiscal Consolidation Project, which provided clearer strategies and measures for local governments to cope with fiscal imbalances. The project contains 27 practical measures under four main headings: income source diversification, expenditure reduction, debt management and financial counselling. In pursuing financial counselling, the central government wants to help lower-level governments to exercise fiscal autonomy and control their debt.

To broaden sources of income and improve fiscal autonomy, some practical measures were suggested, including reviewing credits for local taxes and enhancing the assessment of real estate values. These aim to increase revenue by means of broadening the local tax base. According to the National Treasury Administration, in 2013, every municipality's tax revenue increased (the maximum was New Taipei City's, at 18.89 per cent, and the minimum was Taipei City's, at 5.17 per cent). These measures seem effective, especially in larger cities such as New Taipei, Taichung and Kaohsiung City. The other measure was to increase non-tax revenue through user pays and developing and activating public assets. Comparatively speaking, these measures have been accepted because of their limited adverse effects, whereas broader revenue measures, such as increased tax rates, did not work because of political resistance.

Expenditure cutting measures suggested by the Local Fiscal Consolidation Project included managing personnel numbers in municipalities, re-engineering organisations, reviewing non-legal financial obligations and reducing educational and personnel expenditure. In 2013, Kaohsiung City and New Taipei City outperformed the other municipalities in reducing their expenditure—decreasing the level of deficit by 3.62 per cent and 8.68 per cent, respectively. Some successes were achieved via land development or where the central and local governments shared the expenditure burden and related political pain via financial grants. However, it is understandable that local governments were reluctant to initiate action to reduce services to the public, by adopting public service cuts in areas such as education and social welfare, and wanted the central government to take the lead in this area.

Finally, the Local Fiscal Consolidation Project attempted to establish an open information mechanism and accountability system to manage and control debt, including making rules for forced budget repayment and establishing public debt administration committees. Tainan City's debt reached 94.5 per cent of its loan cap in 2013, which activated the early warning mechanism, and the city was required to propose a debt management plan and repayment schedule for the following year. With the policy of information transparency, the public and the mass media are better positioned to provide oversight of their governments and to hold local government leaders accountable and prevent them from increasing debt.

To sum up, if the central government wants to be a financial counsellor or controller in cutback management, in Taiwan, as in many other countries, the difficulty is ensuring each level of government accepts responsibility for funding its functions. Politically, it is easier for local governments to blame the central government for insufficient grants and revenue shares and for the central government to push responsibility for functions to local governments without identifying the sources of funding.

References

Bideleux, R. 2011. 'Contrasting responses to the international economic crisis of 2008–2010 in the 11 CIS countries and in the 10 post-communist EU member countries'. *Journal of Communist Studies and Transition Politics* 27(3–4): 338–63. doi.org/10.1080/13523279.201 1.595152.

Borcherding, T., B. Burnaby, W. Pommerehne and F. Schneider. 1982. 'Comparing the efficiency of private and public production: The evidence from five countries'. *Journal of Economics* 2: 127–56.

Chen, S. Z. 2012. 'Exploration of financial autonomy after five municipalities' adjustment'. [In Chinese]. *Taiwan Economic Forum* 10(12): 52–81.

Dabrowski, M. 2009. *The global financial crisis: Lessons for European integration.* CASE Network Studies & Analyses No. 384. Warsaw: Center for Social and Economic Research.

Daft, R. L. 2007. *Understanding the Theory and Design of Organization.* Mason, OH: Thomson South-Western.

Department of Land Administration. 2015. 'Ministry of Interior estimates the present value of the land in 2015 raised the national average of 12.04%'. [In Chinese]. Press release. Taipei: Ministry of the Interior. Available from: www.land.moi.gov.tw/pda/hotnews.asp?cid=413&mcid=3281 (accessed 3 May 2015).

Directorate-General of Budget, Accounting and Statistics (DGBAS). 2014. *National Statistics: Main municipalities' statistics index.* [In Chinese]. Taipei: DGBAS. Available from: statdb.dgbas.gov.tw/pxweb/Dialog/varval.asp?ma=CS2501A1A&ti=&path=../database/CountyStatistics/&lang=9 (accessed 16 August 2017).

Fang, K.-H. 2006. 'Exploring fiscal decentralization and its meaning in Taiwan'. [In Chinese]. *Policy Research* 6: 51–88.

Gieve, J. and C. Provost. 2012. 'Ideas and coordination in policymaking: The financial crisis of 2007–2009'. *Governance: An International Journal of Policy, Administration, and Institutions* 25(1): 61–77. doi.org/10.1111/j.1468-0491.2011.01558.x.

Hsu, J. H. and M. H. Zheng. 2011. 'Challenges and prospects of local finance in new municipalities ages'. [In Chinese]. *Government Resource Planning* 35(6): 57–70.

Kattel, R. and R. Raudla. 2013. 'The Baltic republics and the crisis of 2008–2011'. *Europe–Asia Studies* 65(3): 426–49. doi.org/10.1080/09668136.2013.779456.

Kickert, W. 2012. 'State responses to the fiscal crisis in Britain, Germany and the Netherlands'. *Public Management Review* 14(3): 299–309. doi.org/10.1080/14719037.2011.637410.

Krueathep, W. 2013. 'Municipal responses to fiscal austerity: The Thai case'. *International Journal of Public Administration* 36(7): 453–68. doi.org/10.1080/01900692.2013.772631.

Land Administration Bureau of Taichung City Government. 2013. *Open Sources and Throttle Practice and Outcome*. [In Chinese]. Taichung City: Land Administration Bureau of Taichung City Government. Available from: www.land.taichung.gov.tw/archive/82/file/地政局開源節流績效.pdf (accessed 5 May 2015).

Lee, Y. J., K. N. Sun, X. F. Li and B. W. Lin. 2007. *Government Finance and Budget*. [In Chinese]. Taipei: Wu-Nan Culture Enterprise.

Levine, C. H. 1978. 'Organizational decline and cutback management'. *Public Administration Review* 38(4): 316–25. doi.org/10.2307/975813.

Levine, C. H. 1979. 'More on cutback management: Hard questions for hard times'. *Public Administration Review* 39(2): 179–83. doi.org 10.2307/3110475.

Levine, C. H., I. S. Rubin and G. G. Wolohojian. 1981. *The Politics of Retrenchment: How local governments manage fiscal stress*. Beverly Hills, CA: Sage Publications.

Liao, K. J. and C. C. Wu. 2005. 'Unbearable future: Local financial dilemma, case analysis of township-level public authorities of Chia-Yi County'. [In Chinese]. *Journal of Public Administration* 14: 79–124.

Liu, C. H. and N. L. Kuo. 2012. 'Revenue diversification and revenue stability: Empirical evidence from local governments in Taiwan'. [In Chinese]. *Public Administration & Policy* 54: 83–120.

Lin, X. C. 2012. 'Taipei Q1 "double floor right" + "dual urban renewal" Tender'. [In Chinese]. *MyGoNews*, 31 January. Available from: www.mygonews.com/news/detail/news_id/8019 (accessed 3 May 2015).

Lodge, M. and C. Hood. 2012. 'Into an age of multiple austerities? Public management and public service bargains across OECD countries'. *Governance: An International Journal of Policy, Administration, and Institutions* 25(1): 79–101. doi.org/10.1111/j.1468-0491.2011.01557.x.

Massey, A. 2011. 'Nonsense on stilts: United Kingdom perspectives on the global financial crisis and governance'. *Public Organization Review* 11: 61–75. doi.org/10.1007/s11115-010-0147-y.

Ministry of Finance (MoF). 2014. *Yearbook of Financial Statistics, Republic of China 2013*. [In Chinese]. Taipei: Ministry of Finance.

National Treasury Administration (NTA). 2014. *Fiscal Consolidation Project: Key planning and outcomes.* [In Chinese]. Taipei: NTA. Available from: www.nta.gov.tw/web/Eng/Default.aspx (accessed 17 July 2017).

Overmans, T. and M. Noordergraaf. 2014. 'Managing austerity: Rhetorical and real responses to fiscal stress in local government'. *Public Money & Management* 34(2): 99–106. doi.org/10.1080/09540962.2014.887517.

Pammer, W. J. 1990. *Managing Fiscal Strain in Major American Cities: Understanding retrenchment in the public sector.* Westport, CT: Greenwood Press.

Pandey, S. K. 2010. 'Cutback management and the paradox of publicness'. *Public Administration Review* 70(4): 564–71. doi.org/10.1111/j.1540-6210.2010.02177.x.

Peters, B. G. 2011. 'Governance responses to the fiscal crisis: Comparative perspectives'. *Public Money & Management* 31(1): 75–80. doi.org/10.1080/09540962.2011.545551.

Peters, B. G., J. Pierre and T. Randma-Liiv. 2011. 'Economic crisis, public administration and governance: Do new problems require new solutions?' *Public Organization Review* 11(1): 13–27. doi.org/10.1007/s11115-010-0148-x.

Pollitt, C. 2010. 'Cuts and reforms: Public services as we move into a new era'. *Society and Economy* 32(1): 17–31. doi.org/10.1556/SocEc.32.2010.1.3.

Posner, P. and J. Blöndal. 2012. 'Democracies and deficits: Prospects for fiscal responsibility in democratic nations'. *Governance: An International Journal of Policy, Administration, and Institutions* 25(1): 11–34. doi.org/10.1111/j.1468-0491.2011.01554.x.

Raudla, R., R. Savi and T. Randma-Liiv. 2013. *Literature Review on Cutback Management.* Rotterdam: COCOPS. Available from: hdl.handle.net/1765/40927 (accessed 17 July 2017).

Schick, A. 1998. *A Contemporary Approach to Public Expenditure Management.* Washington, DC: The World Bank.

Shan, C. C. 1996. 'Managing fiscal stress in local governments'. [In Chinese]. *The Chinese Public Administration Review* 5(3): 123–42.

Thynne, I. 2011. 'Symposium introduction: The global financial crisis, governance and institutional dynamics'. *Public Organization Review* 11: 1–12. doi.org/10.1007/s11115-010-0144-1.

Van de Walle, S. and S. Jilke. 2012. *Savings in public services: A multilevel analysis of public preferences in the EU27.* COCOPS Working Paper No. 8. Rotterdam: COCOPS.

Verick, S. and I. Islam. 2010. *The great recession of 2008–2009: Causes, consequences and policy responses.* IZA Discussion Paper No. 4934, May. Bonn: Institute for the Study of Labor.

Walzer, N., W. Jones, Bokenstrand and H. Magnusson. 1992. 'Choosing fiscal austerity strategies'. In P. E. Mouritzen (ed.) *Managing Cities in Austerity: Urban Fiscal Stress in Ten Western Countries.* London: Sage Publications.

Wolman, H. 1980. 'Local government strategies to cope with fiscal pressure'. In C. Levine and I. S. Rubin (eds) *Fiscal Stress and Public Policy.* Beverly Hills, CA: Sage Publications.

Zhou, Z.-L. 2014. 'Metropolitan urban area growth and multi-scale governance challenges of globalization in Taiwan'. [In Chinese]. *Humanities and Social Sciences Newsletter Quarterly* 15(2): 67–77.

13

Australia's employment services, 1998–2012: Using performance monitoring and evaluation to improve value for money

Wendy Jarvie and Trish Mercer

The reform of employment services delivery in Australia

Australia, together with the Netherlands, has been recognised as a world leader in the introduction of market competition for the provision of employment assistance to unemployed jobseekers. Yet as Struyven (2004: 3) has observed, the creation of a quasi-market in employment service provision is not a simple choice for government and requires a continual and complex 'balancing act' between government regulation and creating sufficient room for market competition, and also between the goals of efficiency and equity. This chapter investigates the intensive evaluation and performance monitoring processes that the Australian Government invested in and utilised over the 15 years from 1998 to support the development and fine-tuning of the market delivery of employment services, and to drive continual improvement in value for money.

In the early 1990s, a period of experimentation had begun in the delivery of employment assistance, which is a national government function in Australia. The Labor Government of Paul Keating had moved beyond the traditional provision of such assistance by its public provider (the Commonwealth Employment Service) to encourage contestability in employment services, including an innovative case management approach for the long-term unemployed delivered by the community sector and private contracted case managers and a billion-dollar investment in training programs under the Working Nation program (Davidson and Whiteford 2012: 53). By 1995, the last year of the Keating Government, the annual cost of employment and labour market assistance programs was over $4 billion. Following the election of John Howard's Coalition Government in 1996, what was seen as a more radical experiment was introduced, in May 1998, which involved the Department of Employment[1] contracting a Job Network of community-based and private providers who would provide employment assistance to unemployed jobseekers and also employers (Thomas 2007: 1–2). While it delivered significant budget savings, this reform, the government contended, would address known deficiencies in the current provision of employment assistance, which had not achieved any significant difference in getting the unemployed into regular employment, while retaining the case management approach with its emphasis on flexible and individualised assistance. At the same time, the government tightened the requirements on those receiving unemployment benefits to actively look for work (known as 'activity testing') and increased the sanctions for failing to do so (Thomas 2007: 10–11).

The rationale for outsourcing employment services was that it would ensure a greater focus on achieving *outcomes for clients* at *lower cost to government* through:

1. *paying for client outcomes* rather than inputs
2. *creating competition* between providers for
   a. employment services contracts (through tendering arrangements)
   b. jobseeker clients (who could choose their employment service provider).

---

1   The Department of Employment has experienced a number of machinery-of-government (and thus name) changes since 1998. For simplicity, it is referred to as the Department of Employment in this chapter.

It was thus intended to focus provider strategies, energies and resources on achieving outcomes for clients, at the lowest costs possible, and not on providing activities for clients to do. This was in line with the prevailing New Public Management (NPM) public administration theory to shift focus from inputs to outcomes. A declared objective of the reforms was to obtain better value for money (PC 2002: 3.2).

The Job Network system was managed by the Department of Employment (for an explanation of its role, see Appendix 13.1). It operated through the referral by the newly established public benefits agency, Centrelink, of jobseekers receiving government income support to the contracted providers, who had flexibility in determining what 'employment assistance' (rather than a conventional labour market program, as under the previous system) would be appropriate for an individual jobseeker. Fees paid to providers comprised two components: one fee when a jobseeker commenced with them and a second when an employment or other outcome was obtained. Fees were on a sliding scale, with higher fees set for those who remained in employment for 26 weeks or more. Fees for both components also varied depending on the level of jobseeker disadvantage the client faced, as assessed by Centrelink through the Job Seeker Classification Instrument (JSCI). The higher fees were intended to offer providers an incentive to make the greater effort required to help more disadvantaged jobseekers.

While the key principles of the system remained unchanged—such as having contracted employment service providers and payments for outcomes—the system itself underwent significant development and modification between 1998 and 2012. Broadly, there were three main phases (see Table 13.1):

1. The Job Network 'Black-box'[2] Market (1998–2003): The initial development phase, in which contracted providers had significant discretion as to what 'employment assistance' they provided and which focused on outcomes over processes (i.e. 'black-box' methods).

2. The Job Network 'Regulated Market' (2003–09) (also called the Active Participation Model [APM]): The second phase, in which there were increased government regulation and monitoring of providers with

---

2   This was the term commonly used for this first phase of the Job Network.

a prescribed continuum of services for jobseekers, in response to the discovery that providers were not investing sufficient resources in their most disadvantaged jobseekers.

3. The Job Services Australia (JSA) *'Inclusive Market'* (2009–12): The revamping of the system under the new Labor Government of Kevin Rudd, which rolled seven schemes into one with four 'streams' of assistance for the unemployed, greater focus on the most disadvantaged and more transparent provider star ratings.

Improving value for money

The budgetary gains for the government from introducing the Job Network were evident from the outset: there was an immediate reduction in the national budget spent on active labour market programs, from $4.08 billion in 1995–96 to $2.56 billion in 1998–99 (Organisation for Economic Co-operation and Development [OECD] 2001: 205). There was an associated decline in gross domestic product (GDP) spending on active labour market programs, from 0.8 per cent to 0.4 per cent over two years (OECD 2001: 13).

As well as clear budget savings, there were significant reductions in the average cost per employment outcome.[3] The employment department, in its evaluation report in 2002, estimated that Job Network costs per employment outcome were the lowest achieved in the previous decade: about $5,000–$6,000 since mid-1998, compared with between $10,000 and $16,000 under Labor's Working Nation programs in the mid-1990s (DEWR 2002b: 4). This decline in costs per employment outcome had been produced through both lower unit costs and higher employment outcomes (Davidson and Whiteford 2012: 108).

The marked change in cost per employment outcome is shown in Figure 13.1. Over time, moreover, this cost continued to decline (Figure 13.2). The sustainability of outcomes achieved by jobseekers was maintained, together with improvements in net impact.[4] Surveys

---

3   'Cost per employment outcome' is the average unit cost of all programs divided by the proportion of participants in employment three months after leaving the program (Davidson and Whiteford 2012: 108).

4   Net impact is the measure of the difference that employment services have made to clients' expected outcomes without assistance. See, for example, DEWR (2003: 98).

showed that both employers and jobseekers were happier with the new arrangements, and the model of provision proved to have sufficient flexibility to deal with changes to labour market conditions, including the reductions in unemployment, the emergence of skills shortages up to 2007 and the worsening employment situation with the Global Financial Crisis (GFC) of 2008. The effectiveness, including cost-effectiveness, of this model of service delivery has been recognised by the OECD (2001: 20; 2012: 13), external researchers (Thomas 2007: 15; Davidson and Whiteford 2012: 57) and through an independent review by the government's research and evaluation body, the Productivity Commission, in 2002.[5] Clearly, the government's objective of improving value for money was being met.

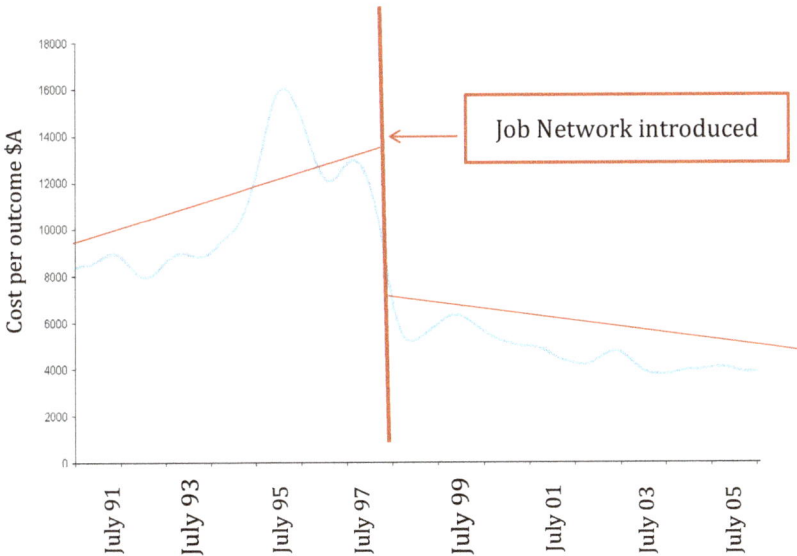

Figure 13.1 Decline in cost per employment outcome, 1991–2006
Source: DEEWR (2007: 138).

5   This report, released in June 2002, contained some criticism of elements of the Job Network system, but was supportive overall, concluding that the advantages of the new market for employment services 'outweigh its limitations' because 'it sets out clear objectives, provides stronger incentives for finding ways of achieving job outcomes and encourages cost efficiency' (PC 2002: xxvi, xxxiii).

Table 13.1 Employment services in Australia, 1998–2012

System[1]	Contract period	No. of providers[2]	Key features	Major departmental evaluations[3]
'Black-box' Market: Job Network (Howard Coalition Government)	1998–2000 2000–03	306 205	Eligible jobseekers referred by Centrelink to Job Network providers, who had significant discretion and were contracted for results Job Network services for jobseekers dependent on assessed needs through Job Seeker Classification Instrument (JSCI)[4] score Tighter activity test requirements for unemployed income support recipients Introduction in 1999 of biannual Star Ratings[5] system for performance evaluation—used to reward higher-performing providers and remove business from poorer performers	Evaluation of Job Network (2000, 2001 and 2002) Performance review of JSCI (2000) Net impact of labour market programs (1997)
Regulated Market: Active Participation Model (APM) (Howard Coalition Government)	2003–06 2006–09	109 103	Level of Job Network services dependent on duration of unemployment as well as JSCI score—greater purchaser oversight 'Intensive Assistance' provided if jobseeker still unemployed after 12 months 'Job Seeker Account' to support provider investment in disadvantaged jobseekers Mandatory IT system for information flow	Job Network best practice (2006) Net impact study of Intensive Assistance and Job Search Training (2003) Job Seeker Account evaluation (2006) APM evaluation (2007)
Inclusive Market: Job Services Australia (JSA) (Rudd Labor Government)	July 2009–2012	116	Seven programs integrated into one, with four 'streams' (levels) of assistance based on extent of jobseeker disadvantage and timing and type of services from providers Greater flexibility in program assistance JSCI score again significant for type of assistance available	Independent review of the jobseeker compliance framework (2010) Net impact study of labour market assistance (2010) Review by expert reference group of Star Ratings (2010)

[1] Descriptors from Considine and O'Sullivan (2014).

[2] Taken from OECD (2012: 76).

[3] Conducted by officers in the employment department or commissioned from experts with departmental support.

[4] Tool that assesses how difficult it will be for the jobseeker to find employment.

[5] A performance management system developed by the employment department that gives providers a rating (between one and five stars) based on their comparative performance in achieving employment or educational outcomes for jobseekers.

Sources: Davidson and Whiteford (2012); OECD (2012); Borland (2014); Considine and O'Sullivan (2014).

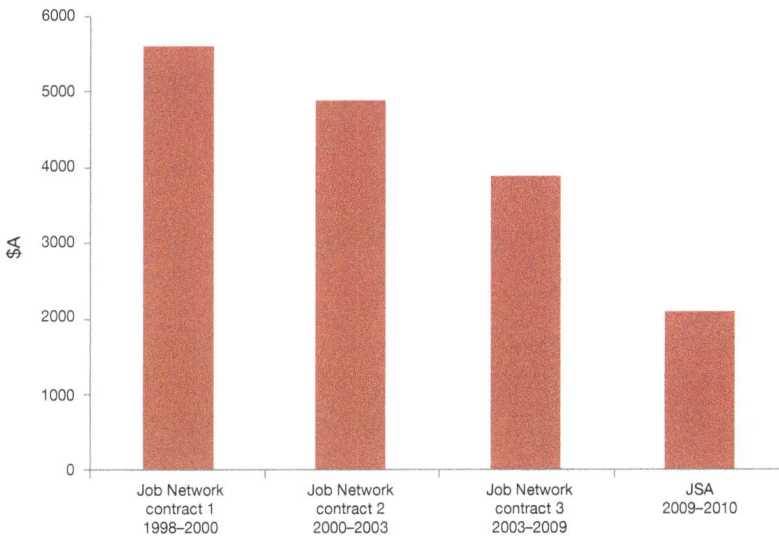

Figure 13.2 Cost per employment outcome
Source: Data from DEEWR (2011).

Evaluation and its role in program design and management

The cost-per-outcome estimates, together with estimates of net impact and other analyses, such as identifying which jobseekers were being successfully assisted and which were less well supported, were obtained from a comprehensive and sustained evaluation and monitoring program that began in 1998 and was continued under both Coalition and Labor governments.

The first major evaluation strategy was announced in April 1998. It was designed to enable the Howard Government 'to assess how well [the] Job Network was working and to provide information for later policy adjustment' (DEWR 2002b: 1). It was also to provide solid public evidence on the impact of such a radical and controversial shift in delivery arrangements.[6] Three stages of evaluation were carried out. The first two reports on the implementation of the Job Network and early indicators of the impact of assistance were published in 2000 and 2001, while the final stage, released in 2002, focused on the lessons learnt from evaluating the Job Network, including its effectiveness in improving the employment prospects of jobseekers on a sustainable basis (DEWR 2000, 2001, 2002b). The evaluation strategy also required that the Productivity Commission review the policy framework for the Job Network.

Each major phase of the Job Network and of JSA had an extensive set of evaluation products (see Table 13.1). The investment was significant; by way of example, the evaluation strategy for the JSA in 2009 was costed at $8.3 million (DEEWR 2009). The employment department managed all the evaluations in-house. Reports were based on both quantitative and qualitative analysis, which was conducted by both in-house experts in data analysis and evaluation and external consultants contracted by the department to undertake research and a major survey program of jobseekers, employment providers and employers. The department conducted several types of evaluations, as the OECD (2012: 228) observed: evaluations of specific programs, processes or jobseeker outcomes, estimates of the net impact of programs and broader strategic reviews employing a range of evidence. The strength of departmental administrative and program monitoring data was crucial to these evaluations. For example, data on jobseeker outcomes from employment assistance were collected from a post-program monitoring survey carried out three months (and sometimes six months) after assistance, and data on jobseeker characteristics were collected through the JSCI. Government income support data were also used. The extensive internal capability was built on an existing foundation of research and evaluation expertise, which had been enhanced following the introduction of the Job Network.

---

6   The driving force inside the Howard Government for these reforms was the Minister for Schools, Vocational Education and Training, David Kemp, who was known for his strong interest in gathering an evidence base to support the government's major reforms (Jarvie and Mercer 2015: 346, 351).

The evaluation and monitoring activities were not only extensive; the findings were also very influential in modifying employment services. Both the OECD and external researchers have commented that a characteristic of Australia's employment services system was the high policy relevance of its evaluations and monitoring, with the one hesitancy being that the detailed evaluations and research have been done within the department, thus detailed evaluative data have not been subjected to external scrutiny (OECD 2012: 225).

The first three evaluations of the Job Network were particularly influential in the design of the second phase, known as the Active Participation Model (APM), which was introduced in 2003 and which responded to several of the early evaluation findings about the Job Network's performance (Table 13.1) (DEWR 2002b: 6; OECD 2012: 6). Through some key contract changes, the Howard Government accepted that the initial design of this radically new system had introduced unintended disincentives in the market to offer sustained services for 'difficult' jobseekers. In particular, the evaluation finding that the most disadvantaged jobseekers often received limited assistance from their provider underpinned the introduction of fixed service fees that were weighted towards those jobseekers who were most difficult to place (Davidson and Whiteford 2012: 58). Additionally, the Job Seeker Account, also introduced in 2003, established a quarantined funding pool to enable providers to expend funds on measures to address barriers to jobseekers. Under this new APM, greater oversight of provider activity was established, with information on provider contact with jobseekers and assistance provided now being reported to the employment department through a central information technology (IT) platform known as EA3000 (Davidson and Whiteford 2012: 58).

The design of the subsequent JSA model, introduced in 2009, was also considerably influenced by the department's evaluation findings— in particular, its net impact studies of labour market assistance. This included the decision to integrate seven existing programs into one and to concentrate assistance on the most disadvantaged jobseekers, given the evidence that the largest net impact from employment providers was associated with this category of the unemployed (OECD 2012: 224). The evaluation also showed that giving intensive support to clients for 12–18 months was too long, and this was subsequently cut back to six months.

With the improved access to information following the introduction of the APM and the EA3000 platform in 2003, the department conducted seminars and published material on 'best practices' in the Job Network and internal analysis of detailed administrative data on employment outcomes (DEWR 2006; Davidson and Whiteford 2012: 66).

Given the significance of the government's investment in employment services and public scrutiny of this new approach, the employment department's evaluation and monitoring activities have been subject to ongoing external scrutiny, such as in the Productivity Commission's independent review in 2002 and in the two major reports by the OECD published in 2001 and 2012. In response to methodological issues identified by the Productivity Commission and the OECD in 2001, the employment department reassessed its approach to measuring the net employment gains provided by the Job Network (Thomas 2007: 15–16).

The role of star ratings in achieving value for money

As described earlier, improved value for money was undoubtedly achieved, although large efficiency gains and cost reductions took time to emerge (Finn, quoted in Borland 2014: 10). What was unexpected was that some of the mechanisms by which these were achieved were quite different to the original conception. For example, the original idea to choose providers on the basis of price tenders was quickly abandoned and replaced with tenders based on expected quality and outcomes. And one element, 'star ratings' for providers, has proved to be much more powerful than originally conceived.

Star ratings of providers—where providers were given a rating of between one and five stars (one star being poor and five stars being the highest rating)—were developed in 1999 with the assistance of the South Australian Centre for Economic Studies at Adelaide and Flinders universities. It was originally designed as a mechanism to signal to jobseekers the relative effectiveness of local providers. It was thus intended to drive competition between providers for clients. In practice, it very rapidly became the major mechanism of rewarding highly performing providers with more business and contracts and removing relatively poorly performing providers. Arguably, it became the key driver in achieving value for money in the employment services program for the past 15 years.

What are star ratings? How are they calculated?

Star ratings are measures of provider performance adjusted for differences in jobseeker characteristics and local labour market conditions. The core features of the ratings have remained broadly constant since they were introduced, although the way they are calculated (including the weightings given to different variables), the distribution and the number of performance levels[7] have varied with different phases of the employment services market.

The main element that determines the star rating of a provider at a site has been the short-term (three to six months) employment or educational outcomes of the jobseekers assisted by that provider at that site. There have also been efficiency variables, such as the time taken to 'place' jobseekers. For each provider site, the outcomes for jobseekers (disaggregated by their characteristics and local labour market conditions), together with other variables, each with a weight, are compared with the national estimate for all providers via a regression (PC 2002: 11.19). The differences at each provider site between the outcomes obtained and the expected outcomes are then allocated a star rating. Overall, the star rating reflects the value added by a provider compared with other providers.

Initially, under the Job Network, the distribution was fixed, so that, even if a provider improved their performance in absolute terms, they would receive an improved star rating only if they improved their performance compared with other providers. After 2009, following an expert review, ratings were based on the percentage difference between each site's performance and the national average, which reduced the number of providers falling into the lowest star bands, and was deemed fairer by providers.

The variables, and particularly the weightings given to them, varied significantly between contracts. Under the first phase of the Job Network (1999–2003), the two performance indicators for star ratings were:

1. The average time taken for jobseekers to achieve employment placements (which was designed to discourage 'parking' and the delaying of outcomes until higher outcome payments were available).

2. The proportions of jobseekers for whom outcome fees were paid (which was designed to reinforce the focus on job outcomes).

---

7   For a period, there were nine levels, with four 'half' stars and five full stars.

Under the second phase—the APM (2003–09)—the greatest weight (attracting 60 per cent of the weightings within the star ratings) was given to outcomes attracting full outcome payments; generally, this was employment sufficient to take jobseekers off benefits for at least three to six months (see Table 13.2).

Table 13.2 Weightings used for the star ratings under the Active Participation Model, from 2005 (per cent)

Interim 'full' outcomes	Final 'full' outcomes	Intermediate outcomes[1]	Job placements
40	20	20	10

[1] Includes a 5 per cent weighting for educational outcomes.

Notes: Final 'full' outcomes are employment outcomes at 26 weeks; interim ones are at 13 weeks. Percentages do not add to 100.

Source: Davidson and Whiteford (2012: 66), based on Australian National Audit Office (ANAO 2005).

There were significant changes for the third phase under the JSA (2009–12). With the change from Howard's Liberal–National Coalition Government to the Rudd Labor Government in 2007, the star ratings system was revised, following a review by an expert reference group. The new calculation was much more complex and reflected the new Labor Government's focus on helping the most highly disadvantaged. Jobseekers were allocated to one of four 'streams', with one being relatively advantaged and four the most disadvantaged. For the purposes of star ratings, the outcomes achieved by the 'stream four' jobseekers were given four times the weight of those in stream one. There was also greater weighting of 26-week outcomes compared with 13-week outcomes, the introduction of a weighting for 'bonus outcomes' for employment obtained after training and a weighting for 'social outcomes' for jobseekers who completed stream four assistance (for details and changes from the previous system, see Appendix 13.2).

How were star ratings used?

As mentioned, initially, it was expected that the star ratings would be used by jobseekers to choose their provider. In line with this, from 2000, the employment department began to regularly publish star ratings of provider performance at over 1,400 individual sites. However, evaluations and jobseeker surveys regularly reported that the ratings were not influencing jobseekers (PC 2002: xxxii; Struyven 2004: 13).

The employment department's 2007 evaluation reported that the regular release of ratings

> coincided with a sustained improvement in the employment outcomes of jobseekers assisted by the Job Network. This improvement seemed greater than the level of improvement which could have realistically been expected from improvement in the labour market. (DEEWR 2007: 141)

It related this to the fact that the star ratings provided Job Network members with a strong incentive to focus on securing outcomes, job placements and interim outcomes because these were the primary performance measures used for the estimation of the ratings. However, later assessments concluded that their major impact was through their use in eliminating employment service providers that performed poorly (OECD 2012: 13). In tender rounds from 2000 onwards, providers with low star ratings lost business, which was reallocated to higher-performing providers and to some new entrants to the market.

The first major use of the star ratings for allocation of business occurred in the 2003 Job Network tender. In this tender round, the 'top' 60 per cent of providers based on star ratings had their contracts rolled over via an 'invitation to treat', leaving the bottom 40 per cent to compete with new entrants to the market (Davidson and Whiteford 2012: 65–6).[8] After this tender, the number of organisations in the network was almost halved (to 109), with just seven new entrants (Finn 2008).

In 2006, the same process was repeated but a much lower proportion of the business was put out to tender; only 8 per cent of the (lowest-performing) providers were required to tender. This was partly to reduce the disruption that occurs from a major turnover of providers (Finn 2008). In place of regular and major tender processes, a system of rolling six-monthly performance reviews was introduced. Providers whose sites within a given area had consistently low star ratings had their market share reduced, sometimes to zero, with remaining business allocated by the department to other local providers or put out to tender.

In the JSA period (2009–12), star ratings continued to be used to determine future 'business shares' among local providers, but reallocations occurred on an 18-month cycle rather than the previous six-month cycle.

---

8   There was also a quality indicator that was expected to be used only rarely to adjust provider business shares.

This was in response to the widespread criticism of the six-monthly cycle from providers on the grounds that it encouraged 'short-termism' in service delivery strategies and contributed to instability in the Job Network, especially a high turnover of staff who could not be guaranteed employment throughout the three-year tender period (O'Connor 2008, quoted in Davidson and Whiteford 2012: 65–6).

While the removal of poorer-performing providers is regarded as having had the greatest impact on the operation of the market, star ratings were useful in:

1. driving servicing efficiency in terms of reducing time to achieve outcomes for clients

2. encouraging provider focus on government priorities such as achieving outcomes for the most disadvantaged clients

3. reducing workload for the department associated with new contract periods (through rolling over of contracts).

From early on, this rating system was seen as performing an 'essential function' in the operation of the market (DEWR 2002a: 1). Both Coalition and Labor governments clearly viewed star ratings as a useful tool. Star ratings were gradually extended to other providers of employment-related services, with the first star ratings of provider performance published for Disability Employment Services in July 2006 and for Vocational Rehabilitation Services in 2007. Star ratings have also been continued for subsequent employment services arrangements under the JSA, 2012–15, and the Job Active 2015 model.

Acceptance of star ratings

While the introduction of star ratings had an immediate impact on effectiveness and cost (see Boxall 2003), it took some time before they were fully accepted by the industry. Originally, there was relatively little publicly available information on how the ratings were calculated and their composition, but, after the expert review in 2009, which led to greater transparency and less frequent reallocation of business, there was much greater acceptance.[9] The Australian National Audit Office (ANAO) reported in a 2013–14 audit that '[t]he approach to

---

9   Interview with S. Sinclair, Chief Executive Officer, National Employment Services Association, September 2015.

measuring performance was generally accepted' by JSA providers and '[t] he Department has consulted with providers, and as a result aspects of the performance measures have been adjusted over time to improve its operation' (2014: 2.43).

There was general acceptance by the providers' peak body that the variables used, and the behaviour they reward, have been a key driver of performance.[10] 'The Star Rating System is defensible, with a sound mathematical basis, and essentially the best methodology to normalise each site and contract ESA (Employment Services Area)' (NESA 2015: 6).

One reason that star ratings and their component performance measures have driven performance is the confidence these employment providers and their peak body have had in the integrity of the system, which was managed by the Department of Employment. While there was always the danger of fraud (for example, DEEWR 2012), there was confidence in the data in the system.[11] There was also confidence in the integrity of tender processes and mechanisms to get feedback on provider performance (for audit and fraud controls, see Box 13.1).

Box 13.1 Audit and fraud controls

- Tendering process: External probity adviser.
- Contract managers in each state. Providers assigned a risk rating, which determines the level of monitoring.
- IT system: Verifies providers' claims against social security data.
- Surveys of 400,000 jobseekers annually to gain feedback on their providers.
- Jobseeker complaints process and a 'tip-off' line.
- Internal and special audits.

Supplemented by broader controls, including the ANAO, parliamentary inquiries and the ombudsman.

Source: DEEWR (2012).

Conclusion

The outsourcing of service provision from government to private and community providers is conceptually simple and attractive to governments seeking to improve value for money. This example from Australia shows that improved value for money can be achieved, but it has required

---

10   ibid.
11   ibid.

a complex system of management, including an intense focus on the performance of providers and the outcomes of the system. It has required experimentation and an acceptance that some elements have been more effective than others (Table 13.3).

Table 13.3 Employment services: Design features to drive better outcomes at lower cost

System features	Effective?	Comments
Payment for outcomes	Yes—in focusing providers on getting employment outcomes	While it was effective, it required constant fine-tuning and supplementation with other mechanisms to prevent 'parking' of hard-to-help clients (where 'parking' means clients were given very minimal assistance). It also required constant monitoring for fraud.
Targeting jobseekers using the JSCI: An assessment of how difficult it will be for the jobseeker to get a job	Generally, yes— very important for targeting support to most disadvantaged	Greater fees were paid when outcomes were achieved for jobseekers with a high JSCI. Use of the JSCI in determining what services a jobseeker would get and the outcome fees paid changed between phases/contracts.
Tendering	Effective when tendering on quality and outcomes Ineffective when tendering on price	Tender rounds created major disruption to services for clients when there was large turnover of providers— for example, in 2009.
Jobseeker clients able to choose provider	Not effective	Jobseekers would tend to use closest provider. Very few exercised choice based on provider performance.
Star ratings of providers	Very effective in driving value for money over the period 2000–12	Used by the employment department to 'roll over' the contracts of best-performing providers, awarding of tenders and removal of poor performers. Needed regular fine-tuning to reflect changes in labour market conditions, and constant monitoring for fraud. Not effective in rating performance of specialist providers working with very hard-to-help clients.

Source: Author's work.

There have been many elements that have contributed to the results achieved in the privatised employment services system. One element was the fact that, while it was a radical change, the reform was built on previous experience with the outsourcing of some employment services and learnings from a long investment in research, evaluation and stakeholder engagement. Another important contributor was the targeting of highly disadvantaged jobseekers through the JSCI tool. The third element was its outcomes focus—its clear performance framework, payment for outcomes and, in particular, the use of provider star ratings in contract renewal and reallocation of business.

Underpinning all of these were the sustained and extensive public monitoring and evaluation, which provided the star ratings and other measures of provider and system outcomes, to enable regular fine-tuning of the system. In addition, it has required a core group of public officials with analytical and management capacity and who were trusted by providers; a strong audit and fraud system; and management based on a clear focus on the evidence of 'what works' and what needs to change and preparedness to modify the system in line with that evidence.

References

Australian National Audit Office (ANAO). 2005. *Implementation of Job Network employment services contract 3, Department of Employment and Workplace Relations; Centrelink.* Audit Report No. 6 2005–06. Canberra: ANAO.

Australian National Audit Office (ANAO). 2014. *Management of services delivered by Job Services Australia, Department of Employment.* Audit Report No. 37 2013–14. Canberra: ANAO.

Borland, J. 2014. 'Dealing with unemployment: What should be the role of labour market programs?' *Evidence Base* 4. Melbourne: Australia and New Zealand School of Government. Available from: journal. anzsog.edu.au (accessed 17 July 2017).

Boxall, P. 2003. Measuring performance: The state of the art. Presentation to the Australia and New Zealand School of Government.

Considine, M. and S. O'Sullivan. 2014. 'Introduction: Markets and the new welfare—Buying and selling the poor'. *Social Policy and Administration* 48(2)(April): 119–26. doi.org/10.1111/spol.12052.

Davidson, P. and Whiteford, P. 2012. *An overview of Australia's system of income and employment assistance for the unemployed.* OECD Social, Employment and Migration Working Papers No. 129. Paris: OECD Publishing. doi.org/10.1787/5k8zk8q40lbw-en.

Department of Education, Employment and Workplace Relations (DEEWR). 2007. *Active Participation Model Evaluation. July 2003–2006.* November. Canberra: Australian Government.

Department of Education, Employment and Workplace Relations (DEEWR). 2009. *Evaluation Strategy for Job Services Australia 2009 to 2012.* Canberra: Australian Government.

Department of Education, Employment and Workplace Relations (DEEWR). 2011. *Taskforce on Strengthening Government Service Delivery for Job Seekers. Report to the Secretary of the Department of Education, Employment and Workplace Relations and the Secretary of the Department of Human Services.* 30 March. Canberra: Australian Government.

Department of Education, Employment and Workplace Relations (DEEWR). 2012. *Job Services Australia provider brokered outcomes.* Audit Report. Canberra: Australian Government.

Department of Employment and Workplace Relations (DEWR). 2000. *Job Network evaluation stage one: Implementation and market development.* Evaluation and Program Performance Branch Labour Market Policy Group EPPB Report 1/2000. Canberra: Australian Government.

Department of Employment and Workplace Relations (DEWR). 2001. *Job Network evaluation stage two: Progress report.* Evaluation and Program Performance Branch Labour Market Policy Group EPPB Report 2/2001. Canberra: Australian Government.

Department of Employment and Workplace Relations (DEWR). 2002a. *Government Response to the Productivity Commission Independent Review of Job Network.* Canberra: Australian Government.

Department of Employment and Workplace Relations (DEWR). 2002b. *Job Network evaluation stage 3: Effectiveness report.* Report 1/2002. Canberra: Australian Government.

Department of Employment and Workplace Relations (DEWR). 2003. *Intensive assistance and job search training: A net impact study.* Evaluation and Program Performance Branch, Employment Analysis and Evaluation Group December EPPB Report 2/2003. Canberra: Australian Government.

Department of Employment and Workplace Relations (DEWR). 2006. *Job Network Best Practice.* Canberra: Australian Government.

Finn, D. 2008. *The British 'Welfare Market': Lessons from contracting out welfare to work programmes in Australia and the Netherlands.* York, UK: Joseph Rowntree Foundation. Available from: www.jrf.org.uk (accessed 17 July 2017).

Jarvie, W. and T. Mercer. 2015. 'Championing change in a highly contested policy area: The literacy reforms of David Kemp, 1996–2001'. In J. Wanna, E. A. Lindquist and P. Marshall (eds) *New Accountabilities, New Challenges.* Canberra: ANU Press.

National Employment Services Association (NESA). 2015. *Employment Services Australia: Roadmap for the future (detailed proposals).* Melbourne: NESA. Available from: nesa.com.au (accessed 17 July 2017).

O'Connor, B. 2008. *The Future of Employment Services in Australia.* Canberra: Department of Education, Employment and Workplace Relations.

Organisation for Economic Co-operation and Development (OECD). 2001. *Innovations in Labour Market Policies: The Australian way.* Paris: OECD Publishing.

Organisation for Economic Co-operation and Development (OECD). 2012. *Activating Jobseekers: How Australia does it.* Paris: OECD Publishing.

Productivity Commission (PC). 2002. *Independent review of the Job Network inquiry report.* Report No. 21, June. Melbourne: Productivity Commission.

Struyven, L. 2004. *Design choices in market competition for employment services for the long-term unemployed.* OECD Social, Employment and Migration Working Papers No. 21. Paris: OECD Publishing.

Thomas, M. 2007. *A review of developments in the Job Network*. Research Paper No. 12, 2007–08, 24 December. Canberra: Department of Parliamentary Services, Parliament of Australia.

Appendix 13.1 The role of the Department of Employment

The Department of Employment (with different titles since 1998) administers the employment services market by:

1. defining purchaser provider arrangements and detailed in-service contracts with private and community-based providers

2. organising public tenders and the award of contracts

3. monitoring and supervision of the contract implementation.

In 2012, the department oversaw contracts with more than 100 private and community-sector providers. It paid providers fees for contracted services and placement outcomes, supervised contract implementation at the level of the department and through its state, territory and district offices and monitored provider performance at the level of about 2,300 individual sites through star ratings assessments and other performance indicators (OECD 2012: 63, 75).

Appendix 13.2 Star ratings for the JSA, 2009–12

Appendix Table A13.1 Weightings used for JSA star ratings (per cent)

	Stream 1 (overall weighting of 10%)	Stream 2 (overall weighting of 20%)	Stream 3 (overall weighting of 30%)	Stream 4 (overall weighting of 40%)
KPI1: 'Speed to place'	18	7	5	2
KPI2: Interim 'full' outcomes	10	23	25	19
KPI2: Final 'full' outcomes	10	30	30	21

	Stream 1 (overall weighting of 10%)	Stream 2 (overall weighting of 20%)	Stream 3 (overall weighting of 30%)	Stream 4 (overall weighting of 40%)
KPI2: Intermediate outcomes	10	20	20	18
KPI2: Paid placements	42	10	10	10
KPI2: Completion of Stream 4	n.a.	n.a.	n.a.	20
KPI2: 'Bonus' outcomes	10	10	10	10
Total	100	100	100	100

Notes: 'Speed to place' refers to the time taken to achieve outcomes; 'interim and final full outcomes' refers to employment outcomes sufficient to remove entitlements to income support or participation in an educational program that is sustained for 13 and 26 weeks, respectively; 'intermediate outcomes' refers to part-time employment or a less substantial educational program; 'paid placements' refers to employment that is sustained for at least 50 hours; 'bonus outcomes' refers to employment outcomes attained within 12 months of completion of a qualifying training program or outcomes attained by Indigenous people.

Source: Davidson and Whitehead (2012: 80).

Changes in the star ratings framework compared with the Job Network framework include:

- greater complexity, with 36 weights (previously only seven weights)
- higher weighting on outcomes attained by the most disadvantaged jobseekers: 40 per cent for those in stream four, compared with 10 per cent for those in stream one (previously, outcomes achieved after one year of unemployment or three years had the same weight)
- higher weighting on 26-week outcomes compared with 13-week outcomes (previously, 40 per cent on 13-week outcomes and 20 per cent on 26-week outcomes)
- 10 per cent weight on 'bonus outcomes', which include training/ apprenticeship outcomes (previously, there was a 10 per cent weight on the disadvantaged jobseeker share in the 13-week outcomes)
- weight on 'social outcomes' for jobseekers who complete stream four assistance (previously, 'social outcomes' were paid for completion of two years in the personal support program).

14

Case study of the role of third-party evaluators in performance-based budgeting reform at the local government level in China

Zaozao Zhao

Introduction

Performance-based budgeting (PBB) focuses on using performance measurements during the budgetary process to help governments manage public resources more efficiently and effectively and to heighten the transparency of, and accountability for, how public resources are used (Curristine 2005; Schick 2014; Moynihan and Beazley 2016). In the past half-century, there have been two waves of PBB reform in China—the first in the 1960s and the latest in the 1990s.

Central to the success of PBB has been China's administrative capacity, including its capacity to collect and analyse data, to write reports and, more generally, to manage budget processes and administer programs and projects (Ho and Im 2015; Moynihan and Beazley 2016). However, it is not easy for governments to improve their administrative capacities to a high level in a short time, thus presenting an obstacle to the success of PBB in developing countries.

Seeking help from consultants is a simple and popular option for improving capabilities and meeting PBB requirements; however, this approach has its shortcomings (Moynihan and Beazley 2016). First, many consultants pay too much attention to theory and too little to the particular characteristics of the country concerned. Second, a government must have the financial means to employ a consultant, and low-income countries often lack sufficient resources to do so. Finally, a government with little motivation to improve its own capacities will likely depend too much on its consultants, thereby slowing its capacity-building efforts that much more.

In China, over the past 10 years, PBB has been introduced and developed, with many changes in implementation added, including the increasing role of PBB third-party evaluation institutions (PBB third parties) (Niu 2012). In this research, the PBB third parties examined are those with a degree of independence, including for-profit organisations, such as enterprises, accounting firms, asset evaluation companies and non-profit entities, such as universities and their research centres, public scientific research institutions and other community organisations. Although there is some literature on the use of third parties in performance evaluation, it is focused on the post-performance evaluation of public services, and the role of PBB third parties in the PBB process as a whole has not been investigated.

As found in previous studies of PBB, local governments in China need the support of PBB third parties for their public service post-performance evaluations for four reasons. First, it makes governance more transparent and accountable; a third-party evaluation ensures some outside involvement and a degree of independence rather than relying on an evaluation from inside the government (Bao et al. 2005; Zheng et al. 2009; Ma and Yu 2013; Li and Huang 2016). Second, it helps shift a government's focus from gross domestic product (GDP) alone to improving its governance capability and improving the quality and effectiveness of its public services (Bao et al. 2005; Zheng and Bi 2009). Third, it compensates for the often-limited performance evaluation capabilities of a local government. And, last but not least, it facilitates learning from developed countries (Bao et al. 2005).

Much is known about why local governments need PBB third parties, but there has not yet been a description or explanation of how PBB third parties contribute to the PBB process and to PBB reform. This study fills that gap.

This research focuses on the role of PBB third parties in the PPB process as a whole and the relationship between PBB third parties and local governments in the PBB reform process using a number of case studies. By analysing three typical cases, the following issues are addressed:

1. Why do local governments in China increasingly rely on PBB third-party evaluators in the PBB process?

2. What is the relationship between a financial department and a PBB third party (e.g. a principal–agent relationship or something else)?

3. How does this relationship influence PBB practices in China?

PBB third parties' contribution to PBB reform: Three cases

Three typical cases were selected for this research: a non-profit organisation, the China Development and Research Foundation (CDRF); a for-profit organisation, Horizon; and a public institution, the Shanghai University of Finance and Economics Institution of Public Policy and Governance (IPPG).

These three organisations were chosen for two reasons. First, they represent the three major types of PBB third-party performance evaluation agencies used in China. Second, they were among the first PBB third parties to participate in the Chinese Government's performance budget management reform. The author participated as an expert in performance evaluation for both the CDRF and Horizon, and also gained a good understanding of the IPPG's role as a PBB third party through detailed interviews with its employees and analysis of relevant documents. The following briefly describes the three cases.

Case 1: The CDRF, a non-profit organisation

The CDRF is a non-profit, non-governmental organisation (NGO) established by the State Council's Development Research Center. Although it has a strong government background and resources, it also has NGO status and uses the NGO management model. The CDRF established its own financial performance study team before 2014, has a wide range of specialists and, importantly, works in close cooperation with local governments. In other words, the CDRF was often selected as a PBB third party by government because of its three influential advantages: knowledge structure, expert resources and government trust.

For example, in 2008, Jiaozuo City, Henan Province, commissioned the CDRF to evaluate the performance of the city's transfer payments that were meant to equalise public services between urban and rural areas. Both the provincial government and the central Ministry of Finance (MoF) paid close attention to the evaluation and its findings.

Between 2008 and 2009, the CDRF was responsible for helping Jiaozuo City set up a performance evaluation system, inviting and managing the participation of experts, organising the performance evaluation process and completing final performance reports, which were submitted to the city's executive leader. In short, the CDRF participated in the entire performance evaluation of the PBB process as a whole. The CDRF completed performance evaluations independent of the city's government. The final performance evaluation reports were used by the government and submitted to the MoF. After completing the program, the CDRF gained the full trust of the city's financial department, and the evaluation system it designed is still in use today.

In 2012, the CDRF won another performance evaluation program, for Nanhai County, Guangdong Province, through a competitive bidding process. In that case, because Nanhai's finance department had considerable self-confidence in applying PBB, the CDRF faced demands different from those for Jiaozuo City. Nanhai had already pursued PBB reform for about five years, and had established a whole performance evaluation system that had then been introduced to other local governments by the MoF. When the CDRF accepted the Nanhai finance department's PBB third-party role, it made the decision to first adopt and then build on Nanhai's existing PBB system and culture. The CDRF's performance reports were always submitted to the city leader directly, not only because of their excellent quality but also because of the complete trust between the Nanhai Government, the finance department and the CDRF.

Despite this success, however, the CDRF changed its corporate strategy after 2014. It withdrew from the PBB third-party market after completing a three-year evaluation of Nanhai District, Foshan City, Guangdong Province. It did so for three reasons: a decision to pursue a new strategic direction, the loss of some of its leading researchers, making it difficult to support large-scale evaluations, and the costs involved.

Case 2: Horizon Co. Ltd

Horizon is a private consulting company that focuses on social studies. It has achieved considerable success in a competitive market. Since 2012, Horizon has been trying to enter the field of PBB performance and evaluation. As a competitor of the CDRF, Horizon seized the opportunity during 2012–14 presented by the CDRF's decision to begin withdrawing from the PBB third-party market. Horizon worked hard to gain the trust of local governments with close communication and by proving its capacity through the evaluation of small projects. It also upgraded its professional knowledge and skills by learning from these experiences, and set up an expert team using its social connections.

After 2014, Horizon became the most important PBB third party for the finance department in Nanhai District. In the 2014 budget, it undertook more than 1,000 performance evaluations of projects costing more than RMB300,000 (A$57,000). Horizon has also expanded throughout the country, progressively undertaking performance evaluations for finance departments in Shandong Province, Jiangsu Province and Guizhou Province.

Overall, Horizon has been responsible for providing PBB third-party evaluations of public investment projects involving more than RMB60 billion (A$11.4 billion) over the past four years, including RMB25 billion (A$4.8 billion) for pre-performance evaluations (41.3 per cent), RMB120 million (A$23 million) for operating performance reviews (0.2 per cent) and RMB35 billion (A$6.7 billion) for post-performance evaluations (58.5 per cent).

Case 3: IPPG and Wenzheng Management Co. Ltd

The IPPG is not an independent legal body but part of Shanghai University of Finance and Economics. It has had a long-term working relationship with Shanghai's city government and the city's finance department. In 2009, the IPPG collaborated with Shanghai's Minhang District to conduct theoretical research for PBB reform, which laid the foundation for the IPPG to enter the PBB third-party market. In 2013, the IPPG established Wenzheng Management Co. Ltd, which has been a very important PBB third party in Shanghai.

Wenzheng has unique advantages: it has access to the IPPG's expert team, it has information and performance evaluation software connected directly to the electronic system of budget management for the city's finance department and it has developed long-term trust not only with Shanghai's finance department but also with neighbouring provinces and cities. Thus, the IPPG and Wenzheng have combined to become the major PBB third party in eastern China. Many local governments in the area have been using the performance evaluation software system developed by Wenzheng. Because the IPPG has this key technology for performance evaluation, it has expanded very quickly in recent years.

Analysis of the role of PBB third parties and their relationship with local government

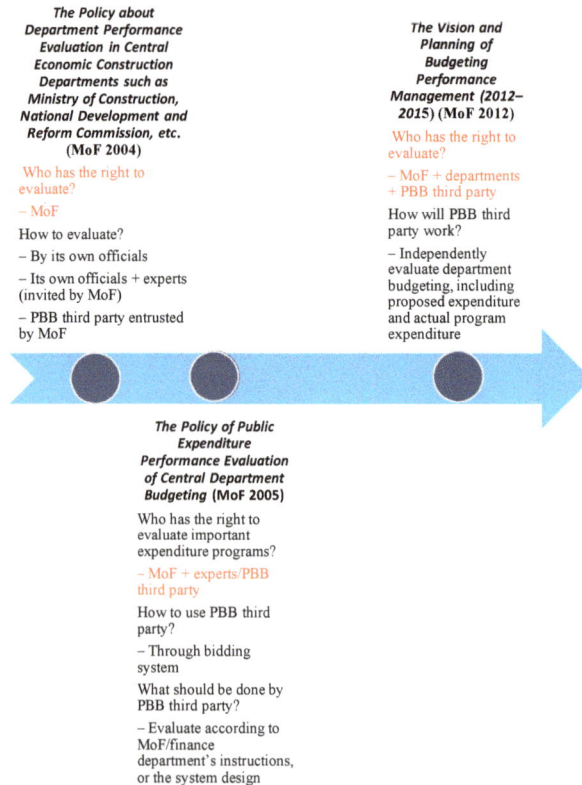

The Policy about Department Performance Evaluation in Central Economic Construction Departments such as Ministry of Construction, National Development and Reform Commission, etc. (MoF 2004)

Who has the right to evaluate?

– MoF

How to evaluate?

– By its own officials

– Its own officials + experts (invited by MoF)

– PBB third party entrusted by MoF

The Vision and Planning of Budgeting Performance Management (2012–2015) (MoF 2012)

Who has the right to evaluate?

– MoF + departments + PBB third party

How will PBB third party work?

– Independently evaluate department budgeting, including proposed expenditure and actual program expenditure

The Policy of Public Expenditure Performance Evaluation of Central Department Budgeting (MoF 2005)

Who has the right to evaluate important expenditure programs?

– MoF + experts/PBB third party

How to use PBB third party?

– Through bidding system

What should be done by PBB third party?

– Evaluate according to MoF/finance department's instructions, or the system design

Figure 14.1 Changing rules for PBB third parties since 2004

Sources: MoF (2004, 2005, 2012).

With the development of PBB reform practices in China, government policy on the role and functions of PBB third parties and their relationship with local governments has evolved since 2004, as shown in Figure 14.1.

Relationship in three periods

The first step of PBB reform in China was the MoF's departmental performance evaluation policy of 2004 (MoF 2004). Under this policy, the MoF organised individual experts and consultants from different fields to complete evaluation work. However, local governments found it was very difficult to depend on the individual experts or consultants selected by the MoF to complete departmental evaluations, as the work was very complicated and the number of programs and projects to be evaluated was large and growing rapidly.

In response, the MoF modified the reform policy in 2005 (MoF 2005). PBB third parties were allowed a greater role and local governments were given more authority to contract PBB third parties. In several local governments, PBB third parties gained the right to take part in the whole PBB process, including pre-evaluation of a department's program budget planning, mid-term evaluation of approved programs and projects as well as post evaluation of program and project results. The performance evaluation results were submitted to the local government leadership and legislatures. Parts of the evaluation reports were also available to citizens. It is difficult, however, to draw firm conclusions about whether and how the evaluation results affected budget decisions and the allocation of public resources each year.

After the National People's Congress passed the new Budget Law in 2014, PBB reform entered its third stage. The new law introduced a number of significant changes, including affirming the positive functions of PBB reform and performance evaluation (Han 2014; Ma and Xiao 2014). Since the passage of the new Budget Law, fewer local governments have used individual consultants or experts from different fields to help their own officials evaluate projects and proposals in their budget processes, and have instead increasingly made use of contracts with PBB third parties. Accordingly, the relationship between local governments and PBB third parties has become closer but also more complex.

Although the central government and the MoF have the power to modify policy, local government plays the key role in building relationships between PBB third parties and governments. A local government's success and confidence accumulate as lessons are learned and new problems identified (Jing 2016). The experiences of local government are useful for the central government and the MoF when they decide to refine the PBB third-party policy.

For instance, Nanhai's practices provided the MoF with a good example. Nanhai District is an economically developed area in southern China. Before 2008, Nanhai's finance department had set up its own performance evaluation system, and its practice had been to use individual consultants who had limited authority and could evaluate only the less complex public programs. However, too many programs that should have been evaluated were not, and Nanhai's finance department found that it was not possible to complete the whole PBB process even with consultants. So, in 2008, it signed a government procurement contract with a PBB third party to provide performance evaluations and to set up a performance indicators system.

After 2008, the Nanhai finance department gave its PBB third parties considerable flexibility regarding the evaluation process. This was especially true during the period 2012–14 when Nanhai entrusted the CDRF as an important PBB third party. The CDRF was allowed to invite the participation of all kinds of experts, to organise the program evaluation process, to write and submit independent evaluation reports about the allocation of resources and even to give suggestions about how to improve the PBB evaluation system. Along the way, real trust built up between PBB third parties and the Nanhai finance department.

Nanhai's experience gave the MoF an example of the wider role that could be played by third parties and led to the MoF adjusting its policy in 2012. Between 2004 and 2012, PBB third parties, local governments and their finance departments gained considerable experience and knowledge about how to work cooperatively with each other. The MoF adjusted its rules in 2012 and allowed PBB third parties to take a wider part in PBB. Since 2012, PBB third parties can be invited to take part in the entire budgeting resource allocation process, including procedures for both operating and capital expenditures.

Through analysis of the development of policy and these three cases, it is possible to see the practical impact of the changing policy regarding the role of PBB third parties over the period of PBB reform (see Figure 14.1) and also how that policy has been informed by local government experience. The MoF has been adjusting PBB policy regularly, including encouraging greater cooperation with PBB third parties. In line with the central government's demands, local government finance departments have been building closer relationships with PBB third parties since 2005.

Reasons for entrusting a PBB third party

There are several reasons a local government needs a PBB third party in the PBB process.

First, a local government and its finance department need effective institutions and approaches to make up for their limited capability and to ease the pressure of PBB reform. Local governments are eager to get more professional expert support to set up their evaluation systems. As reforms deepen, government programs and projects become more complex, as does the process of evaluating them. Along with complexity, the resources required for the PBB process have also increased.

Local finance departments, however, have limited capacity. According to interviews with local officials from Nanhai District, Foshan City, Guangdong Province, between 2010 and 2013, there were an average of 500–600 projects worth around RMB30 million (A$5.7 million) each that went through the pre-evaluation process each year. The local finance department had to devote much more effort to completing these tasks and found the additional work challenging. Lacking the necessary skills themselves, the finance department had to turn to a PBB third party.

Second, the nature of public budgeting is political and PBB necessarily has a political character. According to the budgeting reform experiences of other countries over the past century, any reform to the budgetary process affects power structures and the way conflicting interests over resource allocation are settled. China's local governments, consistent with central government policies, have been looking forward to ensuring the debate over resource allocation is not confined to internal parties but also involves external players. This attracts wider public support and reduces the risk of protests against government decisions on projects and programs. Previously, finance departments took the leadership role in reform and had to address and deal with the many conflicting interests and priorities themselves. As a result, local finance departments became solely responsible for resource allocation decisions and were criticised and questioned by other departments, citizens and stakeholders. Common areas of criticism included the adequacy of evaluation technology as well as the fairness and impartiality of evaluation findings. Local governments and finance departments now hope to avoid this awkward situation by introducing PBB third parties into the PBB process and evaluations, and ensuring PBB third parties engage with groups outside the finance department and the local government.

Third, local governments and finance departments are required to implement a top-down policy of PBB reform and evaluation. Beginning in 2015, local governments have been required to build a PBB institutional system and performance evaluation approach including a comprehensive evaluation system and a management system for PBB third-party involvement (MoF 2012). In addition, the central government will be assessing how counties have introduced PBB reforms and will reward the 200 best-performing counties through a special fund (MoF 2012). To meet the top-down requirements of PBB reform, many local governments and financial departments have considerable incentive to quickly seek the cooperation of PBB third parties.

Finally, local governments are conscious of the disadvantages of internal evaluations and are keen to ensure any such evaluations are publicly credible. It was inevitable that local finance departments would initially dominate PBB reform and performance evaluation in China, because the role and capacity of the people's congresses were limited. As a result, however, the objectivity, scientific integrity and professionalism of evaluation findings were often questioned. To ensure impartiality, scientific integrity and professionalism of performance evaluation, the Chinese Government turned to more independent PBB third parties, giving them appropriate authority. In theory at least, this should avoid the disadvantages of internal evaluation and make the evaluation findings more credible.

Evaluating PBB third parties

PBB third-party participation is not always ideal, however, and this was particularly true in the early days of China's PBB reform. Some third parties had insufficient knowledge of government processes and programs, oversight of their evaluations was inadequate and financial departments were not entirely sure of what they wanted to do with PBB (Hu 2014). These problems negatively affected PBB third-party work and the quality of their performance evaluations. Moreover, some of the experts who were invited by PBB third parties to participate in the PBB and evaluation process did not fully understand the background of the public programs they were evaluating, so it was difficult for them to make the necessary professional judgments or to draw appropriate scientific evaluation conclusions.

Analysis of the demands of the central government's policy and applying its criteria for success provides some insight into the extent to which PBB third parties have contributed to improved allocation of resources through independent, impartial, scientific, effective, efficient, authoritative and professional evaluation advice. Using the official political requirements (MoF 2012), this research applies the following conceptual definitions and standards:

1. Independence: The procedure should be independent, including independently inviting experts to participate, organising the evaluation and writing the accreditation report. There must be no conflict of interest in the third party's relationship with the institutions being evaluated, and the PBB third party should not be unduly influenced by the party employing them in setting out the evaluation methodology, developing the indicator system or preparing the evaluation results.

2. Impartiality means treating all subjects equally without prejudice by using the same evaluation system, standards, rules and procedures.

3. Scientific integrity means the performance evaluation method should be based on known theories.

4. Effectiveness and efficiency refer to the evaluation providing more credible findings and involving lower cost than internal evaluations.

5. Authority refers to the degree of impact exerted by the evaluation result on performance budgeting management, identified as 'no impact', 'just as a reference' or 'as an important basis'.

6. Professionalism refers to the use of professional indicators, organisation and management methods and team members.

These criteria and how they can be measured are set out in Table 14.1.

Table 14.1 Definition of standards and ranking of PBB third-party performance

Rank standards	+++	++	+
1. Independence	1.1 Completely independent procedure (inviting experts, organising evaluation and writing accreditation report) 1.2 No interest relationship with evaluated unit 1.3 Completely independent evaluation principle	One is not satisfied	Two or above are not satisfied
2. Impartiality	2.1 To treat all subjects equally without prejudice 2.2 To use the same evaluation system, standards, rules and procedures	One is not satisfied	Two are not satisfied
3. Scientific integrity	3.1 The performance evaluation method should be scientific and based on clear theories	On relatively clear theories basis	No theories basis
4. Effectiveness	4.1 To improve result of evaluation 4.2 To reduce the cost of internal evaluation for the government	One is not satisfied	Two are not satisfied
5. Authority	5.1 'As an important basis'	'Just as a reference'	'No impact'
6. Professionalism	6.1 Professional organisation 6.2 Management and professional team	One is not satisfied	Two are not satisfied

Source: Author's drawing on MoF (2004, 2005 and 2012).

Using these criteria, the performance of the three PBB third parties included in this case study was assessed via interviews with the relevant financial department officials. The results are summarised in Table 14.2.

Broadly speaking, the NGO (CDRF) and the Shanghai University–based organisation (the IPPG/Wenzheng) were assessed to have contributed more successfully than the for-profit organisation (Horizon). The CDRF and the IPPG have almost the same performance score. This can be explained as follows.

Local governments tend to believe not-for-profit organisations are more independent than for-profit organisations so they scored higher than Horizon. Furthermore, the CDRF and the IPPG had their own academic research teams and did not rely on outside experts and consultants, so they had the academic abilities to improve PBB reform and relevant performance evaluation systems. They also had higher scores than Horizon when it came to the scientific integrity, effectiveness and professionalism criteria. However, all three PBB third parties were assessed as having room for improvement regarding their scientific integrity and effectiveness performance; none of the local governments and financial departments was fully satisfied with any of the performance index systems set up by the three PBB third parties.

That said, these results do not take into account the different contexts in which the PBB third-party organisations were operating. In fact, despite some disappointment about aspects of their performance, all three PBB third parties were considered by the respective finance departments to have made positive contributions.

Table 14.2 Assessment of PBB third-party performance in the three cases

Rank standards	CDRF (NGO)	IPPG (NGO) and Wenzheng Management Co. Ltd	Horizon
1. Independence	+++	+++	+
2. Impartiality	+++	+++	+++
3. Scientific integrity	++	++	+
4. Effectiveness	++	++	+
5. Authority	+++	+++	++
6. Professionalism	+++	+++	++

Reviewing these three cases, a number of key factors can be identified that affect how well the PBB third parties contributed to performance evaluation or the PBB process.

First, trust between the PBB third party and the local government finance department was a very important factor. If the local government trusted the PBB third party, they were allowed more independence and autonomy. Equally, if the PBB third party had adequate professional knowledge, management skills and good internal organisational arrangements, local governments trusted them more and recognised the effectiveness of their suggestions and final reports.

Second, the characteristics of the local government and its finance department may affect the PBB third party's contribution. In the cases studied, the finance departments of Minhang District in Shanghai City,

Nanhai District in Foshan City in Guangdong Province and Jiaozuo City had different characteristics. Shanghai Minhang and Foshan Nanhai districts are in eastern China and have experienced rapid economic development. Their finance departments are also very receptive to new ideas. The two governments in these regions were among the first to experience PBB reform, at the beginning of which they chose to cooperate with a research agency to build their institutional framework and the evaluation system for performance budgeting. They were therefore in a good position to closely oversee a PBB third party and to require it to follow the finance department's initiatives.

However, Jiaozuo City, in central China and with a more modest economic base, depended much more on its PBB third party. The PBB third party in that case was responsible for developing the evaluation process and designing the system as well as preparing evaluation reports and so on. The control and quality monitoring of the PBB third party were not as strict as in the other two cities.

The research also found that different developed cities may choose different PBB and evaluation approaches, as occurred with Minhang and Nanhai districts. There are two differences between these districts. One relates to the time allowed to develop the necessary trust with a PBB third party: Minhang District trusted the PBB third party's evaluation work from the beginning, while Nanhai District did not fully trust the PBB third party until after a year of reform experience. The other difference relates to the range and scale of the evaluation work. Since 2015, Nanhai District has included all government finances in pre-performance evaluations while Minhang District subjects only key projects to pre-performance evaluation.

Last but not least, the three PBB third parties' abilities, including those in academic research and organisation, were the most important factors directly affecting their performance. With the development of PBB reform, local governments' abilities have improved and their demands on the three PBB third parties have been more complex and more strict as their relationships progressed. Just as importantly, the performance of the three PBB third parties affected the trust they gained from the local government, which in turn affects their own development and future.

Findings and conclusions

This study finds that, during the early period of improving PBB reform in China, PBB third parties have become one of the most important parts of the performance budgeting management system. Performance budgeting evaluations at all levels of government, especially for finance departments, now depend on PBB third parties. This allows local governments in China to pursue PBB reform despite their own limited capabilities, making use of a range of different types of PBB third-party organisations. PBB third parties also now take part in the whole PBB process for local governments, including the post-performance evaluation, pre-performance evaluation and operating performance evaluation.

In the PBB system, however, the government, and especially its finance department, remains the central authority for the allocation and evaluation of financial resources. Essentially, this means the PBB third party and the finance department relate to one another as agent and principal, as the latter controls the rules for financial allocation. The success of the relationship depends crucially on the PBB third party gaining the complete trust of the government. The nature of the relationship also varies with the context in which the local government is operating.

In general, the role of a PBB third party is to evaluate the necessity for, benefits and feasibility of particular project proposals, to apply the finance department's general rules and to organise the input of experts to improve the quality and effectiveness of performance evaluation. The results of the pre-performance evaluation, in particular, are subject to final decisions by the government and finance department. In the end, a PBB third party's own capacity and familiarity with the budgetary management practices will affect its performance and contribution to PBB.

References

Bao, G., Y. Sha, Z. Jiang, H. Wang and F. Shi . 2005. 'Lanzhou experiment: New exploration of third parties for government performance evaluation'. *Journal of Shanghai Urban Vocational and Technical College* 14(3): 22–5.

Curristine, T. 2005. 'Performance information in the budget process: Results of the OECD 2005 questionnaire'. *OECD Journal on Budgeting* 5(2): 87–131. Paris: OECD Publishing.

Han, J. 2014. 'Walk towards modern finance: Minister of Finance Lou Jiwei explains the New Budget Law'. *Xinhua News Agency*, 10 September. Available from: news.xinhuanet.com/fortune/2014-09 /10/c_1112430189.htm (accessed 15 August 2017).

He, Q. 2009. 'The application and management of experts in performance budgeting'. *Local Financial Research* (1): 24–37.

Ho, A. T.-K. 2011. 'PBB in American local governments: Not just for budgeting, and more than a management tool'. *Public Administration Review* 71(3): 391–401. doi.org/10.1111/j.1540-6210.2011.02359.x.

Ho, A. T.-K. and T. Im. 2015. 'Challenges in building effective and competitive government in developing countries: An institutional logics perspective'. *American Review of Public Administration* 45(3): 263–80. doi.org/10.1177/0275074013501856.

Hu, C. 2014. 'Intermediary organizations in the study of budget performance evaluation: Based on the questionnaire survey of Anhui Province'. *Financial Communication* (11): 84–6.

Jing, Y. 2016. 'The transformation of Chinese governance: Pragmatism and incremental adaption'. *Governance* 30(1): 1–7.

Li, W. and Y. Huang. 2016. 'A theoretical perspective on performance evaluation of fiscal special funds based on logical model: A case study of Guangdong Province People's Congress'. *Journal of Public Management* (3): 111–21.

Lu, Y. 2011. 'Individual engagement to collective participation: The dynamics of participation pattern in performance budgeting'. *Public Budgeting & Finance* 31(2): 79–98. doi.org/10.1111/j.1540-5850.2011.00980.x.

Lu, Y., Z. Mohr and A. T.-K. Ho. 2015. 'Taking stock: Assessing and improving performance budgeting theory and practice'. *Public Performance & Management Review* 38: 426–58. doi.org/10.1080/15 309576.2015.1006470.

Ma, H. and P. Xiao. 2014. 'On revision of China's Budget Law on the background of deepening fiscal and taxation system reform: An analysis of revision background, content and effect of China's Budget Law'. *Finance & Economics of Xinjiang* 6: 5–11.

Ma, L. and W. Yu. 2013. 'Assessing third-party public service performance assessments: A comparative case study'. *Social Sciences in Nanjing* (5): 55–63.

Ministry of Finance (MoF). 2004. *The Policy about Department Performance Evaluation in Central Economic Construction Departments such as Ministry of Construction, National Development and Reform Commission, etc.* Beijing: Ministry of Finance. Available from: www.51wf.com/print-law?id=1240077 (accessed 15 August 2017).

Ministry of Finance (MoF). 2005. *The Policy of Public Expenditure Performance Evaluation of Central Department Budgeting.* Beijing: Ministry of Finance. Available from: jl.mof.gov.cn/lanmudaohang/ zonghecaizheng/zhengcejieshao/201105/t20110516_548790.html (accessed 15 August 2017).

Ministry of Finance (MoF). 2012. *The Vision and Planning of Budgeting Performance Management (2012–2015).* Beijing: Ministry of Finance. Available from (accessed 15 August 2017).

Moynihan, D. and I. Beazley. 2016. *Toward Next-Generation Performance Budgeting: Lessons from the experiences of seven reforming countries.* Washington, DC: World Bank Group. doi.org/10.1596/978-1-4648-0954-5.

Niu, M. 2012. 'Ten years' review of local performance budgeting reform in China: Success and challenges'. *Wuhan University Journal (Philosophy & Social Science)* (6): 85–91.

Schick, A. 2014. 'The metamorphoses of performance budgeting'. *OECD Journal on Budgeting* 13(2): 49–79. Paris: OECD Publishing.

Xu, Y. and Q. Yang. 2015. 'New development: China's Budget Law and local debt'. *Public Money and Management* 35(6): 447–50. doi.org/ 10.1080/09540962.2015.1083691.

Zheng, F. and Z. Bi. 2009. 'Third-party performance evaluation and service-oriented government building'. *Journal of South China University of Technology (Social Science Edition)* 11(4): 33–8.

15

Education outlay, fiscal transfers and interregional funding equity: A county-level analysis of education finance in China

Ping Zhang, Zizhou Bu, Youqiang Wang and Yilin Hou

Introduction

Equity in education finance has been a key policy and social issue since the mid-twentieth century. Governments worldwide have made great efforts to provide more equitable opportunities for education for their citizens as an investment in human capital. Local governments often shoulder the largest share of education costs, so, to address the issue of intraregional inequity resulting from local funding, subnational governments often redistribute resources collected from progressive taxes. In some countries, the central government also takes on some funding responsibility to address interregional inequity.

In the past three decades, against the background of high economic growth and rapid sociopolitical development, education finance in China has transitioned from a local government–only regime to a new regime that involves a combination of local, provincial and central government funding. This fast-tracked transition provides a good window for scholars to study the impact of the changing education finance regimes. Since reform of the country's central–local government tax-sharing system in

1994 and income tax reform in 2002, transfer payments from higher levels of government (central and provincial) to lower levels (county) have been a critical policy tool to improve equity in the provision of basic education. Beginning in 2000, the central government stepped in (with requirements for provincial shares of funding), aiming to drastically reduce interregional disparity and improve equity as well as the overall quality of basic education throughout China's vast rural areas. For example, in 2001, the State Council issued the 'Decision on Basic Education Reform and Development' to establish a county-oriented rural compulsory education system and to shift responsibility for setting rural teacher salaries from the township to the county level. To promote compulsory education, there were also two waves of initiatives under the Poor Region Compulsory Education Program, in 1995–2000 and 2000–05.

This chapter examines the effects of these funding reforms on education funding equity in China, with a particular focus on intraprovincial equity and funding for rural communities. We will test the differential effects of the regime's transition on the equity of education finance, taking advantage of provincial-level data and a panel dataset of county-level jurisdictions across the country. We will control for local own-source revenue, transfers (total and by type), local economic conditions, local demographics, policy shocks, the urban–rural divide and the region (east, central and western China). The chapter contributes to the literature in several important ways. It will dissect the differential effects of local, provincial and central funding levels on intraprovince equity of overall education finance and provide evidence on how policy shocks in a fast-growing economy affect education provision in a transitioning system. The chapter will also shed light on how elements of fiscal federalism work in a unitary state system.

The chapter is organised as follows. The next section briefly reviews the relevant literature, while section three explains our concept of education funding equity and our modelling methodology in the context of China's current rapid socioeconomic transition. Section four presents and discusses the empirical results and the final section provides some concluding comments.

Literature review

Adequacy, equity and efficiency are among the key issues in education finance. Research on education finance equity is targeted primarily towards examining whether education as a public good is provided equitably to students or whether schools and districts are funded equitably with sufficient resources to cover teachers, supplies and infrastructure for the equitable provision of education services to students. Equitable education investment across districts and groups helps to narrow future productivity gaps and achieve sustained growth, broader equity and access to decent living standards. As a public good, basic education is financed mainly through taxation and is mostly managed by government; thus, government shoulders the responsibility for resource equity as well as adequacy.

Measuring equity and setting equity standards present a research challenge. Berne and Stiefel (1994) explore conceptual, methodological and empirical issues in resource allocation at the intradistrict and school levels. They suggest that equity concepts can be applied at the school level; they also identify a series of methodological issues and include an empirical analysis of equity at the intradistrict and school levels in New York. Duncombe and Yinger (1998) show how to estimate comprehensive educational cost indexes that control for school district inefficiency, and include them in state aid formulas aimed at achieving equity. They simulate for New York the impact of several aid formulas on educational performance and evaluate them using several equity criteria. Murray et al. (1998) use variations across states over time to investigate the impact of reform on the distribution of school resources. Their results suggest that court-ordered finance reform reduced intrastate inequality in spending by 19 to 34 per cent. Successful litigation reduced inequality by requiring increased spending in the poorest districts while leaving spending in the richest districts unchanged, thereby increasing aggregate spending on education. Rubenstein et al. (2008) use an 11-year panel dataset containing information on revenue, expenditure and demographics for every school district in the United States; they examine the effects of state-adopted school accountability systems on the adequacy and equity of school resources. They find little relationship between state implementation of accountability systems and changes in school finance equity, although they do find evidence that states in which courts overturned the school finance system during the decade of their study exhibited significant equity improvements. Additionally, while implementation of accountability per se does not appear to be linked to changes in resource adequacy, states that implemented strong accountability systems did experience improvements.

The type of system used for financing and providing education can have a number of practical implications. Baicker and Gordon (2006) find that, in the United States, states finance the required increase in education spending in part by reducing their aid for other programs. Thus, while court-ordered school finance equalisations do increase total state aid to localities for education, they do so at the expense of drawing state intergovernmental aid away from programs such as public welfare, health, hospitals and general services. These results have significant implications for redistribution policy in a federal system—both across programs and across localities. Besley and Coate (2003) suggest that modelling the details of political decision-making is important for understanding the trade-off between centralisation and decentralisation. They show why even relatively homogeneous polities may face a cost from centralisation whether or not the (central) legislature is cooperative. This insight is underpinned by the way in which different interests play out in the legislature in a system of pooled finances. Moreover, even with a cooperative legislature, the familiar presumption that centralisation facilitates higher spillovers (and greater equity in resource distribution) does not always emerge. Andrews et al. (2002) define the factors affecting economies of size, updating the literature from 1980. Cost function studies suggest that sizeable potential savings in instructional and administrative costs may exist by moving from a very small district (500 or fewer pupils) to a district with 2,000–4,000 pupils. The findings from production function studies of schools are less consistent, but there is some evidence that moderately sized elementary schools (300–500 students) and high schools (600–900 students) may optimally balance economies of size with the potential negative effects of large schools. Program evaluation research on school consolidation is limited, however, and the potential diseconomies of size in large central city school districts have yet to be fully explored. The optimal size of schools is an important factor in education resourcing, including the achievement of efficient and equitable resource distribution.

The case of China

Since the early 1980s, the financing of basic education in China has moved rapidly away from a centralised system with a narrow revenue base to a decentralised system with a diversified revenue base. This chapter provides a critical assessment of the impacts of the financial reform of basic education in China, focusing on issues of structure, resource mobilisation, inequality and inefficiency. It concludes that, while the reform has been successful in achieving the objectives of structural change and mobilisation of additional government and non-government resources, the current system is marked by notable weaknesses in terms of glaring inequalities and significant inefficiencies. Further improvements of the financing system require interventions both inside and outside the education sector.

The Chinese Government has long realised the key role of basic education in the country's strategic development and hence made it a statutory requirement to guarantee adequate input into education; the revised Law on Compulsory Education (2006, revised version) stipulates that the state (i.e. government at all levels) bears responsibility for adequately funding education through its annual budgets.

Since 2000, the central government, with more revenue from large central taxes, began to invest heavily in education by granting increasingly large annual transfers specifically designated for teacher salaries, school construction, subsidies for student meals and supplies, as well as boarding (dormitory) costs, in poor, rural and remote (mountain and pastoral) areas. In the meantime, provincial governments, at the direction of the centre, have also started providing more funding than previously for education. These fiscal transfers have provided an avenue for funding equity that has become a new priority, and education funding is now provided through a new, more centralised scheme.

Wang (2004) provides a discussion of county-level budgeting in China. Based on field studies in three poverty-stricken counties in north-western China, she argues that the existing institutional arrangement for budget formulation does not enable wide participation in the budget process, and the separation of citizen demands from the spending priorities of county governments has contributed to a lack of social equity in the provision of public services. The most serious problem is that the needs of the poorest and thus the most needy citizens are overlooked. Because of this separation, citizens have to be self-reliant in solving problems outside the purview of government budgeting. Wang (2004) argues that the elimination of extra-budgetary funds as a key measure in financial reform in rural areas is not the solution to the problem. The spending priorities of county governments have to be changed and the political configuration behind such priorities has to be challenged. Liu (2005) points out that the newly introduced market mechanisms have profoundly influenced education finance in China, presenting challenges to education equity. As a result, an ethical appeal is now being made for education equity to be a central feature of education policy. It must be one of the main goals of the education market. As a result, education equity must also incorporate new concepts and ideas such as new definitions of equity and inequity and principles about acceptable differences. New educational institutions may need to be created to cope with conflicts between China's growing market economy and education equity. Yang (2006) analyses the institutional characteristics of education equity in four different phases in modern China, arguing that, since 1977, the main emphasis has shifted from equality of educational rights to equal educational opportunities, raising the bar regarding education quality as well as equity.

The Chinese research community focused on education finance has paid attention to issues of funding adequacy, equity and efficiency. Studies on equity, as mentioned above, are the most rapidly developing field. Quantitative studies are common, utilising national and provincial data collected by the National Bureau of Statistics, the Ministry of Education and the Ministry of Finance on local-level school enrolments, the number and salaries of teachers, school buildings and teaching facilities. While provincial aggregates have been available, lower-level statistics have not.[1] A big advance of this study is that we have put together a dataset of all county-level governments in China (rural counties, urban districts and county-level cities) for the period since the new, more centralised scheme of education financing was put in place. For this reason, this study carries important significance both for theoretical exploration and for policy formulation.

---

1   Even though they were not published, statistics on these were collected by relevant government agencies. Wang (2001) and Zeng and Ding (2003, 2005) used local-level education finance statistics collected by the Ministry of Education.

Modelling funding equity

The concept of *inequity* used in this study refers to the gap in the adequacy of education finance between economically more developed and underdeveloped counties within provinces. The gap is an index at the county level—our unit of analysis—and not at the individual student or school level. It measures the dispersion of county-level funding adequacy from the provincial mean. We call it the inequity index: the larger the index, the higher is the inequity within provinces across China.

Dependent variable

The inequity index is developed from the adequacy index used in an earlier paper by the authors (Hou et al. 2010), as the square of deviation from the mean level of education funding in a province. Constructing an inequity index of basic education inputs in the Chinese context is a dauntingly complex task. We outline below the major steps in constructing this index and the elements we use in the process. This index is our dependent variable.

First, we need to calculate the index from the indicator of adequacy. The calculation of adequacy is based on input and output standards at the provincial level, for two important reasons. First, provinces, not the central government, set the regional standards for all major input and output factors of production. This point is often ignored and misunderstood by people unfamiliar with Chinese government operations; the conventional understanding about China is that, since it is a highly centralised country (under a single dominant political party), everything is set by the central government. That is an oversimplification. On fiscal and managerial matters, the central government has, in fact, decentralised many powers to the provinces in recent years because of its lack of information and for management convenience and the sake of efficiency. Second, provinces, not the central government, redistribute within provincial boundaries, whereas the central government redistributes between provinces according to their level of economic development.

We consider the following elements: 1) enrolments in elementary and middle schools; 2) different ratios of school-age children in rural and urban populations; 3) governmental budgetary input and non-governmental input; 4) teacher–student ratios for elementary and middle schools, and the two ratios for urban versus rural areas; 5) teachers' average salary levels in comparison with civil servants at the stipulated provincial level or standard; and 6) operational and facility costs. All factors of production are calculated according to the central government standards set in the 1990s by the Ministry of Education, in 2001 by the Central Office of Government Establishment, the Ministry of Finance, the Ministry of Education and the National Development and Reform Commission in conjunction with the Ministry of Housing and Construction. Thus, we obtain the amount of resources needed to provide the basic, standard level of education in each county-level jurisdiction.

We then calculate the adequacy variable by comparing the difference between our calculated amount and the actual outlay in each county jurisdiction. The difference between the two is the gap between the required and actual amount in a specific county. This gap varies by year and by county. Finally, we get the equity variable from the difference between the individual county's adequacy and the average level within the same province and year. The formulas are provided in Equation 15.1.

Equation 15.1

$$Equtiy_{c,t} = A_{c,t} - \frac{1}{n^*}\sum_{c \in C^*} A_{c,t}$$

$$\text{where} \quad A_{c,t} = \frac{E_{\text{Real }c,t}}{E_{\text{Standard }c,t}} = \frac{E_{\text{Real }c,t}}{\sum_{j}\sum_{i} S_{i,c,t} \times \frac{P_{j,c,t}}{P_{T,c,t}} \times R_{i,j} \times s_{p,t} \times p_{j,p,t} \times e_{p,t}}$$

$Equity_{c,t}$ is the equity of access to education for each year and county (county-level city and district, equivalently); $c \in C^*$ represents all the counties in the same province as the target county; n^* is the number of counties in the same province as the target county; $A_{c,t}$ is the adequacy of education for each year and county (county-level city and district, equivalently); $E_{\text{Real}c,t}$ is the real expenditure on education for each year and county (county-level city and district, equivalently); $E_{\text{Standard}c,t}$ is the standard expenditure on education for each year and county (county-level city and district, equivalently); $S_{i,c,t}$ is the number of students for each year (t) and county (c) (county-level city and district, equivalently), by primary/secondary school (i); $P_{j,c,t}$ is the population for each year and county (county-level city and district, equivalently), by rural/urban (j); $R_{i,j}$ is the teacher–student ratio, by primary/secondary school and by rural/urban; $S_{p,t}$ is the average public sector salary for each year and province (or equivalent administrative region); $p_{j,p,t}$ is the consumer price index (CPI) for each year and province (or equivalent administrative region), by rural/urban; and $e_{p,t}$ is the index for adjusting conceptual and statistical consistency for each year and province (or equivalent administrative region).

We then exclude non-governmental resources from the input side and drop extreme outliers (the top and bottom 5 per cent). Diagnostic analysis shows that this gap (before square) is approximately normally distributed around a mean of zero (though with a longer positive tail than a negative one), as shown in Figure 15.1.

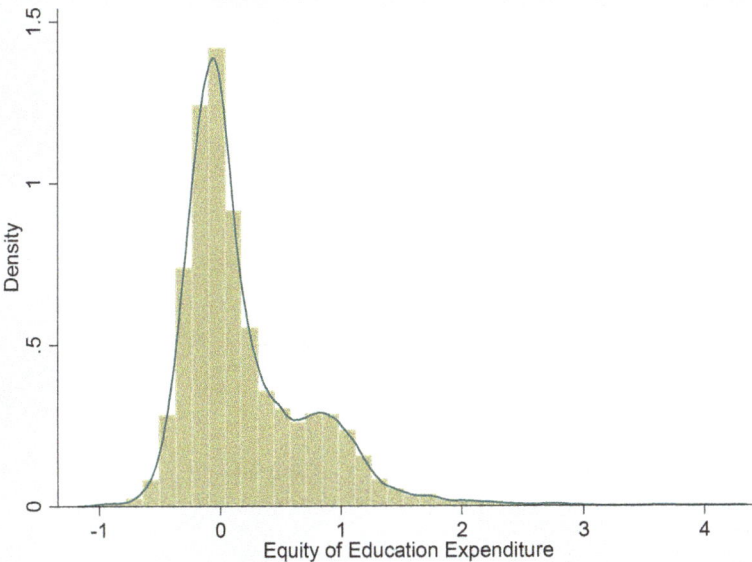

Figure 15.1 Density distribution of the adequacy index with extreme outliers included (all counties in all provinces)
Source: Authors' work.

Based on the equity variable, we use the square of relative mean difference as the dependent variable, which can capture the inequity of education finance in a county (the higher the value in this index, the lower is the funding equity in education finance). Here, A_{it} can be seen as an indicator of education funding adequacy (i is county and t is year) (Equation 15.2).

Equation 15.2

$$Inequity_{it} = (\frac{A_{it} - \mu_i}{\mu_i})^2$$

From 2000 to 2006, the aggregate mean of this index trended upwards over time, as shown in Figure 15.2.

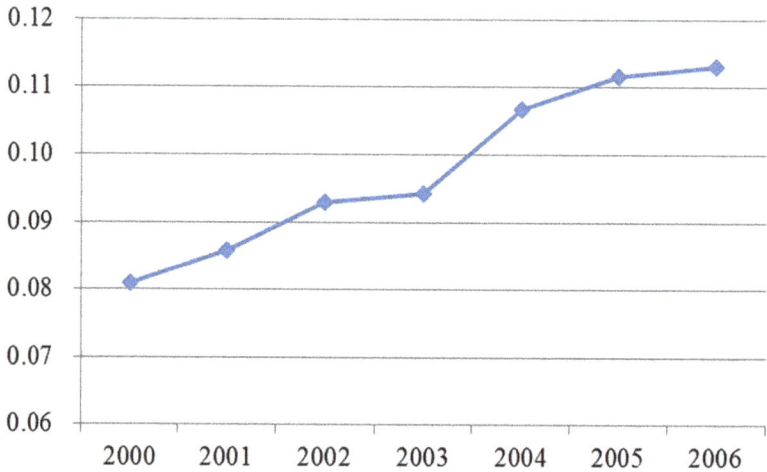

Figure 15.2 Trend change of inequality index over sample period (adequacy)

Source: Authors' work.

Empirical model

We model the equity of education financing in the Chinese context as follows (Equation 15.3).

Equation 15.3

$$E_{c,t} = f (ECN/FIN, POL, S, X, T, C)$$

In Equation 15.3, **E** is the funding equity in county *c* in year *t*. The influencing factors include the local economy, **ECN**, and government revenue, **FIN**, as the base of its finance; the two will be used exclusive of each other in any model specifications due to their strong correlation. **POL** (policy) is our key variable block, which includes the chosen level of education expenditure at the per capita level and the amount of fiscal transfers from the central and provincial (subcentral) governments by type and use. S, the total enrolment of local elementary and middle schools, is also among our key variables. These are all exogenous to local government. X represents the vector of control variables, including demographics, rural–urban divide, financial and geographical typology, employment and major outlay programs. T and C are year and county fixed effects to control for time-invariant and locality-invariant factors.

Explanatory variables

Our key independent variable is per capita education expenditure. Other key variables are the number of elementary students per village and the number of middle school students per town, both calculated from the ratio of the rural population in the total population, total county enrolments in elementary and middle schools and the number of villages and towns in each county/city. In regard to the local economy, we have per capita gross domestic product (GDP), total employment in public institutions, employment in the agricultural sector and per capita personal savings in the bank. GDP per capita captures the value of the economy in terms of average expenditure per person; employment reflects the degree of urbanisation; and personal savings is a proxy for disposable personal income, which is not available.[2]

As for government finance, we have per capita government revenue from taxes and fees and revenue by its source from the value-added tax (VAT), personal income tax and agricultural tax. The VAT is by far the most important revenue source. This revenue is divided 3:1 between central and provincial governments; within each province, the province, prefecture and county shares of that 25 per cent vary considerably, decided by provincial (sometimes also by prefectural) governments. Personal income tax is important in urban areas where salaries are much higher than in rural areas. This revenue is divided 6:4 between central and provincial governments; each province determines its own division of its 40 per cent share between its layers of government. Agricultural tax refers to a basket of multiple taxes on farm products with different rate structures. In the past few years, the central government has repealed most of these taxes, fundamentally relieving the tax burden on farmers. The remaining few taxes apply primarily to specialty products.

---

2   Note that some of the four variables may be highly correlated, especially GDP and savings in the bank. We tested the correlation between each pair and confirmed that there is no collinearity problem in the regressions.

Fiscal transfers represent a major policy change over the past decade of fiscal administration reform. Since 1998, the amount of transfers to localities, especially to poor and rural areas, has increased exponentially. Transfers flow down from the central Ministry of Finance (as well as some other ministries) under multiple names, types and uses; however, they all fall into two categories: one for improving local fiscal capacity and the other for designated purposes.[3] The former can be used with local discretion; the latter has to be spent on specific projects. Here, we use the total transfers as a ratio against total own-source revenue and also per capita discretionary transfers and per capita special-purpose transfers. For government size and functions, we include expenditure on economic development, administration and law enforcement (public safety, legal and judicial agencies). These three are in per capita terms, converted as the ratio against the provincial average. All financial variables used in this study are deflated by the CPI (with 1993 as the base year).

We control various other aspects of each locality. For demographics, we use population density (per square kilometre) and the natural population growth rate. (We also use the percentage of 0–14-year-olds and the percentage of those aged 65 years and over, the average years of educational attainment and the illiteracy rate of the population, as well as ethnic minority status [dummy] of the county in the cross-section model.) We also categorise the financial status of localities, controlling for rich counties, subsidy counties and deficit counties—all three as binaries. Rich counties are those that have long been able to collect own-source revenue of more than RMB100 million (A$18.7 million) each year and that have generally stable and healthy tax collection systems. Subsidy counties are those that received subsidies in addition to the above transfers; such institutional arrangements started before the transfer scheme began in 1998. Deficit counties are those that have a very limited revenue base and have constantly incurred deficits. Through reviews between county, provincial and central governments, subsidies and deficit allowances are agreed special institutional arrangements. The difference between these two types is, we can reasonably assume, that counties on a preset amount of subsidy face hard budget constraints, while those allowed to incur deficits face a softer budget constraint. In the cross-section model, mountain, minority, pastoral and poverty dummies are used for geographic typology.

---

3   A third category is called 'tax returns', which are not transfers but a transitional measure as a result of central–provincial bargains in the 1994 tax reform. In this study, we do not consider tax returns as real transfers; however, these are included in the total transfers.

Data sources are the authoritative annual series for nationwide data: *Countrywide Prefecture, City and County Financial Statistics* by the Ministry of Finance, *China County/City Socio-Economic Annual* by the State Statistics Bureau and *Countrywide County/City Population Statistics* by the Ministry of Public Security. Summary statistics are in Table 15.1. All data are for the period 2000–06.

Table 15.1 Summary statistics of main variables

Variable	No.	Mean	SD	Min.	Max.
EquityEdu (deviation from the mean divided by mean)	2,604	0.15	0.36	–0.37	1.17
Inequity index (squared)	2,604	0.15	0.26	0.00	1.38
Per capita education expenditure in 1,000	2,604	0.10	0.06	0.02	0.48
Elementary student/village in 1,000	2,604	0.14	0.07	0.00	0.48
Middle school student/town in 1,000	2,604	1.81	1.00	0.00	6.19
Per capita local GDP (10,000)	2,604	0.61	0.60	0.00	8.23
No. of institutional employees per 100 population	2,604	5.37	3.82	0.97	48.95
No. of agricultural employees per 100 population	2,604	53.82	6.80	6.94	71.85
Per capita personal savings in the bank	2,604	0.34	0.29	0.02	4.22
Per capita tax revenue (1,000)	2,604	0.52	0.47	0.07	6.82
Revenue from value-added tax (per capita in 1,000)	2,604	0.04	0.09	–0.14	1.41
Revenue from personal income tax (per capita in 1,000)	2,604	0.01	0.02	0.00	0.25
Revenue from agricultural taxes (per capita in 1,000)	2,604	0.02	0.03	0.00	0.52
Fiscal transfer/own-source revenue ratio	2,604	0.43	0.23	0.00	1.36
Fiscal transfers—discretionary in 1,000	2,604	0.04	0.06	–0.03	0.68
Fiscal transfers—special purpose in 1,000	2,604	0.16	0.12	0.00	1.34
Per capita expenditure on economic development in 1,000	2,604	0.03	0.04	0.00	0.69
Per capita expenditure on administration in 1,000	2,604	0.06	0.05	0.01	0.62
Per capita expenditure on law enforcement in 1,000	2,604	0.03	0.03	0.00	0.38
Population density (10,000/km sq)	2,604	0.05	0.08	0.00	3.81
Population growth rate	2,604	0.00	0.04	–0.52	1.08

Variable	No.	Mean	SD	Min.	Max.
Rich county (binary)	2,604	0.54	0.50	0.00	1.00
County on financial subsidy (binary)	2,604	0.23	0.42	0.00	1.00
County allowed deficit (binary)	2,604	0.27	0.45	0.00	1.00
Year 2000 population growth rate	606	5.77	3.38	−2.70	17.81
Percentage of population aged 0–14 years	606	24.40	4.46	13.10	39.36
Percentage of population aged 65 and over	606	7.42	1.61	2.92	13.47
Average educational attainment	606	7.17	0.65	3.35	9.42
Rate of illiteracy	606	9.92	5.78	1.33	57.59
Percentage of employment in industry	606	13.07	11.71	0.62	67.39
Percentage of employment in services	606	14.16	6.63	2.56	45.11
Mountainous county (binary)	607	0.35	0.48	0.00	1.00
County of minorities (binary)	607	0.11	0.32	0.00	1.00
Pastoral county (binary)	607	0.04	0.20	0.00	1.00
Poor county designation (binary)	607	0.18	0.39	0.00	1.00
VAT shared by provincial government	563	0.05	0.04	0.00	0.13
Business tax shared by provincial government	537	0.18	0.15	0.00	0.57
Personal income tax shared by provincial government	552	0.12	0.04	0.05	0.24
Corporate income tax shared by provincial government	552	0.12	0.08	0.00	0.24

Source: Author's calculation based on compiled data set.

Empirical methodology and results

We use a fixed-effects estimator with robust standard errors in all the model specifications. We first take a subsample of the total dataset, involving balanced panels of 372 counties across the country. With this set, we use lag operators to identify the effects of the key variables. We then take first difference terms to investigate the effect of changes. Finally, to tease out any endogeneity issues as much as possible, we take the absolute difference in the change of the inequity index between 2000 and 2006, and the independent variables, plug in exogenous controls from the year 2000 census for a cross-sectional examination and use ordinary least squares (OLS) to run the cross-section analysis.

Model identification

Table 15.2 illustrates our exploration of a model. The four columns show results of different model specifications. The results show whether the variables fit well in each model and whether their effects are consistent across the four specifications, with different control variables and with or without year dummies. Per capita education expenditure is consistently significant across the different model specifications; it is positive and its magnitude is stable. The positive coefficients illustrate that education expenditure may decrease funding equity, probably because education expenditure is a function of local wealth—that is, localities with high concentrations of wealth tend to invest more heavily in education whereas poor regions cannot.

Table 15.2 Four model specification results without time differences: Impact on inequity index (dependent variable) (fixed-effects estimator with robust standard errors)

Variables	(1)	(2)	(3)	(4)
Per capita education expenditure in 1,000	1.3674*** (0.3220)	1.2163*** (0.3424)	1.1067*** (0.2633)	0.9322*** (0.3004)
L. Elementary student/village in 1,000	–0.0104 (0.0833)	–0.0355 (0.0826)	0.0132 (0.0809)	–0.0040 (0.0778)
L. Middle school student/town in 1,000	–0.0057 (0.0069)	–0.0086 (0.0069)	–0.0083 (0.0068)	–0.0127* (0.0068)
L. Per capita local GDP (10,000)	0.0387 (0.0316)		0.0271 (0.0322)	
L. No. of institutional employees per 100 population	–0.0007 (0.0012)		–0.0006 (0.0012)	
L. No. of agricultural employees per 100 population	–0.0016* (0.0008)		–0.0023** (0.0009)	
L. Per capita personal savings in the bank	–0.0286 (0.0272)		–0.0450 (0.0323)	
L. Per capita tax revenue (in 1,000)		0.0256 (0.0687)		–0.0052 (0.0732)
L. Revenue from VAT (per capita in 1,000)		0.2364* (0.1425)		0.2767* (0.1476)
L. Revenue from personal income tax (per capita in 1,000)		0.5922 (0.4731)		0.8826** (0.4367)
L. Revenue from agricultural taxes (per capita in 1,000)		0.3420** (0.1564)		0.3236** (0.1460)
L. Fiscal transfer/own-source revenue ratio	0.1271** (0.0514)	0.1708*** (0.0603)	0.0335 (0.0473)	0.0618 (0.0546)

Variables	(1)	(2)	(3)	(4)
L. Fiscal transfers—discretionary in 1,000	0.0893 (0.1404)	0.0809 (0.1522)	−0.0306 (0.1349)	−0.0248 (0.1576)
L. Fiscal transfers—special purpose in 1,000	−0.0551 (0.0929)	−0.0473 (0.0982)	−0.1192 (0.0900)	−0.0903 (0.1103)
L. Outlay on economic development as ratio of provincial average	−0.0012 (0.0042)	−0.0033 (0.0044)	0.0012 (0.0042)	−0.0007 (0.0043)
L. Outlay on administration as ratio of provincial average	0.0238 (0.0181)	0.0106 (0.0192)	0.0259 (0.0187)	0.0118 (0.0203)
L. Outlay on law enforcement as ratio of provincial average	0.0126 (0.0195)	0.0018 (0.0173)	0.0217 (0.0206)	0.0102 (0.0182)
Population density (10,000/km sq)	0.0029 (0.0056)	0.0028 (0.0056)	0.0049 (0.0053)	0.0045 (0.0054)
Population growth rate	−0.0007 (0.0394)	−0.0165 (0.0435)	−0.0001 (0.0382)	−0.0169 (0.0428)
Rich county (binary)	0.0135 (0.0106)	0.0141 (0.0108)	0.0060 (0.0104)	0.0070 (0.0107)
County on financial subsidy (binary)	−0.0277*** (0.0100)	−0.0276*** (0.0101)	−0.0286*** (0.0092)	−0.0282*** (0.0094)
County allowed deficit (binary)	−0.0084 (0.0190)	−0.0081 (0.0192)	−0.0058 (0.0189)	−0.0055 (0.0191)
y2002	−0.0191** (0.0076)	−0.0241*** (0.0075)		
y2003	−0.0238** (0.0109)	−0.0305*** (0.0107)		
y2004	−0.0322** (0.0132)	−0.0407*** (0.0129)		
y2005	−0.0616*** (0.0185)	−0.0676*** (0.0171)		
y2006	−0.0714*** (0.0247)	−0.0777*** (0.0224)		
Constant	0.0573 (0.0545)	−0.0229 (0.0378)	0.1410*** (0.0501)	0.0270 (0.0312)
Observations	2232	2232	2232	2232
R-squared	0.197	0.209	0.178	0.188

* $p < 0.10$

** $p < 0.05$

*** $p < 0.01$

Note: Robust standard errors in parentheses. L = one-year lag.

Source: Regression result based on compiled data.

The number of elementary school students per village and the number of middle school students per town are both negative but not significant. This result is broadly consistent across the specifications, indicating that there are no direct effects of school enrolment on funding equity. Among measures of the local economy, only employment in the agricultural sector shows a significant effect on the inequity index in the two models testing this variable. Since counties with higher levels of agricultural employment usually are less developed, the negative sign indicates that, as agricultural employment drops towards the provincial mean, equity is likely to improve even though a more developed county may be higher than the mean, increasing the inequity index. However, the coefficient of this variable is very small. Among government finance variables, most of the revenue. sources seem to work towards increasing inequity (the index). Revenues from the VAT and the agricultural tax are consistently significant. While more own-source revenue provides the average county an edge in funding adequacy, it decreases equity across counties in the province due to the effect of resource concentration. In other words, counties with more own-source revenue are those that are likely to achieve funding adequacy (or higher).

Fiscal transfers to poor localities are a major policy instrument that the Chinese central and provincial governments have been using in recent years to improve education funding equity. Here they are measured as a ratio against total own-source revenue on a per capita basis. Perhaps surprisingly, fiscal transfers are significant and positive, decreasing equity. The reason could be that the total fiscal transfer is an aggregate measure that includes tax returns, which, to a large extent, reflects the level of local economic development.[4] Discretionary transfers and special-purpose transfers are not significant. This may be because these transfers are mainly directed towards reducing interprovincial disparity and do not help to decrease intraprovincial inequity, which is what is measured in this chapter. The results are also consistent with the conclusion by Wu and Wang (2013) that provincial governments may have grabbed central grants for their own self-interest. Variables on government size and functions do not have statistically significant effects on funding equity.

---

4   As the tax returns are generated entirely locally, we also add them to the own-source revenue as alternative tests for each regression and find that the effects are even more significant, which confirms our overall results.

Of the other control variables, demographic factors are not significant in any of the model specifications. In the financial category of localities, the coefficients of subsidy counties are consistently significant. The likely reason is that subsidy counties tend to have more rural areas, where the subsidy can greatly help to raise the level of education funding and thereby increase the adequacy and equity of funding. Coefficients on the year effects are consistently negative and significant in all the years (year 2001 as default) across most models. The coefficients become largely negative from 2002 each year until 2006, indicating that the macro policy became more effective over the sample period—that is, some fixed factors across years have increased the equity of education funding, such as policies to widen economic growth in western and central provinces.

Difference measures of education expenditure: Full model specification

Next we use a full model specification with the difference measure (current year minus previous year). There are several reasons for this operation. Since we found in the above results (Table 15.2) that the coefficients on the year effects are consistently negative and significant over all the years compared with 2001, we want to estimate the effects of the year-by-year change in education outlays. Also, using the difference measure can effectively help eliminate multicollinearity in the variables. Finally, the mismatch between the fiscal year (January–December) and the school year (September–August) may extend the impact of a current budget on schools over two years. The results are presented in Table 15.3 with the dependent variable (inequity index) in both the level scale (DV = $inequity$ $index$) and the difference scale (DV = $inequity_t - inequity_{t-1}$).

Table 15.3 Model including difference measures (inequity index)

Variables	DV in level		DV in first difference	
	(1)	(2)	(3)	(4)
D. Per capita education expenditure in 1,000	1.5515*** (0.3238)	1.7239*** (0.3186)	2.5970*** (0.5161)	2.7818*** (0.5199)
D. Elementary student/village in 1,000	0.1445 (0.0903)	0.1246 (0.0819)	0.1453 (0.1044)	0.1487 (0.0944)
D. Middle school student/town in 1,000	−0.0115** (0.0050)	−0.0036 (0.0047)	−0.0066 (0.0073)	−0.0000 (0.0071)
D. Per capita tax revenue (1,000)	0.3002** (0.1290)	0.2655** (0.1233)	−0.0348 (0.0934)	−0.0539 (0.0876)

Variables	DV in level		DV in first difference	
	(1)	(2)	(3)	(4)
D. Revenue from VAT (per capita in 1,000)	−0.0883 (0.0649)	−0.0525 (0.0661)	0.0444 (0.0784)	0.0580 (0.0799)
D. Revenue from personal income tax (per capita in 1,000)	−0.1779 (0.3577)	0.2326 (0.3992)	−0.5458 (0.3701)	0.0729 (0.4282)
D. Revenue from agricultural taxes (per capita in 1,000)	−0.2604 (0.1766)	−0.2571 (0.2251)	0.1203 (0.1130)	0.0835 (0.1361)
D. Fiscal transfer/own-source revenue ratio	0.0550 (0.0679)	0.2166*** (0.0737)	−0.0406 (0.0547)	0.1296* (0.0668)
D. Fiscal transfers−discretionary in 1,000	−0.5089*** (0.1857)	−0.5685*** (0.1691)	−0.2184* (0.1185)	−0.2671** (0.1106)
D. Fiscal transfers−special purpose in 1,000	−0.4118** (0.2047)	−0.5517*** (0.1934)	−0.1148 (0.1423)	−0.2481* (0.1441)
D. Outlay on economic development as ratio of average	−0.0083* (0.0046)	−0.0061 (0.0045)	−0.0003 (0.0047)	0.0014 (0.0048)
D. Outlay on administration as ratio of average	−0.0587*** (0.0176)	−0.0523*** (0.0168)	−0.0590*** (0.0184)	−0.0558*** (0.0187)
D. Outlay on law enforcement as ratio of average	−0.0400*** (0.0120)	−0.0342*** (0.0117)	−0.0342** (0.0144)	−0.0313** (0.0147)
D. Population density (10,000/km sq)	0.0086*** (0.0033)	0.0097*** (0.0035)	0.0094*** (0.0027)	0.0114*** (0.0032)
Population growth rate	0.0350 (0.0439)	0.0379 (0.0440)	−0.0186 (0.0599)	−0.0108 (0.0597)
Year dummies	No	Yes	No	Yes
Observations	2232	2232	2232	2232
R-squared	0.156	0.196	0.168	0.198

* $p < 0.10$

** $p < 0.05$

*** $p < 0.01$

Notes: Coefficients of dummy variables for financial status of counties are not shown in the table (available from the authors on request). Robust standard errors are in parentheses. Dependent variable (DV) in level indicates that the dependent variable is the inequity index, while DV in first difference indicates that the dependent variable is measured by first difference—that is, $(DV = inequity_t - inequity_{t-1})$. D = first difference.

Source: Regression result based on compiled data.

The results show that increases in the difference of per capita education outlay may raise the inequity index (i.e. decrease funding equity). Both the per village elementary student variable and the per town middle school student variable keep their insignificance in effect on equity, as they did in Table 15.2 across most models. One significant coefficient for per town middle school students may imply a large student body can be an indicator of economic scale. For a county with high education funding adequacy, larger student bodies drag down spending relative to the provincial average and thereby increase equity. For a county with low adequacy, by contrast, larger student bodies may be correlated with more funding sources and therefore can increase both adequacy and equity.

On the revenue side, the difference in per capita total tax revenue has a significant positive coefficient while the difference in tax structure has no significant impact in the difference model. This makes sense since the tax structure is an indicator of the status of a county that does not change much in a short time. That is why the level of different tax revenue matters while the change in the structure does not give us more information about education funding. The change in total tax revenue can increase funding and, from the positive coefficients, we can conclude that the change in tax revenue is larger for rich counties (with higher adequacy) so the change increases the index and decreases funding equity. China has now abolished agricultural taxes on most staple farm produce, which effectively eliminates any potential effect of the agricultural tax on education outlay. Previously, however, the agricultural tax helped to raise the education funding level (adequacy).

On the policy side, changes in both discretionary and special transfers become very significant and are negative—improving equity—in this comprehensive model using differences rather than just levels. This makes sense because the changes are very different from the levels of transfers. The model eliminates the basic level of transfers, including tax rebates, a large part of which reflects the extent of economic development. The change in fiscal transfer payments is helping local governments to improve public services such as basic education, as intended by central and provincial governments. The transfers–own-source revenue ratio, however, turns out to be positive and significant in some models, reducing equity, which is understandable since the ratio change depends on the changes of both transfers and own-source revenue. Changes in government size and functions also help to increase the funding equity level, which illustrates the role of government in public service provision, including education.

Of the control variables, the population growth rate is not significant in the short term. Population density is significantly positive. Changes in population density in the short term would largely be due to the influx (or outflow) of population. An influx increases the index level and thus decreases funding equity, which probably relates to rich counties attracting labour from other places, and these counties having higher funding inequity. Most of the dummies for the financial status of counties are not significant since they do not change much in the difference model.

Explaining the six-year difference

As Figure 15.2 indicates, the education funding inequity index trends upwards (increasing gap) over the sample period, which is in line with China's economic development and drastic increases in (especially local) government input into education in wealthier counties. In general, it can be said that the central and provincial governments' policy for redistribution and equity has not shown the expected achievements in reducing the interregional gap within provinces, though it may have dampened the increasing trend of inequity (and may also have decreased interprovincial inequity, which is not examined in this study). To better capture this effect, we calculate the difference in the index between 2000 and 2006, also taking the six-year difference for most independent variables used in the above analysis. We then plug in county-level control variables from the 2000 census as exogenous background. With this exercise, we may be able to offer another perspective on the overall effects of the policy shock in the sample period. The sample size of this cross-sectional analysis ranges from 525 to 606 counties in four specifications. Results of the OLS analysis are offered in Table 15.4.

Table 15.4 Cross-section model, dependent variable = inequity index difference between 2006 and 2000

	(1)	(2)	(3)	(4)
Variables	Dependent variable = 2006–2000			
Per capita education expenditure in 1,000	0.0004** (0.0002)	0.0005** (0.0002)	0.0007*** (0.0002)	0.0012*** (0.0002)
Elementary student/village in 1,000	−0.1487 (0.0986)	−0.1178 (0.0999)	−0.1221 (0.1051)	−0.0822 (0.1189)
Middle school student/town in 1,000	−0.0113 (0.0092)	−0.0106 (0.0096)	−0.0117 (0.0096)	−0.0060 (0.0106)
Per capita tax revenue (1,000)	0.9064* (0.4701)	0.7539 (0.4926)	0.8247* (0.5006)	−0.6449 (0.5735)
Revenue from VAT (per capita in 1,000)	0.0003* (0.0002)	0.0003* (0.0002)	0.0003* (0.0002)	−0.0000 (0.0002)
Revenue from personal income tax (per capita in 1,000)	−0.0008 (0.0007)	−0.0007 (0.0007)	−0.0007 (0.0007)	−0.0010 (0.0007)

Variables	(1)	(2)	(3)	(4)
	Dependent variable = 2006–2000			
Revenue from agricultural taxes (per capita in 1,000)	0.0013*** (0.0003)	0.0013*** (0.0003)	0.0013*** (0.0003)	0.0016*** (0.0003)
Fiscal transfer/own-source revenue ratio	0.2251*** (0.0481)	0.2062*** (0.0489)	0.2079*** (0.0526)	0.0916 (0.0573)
Fiscal transfers—discretionary in 1,000	0.3958*** (0.1163)	0.4294*** (0.1185)	0.3640*** (0.1257)	0.3674*** (0.1297)
Fiscal transfers—special purpose in 1,000	−0.0331 (0.0829)	−0.0482 (0.0843)	−0.1661* (0.0935)	0.0917 (0.0998)
Outlay on economic development as ratio of average	0.0023 (0.0050)	0.0027 (0.0050)	0.0028 (0.0051)	0.0023 (0.0053)
Outlay on administration as ratio of average	0.0373 (0.0247)	0.0363 (0.0247)	0.0399 (0.0254)	0.0492* (0.0285)
Outlay on law enforcement as ratio of average	0.0411* (0.0234)	0.0406* (0.0235)	0.0446* (0.0236)	0.0360 (0.0271)
Population density (10,000/km sq)	1.4092 (1.3095)	1.5444 (1.3511)	1.3366 (1.3543)	1.5312 (1.3407)
Rich county (binary)	0.0117 (0.0150)	0.0046 (0.0155)	0.0039 (0.0158)	0.0031 (0.0164)
County on financial subsidy (binary)	−0.0122 (0.0154)	−0.0167 (0.0158)	−0.0203 (0.0177)	−0.0297 (0.0208)
County allowed deficit (binary)	0.0101 (0.0139)	0.0068 (0.0140)	0.0066 (0.0144)	−0.0030 (0.0144)
Year 2000 population growth rate		−0.0051* (0.0027)	−0.0061** (0.0028)	−0.0095*** (0.0033)
Percentage of population aged 0–14 years		−0.0005 (0.0021)	−0.0003 (0.0023)	0.0036 (0.0027)
Percentage of population aged 65 and over		−0.0080 (0.0052)	−0.0053 (0.0054)	−0.0035 (0.0060)
Average educational attainment			0.0076 (0.0197)	0.0374* (0.0222)
Rate of illiteracy			−0.0023 (0.0020)	0.0013 (0.0022)
Percentage employment in industry			−0.0028*** (0.0010)	−0.0008 (0.0012)
Percentage employment in services			0.0030* (0.0015)	0.0034** (0.0015)
Mountainous county (binary)			−0.0055 (0.0145)	−0.0019 (0.0148)
County of minorities (binary)			0.0363 (0.0279)	−0.0371 (0.0360)

Variables	(1)	(2)	(3)	(4)
	Dependent variable = 2006–2000			
Pastoral county (binary)			−0.0329 (0.0354)	−0.0242 (0.0370)
Poor county designation			0.0366* (0.0189)	0.0307 (0.0193)
VAT shared by provincial government				0.3539 (0.2283)
Business tax shared by provincial government				−0.3177*** (0.0763)
Personal income tax shared by provincial government				0.8621*** (0.2771)
Corporate income tax shared by provincial government				−0.3971*** (0.1289)
Constant	−0.1309*** (0.0252)	−0.0143 (0.0766)	−0.0735 (0.1799)	−0.4305* (0.2266)
Observations	607	606	606	525
R-squared	0.233	0.241	0.265	0.230

* $p < 0.10$

** $p < 0.05$

*** $p < 0.01$

Notes: Coefficients for other control variables are not shown in the table (available from the authors on request). Robust standard errors are in parentheses.

Source: Regression result based on compiled data.

For intergovernmental transfers, the coefficients of discretionary transfers are positive and significant, while special transfers are negative but with less statistical significance. The transfer–tax revenue ratio is also positive and significant. These results suggest that transfers have not led to more equitable funding for poor counties in central and western provinces, but have adversely increased intraprovincial inequity, probably because the 'tax return' embedded in the transfer mechanism led to higher local revenue in the more rapidly developing areas.

As in previous models, changes in the number of primary or middle school students do not have an effect on the inequity index. For total tax revenue and revenue by tax type, some are significant and positive. For example, agricultural taxes were repealed during this period, stripping rural counties of their stable own-source revenue, thus increasing the inequity index. By taking the 2006–2000 difference, we capture the effect of this change. Government outlays do not have a consistent effect on the inequity index and the same is true of the financial status of these counties.

Of the control variables from the 2000 census, the natural population growth rate negatively impacts the inequity index, increasing funding equity, which is probably because the funding formula contains a factor of population and school enrolment. The change in average educational attainment exerts a positive impact on the inequity index and decreases funding equity since higher educational attainment indicates better economic conditions for the county—that is, localities with higher average education levels will favour more spending change on education. The status of rural, minority and poor counties, as expected, has no effect on how funding equity changed over the 2000–06 period.

Some major taxes are shared between central, provincial and local governments in China. The central government determines the ratio of shares between central and provincial governments and each provincial government determines the ratio of shares between it and local governments. We calculate the rate of tax shares by provincial governments (relative to local governments) to examine the link between tax sharing and education funding equity. The VAT and personal income tax shared by provincial governments show positive impact, while business tax and corporate income tax are negative. Note that a large provincial tax share indicates less local fiscal capacity, thus the increased share of VAT and personal income tax increases inequity, while the increased business tax and corporate income tax may dampen the incentive for economic development accompanied with less inequity.

Conclusion

Against a background of high economic growth and rapid sociopolitical development in the past three decades, education finance in China has transitioned from a local government–administered regime to one that is a combination of local, provincial and central government funding. Beginning in 2000, the central and provincial governments have stepped in to try to drastically reduce interregional disparity within and across provinces and to improve equity and the overall quality of basic education throughout China's vast rural areas. The fast-tracked transition provides a good window for scholars to investigate the impacts of external policy shocks on education finance. In this chapter, we have attempted to test the effects of the Chinese Government's new funding scheme on the intraprovincial equity of education funding. With a constructed inequity index, we have examined the impact of policy shocks, controlling for multiple factors.

The regression results indicate that the key independent variable, education expenditure decreases funding equity, probably because education expenditure is a function of local wealth—that is, localities with high concentrations of wealth tend to invest more heavily in education, whereas poor regions cannot. Among government finance variables, most of the revenue sources seem to work towards increasing inequity (the index), thus decreasing funding equity. On the policy side, since total fiscal transfer is an aggregate measure that includes tax returns, which, to a large extent, captures the level of local economic development, it seems that total fiscal transfers decrease education finance equity, while discretionary transfers and special-purpose transfers are not significant. However, after taking out the basic level of transfers, including tax rebates, changes in both discretionary and special transfers become very significant and negative, indicating they are indeed helpful in increasing equity (or at least in dampening increases in inequity). The policy target of the change in fiscal transfer payments is therefore helping local governments to improve public services such as basic education. Coefficients on the year effects indicate that the macro policy became more effective over the sample period, improving the funding equity of education. Nevertheless, the changes in transfers are relatively small compared with the primary funds for education, limiting their dampening impact on the large and growing disparity. The inequity index trended continuously upwards from 2001 to 2006. Under the current education finance regime, the issue of equity in education funding across counties (even within provinces) still has a long way to go to be resolved and deserves more policy attention.

In summary, since the inequity index is highly related to local fiscal capacity, two conclusions can be drawn based on the results. First, almost all variables related to the local economy—wealthy or poor—show a significant effect on funding equity. Second, variables that increase the wealth of rich counties drag down their equity, while those increasing the wealth of poor counties increase their equity—both converging to the mean. Therefore, our results do not show evidence of improved equity from the new financing scheme and policies, and the disparity is still obvious between developed and less-developed counties. Given the rapidly growing economy during the period of analysis, there is a significant increase in intergovernmental transfers. These transfers may be helpful in decreasing interprovincial disparities; however, in relation to our focus on intraprovincial inequity, the transfers are not very effective in decreasing intraprovincial inequity of education funding. The results, however, are still preliminary, with limitations on the data range and lack of rigorous analysis of causal relationships. Further exploration and improvements in the reliability of estimates should be conducted in future research.

References

Andrews, M., W. Duncombe and J. Yinger. 2002. 'Revisiting economies of size in American education: Are we any closer to a consensus?' *Economics of Education Review* 21(3): 245–62. doi.org/10.1016/S0272-7757(01)00006-1.

Baicker, K. and N. Gordon. 2006. 'The effect of state education finance reform on total local resources'. *Journal of Public Economics* 90(8–9): 1519–35. doi.org/10.1016/j.jpubeco.2006.01.003.

Berne, R. and L. Stiefel. 1994. 'Measuring equity at the school level: The finance perspective'. *Educational Evaluation and Policy Analysis* 16(4): 405–21. doi.org/10.3102/01623737016004405.

Besley, T. and S. Coate. 2003. 'Centralized versus decentralized provision of local public goods: A political economy approach'. *Journal of Public Economics* 87(12): 2611–37. doi.org/10.1016/S0047-2727(02)00141-X.

Duncombe, W. and J. Yinger. 1998. 'School finance reform: Aid formulas and equity objectives'. *National Tax Journal* 51(2): 239–62.

Hou, Y., Z. Bu and Y. Wang. 2010. 'Central financing, sub-central redistribution, and funding adequacy in heterogeneous localities: Evidence from China's recent reform'. 26 April. Available from: ssrn.com/abstract=1596289 (accessed 19 July 2017). doi.org/10.2139/ssrn.1596289.

Liu, F. 2005. 'Education equity under market economy: Problems and institutional arrangement'. *Journal of Beijing Normal University (Social Science Edition)* 187(1).

Murray, S., W. Evans and R. Schwab. 1998. 'Education finance reform and the distribution of education resources'. *American Economic Review* 88(4): 789–812.

Qin, W. and Y. Li. 1992. *Decision Making in Education Input.* Beijing: Peking University Press.

Rubenstein, R., S. Ballal, L. Stiefel and A. E. Schwartz. 2008. 'Equity and accountability: The impact of state accountability systems on school finance'. *Public Budgeting & Finance* 28(3): 1–22. doi.org/10.1111/j.1540-5850.2008.00908.x.

Tsang, M. 1996. 'Financial reform of basic education in China'. *Economics of Education Review* 15(4): 423–44. doi.org/10.1016/S0272-7757(96)00016-7.

Wang, R. 2001. *Region differentials in China's education funding: A preliminary report on poverty relief.* Beijing: Ministry of Education. Available from: en.moe.gov.cn/ (accessed March 2010).

Wang, R. 2004. 'County government educational budgeting in China: A case study'. *Peking University Education Review* (2).

Wu, A. M. and W. Wang. 2013. 'Determinants of expenditure decentralization: Evidence from China'. *World Development* 46(2): 176–84. doi.org/10.1016/j.worlddev.2013.02.004.

Yang, D. 2006. 'From equality of right to equality of opportunity: The slot of educational equity in new China'. *Peking University Education Review* (2).

Zeng, M. and Y. Ding. 2003. 'Education fiscal transfer and financial challenges for China's compulsory education'. *Peking University Education Review* 1(1): 84–94.

Zeng, M. and Y. Ding. 2005. 'A study of resource use and imbalanced allocation in China's compulsory education'. *Education and Economy* 2: 34–40.

Zhang, X., S. Fan, L. Zhang and J. Huang. 2004. 'Local governance and public goods provision in rural China'. *Journal of Public Economics* 88(12): 2857–71. doi.org/10.1016/j.jpubeco.2003.07.004.

16

Timely help or icing the cake? Revisiting the effect of public subsidies on private R&D investment in Taiwan

Hsini Huang and Nailing Kuo[1]

Introduction

Ever since Solow's (1957) pioneering work, it has been widely acknowledged that research and development (R&D) and technological innovation are key drivers of economic growth and national competitiveness (Coe and Helpman 1995). However, it is also commonly agreed that the market will fail to invest sufficiently in R&D if it creates non-rival and non-excludable outcomes—that is, if the outcomes are 'public goods'. Private firms are afraid of having limited capacity to capture the returns from their R&D activities. As a result, the allocation of financial resources to R&D is likely to be at a suboptimal level, as R&D can yield positive spillover effects to the relevant industry or even to society more broadly. Scholars argue that, in addition to direct public R&D where spillover effects are greatest (e.g. from 'basic' research), governments should use various policy tools to provide incentives for firms to expand their R&D spending—for example, strengthening the

1   The authors acknowledge valuable comments from Professor Andrew Podger, Tsai-tsu Su and the anonymous reviewers who helped to shape this chapter. In addition, we are thankful to our graduate students Tzu-Hao Chen and Wei-Jie Liao for their assistance with the collection of these data.

intellectual property system, providing direct financial support to conduct R&D projects, offering R&D tax credits (Hall and Van Reenen 2000), providing public venture capital (Lerner and Hall 2010) and government R&D grants or providing government loans with low interest rates.

Over the past three decades, as a latecomer in the global economy, Taiwan has performed well in manufacturing production and technological development, especially in the precision instrument and electronics industries. Figure 16.1 shows an international comparison of the gross domestic spending on R&D of Taiwan with a selection of Organisation for Economic Co-operation and Development (OECD) countries, illustrating that Taiwan, as a small-scale economy, ranks high in terms of nationwide R&D expenditure as a share of gross domestic product (GDP) (a simple measure of R&D intensity for a country). According to the OECD's *Frascati Manual*, the measure of R&D expenditure 'consists of the total expenditure (current and capital) on R&D carried out by all resident companies, research institutes, university and government laboratories' (OECD 2015). For more balanced international comparison, government tax incentives are not included in the calculation of R&D expenditure.

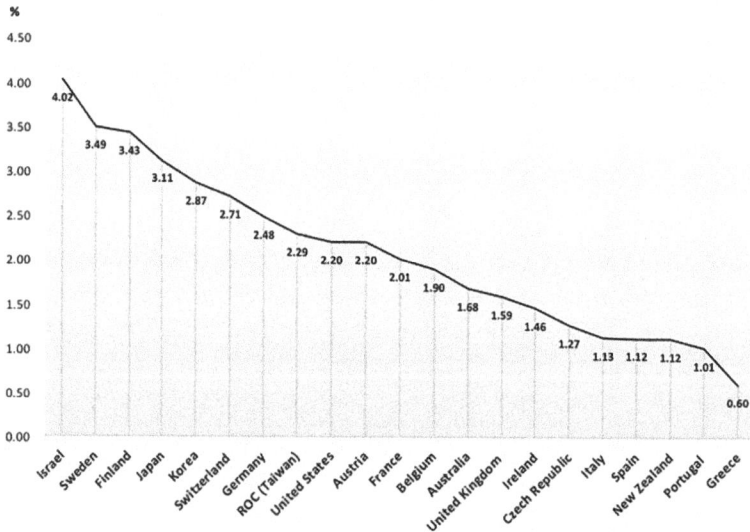

Figure 16.1 Comparison of civil R&D expenditure as a percentage of national GDP across Taiwan and OECD countries: A 1996–2012 average

Note: Civil R&D expenditure refers to all but national defence–related R&D investments and tax expenditure by business, government, higher education and non-profit organisations.

Sources: Ministry of Science & Technology and Taiwan Institute of Economic Research (2006, 2014).

Studies of developing countries are, however, scarce. A survey of relevant empirical studies conducted by Zúñiga-Vicente et al. (2014) found that, of all the surveyed papers published between the mid-1960s and 2011, approximately 40 per cent of the studies of R&D investment used data from the United States, while the rest drew from data for the European Union or other developed countries, such as Ireland, Australia and Japan. Few studies of the effects of policy schemes created by the public sector on private R&D use data from developing or newly industrialised countries, such as Taiwan (Yang et al. 2012). Meanwhile, a large academic literature has investigated whether the provision of R&D tax incentives promotes R&D in firms and, to a lesser extent, explores the effects of other policy schemes (e.g. government grants) on inducing private firms' expenditure on R&D.

As an export-oriented country, Taiwan is one of the best-performing economies among the developing countries who specialise in the electronics and precision machinery industries. Figure 16.2 depicts Taiwan's R&D/GDP ratio during the period 1996–2013 as a simple measure of the knowledge intensity in the economy and the amount of government R&D funding used to support business enterprise R&D expenditure. For the two measures plotted in Figure 16.2, tax expenditure (i.e. tax relief) is separate from the measurement. The R&D/GDP ratio increased steadily from 1.8 per cent in 1996 to 2.28 per cent in 2001, followed by a slight downward trend between 2002 and 2006, reflecting the global economic recession in 2000 and 2001. It then gradually increased from 2007 and reached 2.9 per cent in 2013. The amount of government funds used to support private R&D expenditure has increased rapidly since 2002, reaching NT$4.7 billion (A$198 million) in 2004 and climbing again after 2007, with a second spike, of NT$6.4 billion (A$270 million) in 2010, after the old industrial technology policy, the Statute for Upgrading Industries (SUI), was annulled, in May 2010. The new Statute for Industrial Innovation (SII) reduces the tax relief for conducting R&D, lowers corporate tax and provides more diverse financial support, including direct and indirect subsidies, such as R&D grants, innovation grants, national development fund support and venture capital investment for start-ups. The Taiwanese Government has emphasised subsidising firms for their R&D hiring, R&D projects and product commercialisation based on applications for grants, and so on. Figure 16.2 also illustrates that the amount of funds on offer to private enterprise for conducting R&D activities declined after 2010. Some observers suggest that, due to the burden of low corporate tax following the change of the SII, the total government budget has decreased in response.

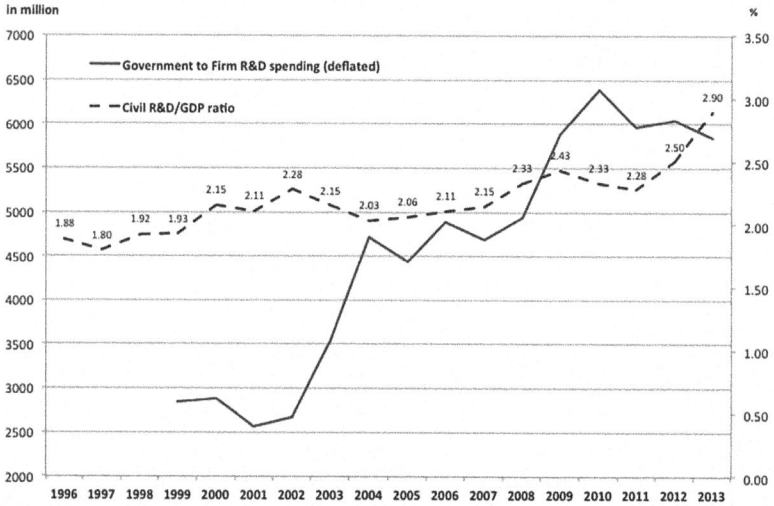

Figure 16.2 Taiwan's civil R&D/GDP ratio and government R&D spending to private firms, by year, 1996–2013

Sources: Ministry of Science & Technology and Taiwan Institute of Economic Research (2007–14).

By looking at public innovation support (not including tax expenditure) relative to private R&D expenditure (see Figure 16.3), the data show that the ratio fluctuated over the period 1999–2014, with a maximum of 2.5 per cent recorded in 2004. After that peak, public innovation support relative to private R&D expenditure gradually declined, to 2.0 per cent in 2008, and continued downwards, to 1.5 per cent in 2014. Overall, since 2004, we see a general downward trend in government R&D support as a percentage of private R&D investment. The descriptive results from Figures 16.2 and 16.3 suggest that public support for private R&D expenditure is not a level trend but has varied over time.

Drawing on these data of changes in public R&D support over the past 15 years, our research examines whether the input of public grants or support for R&D invokes companies' subsequent R&D expenditure in Taiwan. The findings of this research contribute to discussion about the direct effect of government subsidies on private firms' R&D investment. The more we know about the impacts of public subsidisation, the more likely it is we can improve the effectiveness of and value for government money. Additionally, given the existence of sectoral differences, this chapter will further investigate the effects of public subsidies on the inducement of private R&D across different industries.

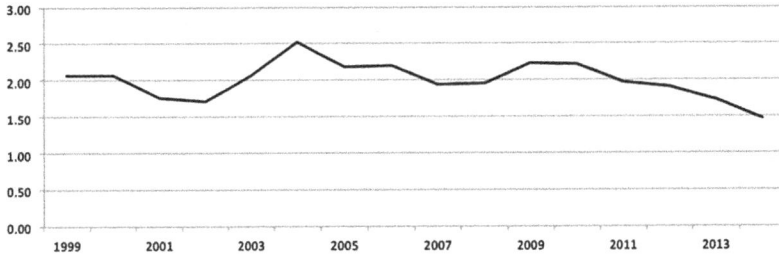

Figure 16.3 Public R&D support to the private sector as a percentage of private R&D expenditure in Taiwan, 1999–2014

Sources: Ministry of Science & Technology and Taiwan Institute of Economic Research (2007–14).

The chapter is structured as follows. The next section provides a brief review of the literature about the effects of government intervention on R&D activities. Section three describes the method and data used for analyses. The results are presented in section four and the chapter concludes with discussions of our findings and potential avenues for future research.

Literature review

Public support for private R&D

Two policy tools have commonly been applied to stimulate industrial R&D: tax incentives and direct government financial support. There have been many studies on the relationship between tax incentives and industrial R&D. Tax incentives for R&D have long been identified as a suboptimal remedy for failures in the market (Hall and Van Reenen 2000). Tax incentives—the major policy instrument used to encourage the supply of R&D activities in the past two decades—have been receiving criticism in Taiwan. According to Yang et al. (2012), one big criticism of R&D tax credits is lack of fairness—that is, the system essentially favours large enterprises and specific industries instead of small and medium-sized firms. Moreover, large companies are more likely to claim substantial expenses even for costs of questionable relevance to genuine R&D activities (Bozeman and Link 1985). Figure 16.4 shows that the amount of tax expenditure grew steadily from 1993 to reach a peak in 2007 of about NT$200 million (A$8.4 million). During this period and through to 2010, the SUI was the most important industrial technology policy. The main tool for increasing industrial upgrading under the statute was the provision of tax relief for R&D activities, R&D-related personal training, automation, pollution control and investment in risky areas. As Figure 16.4 illustrates, the amount of tax credit for R&D has been increasing rapidly since 2004, raising concerns from stakeholders about the excessive use of tax incentives.

To address concerns about the effectiveness and fairness of the R&D tax incentive policies, in December 2009, the SUI was replaced with a new policy, the SII. This reduces the credit rate of R&D spending to 15 per cent from the effective rate of 30 per cent, annuls the incremental credit rate (up to 50 per cent) for the excess of current-year R&D spending amounts over the average of the preceding two years' R&D spending amount and limits the use of credit to only the current year's income tax payable (disallowing any unused credit to be carried forward to subsequent years). Together, these changes have caused a sharp fall in tax reductions for R&D, as shown in Figure 16.4.

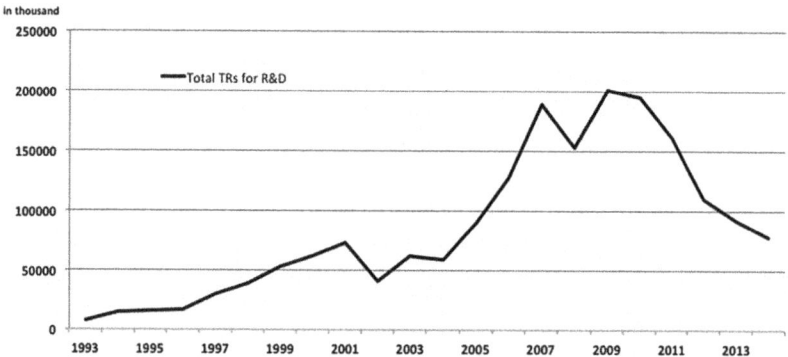

Figure 16.4 Total tax reductions for R&D in Taiwan, 1993–2014

Note: Dollar values are in 2011 dollars using the consumer price index (CPI) reported by the Directorate-General of Budget, Accounting and Statistics of the Executive Yuan, Taiwan.

Source: Department of Statistics (various years).

While the reduced emphasis on tax expenditure was informed by research that questioned the impact of tax credits, the impact of direct public R&D subsidies (e.g. grants, public loans, venture capital investment or contracts) on private R&D has so far received less attention, despite the scale of public expenditure. Proponents such as Girma et al. (2008) argue that public R&D subsidies induce employment creation and increase wages. There are doubts, however, about whether subsidisation policy does spur innovation (Wallsten 2000; Czarnitzki and Fier 2002). For instance,

Wallsten (2000) questioned the optimistic view that says the government will be able to rectify market failure, suggesting that the government is also picking the winners. In this regard, the evidence is mixed. As with the criticisms of tax credits, politicians or industrial interest groups could improperly use government subsidies to reward their own interests.

Mansfield (1986) was a pioneering scholar who distinguished between the social return and private return of money invested in R&D. His findings demonstrated that the social benefits—both measurable and intangible—of industrial innovation were significantly larger than private benefits, which usually refer merely to tangible benefits that can be measured in terms of monetary values. Put differently, public support for private R&D is seen to enlarge social welfare in addition to the money or tax deduction received by companies. However, as Bozeman and Link (1985: 377) suggest, the fundamental question is 'how much social value is enough to warrant public support?'. This remains an open issue given the mixed results of research to date. The following section summarises the two major arguments regarding the net effect of government support for R&D, the complementary effect and the substitution effect.

The net effect of government support for R&D

A large number of empirical studies across the world have tried to answer the question of whether public R&D subsidies and privately financed R&D are substitutes or whether they complement each other (David et al. 2000).

For the substitute (or crowding-out) effect, using data on Israeli manufacturing firms, Lach's (2002) study shows that government funding is actually replacing private firms' R&D investment. Assuming private firms aim to maximise profits, the crowding-out effect is expected to occur when applying for a grant is cheap and the probability of getting the funding is high compared with private firms' alternative financing sources, such as applying for bank loans (Aschhoff 2009). Empirically, Wallsten (2000) found crowding-out effects using a sample of Small Business Innovation Research (SBIR) program awardees in the United States and the tendency to pick previous winners to assure program success. Despite the almost dollar-to-dollar crowding-out effect of awards, Wallsten also argued that the direct support from the SBIR had some positive effect by keeping the award-receiving firms' R&D activities at a constant level.

Another thread of the international literature supports the positive effect of government funding for R&D, suggesting that public support reduces risks for private firms and induces them to invest more in R&D. Moreover, public financial support addresses the externality problem that the original investor in the new technology is not able to capture the full returns (Lerner and Hall 2010). Public funding is viewed as a way to mitigate market failure and may increase incentives for the private sector to invest in R&D (Arrow 1962). Conventional wisdom suggests projects with high rates of return are those with higher risk. But, as Aschhoff (2009) noted, riskier private R&D projects often benefit more from the assistance of government subsidies. Compared with private venture capital or investment organisations, a government agency with a group of relevant experts may be better able to identify the most risky but promising projects among all the applicants for funding (Lerner 1999). This may suggest that, when the R&D project has high risk, government support is likely to stimulate additional investment (measured as R&D expenditure) by the private sector.

Possible mechanisms driving the additionality effect may be complex. For instance, government funding (i.e. subsidy) can provide a good signal for firms to acquire external private funding (Meuleman and De Maeseneire 2012). Obtaining a government grant may indicate to banks or other external private financial institutions that the investment is worthwhile. In Görg and Strobl's (2007) study, the amount granted also affects the impact of the R&D. They found that the additionality effect occurs when firms receive small grants, while large grants could serve to decrease private R&D spending. Using Spanish data for manufacturing firms, González and Pazó (2008) found the additionality effect of public funds on private R&D investment was relatively weak for those firms that would conduct R&D in the absence of government support. Various studies have provided some evidence to support this conclusion, including in the case of R&D investment by German manufacturing firms (Almus and Czarnitzki 2003), German service companies (Czarnitzki and Fier 2002) and Spanish manufacturing firms (González and Pazó 2008).

In practice, the effects of public subsidies on private R&D expenditure can be subtle. Aschhoff (2009) summarised four kinds of possible effects of direct public funding on a firm's R&D expenditure: full crowding-out, partial crowding-out, additionality and no effect (see Figure 16.5). In the case of full crowding-out, private R&D expenditure is expected to be lower than the full amount of public funding supplied. The partial crowding-out situation is slightly better than the full crowding-out story, with some net increase in total (public and private) R&D expenditure. Additionality is exhibited when firm-financed R&D investments increase when they receive public subsidies. The fourth type of effect is no effect, which suggests that the amount of privately financed R&D expenditure remains the same regardless of receipt of government subsidies.

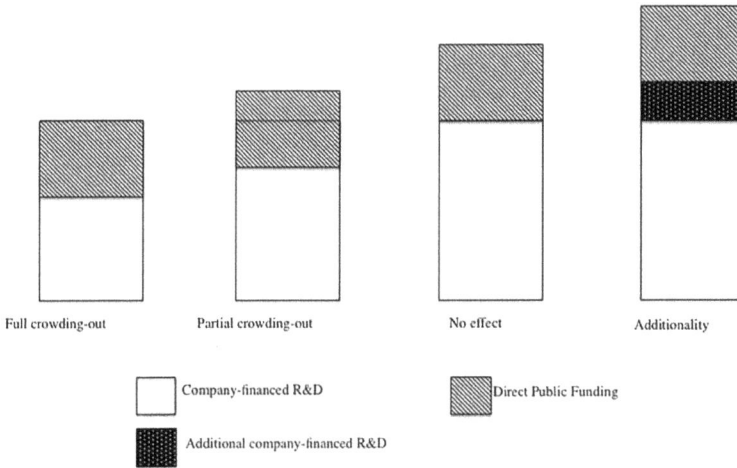

Figure 16.5 Possible effects of public R&D funding on firms' R&D expenditure
Source: Authors' illustration based on concepts in Aschhoff (2009).

The effect on private R&D investment of public support could vary due to firm heterogeneity. Wallsten (2000) evaluated payments through the SBIR program and found they have no impact on young R&D-intensive firms. Toivanen and Niininen (2000) observed some substitution effect in the case of subsidies to large firms, while, for small firms, the public funding had no effect on privately financed R&D, indicating that the scale of financial and industrial resources is likely to change firms' strategies for R&D spending. In contrast, using panel data for Israeli firms, Lach (2002) reveals a significant increase in private R&D spending for small and medium-sized firms, but no effect in large firms.

Summarising the above literature, existing evidence on the direct effect of government subsidies is mixed, although there has been an increase in empirical studies using advanced econometrics models to examine this issue. Moreover, scholars also warn that empirical methods with which to investigate this topic should control for selection and endogeneity bias in the samples. For example, studies should account for industrial heterogeneity, as firms in different sectors do not participate in R&D

equally (Blanes and Busom 2004). The contribution of this chapter is to continue this discussion along the same theoretical thread to test whether the effect of public subsidies is a story of crowding-out or one of additionality across industries at different levels of technological intensity.

Data, method and results: An exploratory analysis of the effects of government R&D funding

The data used here are mostly extracted from the indicators of the science and technology sectors compiled by Taiwan's Ministry of Science and Technology. The information collected corresponds to the sectoral level, suggesting this as the unit of analysis. The dataset consists of an unbalanced panel of all 24 sectors[2] during the period 2001–13 in Taiwan, including five high-technology sectors, five medium- to high-technology sectors, six medium–low-technology sectors and eight low-technology sectors based on the industrial classification[3] defined by the OECD's *Frascati Manual* in 2002. To measure the causality between government funding and private firms' R&D investment, information about lagged variables is important for determining the persistence of innovation activities. As a result, we construct a panel sample of 304 observations from 24 industries.

Many empirical studies have shown that most private R&D projects are financed internally (Hall 1992; Hao and Jaffe 1993; Brown et al. 2009). This is also true for private companies conducting R&D research in Taiwan. Figure 16.6 illustrates the percentage of private R&D expenditure funded by government, which is actually very low, yet the proportion of government support is observed to be higher in medium- to high-technology sectors (mean = 2.7 per cent) than in the high-technology sectors (mean = 1 per cent).

---

2   The aircraft and spacecraft sector is the only high-technology sector that covers data only from 2001 to 2006. The other 23 sectors have data for the whole period, from 2001 to 2013.

3   The five high-technology sectors are: pharmaceuticals; office, accounting and computing machinery; radio, TV and communications equipment and apparatus; medical, precision and optical instruments, watches, clocks and related instruments; and aircraft and spacecraft. The five medium- to high-technology sectors are: chemicals and chemical products; machinery and equipment; electrical machinery and apparatus; motor vehicles, trailers and semi-trailers; and transport equipment. The rest are either low–medium or low-technology industries, such as rubber and plastic products, basic metals, food products and beverages and recycling.

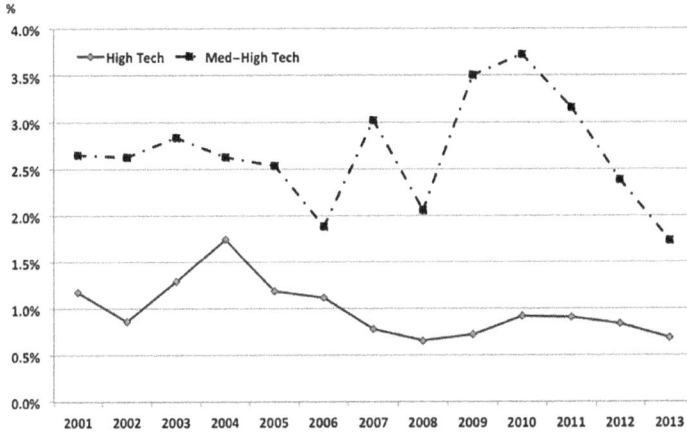

Figure 16.6 Enterprise R&D funded by the Taiwanese Government, 2001–13 (per cent)

Sources: Ministry of Science & Technology and Taiwan Institute of Economic Research (2006, 2014).

Granger causality models are applied to explore the relationship between government R&D funding and private R&D spending. According to Granger (1988), the independent variable 'X' can be used as a Granger cause of the dependent variable 'Y' if it satisfies the following two principles: '(a) The cause occurs before the effect and (b) the causal series contains special information about the series being causal that is not available in the other available series' (Granger 1988: 200; Stock and Watson 2011). We use Equations 16.1 and 16.2 as examples.

Equation 16.1

$$Y_t = f(Y_{t-1}, \ldots, Y_{t-n-1}, X_{t-1}, \ldots, X_{t-n-1})$$

Equation 16.2

$$X_t = f(X_{t-1}, \ldots, X_{t-n-1}, Y_{t-1}, \ldots, Y_{t-n-1})$$

'X' is considered to be a Granger cause of 'Y' if the following two rules are true. In Equation 16.1, the joint test of the lag of 'X' on 'Y' is statistically significantly different from 0. And, in Equation 16.2, lags of 'Y' are not causing 'X'. Vector autoregressive (VAR) models are adopted to investigate the effects of government fiscal support on private R&D investment.

For the following analyses, the key dependent variable is, separately, private R&D investment, operationalised by private R&D spending, R&D labour costs and R&D capital investment. The independent variable is assessed as government R&D spending provided to business, by industry.

Findings

The results of Granger causality are sensitive to the number of lagged years selected for analysis. Holtz-Eakin et al. (1988) suggest that the number of lagged years should be less than one-third of the total years to avoid the problem of over-identification. Given that there are 13 years in the data for each industry, this study uses no more than lagged level t–4. The analysis begins with running VAR models with four-year lagged variables and below. Subsequently, the Akaike information criterion (AIC) and the Schwarz Bayesian Information Criterion (SBIC) were checked to find the optimal lagged years, with the results showing that lagged level t–2 has the smallest AIC and SBIC values.

Table 16.1 illustrates models that test the correlation between government R&D support and total private R&D expenditure, including current and capital expenditure. Using the full sample, the VAR models (Models 1 and 2) fail the Granger causality test of the relationship between lagged government support (GOV_{t-1}) and private R&D spending ($RDEXP_t$). The elasticity test results reveal that a 1 per cent increase in government funding in the previous year (GOV_{t-1}) leads to a 4 per cent unit increase in private R&D expenditure ($RDEXP_t$). On the other hand, previous government funding at t–1 seems to induce more government funding at time t.

When the sample is divided by the technological level of industries into high-technology industries, medium- to high-technology industries and low-technology industries (including both medium–low and low-technology sectors), the effects of government funding across various industries are tested by VAR models. Results from Models 3 and 4 suggest that government R&D support for high-technology industries is likely to be a Granger cause of private R&D spending: government financial support for R&D is positively associated with private investment in R&D, consistent with the optimistic crowding-in argument of public support. The elasticity analysis reveals that a 1 per cent increase in government support is associated with a 6 per cent increase in firm-financed R&D. In contrast, for medium-technology industries, VAR Models 5 and 6 fail the Granger causality test relating to public R&D assistance and private R&D spending. For low-technology industries, in Model 7, the coefficient of $RDEXP_{t-1}$ is negative but insignificant. In Model 8, the privately financed R&D expenditure in the previous year is positively associated with government spending. Taking these two models together, the Wald test indicates that the relationship between public R&D funding and private R&D spending has an inverse Granger causality: private R&D expenditure increased and then government funding for R&D followed up. In other words, public R&D support for low-technology sectors is likely to have, at best, no positive effect. A grant is likely to simply allow firms in low-technology sectors to continue what they have done in terms of R&D at a constant level (Wallsten 2000). Even worse, findings suggest that government agencies' funding decisions are heavily based on firms' previous R&D inputs. This may be because of the limited ability of the government to identify promising and capable awardees in this industry sector.

Total private R&D expenditure was also divided into R&D-related labour costs and R&D-related capital costs, with regression results presented in Tables 16.2 and 16.3, respectively. Table 16.2 demonstrates the relationship between government R&D support and private R&D-related labour costs, while Table 16.3 shows the relationship between government support and private R&D spending on capital costs. Using the whole industry sample, the models again fail the Granger causality test between government spending and private R&D costs (see Models 1 and 2). But, for high-technology industries, the Granger causality test indicates that government funding does induce private enterprises to invest more in R&D-related activities in terms of both labour costs and capital costs (see Models 3 and 4 in Tables 16.2 and 16.3). However, for medium- to high-technology and low-technology sectors, the story is quite different. Models 5 and 6 in Table 16.2 show that, for medium- to high-technology industries, public funding has no impact on private R&D-related labour costs. The results of Models 5 and 6 in Table 16.3, however, reveal the existence of an inverse Granger causality between government R&D assistance and private R&D-related capital costs for medium- to high-technology industries. Similarly, Models 7 and 8 in Tables 16.2 and 16.3 show again that inverse Granger causality relationships are found between public funding and private R&D-related labour costs and capital investment within the low-technology sector, implying that the government is likely to act as a risk-adverse investor. The findings for medium–high and low-technology industries support our conjecture that government funding is perhaps just the icing on the cake: the government supports and assists those firms that are already successful and does not focus on small, promising firms that actually need public funding to grow.

Table 16.1 Granger causality test: Government R&D expenditure versus private R&D expenditure

	Model 1 All industries	Model 2 All industries	Model 3 High-tech industries	Model 4 High-tech industries	Model 5 Medium–high-tech industries	Model 6 Medium–high-tech industries	Model 7 Low-tech industries	Model 8 Low-tech industries
	$RDEXP_t$	$GOVRD_t$	$RDEXP_t$	$GOVRD_t$	$RDEXP_t$	$GOVRD_t$	$RDEXP_t$	$GOVRD_t$
$RDEXP_{t-1}$	1.145*** (0.064)	-0.004 (0.005)	0.934*** (0.155)	-0.005 (0.012)	1.102*** (0.126)	0.023 (0.021)	0.691*** (0.077)	0.043*** (0.013)
$RDEXP_{t-2}$	-0.096 (0.068)	0.007 (0.006)	0.093 (0.161)	0.008 (0.013)	-0.185 (0.131)	-0.007 (0.021)	0.343*** (0.080)	-0.031** (0.013)
GOV_{t-1}	1.974** (0.748)	0.720*** (0.065)	3.984*** (1.858)	0.676*** (0.155)	0.542 (0.925)	0.649*** (0.151)	-0.065 (0.468)	0.635*** (0.078)
GOV_{t-2}	0.426 (0.764)	0.118* (0.066)	2.043 (1.863)	0.074 (0.154)	-0.179 (0.930)	0.062 (0.152)	-0.453 (0.509)	0.158* (0.085)
Obs	256	256	47	47	55	55	154	154
R^2	0.997	0.851	0.996	0.782	0.899	0.674	0.942	0.709
Granger causality Wald test (chi²)	19.34***	13.91***	11.515**	4.122	0.449	3.263	1.426	16.872***
Granger causality	Fail		Granger causality		Fail		Inverse Granger causality	

*** significant at the 99 per cent level

** significant at the 95 per cent level

* significant at the 90 per cent level

Note: The year variable is controlled as the exogenous variable in the analysis.

Source: Authors' calculations.

Table 16.2 Granger causality test: Government R&D expenditure versus R&D labour costs

	Model 1 All industries		Model 2 All industries	Model 3 High-tech industries	Model 4 High-tech industries	Model 5 Medium–high-tech industries	Model 6 Medium–high-tech industries	Model 7 Low-tech industries	Model 8 Low-tech industries
	RDLAB		GOVRD	RDLAB	GOVRD	RDLAB	GOVRD	RDLAB	GOVRD
$RDLAB_{t-1}$	1.199*** (0.065)		−0.004 (0.005)	1.134*** (0.154)	−0.006 (0.012)	1.009*** (0.126)	0.108 (0.026)	0.670*** (0.077)	0.037** (0.016)
$RDLAB_{t-2}$	−0.151** (0.070)		0.007 (0.005)	−0.095 (0.164)	0.0095 (0.012)	−0.049 (0.131)	0.013 (0.027)	0.353 (0.080)	−0.025 (0.017)
GOV_{t-1}	−2.013** (0.825)		0.738*** (0.068)	−1.887 (2.12)	0.706*** (0.160)	0.651 (0.745)	0.639*** (0.154)	0.450 (0.380)	0.636*** (0.078)
GOV_{t-2}	4.179*** (0.818)		0.115* (0.067)	5.772** (2.038)	0.071 (0.154)	−0.405 (0.757)	0.030 (0.156)	−0.551 (0.417)	0.167* (0.086)
Obs	256		256	47	47	55	55	154	154
R^2	0.995		0.850	0.993	0.780	0.919	0.673	0.951	0.698
	31.63***		12.32**	9.854***	3.674	0.768	3.080	1.997	10.245**
Granger causality test	Fail			Granger causality		Fail		Inverse Granger causality	

*** significant at the 99 per cent level

** significant at the 95 per cent level

* significant at the 90 per cent level

Note: The year variable is controlled as the exogenous variable in the analysis.

Source: Authors' calculations.

Table 16.3 Granger causality test: Government R&D expenditure versus R&D capital costs

	Model 1 All industries	Model 2 All industries	Model 3 High-tech industries	Model 4 High-tech industries	Model 5 Medium-high-tech industries	Model 6 Medium-high-tech industries	Model 7 Low-tech industries	Model 8 Low-tech industries
	RDCAP	GOVRD	RDCAP	GOVRD	RDCAP	GOVRD	RDCAP	GOVRD
$RDCAP_{t-1}$	1.032*** (0.060)	0.016* (0.010)	0.751*** (0.146)	0.028* (0.025)	0.065*** (0.132)	0.094** (0.039)	0.429*** (0.084)	0.071** (0.023)
$RDCAP_{t-2}$	-0.126** (0.056)	0.0004*** (0.009)	-0.060 (0.114)	-0.003 (0.019)	0.060 (0.132)	-0.068* (0.039)	0.146* (0.086)	-0.002 (0.024)
GOV_{t-1}	4.252*** (0.397)	0.723*** (0.064)	5.939*** (0.865)	0.599*** (0.145)	-0.125 (0.552)	0.869*** (0.163)	-0.095 (0.281)	0.648*** (0.078)
GOV_{t-2}	-2.678*** (0.465)	-0.052 (0.075)	-0.181 (1.339)	-0.027 (0.225)	0.103 (0.542)	0.003 (0.160)	0.508* (0.299)	0.196** (0.083)
Obs	256	256	47	47	55	55	154	154
R^2	0.967	0.861	0.976	0.837	0.578	0.794	0.385	0.716
F	123.0***	16.25***	55.61***	4.28	0.053	5.735*	3.917	11.255***
Granger causality test	Fail	Granger causality	Granger causality		Inverse Granger causality		Inverse Granger causality	

*** significant at the 99 per cent level

** significant at the 95 per cent level

* significant at the 90 per cent level

Note: The year variable is controlled as the exogenous variable in the analysis.

Source: Authors' calculations.

Concluding remarks

In 2009, the Taiwanese Government appropriately switched its emphasis in R&D support away from tax expenditure to direct subsidies, responding to evidence of the limited effectiveness of tax expenditure. The research here suggests there is a strong case for a more differentiated approach to the allocation of direct R&D subsidies to improve effectiveness and value for money.

Our findings suggest that industries are not risk neutral: sectors with different levels of technological intensity respond differently to public R&D support. Government subsidies are found to induce increased private R&D investment in high-technology sectors, corresponding to some of the current literature, which suggests an 'additionality' effect of public spending on private R&D. Nevertheless, there is not enough evidence to support the same effect for medium- to high-technology industries; no effect between public support and private R&D expenditure was found in the empirical model. For low-technology sectors, the relationship between our two major variables is reversed, implying that the government might be failing to make good judgments about what are risky but worthwhile R&D projects in which it should invest.

Many observers suspect the government's process for selecting who receives public R&D subsidies is not as robust as people expect. Blanes and Busom (2004) note that public funding is more likely to go to those firms that already conduct a lot of R&D or have had successful experience in the past. In the low-tech sectors, consistent with Bozeman and Link's (1985) suspicion about the actual use of public support, many firms may be using government funding merely to upgrade manufacturing automation, rather than conducting R&D projects. Findings of an inverse Granger causality between public funding and private investment in labour costs and R&D-related capital indicate risk-adverse behaviour by the government in reviewing applications from low-tech sectors.

We also find evidence that direct public support is a Granger cause of increased private investment in R&D labour and R&D-related capital investment in high-technology sectors. For medium- to high-technology sectors, such as electrical machinery and chemicals, government support does not affect decisions about private R&D investment, suggesting a deeper reluctance to undertake risky R&D or introduce new technologies even with the assistance of public funding in those manufacturing-oriented industries. In particular, the findings not only suggest a crowding-out phenomenon in medium- to high-tech and low-tech sectors, but also the inverse Granger relationship between public funding and private R&D-related capital costs implies that the government tends to offer financial support to those industries that performed well in the past, consistent with Wallsten's (2000) concern.

To summarise, we argue that government R&D support is likely merely to provide the icing on the cake, especially for medium- to high-technology and low-technology sectors. To maximise value for money, the Taiwanese Government needs to pay more attention to the allocation of public funds to private R&D. As suggested above, the funds should not be a reward to those industries that have already performed well, but should be designed as an incentive for industries with R&D potential to invest more. Therefore, a proper review mechanism is needed to monitor and evaluate the effectiveness of the public funding of private R&D. The SBIR program in the United States is an example. It has decentralised so that 11 federal agencies—including the Department of Defence and the Department of Energy—each administer their own programs based on general guidelines approved by the US Congress. In Taiwan, the Ministry of Economic Affairs is the major agency in charge of the distribution of all SBIR funds. The disadvantage of having one centralised agency is that the Ministry might not have enough expertise in the selection of the right investment targets for every sector. If this program was designated to different agencies, they could each accept proposals based on their professional judgment in line with their agency's specialty.

Finally, in shedding some light on the efficacy of government endorsement of private R&D, the findings in this chapter have important policy implications for the government in shaping Taiwan's national and regional innovation programs. Accordingly, R&D subsidies can be expected to have very diverse effects on private R&D investment and on productivity across industries. The lesson learned from our empirical findings is that we are more aware of the need for an effective approach to distribute the direct subsidies that will ultimately increase the value of government money.

References

Almus, M. and D. Czarnitzki. 2003. 'The effects of public R&D subsidies on firms' innovation activities: The case of Eastern Germany'. *Journal of Business & Economic Statistics* 21(2): 226–36. doi.org/10.1198/073500103288618918.

Arora, A. and W. M. Cohen. 2015. 'Public support for technical advance: The role of firm size'. *Industrial and Corporate Change* 24(4): 791–802. doi.org/10.1093/icc/dtv028.

Arrow, K. 1962. 'Economic welfare and the allocation of resources for invention'. In K. Arrow *The Rate and Direction of Inventive Activity: Economic and social factors.* Princeton Legacy Library. Princeton, NJ: Princeton University Press. Available from: ideas.repec.org/h/nbr/nberch/2144.html (accessed 15 July 2011).

Aschhoff, B. 2009. *The effect of subsidies on R&D investment and success: Do subsidy history and size matter?* ZEW Discussion Paper. Mannheim, Germany: Center for European Economic Research. Available from: econpapers.repec.org/paper/zbwzewdip/09032.htm (accessed 1 February 2016).

Blanes, J. V. and I. Busom. 2004. 'Who participates in R&D subsidy programs? The case of Spanish manufacturing firms'. *Research Policy* 33(10): 1459–76. doi.org/10.1016/j.respol.2004.07.006.

Bozeman, B. and A. Link. 1985. 'Public support for private R&D: The case of the research tax credit'. *Journal of Policy Analysis and Management* 4(3): 370–82. doi.org/10.2307/3324191.

Brown, J. R., S. M. Fazzari and B. C. Petersen. 2009. 'Financing innovation and growth: Cash flow, external equity, and the 1990s R&D boom'. *The Journal of Finance* 64(1): 151–85.

Coe, D. T. and E. Helpman. 1995. 'International R&D spillovers'. *European Economic Review* 39(5): 859–87. doi.org/10.1016/0014-2921(94)00100-E.

Czarnitzki, D. and A. Fier. 2002. *Do innovation subsidies crowd out private investment? Evidence from the German service sector.* ZEW Discussion Paper. Mannheim, Germany: Center for European Economic Research. Available from: ideas.repec.org/p/zbw/zewdip/893.html (accessed 1 February 2016).

David, P. A., B. H. Hall and A. A. Toole. 2000. 'Is public R&D a complement or substitute for private R&D? A review of the econometric evidence'. *Research Policy* 29(4–5): 497–529. doi.org/10.1016/S0048-7333(99)00087-6.

Department of Statistics. Various years. *Yearbook of Financial Statistics.* Taipei: Ministry of Finance.

Girma, S., H. Görg, E. Strobl and F. Walsh. 2008. 'Creating jobs through public subsidies: An empirical analysis'. *Labour Economics* 15(6): 1179–99.

González, X. and C. Pazó. 2008. 'Do public subsidies stimulate private R&D spending?' *Research Policy* 37(3): 371–89. doi.org/10.1016/j.respol.2007.10.009.

Görg, H. and E. Strobl. 2007. 'The effect of R&D subsidies on private R&D'. *Economica* 74(294): 215–34. doi.org/10.1111/j.1468-0335.2006.00547.x.

Granger, C. W. J. 1988. 'Some recent developments in a concept of causality'. *Journal of Econometrics* 39(1–2): 199–211.

Hall, B. H. 1992. *Investment and research and development at the firm level: Does the source of financing matter?* NBER Working Paper No. 4096. Cambridge, MA: National Bureau of Economic Research. Available from: www.nber.org/papers/w4096 (accessed 13 November 2015). doi.org/10.3386/w4096.

Hall, B. and J. Van Reenen. 2000. 'How effective are fiscal incentives for R&D? A review of the evidence'. *Research Policy* 29(4–5): 449–69. doi.org/10.1016/S0048-7333(99)00085-2.

Hao, K. Y. and A. B. Jaffe. 1993. 'Effect of liquidity on firms' R&D spending'. *Economics of Innovation and New Technology* 2(4): 275–82.

Holtz-Eakin, D., W. Newey and H. S. Rosen. 1988. 'Estimating vector autoregressions with panel data'. *Econometrica* 56(6): 1371–95.

Lach, S. 2002. 'Do R&D subsidies stimulate or displace private R&D? Evidence from Israel'. *The Journal of Industrial Economics* 50(4): 369–90. doi.org/10.1111/1467-6451.00182.

Lerner, J. 1999. 'The government as venture capitalist: The long-run impact of the SBIR program'. *The Journal of Business* 72(3): 285–318.

Lerner, J. and B. H. Hall. 2010. 'The financing of R&D and innovation'. In B. H. Hall and N. Rosenberg (eds) *Handbook of the Economics of Innovation. Volume 1.* Amsterdam: Elsevier. Available from: www.hbs.edu/faculty/Pages/item.aspx?num=43501 (accessed 13 November 2015).

Mansfield, E. 1986. 'The R&D tax credit and other technology policy issues'. *The American Economic Review* 76(2): 190–4.

Meuleman, M. and W. De Maeseneire. 2012. 'Do R&D subsidies affect SMEs' access to external financing?' *Research Policy* 41(3): 580–91. doi.org/10.1016/j.respol.2012.01.001.

Ministry of Science & Technology and Taiwan Institute of Economic Research. 2006. *Indicators of Science and Technology ROC.* Taipei: Ministry of Science & Technology.

Ministry of Science & Technology and Taiwan Institute of Economic Research. 2007. *Indicators of Science and Technology ROC.* Taipei: Ministry of Science & Technology.

Ministry of Science & Technology and Taiwan Institute of Economic Research. 2008. *Indicators of Science and Technology ROC.* Taipei: Ministry of Science & Technology.

Ministry of Science & Technology and Taiwan Institute of Economic Research. 2009. *Indicators of Science and Technology ROC.* Taipei: Ministry of Science & Technology.

Ministry of Science & Technology and Taiwan Institute of Economic Research. 2010. *Indicators of Science and Technology ROC.* Taipei: Ministry of Science & Technology.

Ministry of Science & Technology and Taiwan Institute of Economic Research. 2011. *Indicators of Science and Technology ROC.* Taipei: Ministry of Science & Technology.

Ministry of Science & Technology and Taiwan Institute of Economic Research. 2012. *Indicators of Science and Technology ROC*. Taipei: Ministry of Science & Technology.

Ministry of Science & Technology and Taiwan Institute of Economic Research. 2013. *Indicators of Science and Technology ROC*. Taipei: Ministry of Science & Technology.

Ministry of Science & Technology and Taiwan Institute of Economic Research. 2014. *Indicators of Science and Technology ROC*. Taipei: Ministry of Science & Technology.

Organisation for Economic Co-operation and Development (OECD). 2002. *Frascarti Manual 2002: Proposed Standard Practice for Surveys on Research and Experimental Development*. Paris: OECD Publishing.

Organisation for Economic Co-operation and Development (OECD). 2015. *Frascati Manual 2015: Guidelines for collecting and reporting data on research and experimental development*. Paris: OECD Publishing. Available from: www.oecd.org/sti/frascati-manual-2015-9789264239012-en.htm (accessed 18 July 2017).

Solow, R. M. 1957. 'Technical change and the aggregate production function'. *The Review of Economics and Statistics* 39(3): 312–20.

Stock, J. H. and M. Watson. 2011. *Introduction to Econometrics: International edition*. 3rd edn. Boston: Pearson Education.

Toivanen, O. and P. Niininen. 2000. *Investment, R&D, subsidies and credit constraints*. HSEBA Working Paper No. W-264. Helsinki: Helsinki School of Economics and Business Administration, Aalto University.

Wallsten, S. J. 2000. 'The effects of government–industry R&D programs on private R&D: The case of the Small Business Innovation Research program'. *The RAND Journal of Economics* 31(1): 82–100. doi.org/10.2307/2601030.

Yang, C.-H., C.-H. Huang and T. C.-T. Hou. 2012. 'Tax incentives and R&D activity: Firm-level evidence from Taiwan'. *Research Policy* 41(9): 1578–88. doi.org/10.1016/j.respol.2012.04.006.

Zúñiga-Vicente, J. Á., C. Alonso-Borrego, F. J. Forcadell and J. I. Galán. 2014. 'Assessing the effect of public subsidies on firm R&D investment: A survey'. *Journal of Economic Surveys* 28(1): 36–67. doi.org/10.1111/j.1467-6419.2012.00738.x.

17

'Value for money' lessons and challenges

Andrew Podger

Contributors to this book cover a wide range of issues relating to public sector budgeting and financial management in three very different jurisdictions: Australia, the People's Republic of China (PRC) and Taiwan. But, as is evident from the preceding chapters and the original commissioned workshop in Taipei, there is considerable common ground and it is possible to discern some common challenges and identify lessons relevant beyond the three jurisdictions concerned.

The concept of 'value for money'

'Value for money' as discussed throughout this book is not a narrow economic concept nor the product of a set of technical processes for budgeting and managing public finances. It is inherently political, reflecting subjective judgments about the scope and role of government, priorities in allocating scarce resources and optimising impacts among competing policy objectives. It is also affected by institutional contexts, including those that reflect the respective expectations of government, markets and civil society, and the way authority is determined, exercised and held to account.

Budget and financial management processes in the three jurisdictions studied are intended to assist political decision-making, ensuring it is well informed and management decisions follow the policies set by legitimate authority. To use the Australian term, the processes are also aimed at ensuring the 'proper' use of public resources, meaning the 'efficient, effective, economical and ethical' use of resources. In all three jurisdictions, the processes are also aimed at providing feedback from measured results to guide both political and management decision-making.

Drivers of reform

In all three jurisdictions, budget and financial management reform has been one element of a much broader reform process involving economic and social transformations over recent decades. The reform of public finance has been a major contributor to those wider reforms and, in all probability, a prerequisite for their success.

For the PRC, public financial reform has been an essential consequence of its transition from a command economy as China's government has allowed and encouraged the role of market forces and reinvented and restructured the role of government. The past decade has also seen growing appreciation of the need for social programs to build a 'harmonious society' with adequate social protection to dampen inequality. This has raised new challenges for financing, prioritisation and assessments of 'value for money'. For Taiwan, public financial reform has been an essential consequence of democratisation, clarifying authorisation and accountability. It has also been affected by shifting community expectations as the population has become better educated and wealthier, demanding more of government. Australia has experienced its own 'opening up' agenda, particularly in the 1980s and 1990s, with the floating of the dollar and the phasing out of most barrier protectionism. Financial management reform focused on efficiency as governments recognised that global competition affected government activity as well as the private sector. Australia became a pioneer of New Public Management (NPM), emphasising 'management for results' and 'making the managers manage'. This focus on performance management can also be seen in the measures subsequently taken by the PRC and Taiwan.

The reforms have also been affected by external shocks. While initial responses to the 2008–10 Global Financial Crisis (GFC) differed, all three jurisdictions have subsequently had to face serious budget repair challenges. Addressing shocks, and the risks of future shocks and longer-term social and economic change, has driven more disciplined approaches to budget control and increasing interest in risk management, including assessment of longer-term developments such as demographic change.

Sequencing reforms

The varying drivers of budget and financial management reform, despite some alignment, have affected the reform agendas of the three countries. The reforms have also been affected not only by the different institutional arrangements, but also by the varying degrees of maturity or stability surrounding jurisdictions' authorisation and accountability frameworks. The varying capacities to pursue reforms have also affected reform agendas.

The PRC continues to face a formidable task as it transitions to a market economy and moves towards a new stage of economic and social development, extending the role of government to introduce major social protection programs. It faces very substantial capacity constraints yet has made marked progress in building a comprehensive budget process incorporating all revenue and expenditures. The capacity constraint is most marked at local government levels, notwithstanding the major initiatives a number of provincial governments have taken, with considerable uncertainty over local government debt and the sustainability of revenue and expenditures. Despite the formidable agenda and limited capacity, however, China is not limiting its efforts to so-called core or basic reforms, but is also pursuing performance management and evaluation, including by drawing on third parties to assist and fill capacity gaps.

Taiwan now has a more settled institutional arrangement and mature budgeting and financial management arrangements. It is clearly giving priority to reforms that focus more on 'value for money' assessments through performance management, evaluation and auditing, but recognises the need for more capacity-building to be successful. Nonetheless, Taiwan is also at the frontier in experimenting with new participatory budgeting arrangements.

Australian reforms from the 1980s and 1990s clearly had the advantage of building on a strong platform of comprehensive budgeting and sound financial management and auditing. A lesson from Australia is the risk of some backsliding if bureaucratic and political leadership is wanting, although the Australian story is also one of (mostly) continuing enhancement, with its latest work on risk management and capability providing examples, and the refreshment of its main financial management legislation in the *Public Governance, Performance and Accountability Act 2013*.

Together, these three jurisdictional experiences both support the notion of sequencing and cast some doubt on exactly what fundamentals are required on which to build enhancements. They also suggest that, to some extent, enhancements can be pursued simultaneously with the more fundamental requirements of proper and accountable financing and spending.

Challenges of politics and administration

It is widely accepted among democratic countries that a degree of independence of administration from politics provides important advantages, ensuring administration is not only efficient and effective, but also fair and just and serves all citizens, while the political process ensures legitimacy through majority rule.

In Australia and Taiwan, where there is considerable formal separation of politics and administration, recent experience seems to be that budget and financial management reform has had limited impact on political decision-making other than in supporting control of the budget bottom line. The allocation of resources by political leaders generally reflects political factors, not the performance information generated by the reforms. The politicians are also seen to be risk-averse despite reform rhetoric about innovation and risk management. To the extent allocation is guided by performance information and risk analysis, this seems to relate to management decisions by administrators rather than ministers or other politicians, and even here the evidence presented suggests considerable risk aversion among the bureaucrats.

This picture is perhaps too dismal. It may be that the impact on political decisions is more significant than presented here, as performance information and independent analysis by agencies such as Australia's Productivity Commission and the growing number of external think tanks in Australia and Taiwan (and many other countries) inform public debate and indirectly influence political decisions. It is also possible the internal and confidential budget processes not examined in this book make greater use of professional bureaucratic advice than is apparent in public debates. Moreover, the impact on management decisions by administrators should not be undervalued. While there is some disillusionment with the progress of budgetary reform, few observers or practitioners—political or administrative—suggest winding back the budget and financial management reforms on the basis that the benefits are not worth the time and effort involved in gathering and analysing performance information. The challenge ahead is to more adequately align performance information with budgetary decision-making.

To the extent that politicians are not guided by the information and analysis of the reforms, the fault may not lie exclusively with the politicians. Notwithstanding the benefits of separating politics from administration, the separation can go too far. As emphasised above, 'value for money' is fundamentally a political matter. Performance and risk management are not purely administrative responsibilities. They require active engagement between political leaders and administrators, with administrators appreciating the importance of the dialogue with political leaders so that the political leaders are the ones who take responsibility for setting program objectives, endorsing the performance indicators to be used, acknowledging risks and articulating the government's risk appetite.

China, of course, does not separate politics and administration, at least in any formal way, with the Chinese Communist Party (CCP) maintaining control across all arms of government. Indeed, the CCP uses performance management for the career advancement of party cadres. There is increasing interest in applying performance budgeting and other financial management reforms to resource allocation decisions, and in giving more weight to professional expert analysis. Contributors to this book emphasise the need for local leaders—both those with more 'political' roles and those with more 'professional expert' roles—to embrace these reforms and not just pay lip-service to requirements imposed by central governments.

Institutional roles and relationships

An interesting observation that can be drawn from the book is that budget and financial management reform is not only affected by each jurisdiction's particular institutional framework, but also can help to shift or rebalance that framework.

In all three jurisdictions, the reforms have led to some strengthening of the role of the legislature and have been associated with greater transparency and capacity for civil society and the public to influence government decision-making. In Australia and Taiwan, this is demonstrated particularly by the changed role and increased capacity of the national audit office; and, in Australia, it is also evidenced in the creation of the Parliamentary Budget Office. In China, people's congresses are far weaker than the legislatures in the other two jurisdictions, but there is evidence nonetheless that they are playing an increasing role in budget oversight and review.

Within the executive, finance departments appear to have become more powerful, exercising their traditional 'challenge' role with increased information on line agencies' performance. Devolution of detailed financial management controls has not meant reduced central power, but a shift in the way it is exercised. Finance departments still have considerable control over budget aggregates despite line agencies having more flexibility in allocating their resources, but finance departments also play a strong role in advising the political leadership on policy choices, taking advantage of performance information and their capacity to develop alternative policy options. Having final control over budget estimates and ownership of the financial management framework also gives considerable power to finance departments.

The success of the reforms depends, nonetheless, on cooperation and mutual respect between finance and line agencies, in all three jurisdictions. Overreach by the finance department may just lead to lip-service by line agencies; in extreme situations, it may also lead to gaming and worse.

The impact on intergovernmental relations seems to vary. In both the PRC and Taiwan, where there are differing degrees of decentralisation within what are formally unitary states, the impact parallels that of the impact on central and line agency relationships. The central finance department has increased power, but success is dependent on cooperation and mutual respect, and there are dangers of gaming and worse if this is missing. Success is also dependent on capacity at the local level, including the strength of horizontal relationships; this involves also the capacity and authority of both the local executive and the local legislature.

In Australia, where the provincial governments have considerable sovereignty, including quite powerful legislatures, budget and financial management reforms have not been driven solely by the national government, but also by each government in the federation. There has nonetheless been ongoing debate about the extent to which the national government can or should apply performance (or other) conditions to the revenue transfers it provides to provincial governments, and whether the national audit office should have audit authority in this regard. Significant moves have been taken in this direction, but on the understanding that objectives and performance measures be agreed across jurisdictions.

In all three countries, local governments rely to a significant extent on revenue transfers from the centre, and this is unlikely to change. While this may offer scope for national governments to impose firmer performance conditions on the moneys, or other forms of control, the evidence presented in this book shows there are practical limits and the risk of counterproductive responses.

Increasingly, it seems, the reforms are associated with increased roles for outside organisations. In part, this was inevitable as NPM reforms in all three jurisdictions led to some public sector activities being managed by non-governmental organisations, both for-profit and not-for-profit, on the grounds of efficiency and/or effectiveness (particularly in Australia, but much less so in the PRC and Taiwan). But the processes of performance review and evaluation are also involving external organisations including universities, think tanks and for-profit organisations. As mentioned, China's foray in this respect has involved a conscious attempt to address capacity problems within government. In all three jurisdictions, this seems likely to better inform the public, with the potential for wider and more considered public engagement. Whether this potential is being realised is another matter. Taiwan is actively experimenting with participatory budgeting and this may assist the government in selling its budgetary provisions. However, there is little evidence that public discourse in Australia is better informed than in the past—quite the reverse, perhaps, as it appears distrust and disinterestedness in government are increasing, according to social surveys. In China, the push to adopt 'social accountability' seems to have strengthened in recent years, but it remains under close supervision by the CCP.

Leadership

A message in a number of chapters, including ones on each of the three jurisdictions, is the importance of leadership, at both the political and the administrative levels, if the reforms discussed are to be successful. Leadership is also an essential ingredient for building a culture of integrity across the public sector and a commitment to serve the public. Such a culture takes time and effort to develop and nurture, and needs to be supported by both the institutional framework, with its formal rules, and the informal arrangements that accompany that framework. Such a culture can very easily be undermined by lack of good leadership. The many technical advances described in this book will only be successful if leadership commitment is sustained.

Concluding comments

Appreciating the different institutional contexts is essential to understanding the budget and management reforms in each jurisdiction, but there do appear to be some common drivers, challenges and lessons. Apart from the points raised above, it is also important to recognise that 'reform' is not an event but a work in progress, whether in regard to budgeting and financial management or in regard to wider economic, social and political change. Much has been achieved in these three jurisdictions, but the journey is by no means over in any one of them.

www.ingramcontent.com/pod-product-compliance
Lightning Source LLC
Chambersburg PA
CBHW050806270326
41926CB00026B/4573